BIOLOGICAL REPORT 97(1)
AUGUST 1997

SYNOPSIS OF THE BIOLOGICAL DATA ON THE GREEN TURTLE *CHELONIA MYDAS* (LINNAEUS 1758)

Fish and Wildlife Service

U.S. Department of the Interior

BIOLOGICAL REPORT 97(1)
AUGUST 1997

Synopsis of the Biological Data on the Green Turtle

Chelonia mydas (Linnaeus 1758)

by

Harold F. Hirth

Department of Biology
University of Utah
Salt Lake City, Utah 84112
USA

Fish and Wildlife Service
U. S. Department of the Interior
Washington, D. C. 20240

Preparation of this Synopsis

This review of the green turtle, *Chelonia mydas*, has been prepared following the FAO fisheries synopsis outline of Rosa (1965) and as applied to marine turtles by Hirth (1971b).

The main purposes of this synopsis are to bring together the current and salient information on the biology of the green turtle and to draw attention to some of the major gaps in our knowledge of the species. Because of the nature of a synopsis, i.e., that of providing an entry into the literature, researchers should peruse the original papers for details of methodologies and conclusions.

The author is indebted to Ms. Linda Burns, Interlibrary Loan Supervisor, University of Utah, for helpful and timely assistance in obtaining some rare publications. Assistance from the University of Utah Research Committee aided travel to libraries. Ms. Jeanette Stubbe graciously and conscientiously typed several versions of the manuscript. Mr. Kerry Matz prepared the figures. Dr. John Roth, Chairman of the Biology Department, supported the author with some sabbatical leave time.

It is a pleasure to acknowledge Dr. David W. Ehrenfeld, Dr. Nicholas Mrosovsky, Dr. Mark Nielsen and Dr. Peter C. H. Pritchard for their helpful comments after reviewing an earlier version of the manuscript.

The author thanks Drs. Leslie Dierauf and Richard Byles, Ms. Susan MacMullin and Mr. Art Needleman of the Endangered Species Office, U. S. Fish and Wildlife Service, Albuquerque, New Mexico for help and for supporting the publication of this synopsis.

Abstract

This document reviews the salient and current literature on the biology of the green turtle, *Chelonia mydas* (Linnaeus, 1758) including taxonomy, distribution, physiology, morphology, ecology, demography, exploitation and conservation. Fifteen figures and 17 tables supplement the text.

In general, green turtles are large sea turtles well adapted to marine life. They are circumglobal, commonly occurring in warm, tropical seas. They occur in offshore waters or on the nesting beaches of at least 139 countries and territories. Most nesting sites are located between 30° N and 30° S latitudes. The green turtle is a morphospecies, made-up of several distinct populations and metapopulations. The total range of a population—encompassing the nesting beach, epipelagic habitat, feeding grounds and migrations—can be very extensive.

Sex is determined by substrate temperatures during incubation with warmer temperatures producing females. The diploid chromosome number is 56 and there are no heteromorphic sex chromosomes. Hatchlings use visual cues in crawling to the sea and then, in shallow water, they orient by swimming into the waves. Magnetic cues may be used for orientation in deep water. The cues used by navigating adult turtles in their long-distance gametic migrations are unknown. Satellite telemetry may prove useful in this regard. Recent mtDNA research supports a natal homing hypothesis. Hatchlings and small juveniles are chiefly carnivorous (or omnivorous) while subadults and adults are chiefly herbivorous. Trophic level changes are associated with ontogenetic habitat shifts.

Much more is known about females than males because the former are easily studied on the nesting beaches. Green turtles are characterized by slow growth, delayed sexual maturity, high fecundity, iteroparity, and a relatively long reproductive life (under natural conditions). Reproductive data, from many nesting sites, are provided in tabular form: sizes of nesters, clutch sizes and number of clutches per season, egg and hatchling dimensions, remigration intervals and hatching success. Long-range demographic studies on a few nesting beaches have disclosed significant annual fluctuations in numbers of nesters. Under natural conditions there is high predation on eggs and hatchlings and low predation on adults. Long life was probably the norm for those that survived neonatal mortality, before the advent of humans. A green turtle survivorship curve is roughly concave, under natural conditions. Green turtles are host to a large variety of parasites, and fibropapillomatosis is a significant disease in some widely scattered areas. Major food competitors on the seagrass pastures are dugongs, fishes and sea urchins.

As expected, studies have shown how many aspects of the turtles' physiology are related to their feeding habits, reproductive cycles, prolonged swimming, diving and migrations. References are provided on morphological descriptions of the embryo, egg shell, skull, lung, kidney, ovary and oviduct.

Some major gaps in our knowledge of green turtles are speciation rates, natural sex ratios, ecologies of hatchlings and juveniles during the "lost years", biology of males, survival rates of different size classes, and navigation mechanisms. Obtaining information on some of these parameters can be aided by the development of reliable marking and tracking systems.

Because of many decades of overexploitation by humans, most green turtle populations are endangered or threatened today. Degradation of nesting beaches and oceanic pollution are additional threats to green turtle survival almost everywhere now. Conservation of any one population will almost certainly involve regional cooperation. All populations are important because they are the evolving units in nature and because they represent genetic diversity. For conservation purposes, each green turtle nesting population should be viewed as an autonomous demographic entity. Preservation of the turtles' critical habitats, education, and enforcement of existing protective regulations are among the management strategies discussed.

Contents

1. IDENTITY
1.1 Nomenclature
1.1.1 Valid name
Chelonia mydas (Linnaeus), 1758
1.1.2 Synonymy

Testudo mydas Linnaeus, 1758: 197. Type-locality "insulam Adscensionis".

Testudo macropus Walbaum, 1782: 112. Type-locality not stated. Holotype not designated. (illegitimate name).

Testudo viridis Schneider, 1783: 299. Type-locality unknown, restricted to Charleston, South Carolina by Smith and Taylor (1950: 17). Holotype not designated.

Testudo japonica Thunberg, 1787: 178. Type-locality "Japan". Holotype not designated.

Testudo marina vulgaris Lacépède, 1788: 54 and Table. (illegitimate name; substitute name for *Testudo mydas* Linnaeus, 1758).

Testudo viridi-squamosa Lacépède, 1788: 92 and Table. (illegitimate name).

Chelonia mydas Brongniart, 1800: 89 (see generic synonymy 1.2.1)

Testudo rugosa Daudin, 1801: 37. Type-locality, "la mer des Indes...environs trois dégrés des îles Maldives." Holotype not designated.

Testudo cepediana Daudin, 1801: 50. Type-locality, not stated. Holotype not designated.

Chelonia mydas Schweigger, 1812: 291.

Chelonia virgata Schweigger, 1812: 291. Type-locality "mari sub zona torrida," restricted to "Bermuda Islands" by Smith and Taylor (1950: 17). Holotype not designated.

Caretta cepedii Merrem, 1820: 18. (substitute name for *Testudo cepediana* Daudin, 1801).

Caretta esculenta Merrem, 1820: 18. Type-locality, "Oceano Atlantico." Holotype not designated.

Caretta thunbergii Merrem, 1820: 19. Type-locality, Japan (substitute name for *Testudo japonica* Thunberg 1787).

Chelonia lachrymata Cuvier, 1829: 13. Type-locality, not stated. Holotype, possibly in Mus. Nat. Hist. Natur., Paris (Roux, pers. comm.).

Chelonia maculosa Cuvier, 1829: 13. Type-locality, not stated; restricted to "Ascension Island" by Smith and Taylor (1950: 17). Holotype, possibly in Mus. Nat. Hist. Natur. Paris (Roux, pers. comm.).

Chelonia bicarinata Lesson, 1834: 301. Type-locality, "l 'Océan atlantique." Holotype, possibly in Mus. Nat. Hist. Natur., Paris (Roux, pers. comm.).

Chelonia marmorata Duméril and Bibron, 1835: 546. Type-locality, "île de l'Ascension." Holotype, Mus. Nat. Hist. Natur. Paris 7878.

Euchelys macropus Girard, 1858: 448 (=*Testudo mydas* Linnaeus 1758) by monotypy.

Chelonia formosa Girard, 1858: 456. Type-locality, "Feejee Islands". Holotype, U. S. Nat. Mus. 12386, adult carapace, Fiji Islands, U. S. Exploring Expedition, 1840.

Chelonia tenuis Girard, 1858: 459. Type-locality, "Honden Island, Paumotu Group; Tahiti and Eimo; Rosa Island." Holotype, U. S. Nat. Mus. 12390, male carapace, Rosa Island (=Rose Atoll).

Chelonia albiventer Nardo, 1864: 1420. Type-locality, "Adriatico...prossimatà del porto di Malamocco." Holotype, Mus. Civico Storia Natur. Venezia, Italy, unnumbered dry specimen.

Chelonia agassizii Bocourt, 1868: 122. Type-locality, "embouchure du Nagualate...Pacifique (Guatémala). Holotype, Mus. Nat. Hist. Natur., Paris 9537.

Chelonia lata Philippi, 1887: 84. Type-locality, "Insel Chiloe" Chile. Holotype, Mus. Nat. Hist. Natur., Santiago 100201.

Chelonia mydas carrinegra Caldwell, 1962a: 4. Type-locality, "Bahia de Los Angeles, Baja California Norte, Mexico." Holotype, Los Angeles Co. Mus. 1696.

The preceding, abbreviated synonymy is adapted from Hirth (1980b) and Pritchard and Trebbau (1984). More detailed synonymies are in Bourret (1941), Wermuth and Mertens (1977), Smith and Smith (1979) and Pritchard and Trebbau (1984). Wallin (1985) recommends a neotype in the Stockholm Museum.

1.2 Taxonomy
1.2.1 Affinities
—Suprageneric
    Phylum Chordata
        Subphylum Vertebrata
            Superclass Tetrapoda
                Class Reptilia
                    Subclass Anapsida
                        Order Testudines
                            Suborder Cryptodira
                                Superfamily Chelonioidea
                                    Family Cheloniidae
Generic

Chelonia Brongniart, 1800: 89. Type-species designated as *Chelonia mydas* Cuvier, 1832 (=*Testudo mydas* Linnaeus, 1758) by Fitzinger, 1843: 30.

Chelonia Sonnini and Latreille, 1802: 22. Type species designated as *Testudo mydas* Linnaeus, 1758 by Fitzinger, 1843.

Chelonias Rafinesque, 1814: 66. Emendation.

Mydas Cocteau, 1838: 22. Type-species, *Testudo mydas* Linnaeus, 1758 by tautonomy.

Mydasea Gervais, 1843: 457. Type-species, *Testudo mydas* Linnaeus, 1758 by monotypy.

Euchelonia Tschudi, 1846: 22. Type-species, *Testudo mydas* Linnaeus, 1758 by monotypy.

Megemys Gistl, 1848: viii. (substitute name for *Chelonia* Sonnini and Latreille 1802).

Euchelys Girard, 1858: 447. Type-species, *Euchelys macropus* Girard, 1858: 448 (= *Testudo mydas* Linnaeus, 1758) by monotypy.

The preceding abbreviated synonymy is adapted from Wermuth and Mertens (1977), Smith and Smith (1979), Hirth (1980a), and Cogger et al. (1983), and these accounts can be consulted for details.

Smith and Smith (1979) recognize Brongniart as the source for *Chelonia* and they discuss uses of Sonnini and Latreille, 1802, and Schweigger, 1812.

Generic
The genus *Chelonia* is monotypic, in the opinion of the author (see following two sections).

Specific
Diagnosis: Medium to large size turtles well-adapted to marine life (Fig. 1). The elevated carapace has juxtaposed scutes, is oval to heart-shaped, with four pairs of costals (the first separated from the nuchal). The carapace is constricted sharply above the hind flippers in some eastern Pacific populations. Carapace ground color varies from predominantly green to olive, or brown, or gray to black; and, with a varying number of blotches or streaks of yellow, green, brown, copper and black. The adult plastron varies from white to cream-yellow but in some populations has various sized infusions of gray or black. The bridge has four enlarged inframarginal scutes which lack pores. The head has a pair of prefrontal scales, and usually four postoculars. The tomium of the lower jaw is serrate while that of the upper jaw has strong vertical ridges on its inner surface. The single nail on the foreflippers is more elongate and curved in the male. The strongly prehensile tail of the male is much longer than that of the female, extending well beyond the posterior margin of the carapace (Fig. 2). The carapace and plastron of hatchlings are slate black (darker when wet) and white, respectively. Detailed descriptions are in Deraniyagala (1939), Carr (1952), Smith and Smith (1979), Pritchard and Trebbau (1984), Ernst and Barbour (1989) and Márquez (1990).

1.2.2 Taxonomic status
It is the opinion of the author that the green turtle *(Chelonia mydas)* is a circumglobal, morpho-species. The species is made-up of several distinct populations and metapopulations. The populations can be identified by the name of their nesting beach or beaches used in association with *Chelonia mydas* (see following section). All the populations are important because they are the evolving units in nature and because they represent genetic diversity.

1.2.3 Subspecies
Several populations of green turtles have been described, in morphological and biochemical terms, and some have been given specific or subspecific names. Some of the more recent descriptions follow.
Márquez (1990) recognizes the dark *Chelonia* occurring in the eastern Pacific Ocean principally from Baja California to Peru, and with major nesting beaches in Mexico and the Galápagos Islands, as a species, *Chelonia agassizii*. In addition to the species being smaller than the typical *Chelonia mydas*, Márquez (1990) lists some of the diagnostic features: adult carapace often strongly vaulted; the carapace, in dorsal view, is subcardiform and deeply emarginate over the rear flippers; the carapace width becomes relatively narrower with age; adult carapace is slate gray to black with a blotched brown and olive pattern; upper surfaces of the head and flippers dark; plastron varying from whitish-gray to

Fig. 1. A typical adult female green turtle on Ascension Island, the type locality. Standard straight line carapace length of this individual is 112 cm. Females here are among the largest in the world and they migrate to the Island from Brazil, a round-trip distance of about 4,600 km.

Fig. 2. A typical adult male green turtle on Aldabra Atoll. Standard straight line carapace length of this individual is 95 cm. The size of the tail easily identifies adult males, anywhere.

bluish or olive gray. Younger individuals are usually more colorful and similar to those in the Atlantic populations. Further, Márquez (1990) is of the opinion that *Chelonia mydas* is comprised of two subspecies: *C. m. mydas* in the Atlantic Ocean and *C. m. japonica* in the Indian Ocean and in the western and central Pacific Ocean.

Alvarado and Figueroa (1990) also consider the Eastern Pacific green turtle or black turtle a species, *Chelonia agassizi*. Eight morphometric characters in the Michoacan-nesting *C. agassizi* population and in the Tortuguero-nesting *C. mydas* population were compared. A principal component analysis of the data indicated a clear distinction between the two populations (Alvarado and Figueroa 1990).

Kamezaki and Matsui (1995) analyzed twenty cranial traits of 145 green turtle skulls and four mandibular traits of 103 mandibles from six localities in three oceans (Comoros Is., Seychelles Is., Ogasawara Is., Galápagos Is., Guyana and Caribbean Costa Rica). The Galápagos sample was completely separated from the other samples by a canonical discriminant analysis but was not differentiated from the others by any single character dimension relative to skull length. The authors, therefore, support the recognition of the eastern Pacific population, including the Galápagos Is. population, as a distinct subspecies, *C. m. agassizi,* but not as a distinct species.

Dutton and McDonald (1992) found it difficult to distinguish between *Chelonia agassizi* and *Chelonia mydas*, based on carapace color and shape and plastron color, in a small population in San Diego Bay. The D-loop nucleotide sequences of mtDNA from four San Diego Bay turtles were compared with those of five Hawaiian turtles from the French Frigate Shoals colony and with three Mexican black turtles from the Michoacan nesting colony (Dutton et al. 1994). The San Diego Bay turtles appeared to be more like the Mexican turtles, although some differences in the mtDNA suggested that they may not have originated from the Michoacan colony.

Pritchard and Trebbau (1984) consider the East Pacific *Chelonia* populations from the Galápagos Islands and the mainland shores of the Americas a distinct species, *Chelonia agassizi*. Pritchard in Pritchard and Trebbau (1984) also noted occasional sympatry between *C. mydas* and *C. agassizi* in Pacific Mexico, the Galápagos and Papua New Guinea.

Hendrickson (1980) recommended that *Chelonia mydas carrinegra* be elevated to species status. The position of *carrinegra* in green turtle taxonomy was reviewed by Groombridge and Luxmoore (1989).

Earlier, Carr (1975) suggested that the eastern Pacific form of the green turtle, extending from Baja California to the Galápagos Islands and Peru, and westward to the Hawaiian Archipelago and the Marshall Islands, be called *agassizi;* that *japonica* be used for *Chelonia* in the Indian Ocean and the western tropical Pacific; that *Chelonia*

mydas mydas be used for the Ascension Island population; and, that *Chelonia mydas viridis* be used for the Tortuguero colony.

The use of color as a taxonomic index must be used with caution inasmuch as Frazier (1971) illustrated much color variation within a single population at Aldabra Atoll.

More recently, molecular techniques have been used to determine gene flow between green turtle populations. Mitochondrial DNA data do not support the evolutionary distinctness of *C. agassizi*. The mtDNA data suggest that the *Chelonia* complex should probably be divided into Atlantic-Mediterranean and Indian-Pacific subspecies, with additional population-level distinctness recognized within each ocean basin (Bowen et al. 1992). Under this division, the Indian-Pacific subspecies would be named *japonica*. Based on nucleotide sequences from the cytochrome b gene of mtDNA, Bowen et al. (1993) determined that *C. mydas* is paraphyletic with respect to *C. agassizi* in terms of matriarchal phylogeny. An analysis of nuclear DNA indicated some genetic similarity between populations in Michoacan, Mexico, and the Galápagos (Karl et al. 1992). Although nesting populations appear to be isolated with respect to female (mtDNA) lineages, the work of Karl et al. (1992) with nDNA indicates a moderate level of male-mediated gene flow. Moritz (1994a) recommends that the circumglobal green turtle should be managed as two ESUs (Evolutionary Significant Units), i.e. the Atlantic-Mediterranean and the Indo-Pacific, with each ESU consisting of multiple MUs (Management Units). According to Moritz (1994a) "ESUs should be reciprocally monophyletic for mtDNA alleles and show significant divergence of allele frequencies at nuclear loci" and "MUs are therefore recognized as populations with significant divergence of allele frequencies at nuclear or mitochondrial loci, regardless of the phylogenetic distinctiveness of the alleles."

Green turtles (and other Testudines) have slower microevolutionary rates for mtDNA than other vertebrates (Avise et al. 1992). Karl and Avise (1993) discuss the advantages of using polymerase chain reaction (PCR) techniques to generate population genetic data and they use green turtle data to show how this approach is useful. Norman et al. (1994) used PCR to evaluate sequence variation in the hypervariable control region of green turtle mtDNA and concluded that the Indo-Pacific green turtles include a number of genetically differentiated populations with minimal female-mediated gene flow among them. In a mini-review, Moritz (1994b) draws a distinction between the use of mtDNA analysis to identify and manage genetic diversity and its use as a tool for demographic studies of populations. Dutton and Balazs (1995) briefly describe how DNA can be obtained for PCR analysis from small skin tissue biopsies using a relatively non-invasive sampling procedure. In this procedure, a biopsy punch is used to obtain a disc of tissue from the skin in the dorsal axial region of the rear flipper. No suture is necessary.

A distinct division was revealed between western Caribbean nesting populations (Florida and Costa Rica) and eastern Caribbean nesting colonies (Aves Island and Suriname) and an inverse relationship was found between nesting colony size and mtDNA diversity when analyzing mtDNA control region sequences (Lahanas et al. 1994). Encalada (1994) also found greater mtDNA diversity among smaller nesting colonies in the Atlantic Ocean when sequencing the mtDNA control region of nesters from nine colonies.

Fitzsimmons et al. (1993-94) and Fitzsimmons et al. (1994), respectively, very briefly describe the applicability of microsatellite analysis in population structure of marine turtles and the use of microsatellite techniques to study male-mediated gene flow among populations including paternity of clutches. Details of how microsatellite analysis can be a valuable tool to complement assays of sequence variation in sea turtle nDNA and mtDNA is given by Fitzsimmons et al. (1995a).

The genetic information on green turtle populations is accumulating rapidly but as stated by Lahanas et al. (1994) "It should be cautioned that finer-scale genetic data do not necessarily translate into greater geographic resolution of population structure." A short, popular account of the mtDNA work with green turtles was prepared by Bowen and Avise (1994).

After briefly reviewing the state of affairs, Parham and Zug (1996) recommended that the name *Chelonia mydas* be used, with no formal subspecific recognition, for green turtle populations throughout the world.

The size, sample size, and history of the green turtle breeding population being analyzed can have significant bearing on taxonomic conclusions. Small populations are subject to genetic drift and inbreeding. Populations emanating (Founder effect) or being rebuilt (population bottleneck followed by population flush) from a few individuals usually have less genetic diversity than large populations.

1.2.4 Standard common names

Standard common names are: English - green turtle, green sea turtle, edible turtle, greenback turtle; German - Suppenschildkröte; Dutch - Soepschildpad; French - tortue franche, tortue de mer, tortue verte; Portuguese - tartaruga, tartaruga do mar, tartaruga verde; Japanese - ao umigame; Caribbean Spanish - tortuga, tortuga blanca, tortuga verde.

Common and local names of sea turtles are very important tools for field biologists and conservation agents. Common names of *Chelonia mydas* for some countries and regions are: Aldabra Atoll - tortue de mer, tortie de mer (Hirth and Carr 1970); American Samoa - fonu, laumei ena ena, laumei leai se uga (Tuato'o - Bartley et al. 1993); Andaman and Nicobar Islands - dudh kacchua, kap-ka, kap-troeje, yadi-da (Bhaskar 1979); Angola - yofele (Carr and Carr 1991); Anguilla - greenback (Meylan 1983); Argentina - carey, tortuga carey, tortuga franca, tortuga de mar, tortuga verde (Mittermeier et al. 1980; Freiberg 1981); Australia - green turtle, malurrba, waru (Nietschmann 1989; Bradley 1991; Cogger 1992); Barbados - greenback, green turtle (Horrocks 1992); Belize - white turtle (Márquez 1990); Brazil - suruanã, tartaruga, tartaruga do mar, uruana (Mittermeier et al. 1980; Freiberg 1981); Chile - tortuga comestible, tortuga verde (Mittermeier et al. 1980); China - lu gui (Frazier et al. 1988); Cocos-Keeling Is. - penyu (Gibson-Hill 1950); Colombia - caguama, moro (female) and yauc (male), tortuga, tortuga blanca, tortuga de mar, tortuga verde (Mittermeier et al. 1980; Green and Ortiz-Crespo 1982); Costa Rica (Caribbean) - tortuga, tortuga blanca (Carr 1983); Costa Rica (Pacific) - tora, tortuga negra (Cornelius 1976; Márquez 1990); Cuba - tortuga verde (Márquez 1990); Ecuador - tortuga prieta (Márquez 1990); Egypt - biswa, p'saya, tersa (Frazier et al. 1987); El Salvador - tortuga verde (Márquez 1990); Fiji - ika damu, mako loa, vonu damu, vonu loa (Hirth 1971a); French Guiana - kaouane, ouyamoury (Mittermeier et al. 1980); French Polynesia - tortue, honu (Hirth 1971a); Gabon - nkudu, nkunu, ikes, tchiches, ehu, tortue verte (Fretey and Girardin 1989); Galápagos Is. - tortuga negra, tortuga amarilla (Green and Ortiz-Crespo 1982); Gold Coast - anwa, apuhulu, apuhuru, hala, klo (Irvine 1947); Guadeloupe - tortue, tortue blanche, tortue verte (Meylan 1983); Guatemala (Caribbean) - tortuga verde (Márquez 1990); Guatemala (Pacific) - parlama, tortuga negra, tortuga verde (Márquez 1990); Guyana - bettia (Mittermeier et al. 1980); Hawaii - green turtle, green sea turtle, honu (Balazs 1980); Honduras (Pacific) - guiltora (Márquez 1990); Indochina - lemech, vich (Bourret 1941); Indonesia - penyu biasa, penyu daging, penyu nijan, penyu sala, wau kaku (Rhodin et al. 1980; Suwelo et al. 1982); Israel (Red Sea) - turas al abiad (Frazier et al. 1987); Madagascar - fanojoaty (Hughes 1975); Maylaysia - penyu agar, penyu empegit, penyu pulau, penyu pulo (Chin 1971; Tow and Moll 1982); Maldive Is. - vela (Deraniyagala 1956); Masirah Is. - humsa asfah (FAO 1973); Mayotte - fanu, kasa, nyamba, tortue de mer, tortue franche, tortue mangeable, tortue verte (Frazier 1985); Mexico (Caribbean) - tortuga blanca (Márquez 1990); Mexico (Pacific) - caguama negra, caguama prieta, moosni, parlama, sacacillo, tortuga negra, tortuga prieta (Cliffton et al. 1982; Felger and Moser 1985; Márquez 1990); Micronesia - calap, melop, mwon, wel, winimon, won (Pritchard 1977); Moheli - dusi, kasa, nyamba (Frazier 1985); Mozambique - asa, casa, hassa, icaha, pateri, sinembo, tartaruga (Hughes 1971); Netherlands Antilles - greenback, tortuga blanku (Sybesma 1992); Nevis - greenback (Meylan 1983); Nicaragua (Caribbean) - tortuga verde, turtel, wli (Nietschmann 1973); Nicaragua (Pacific) - torita (Márquez 1990); Ogasawara Is. - ao umigame (Fukada 1965); Panama - tortuga verde (Márquez 1990); Papua New Guinea - 50+ names (Rhodin et al. 1980); Peru - tortuga, tortuga blanca, tortuga comestible, tortuga verde (Mittermeier et al. 1980; Brown and Brown 1982; Márquez 1990); Philippines - bildog, katuan, pawikan, payukan, pudno, tortuga (Pawikan Conservation Project Staff 1993); Portugal - tartaruga do mar, tartaruga verde (Osorio de Castro 1954); Ryukyu Is. - ao umigame (Fukada 1965); São Tomé - ambo, mão branco (Graff 1995); Senegal - dumal, mawa, ndumar, tortue franche, tortue verte (Maigret 1977); Solomon Is. - 29 names (Vaughan 1981); Southeast Africa - asa, casa, fano, fanohara, fanojoaty, fanovua, green turtle, groenseeskilpad, hassa, icaha, ifudu, pateri, sinembo, tartaruga, tortie de mer, tortue de mer, tortue franche, tortue verte, tsakoy (Hughes 1974a); Sri Lanka - gal käsbäva, mas käsbäva, pal amai, perr amai, väli käsbäva (Deraniyagala 1939); St. Barthelemy - tortue (Meylan 1983); St. Kitts - greenback (Meylan 1983); St. Martin - greenback (Meylan 1983); Suriname - kadaloe, krapé, ouyamouri, peñung, portoka, soepschildpad (Schulz 1975; Mittermeier et al. 1980); Thailand - tao saeng-atit, tao ta-nu (Nutaphand 1979); Tonga - fonu, fonu tu ' akula, fonu tu ' apolata, fonu tu ' a ' uli, tuai fonu (Hirth 1971a); Turkey - tirros (Hathaway 1972); Uruguay - tortuga verde (Mittermeier et al. 1980); Venezuela - caguamo, tortuga blanca, tortuga comestible, tortuga de sopa, tortuga franca, tortuga verde (Mittermeier et al. 1980; Pritchard and Trebbau 1984); Western Samoa - laumei (Hirth 1971a); Yemen - bissa, hamas, humea (FAO 1973).

Western Islanders in the Torres Strait distinguish 13 kinds of green turtles *(waru)* based on size, sex, age, color, habitat, agility, appearance and taste of the animal's fat (Nietschmann 1989). The least desirable, *gatau waru* ("drying reef turtle") are old, move slowly, are sedentary residents of drying reefs and graze on several algas which the Islanders say produce poor-tasting, black calipash fat. The *kapu waru* ("good turtle") are younger, bigger, faster, eat mostly seagrasses, migrate to nesting beaches on the Barrier Reef, and the Islanders say have good-tasting green calipash fat.

The Yanyuwa hunters in the southwestern Gulf of Carpentaria have a long historical and spiritual association with green turtles and dugongs. The green turtle is known as *malurrba* but there are additional names based on sex, size, coloration, condition and combinations of these traits (Bradley 1991).

In Tonga some fishermen have names for color phases, sizes and sex (Hirth 1971a), and the Raroians have names for different sizes of sea turtles (Danielsson 1956).

The Seri of Pacific Mexico have eight names for the green turtle with *moosni* being commonly used. Other names are based on coloration, size and condition (Felger and Moser 1985).

1.2.5 Definition of size categories
Size categories for green turtles are defined as follows (carapace lengths are standard straight-line measurements):

hatchling—from hatching (still bearing conspicuous umbilical scar) to the first few weeks of life.

juvenile—posthatchling to 40 cm carapace length. This stage is essentially the carnivorous (or omnivorous) pelagic stage. By about 40 cm carapace length most green turtles have entered their nearshore feeding habitat and are chiefly herbivorous (see section 2.2.2)

subadult—from 41 cm to the onset of sexual maturity, about 70 to 100 cm carapace length, depending upon the population.

adult—sexual maturity, >70-100 cm carapace length depending upon the population. The size at sexual maturity for males is presumed to be similar to that of females (but see section 3.1.1).

1.3 Morphology

1.3.1 External/internal morphology and coloration
General external morphology is described in Deraniyagala (1939), Carr (1952), Pritchard (1979b), Pritchard and Trebbau (1984), Ernst and Barbour, (1989), Márquez (1990), Cogger (1992) and Ernst et al. (1994) (see Fig. 3).

A few investigators have given some populations specific or subspecific names based mainly on morphological and biochemical traits and color. These populations and the traits have been discussed in section 1.2.3.

Morphometric measurements of adults and hatchlings from a wide range of locales are described in sections 3.1.2 and 3.2.2, respectively.

Unfortunately, turtle workers have used different names for some shell structures. The scutes (or laminae) of the carapace are the vertebrals (=centrals), costals (=laterals, pleurals), marginals, nuchal (=precentral, cervical), and supracaudals (=12th marginals, postcentrals) (see Fig. 4). There is more uniformity in the terminology of the plastral scutes: intergular, gulars, humerals, pectorals, abdominals, femorals, and anals. The bones of the carapace are the nuchal (=proneural), neurals, pleurals (=costals), peripherals (=marginals), pygal, and suprapygal. The paired bones of the plastron are the

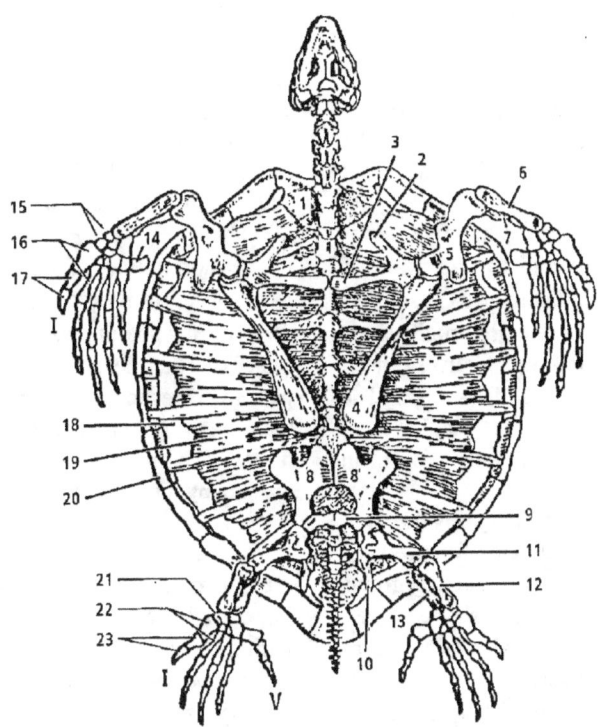

Fig. 3. *Chelonia mydas,* ventral view of skeleton, with plastron removed. 1-nuchal plate; 2-scapula; 3-acromion process of scapula; 4-coracoid; 5-humerus; 6-radius; 7-ulna; 8-pubis; 9-ischium; 10-ilium; 11-femur; 12-tibia; 13-fibula; 14-pisiform; 15-carpals; 16-metacarpals; 17-phalanges; 18-fontanelle; 19-pleural plate; 20-peripheral plate; 21-tarsals; 22-metatarsals; 23-phalanges; I-V-digits. From DeWitte in Vielliers, A. 1958 (with some nomenclatorial additions). Tortues et crocodiles de l'Afrique Noire Française. Initiations Africaines, Institut Français D'Afrique Noire 15: 1-354.

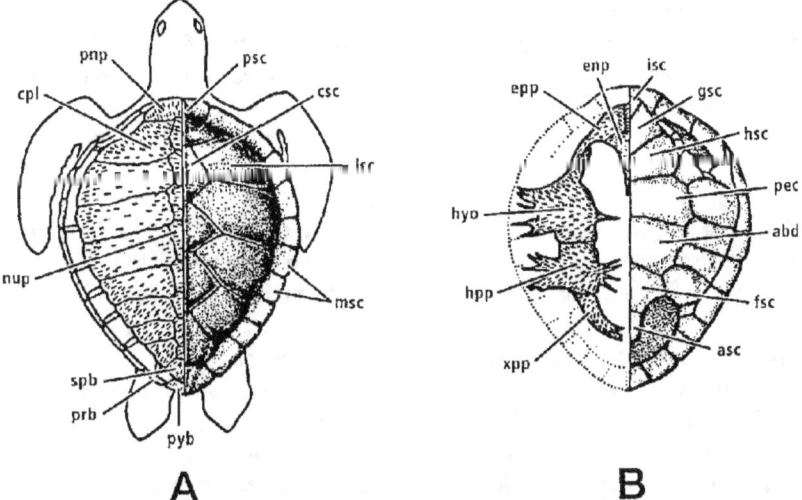

A **B**

Fig. 4. Sketches of *Chelonia mydas* illustrating the epidermal laminae (right) and bony elements (left) of the carapace (A) and the epidermal laminae (right) and bony elements (left) of the plastron (B). abd-abdominal scute; asc-anal scute; cpl-anteriormost of eight costal plates; csc-one of five central scutes; enp-entoplastron; epp-epiplastron; fsc-femoral scute; gsc-gular scute; hsc-humeral scute; hpp-hypoplastron; hyo-hyoplastron; isc-intergular; lsc-anteriormost of four lateral scutes; msc-marginal scutes; nup-neural plate; pec-pectoral; pnp-preneural plate; prb-posteriormost of eleven peripheral bones; psc-precentral scute; pyb-pygal bone; spb-suprapygal; xpp-xiphyplastron. Interlaminar seams are shown by solid lines and sutures by irregular lines. From Legler, J. M. 1993. Morphology and physiology of the Chelonia. Pages 108-119 *in* C. J. Glasby, G. J. B. Ross and P. L. Beesley (eds.), Fauna of Australia, Vol. 2A. Amphibia and Reptilia. Australian Government Publishing Service, Canberra, Australia. Commonwealth of Australia copyright reproduced by permission.

epiplastra, hyoplastra, hypoplastra and xiphiplastra. The single bone anteriorly is the entoplastron. Zangerl (1969), Pritchard and Trebbau (1984) and Ernst and Barbour (1989) discuss the shell terminology used by different investigators.

The streamlined green turtle carapace has five vertebral scutes, four pairs of costals and twelve pairs of marginals. Carapacial scutes are juxtaposed. The relatively small head has a pair of elongate prefontal scales. The minimally retractile neck is thick and relatively short. The strong forelimbs are elongate and paddle-shaped. The hindlimbs are smaller than the forelimbs. A median keel, present on the hatchling carapace, is weakly present in some juveniles and absent in adults.

Wyneken (1994) speculates that the changes in the shell shape of green turtles represent strategies for predator avoidance. In the epipelagic stage the carapace grows from an elliptical shape to a nearly circular shape. Later, when green turtles have entered coastal habitats, the carapace has regained its elliptical appearance.

According to Pritchard and Trebbau (1984) the bones of the carapace are relatively thick in adults; the neural bones are narrow; all peripheral bones except I, II and X bear a pit which receives the end of the rib; there are nine plastral bones with persistent fontanelles along the midline and at the center of each bridge; and, the skull is dorsally flat and extensively roofed.

Zangerl (1980) described the phylogenetic relationships among *Chelonia mydas, Chelonia sismondai* and other cheloniids based on morphology of the carapace, plastron and limb skeleton. The shell of turtles is described and the family Cheloniidae is placed in the metachelydian level of organization by Zangerl (1969).

Solomon et al. (1986) described the heavily keratinized plastron and carapace of the green turtle. The epidermis is generally 2-4 cells thick but at growing points it can attain 6 cell layers. Examination of the bones of *C. mydas* revealed typical chelonian articular surfaces without transphyseal vascularization (Rhodin 1985). Gaffney (1979) reviewed the earlier literature, then updated, the cranial morphology of sea turtles. He gives anatomical descriptions of horizontally (Fig. 5) and medially sectioned skulls of *C. mydas*. Albrecht (1976) described in detail the cranial arteries (Fig. 6). The large stapedial and palatine arteries of the green turtle, and other sea turtles, may be similar to the primitive cranial arterial pattern for turtles.

The papillae along the lateral choanal margin and the nasal cavities are described by Parsons (1968, 1970). Saint-Girons (1991) studied the nasal cavity, histologically. Liebman and Granda (1971, 1975) described the rods, cones and oil droplets in the eyes.

According to Wever (1978), who described the ears of turtles, in *C. mydas* the middle layer of the tympanic membrane is thick and contains a large amount of fatty tissue. This material serves to link the surface layer to the extracolumellar knob. The cochlea attains a length of 1750 μ. Ridgway et al. (1969) measured cochlear potentials and found maximum sensitivities in the regions of 300 to 400 Hz.

The morphology of the pineal-paraphyseal complex, a large structure projecting dorsally and anteriorly above the prosencephalon, was described by Owens and Ralph (1978). They describe two pineal cell types which appear to correspond to the neuroglial supportive cells and the secretory rudimentary photoreceptor cells of other amniotes. The production and role of melatonin was discussed by Owens et al. (1980) and Owens and Gern (1985).

Winokur and Legler (1974) found that green turtles lack typical rostral pores (= epidermal invaginations in the internarial region) but they have a deep sagittal fissure, with an expanded basal portion, between the prefrontal scales, and this may be a pore homologue. In his study of buccopharyngeal mucosa of turtles, Winokur (1988) discovered that green turtles were the only species studied with what he termed "pharyngeal tonsils." These were a series of five to seven pits, lined with cells, in the pharynx, posterior to the glottis.

Quesada and Madriz (1986) give an account of the anatomy of the adult heart and Jaffee (1969) very briefly describes some aspects of the ontogeny of the embryonic heart. Barragán (1994) very briefly described the cardiovascular anatomy of a juvenile Mexican black turtle. The aortas of several, juvenile green turtles from the Cayman Turtle Farm were found to have gross aneurysmal dilations and multiple raised plaques which resembled both the aortic lesions in Marfan's syndrome in humans and those induced by chemical treatments in animals (Toda et al. 1984). Sapsford (1978) reported on a muscular sphincter in the pulmonary arteries of four species of sea turtles, including the green turtle, and suggested that its presence provides a mechanism for the control of blood flow through the heart.

The anatomy of the lung was described by Solomon and Purton (1984) and among their findings were: the respiratory epithelium is typically vertebrate, being pseudostratified columnar with cilia; the gaseous exchange areas appear at all levels from the respiratory bronchi to the alveoli; and the epithelial lining of the alveoli is composed of type I and type II pneumocytes which are morphologically similar to those of birds and mammals. Patterson (1973) reported a lung volume (in [3]) to body mass (oz) ratio of 0.049 in a green turtle.

Solomon and Tippett (1991) determined that the livers of male and female, farm-reared turtles are fat laden and that liver weight and fat accumulation increase with animal weight.

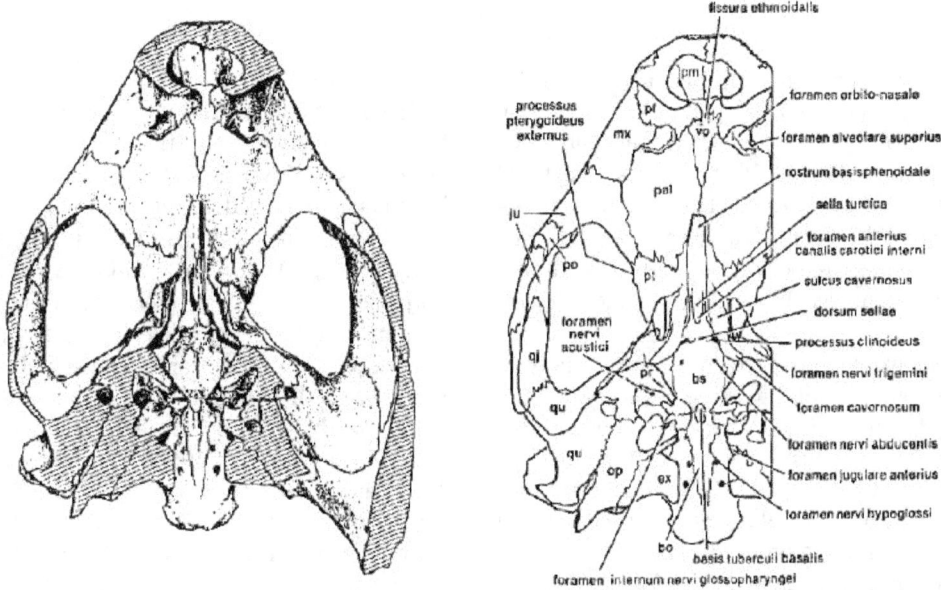

Fig. 5. Cranial morphology of a green turtle. Dorsal view of a horizontally sectioned skull. Hatched areas indicate cut surface. Anatomical abbreviations: bo, basioccipital; bs, basisphenoid; ex, exoccipital; ju, jugal; mx, maxilla; op, opisthotic; pal, palatine; pf, prefrontal; pm, premaxilla; po, postorbital; pr, prootic; pt, pterygoid; qj, quadratojugal; qu, quadrate; vo, vomer. From Gaffney, E. S. 1979. Comparative cranial morphology of recent and fossil turtles. Bull. Amer. Mus. Nat. Hist. 164(2): 65-376. Copyright American Museum of Natural History 1979. Courtesy American Museum of Natural History Library.

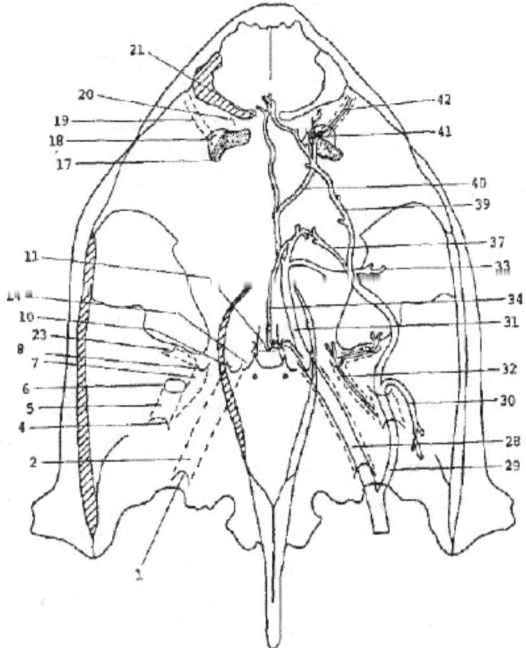

Fig. 6. Semidiagrammatic dorsal view of the cranial arteries (right side) and cranial arterial foramina and canals (left side) of *Chelonia mydas*. 1-F. posterior canalis carotici interni; 2-Canalis caroticus internus; 4-Auditus canalis stapedio-temporalis; 5-Canalis stapedio-temporalis; 6-F. stapedio-temporale; 7-Canalis cavernosus; 8-F. cavernosum; 10-F. caroticum laterale; 11-F. anterior canalis carotici interni; 17-F. orbito-nasale; 18-F. alveolare superius; 19-Canalis alveolaris superior; 20-F. supraorbitale; 21-Fissura ethmoidalis; 23-F. arteriomandibulare; 24-Sulcus caroticus; 28-Internal carotid; 29-Stapedial; 30-Cervical; 31-Palatine; 32-Vestigial mandibular; 33-Mandibular; 34-Orbital; 37-Infraorbital; 39-Supraorbital; 40-Alveolar-nasal; 41-Posterior nasal; 42-Superior alveolar. From Albrecht, P. W. 1976. The cranial arteries of turtles and their evolutionary significance. J. Morphology 149(2): 159-182. Copyright, The Wistar Institute Press 1976.

The kidneys of green turtles are flattened, lobed and closely applied to the posterior wall of the pleuroperitoneal cavity (Solomon 1985). Using light, scanning and transmission microsopy, Solomon (1985) described the functional nephron as being comprised of a glomerulus, proximal tubule, intermediate segment which can be subdivided into a proximal non-secretory segment and a distal mucus secreting segment, distal convoluted tubule, and collecting tubule.

The ovary is a membranous structure with a relatively short attached border resulting in significant folding. In reproductively inactive animals a narrow, compact cortex and spongy medulla are easily recognized (Aitken et al. 1976). The roles of the several subdivisions of the oviduct in egg formation are elucidated by Aitken and Solomon (1976) and Solomon and Baird (1979).

Using light microscopy, Ehrenfeld and Ehrenfeld (1973) described the axillary and inguinal glands. They postulated that the secretion of the glands may serve as a defense substance and/or the secretion may play a role in intraspecies communication. Later, Solomon (1984) using scanning electron microscopy and transmission electron microscopy, as well as light microscopy, elaborated on the structure of the axillary gland.

The phallus of the green turtle is similar in structure to those of the hawksbill, loggerhead and leatherback turtles, in that a single U-shaped fold forms the glans and the seminal groove is single and terminates medially on the inner surface of the fold (Zug 1966).

The major visceral organs of the green turtle are illustrated in the booklet by Rainey (1981), and Wolke and George (1981) have written a guide for conducting necropsies under laboratory and field conditions. Some of the older references to the morphology and physiology of the green turtle are cited in Hirth (1971b).

Miller (1985) reviewed the literature and concluded that the frequency of occurrence of abnormal embryos and hatchlings is low among marine turtles. The most common malformation is variation in scale patterns. From their personal observations and a review of the literature, Rhodin et al. (1984) concluded that the incidence of spinal deformities and kyphosis among a total of 4,207 green turtles, from four localities, was, respectively, 0.14% and 0.10%.

Deviations from normal central and lateral carapace scutes were statistically different in hatchlings from a hatchery (mean 12.8%) and in hatchlings from natural beaches (mean 4.9%) in the Ogasawara Islands (Suganuma et al. 1994). Although not statistically different, 5% of adult females (N=1,252) and 3.3% of adult males (N=661) in the Ogasawara population exhibited similar scute abnormalities.

Demetropoulos and Hadjichristophorou (1995) provide a color photo of an adult green turtle lacking all carapacial shields.

Green turtle hatchlings are blackish above and white below. The plastron usually remains light-colored as the turtle grows. However, Balazs (1986) noted that Hawaiian hatchlings passed through a pronounced color phase in early life. The plastron of Hawaiian neonates (50 mm carapace length) are white but soon become diffused with gray and black pigment (greatest intensity between 70-80 mm carapace length) and then the dark color fades away and usually disappears completely (by 130 mm carapace length) leaving the plastron white again. Albino hatchlings have been reported in Sarawak (Harrisson 1963) Tortuguero (Carr 1967a; Fig. 7) Florida (Fletemeyer 1977), and North Carolina (Schwartz and Peterson 1984). Carr (1967a) stated that four albinos had been found in some one hundred and fifty thousand hatchlings at Tortuguero.

Deraniyagala (1939) described eight color stages in Sri Lanka green turtles. Hatchlings' carapaces are dark greenish bronze and after three or four months they become brownish-red. This background color then is variegated by black, brown and yellow streaks. Ultimately the carapace color is suffused with olive-green and the black and brown streaks are broken-up into small spots. Ventrally, the color is white in the young and light yellow in the adult.

Juvenile carapace coloring is highly variable. Many regional handbooks and field guides give word descriptions of color patterns of immature and/or mature turtles in their respective areas. In an attempt to standarize color descriptions of immature green turtles, Hirth et al. (1992) used Munsell soil color chips to describe pigmentation in Wuvulu Island turtles. Here, the coloration of subadults with carapace lengths of between 45 and 72 cm were basically similar. For example, the large vertebral and costal scutes were, when wet, brown (7.5 YR 4/4) to dark brown (7.5 YR 3/2) at the basal seam with emanating dark brown and olive gray (5Y 5/2) rays of varying length. The plastra varied from white (5Y 8/1) to pale yellow (5Y 8/3).

The coloration of adult males and females is highly variable. Frazier (1971) illustrated a wide range of adult color patterns within the Aldabra population. Pritchard (1971) described several morphotypes in the Galápagos ranging from a "yellow" type to a few with *mydas*-like carapaces to those (majority) with blackish dorsa.

Photographs illustrating coloration and general external morphology are provided by: Carr (1967b), Costa Rica (Caribbean), hatchlings, adult female; Frazier (1971), Aldabra Atoll, adult males and females; Carr (1972b), Australia, sleeping underwater, Costa Rica (Caribbean), nester; Bustard (1973), Australia, large females, male; Ehrenfeld (1974), Australia, copulating, hatchlings, nester, swimming male (cover); Hallowell (1979), Australia, large

Fig. 7. A normal green turtle hatchling and a partial albino from Tortuguero, Costa Rica. Each weighs about 26 g. Hatchlings from this population will increase in weight approximately 4,700X by the time they are reproductively mature. Note that unlike adults, hatchlings crawl using diagonal flippers (i. e. front limb moved in conjunction with hind limb on opposite side).

male; Pritchard (1979b), Australia, large male, Galápagos, nester, Guyana, adult female, captivity, swimming male; Spring (1980), Papua New Guinea, juvenile and large females; Pritchard et al. (1983), locations not given, posthatchling, juvenile, adult male and female; Sheppard (1983), Australia, copulating and stack of four; Pritchard and Trebbau (1984), Suriname, nester, captivity, posthatchling; Bonnett et al. (1985a), Southwest Indian Ocean, hatchlings and nester; Cornelius (1986), Costa Rica (Pacific), large female; Miller (1989), Saudi Arabia, nesters, copulating; Cogger (1992), Australia, copulating stack (2 males, 1 female); Rudloe and Rudloe (1994), Mexico (Pacific) copulating; Demetropoulos and Hadjichristophorou (1995), Mediterranean, adult male and female, juvenile and hatchling; Lindsay (1995), Indonesia, adult male swimming; Wuethrich (1996), Hawaii, adult swimming.

The common name, green turtle, does not refer to its external color, but to the color of its fat.

1.3.2. Cytomorphology

Chelonia mydas has a diploid number of 56 chromosomes. There are no heteromorphic sex chromosomes (Bickham et al. 1980; Bachère 1981).

Using Bkm 2(8) probes, Demas et al. (1990) found male and female-specific DNA fragments in the green turtle. Individual-specific DNA fingerprints are readily identifi-able after hybridization with Bkm 2(8) (Demas and Wachtel 1991).

Frair (1977a) made a comprehensive survey of the turtle literature concerning packed red blood cell volumes (PCV), red blood cell counts (RCC) and red blood cell sizes. The mean PCV of green turtles from several studies ranged from 24.8 to 31.6 $cm^3/100$ cm^3 and the mean RCC in two studies was 523 and $530/mm^3 \times 10^{-3}$. Larger green turtles tend to have higher PCVs, larger red cells and lower RCC (Frair 1977b). There is also a significant positive correlation between carapace length and total serum protein (Frair and Shah 1982). Grumbles et al. (1990) determined that, in wild turtles off the Pacific coast of Mexico, packed cell volumes and red blood cell counts were not significantly different between nesting females, females at sea, and males at sea, but white blood cell counts were significantly lower for males at sea than nesting females or females at sea. Bolten and Bjorndal (1992) found that PCV was not significantly related to differences in body size or sex in a population of juvenile green turtles in the Bahamas. They did find that plasma uric acid and cholesterol were significantly different between females and males. Wood and Ebanks (1984) identified six cell types in the blood: red cells, lymphocytes, eosinophils, basophils, neutrophils and thrombocytes. The infrastructure of thrombocytes are described by Bonnet et al. (1985b). McKinney and Bentley (1985) found that blastogenic and cytotoxic responses of leukocytes to some mitogens and antibody-dependent cell-mediated cytotoxicity were of significant magnitude. Based upon the extinction coefficient, the total carotenoid content in the serum of two Pacific green turtles was determined to be 1.27 µg/ml (Nakamura 1980).

Owens and Ruiz (1980) developed methods for obtaining blood samples from the paired dorsal cervical sinuses and cerebrospinal fluids from the foramen magnum.

Koment and Haines (1982) describe the establishment and characterization of a skin cell line from a young green turtle.

1.3.3 Protein composition and specificity and general physiology

Serum electrophoresis studies indicated that proteins from *Chelonia* are more like those of *Caretta* and *Lepidochelys* than like *Eretmochelys* (Frair 1982). Systematic information derived from immunoelectrophoretic work (Mao and Chen 1982) are in general agreement with taxonomic-relationships established by morphological criteria.

It appears that organic phosphate modulators regulate whole blood oxygen affinity during embryonic development but not in the adult (Isaacks and Harkness 1980). Wells and Baldwin (1994) described how hatchling erythrocyte (red blood cell) mean cell volume is approximately half of the adult value, but hematocrit, blood hemoglobin concentration and blood viscosity of hatchlings and adults are similar. Friedman et al. (1985) found that sea turtle hemoglobins are designed for efficient oxygen transport and release to tissues rather than storage. They also describe how the temperature response of the oxygenated hemoglobin may be related to its ability to maintain metabolically active tissues at several degrees higher than ambient temperatures. This regional endothermy may assist the turtle in long migrations.

Working with Australian green turtles, Reina (1994) found that hatchlings have significantly higher levels of sodium and potassium in their plasma than do adults and the differences may be associated with diet (hatchlings feed on macroplankton: adults on seagrasses). Plasma zinc, analyzed by atomic absorption spectrophotometry, in five green turtles from Costa Rica, averaged 1.00 µg/ml (range 0.67-1.29 µg/ml) (Lance et al. 1995). This average was slightly higher than the means of 0.64 and 0.84 µg/ml reported for five olive ridleys and one Kemp's ridley, respectively.

Using starch gel electrophoresis, Smith et al. (1978) analyzed thirteen biochemical loci in green turtles from Florida and the Caribbean. They found that 46.2 to 69.2% of the loci were polymorphic and that heterozygosity averaged 11.9%.

Osada et al. (1988) determined that the concentration of alpha-macroglobulin in green turtle plasma was about 4 mg/ml and that the concentration of ovomacroglobulin in green turtle egg white was about 0.4 mg/ml. They postulated that the difference was due to divergent evolution. Electron micrographs of alpha-macroglobulin and ovomacroglobulin revealed similarities in their fundamental architecture but differences in some details (Ikai et al. 1988).

Egg lipids from green, loggerhead, leatherback and hawksbill turtles have distinct profiles and this knowledge has been used as a forensic tool to support enforcement of protective regulations (Seaborn and Moore 1994).

Sage and Gray (1979) determined the amino acid composition of elastin in the aorta.

Myoglobins from an Atlantic and a Pacific green turtle exhibited similar amino acid compositions but with possible differences in lysine, histidine, serine, glutamic acid, proline and glycine residues (Williams and Brown 1976). The amino acid sequence of the main component myoglobin from skeletal muscle of the Pacific green turtle was analyzed by Watts et al. (1983).

The complete amino acid sequences of green turtle growth hormone and prolactin consist of, respectively, 190 and 198 amino acid residues (Yasuda et al. 1989 and Yasuda et al. 1990).

The lysine: histidine ratio in the shell keratin of wild green turtles and farm-reared green turtles are significantly different (Hendrickson et al. 1977). These results indicate a dietary influence on shell composition at least up to some point.

Depot fatty acid composition in Caribbean turtles were studied by Joseph et al. (1985) and fatty acids in depot fats of green turtles from Hawaii and Johnston Atoll, which feed principally on marine algae, were analyzed by Ackman et al. (1992).

Measurements made of the water content and fat of standard cores of fat lining the inner carapace of turtles caught off Daru, Papua New Guinea, revealed that the amount of depot fat, total lipid and neutral lipid per core varied with the sex, reproductive status and maturity of the individual (Kwan 1994). Cores from adult females had a significantly greater fat content than those from adult males. Cores from pubescent and vitellogenic females had the highest fat content. Results of this study suggested that sub-carapace depot fat supplies the energy for migrations and egg production.

Penick et al. (1996) determined that Q_{10} values of green fat, small intestine, nonswimming skeletal muscle, pectoralis muscle, liver, heart and kidney tissues ranged from 0.65 to 3.38. Tissue metabolic rates were highest in the kidney and heart tissues and lowest in the green fat and small intestine tissues. Muscle tissue had a high oxygen consumption and this elevated metabolism may be adaptive for long migrations.

Owens and Morris (1985) reviewed the literature on

the comparative endocrinology of *Chelonia, Caretta* and *Lepidochelys*. This review included references to research on pituitary homogenate, follicle stimulating hormone, luteinizing hormone, growth hormone, thyroid stimulating hormone, gonadotropin releasing hormone, arginine vasotocin, melatonin, testosterone, estradiol, progesterone and corticosterone. Subsequent to this review some other accounts of green turtle endocrinology and physiology are provided by Licht et al. (1984) and Licht and Papkoff (1985) on glycoproteins; Licht et al. (1985) on thyroxine and testosterone; Licht et al. (1991) on thyroxine; and, Wibbels et al. (1992) on follicle stimulating hormone, luteinizing hormone, progesterone and testosterone.

Herbst and Klein (1995b) showed how monoclonal antibodies may be useful for immunodiagnostic applications in the green turtle. Shaw et al. (1995a) tested isoflurane on juvenile and subadult green turtles and found it to be a safe and effective anesthetic.

2. DISTRIBUTION

2.1 Total Area

Green turtles are circumglobal, commonly found throughout the tropical seas and as stragglers in a far more extensive area. In general, green turtles are seen between 40°N and 40°S latitudes, but there are a dearth of sightings in the east-central Pacific Ocean and the northeast Atlantic Ocean. They occur on the nesting beaches or in offshore waters of at least 139 countries and territories. Groombridge and Luxmoore (1989) briefly review their occurrence in 126 areas: American Samoa, Angola, Anguilla, Antigua and Barbuda, Ascension and St. Helena, Australia, Bahamas, Bahrain, Bangladesh, Barbados, Belize, Bermuda, Brazil, British Indian Ocean Territories, British Virgin Islands, Burma, Canary Islands, Cape Verde Islands, Cayman Islands, Chile, China, Colombia, Comoro Islands, Congo, Cook Islands, Costa Rica, Cuba, Cyprus, Djibouti, Dominica, Dominican Republic, Ecuador, Egypt, El Salvador, Equatorial Guinea, Eritrea, Federated States of Micronesia, Fiji, French Guiana, French Polynesia, Gabon, Ghana, Grenada and the Grenadian Grenadines, Guadeloupe, Guam, Guatemala, Guinea, Guinea Bissau, Guyana, Haiti, Hawaii, Honduras, Hong Kong, India, Indonesia, Iran, Israel, Jamaica, Japan, Kampuchea, Kenya, Kiribati, Kuwait, Liberia, Madagascar, Madeira and Azores, Malaysia, Maldives, Marshall Islands, Martinique, Mauritania, Mauritius and Dependencies (Rodrigues, St. Brandon Shoals, Mayotte), Mexico, Montserrat, Mozambique, Namibia, Netherlands Antilles (Curacao, Bonaire, Saba, St. Eustatius, St. Maarten), New Caledonia, New Zealand, Nicaragua, Northern Marianas, Oman, Pakistan, Palau Republic, Panama, Papua New Guinea, Peru, Philippines, Pitcairn, Puerto Rico, Qatar, Reunion (Europa, Tromelin, Iles Glorieuses, Juan de Nova), São Tomé and Principe, Saudi Arabia, Senegal, Seychelles, Sierra Leone, Solomon Islands, Somalia, South Africa, Sri Lanka, St. Kitts-Nevis, St. Lucia, St. Vincent and the St. Vincent Grenadines, Sudan, Suriname, Taiwan, Tanzania, Thailand, Togo, Tokelau, Tonga, Trinidad and Tobago, Turkey, Turks and Caicos Islands, Tuvalu, United Arab Emirates, United States of America, U.S. Pacific Islands (Jarvis Island, Johnston Atoll, Howland and Baker Reefs, Palmyra Island, Wake Island), U.S. Virgin Islands, Vanuatu, Venezuela, Viet Nam, Western Samoa, Yemen, Zaire.

To the aforementioned list of areas can be added: Argentina (Frazier 1984a; Richard and Moulin 1990; Scolaro 1990), Canada (Carl 1955), France (Knoepffler 1961), Greece (Margaritoulis et al. 1986), Italy (Gramentz 1989; Basso 1992), Korea (Shannon 1956), Malta (Despott 1930; Brongersma and Carr 1983), Netherlands (Brongersma 1982); Portugal (Brongersma 1982), Spain (Brongersma 1982; Pascual 1985), Tunisia (Laurent et al. 1990; Laurent and Lescure 1992), United Kingdom (Penhallurick 1990), and Uruguay (Gambarotta and Gudynas 1979; Gudynas 1980; Frazier 1984a).

Some recent, detailed accounts of their distribution in some areas of the Pacific Ocean can be found in Hirth (1971a, 1993), Polunin (1975), Pritchard (1977, 1979a), Balazs (1980), UNEP/IUCN (1988c), Lockhart (1989), and Smith and Smith (1979, 1993). On the Pacific coast of the USA, green turtles have been documented from Alaska (Hodge 1981), Washington (Slater 1963) and California (Carr 1952). The following references provide detailed distribution accounts of green turtles in and around the Atlantic Ocean: Villiers (1958), Brongersma (1972), Carr et al. (1982), Meylan (1983), Pritchard and Trebbau (1984), Bacon et al. (1984), Delaugerre (1987), UNEP/IUCN (1988a), Ogren et al. (1989), Groombridge (1990) and Smith and Smith (1979, 1993). Green turtles occasionally stray into the Black Sea (Valkanov 1949; Fuhn and Vancea 1961; Geldiay et al. 1982). In the eastern USA, green turtles have been documented off the Atlantic and Gulf coasts from Massachusetts to Texas (Magnuson et al. 1990) although they are much more common in the warmer waters. In continental USA the main nesting grounds are in Florida. The northernmost nesting record on the U.S. Atlantic coast is North Carolina (Peterson et al. 1985). Some detailed accounts of their distribution in the Indian Ocean are in Peters and Lionnet (1973), Bonnet (1986), UNEP/IUCN (1988b), Miller (1989) and Frazier (1990).

Some worldwide distribution accounts are in Parsons (1962), Hirth (1971b, 1980b), Sternberg (1981) and Bjorndal (1982a).

2.2 Differential Distribution

2.2.1 Hatchlings

After reaching the sea, it is postulated that the hatchlings actively swim (the so-called "swim frenzy") directly away from land until they encounter zones of convergence and/or, where present, sargassum rafts (see Fig. 8). These convergence zones, or rafts, are rich in prey for the hatchlings and provide shelter. At this stage the hatchlings and young juveniles are thought to be chiefly carnivorous but some omnivory may prevail. This time in the lives of green turtles, as well as other marine turtles, was commonly referred to as the "lost year". It is now thought that this epipelagic phase of the green turtle, when it is presumed to be drifting in ocean currents and gyres, may be somewhat more protracted than a year and the plural "lost years" is more accurate. It should be emphasized that the turtles are not "lost"; humans have just not been able to track them. Some post-hatchling recovery sites, although few are recorded, may be quite distant from known nesting beaches. Strong El-Niño years must also have an effect on hatchling distribution. In a couple of seminal papers Carr (1986, 1987a) developed a model showing how hatchling and juvenile loggerheads may drift, perhaps for several years, with major currents and gyres between North America and Europe and this model, where applicable, may be relevant to green turtles.

In laboratory experiments, Mellgren et al. (1994) found that hatchling green turtles, unlike hawksbill and loggerhead hatchlings, did not orient to or congregate in artificial weed beds or in real seaweeds. They concluded that the lost years habitat of the green turtle has yet to be determined.

While not dealing specifically with green turtles, Brongersma (1972) discussed the possible role of currents in carrying sea turtles across the North Atlantic Ocean. Hughes (1989) stated "green turtles nesting on Europa are carried away from the shark-infested inshore waters by an eddy of the Mozambique Current, while the South Equatorial Current carries green turtle hatchlings away from St. Brandon and Tromelin." Witham (1980) reported that tag returns from pen-reared yearling green turtles suggested ocean current dispersal and he concluded "Our data strongly suggest that the initial posthatching period, 'the lost year', is a period of oceanic existence, when turtles opportunistically use ocean currents and food resources for dispersal and survival." The flatback turtle, *Natator depressus*, may be unique among sea turtles in not having a pelagic phase in its life cycle (Walker and Parmenter 1990).

Carr and Meylan (1980) postulated that Tortuguero hatchlings associate themselves with sargassum rafts, and drift in these rafts with currents. Developing this idea further, Carr (1980) posited that "it is therefore possible that both the northern and southern contingents of the Tortuguero breeding population pass their entire life cycles within the Southwest Carribbean Gyre and the region around its perimeter." Coston-Clements et al. (1991) review the literature and report how in addition to four species of sea turtles, pelagic sargassum supports a diverse community of epiphytes, fungi and more than one hundred species of invertebrates and fishes.

Pitman (1992) observed two green turtles, as well as three other species of turtles and a number of unidentified turtles, associated with flotsam in the eastern tropical Pacific Ocean. Witham (1991), however, pointed out that there may be significant predation on marine turtles associated with sargassum and flotsam and he suggested hatchlings may have a higher survival at sea away from sargassum and biomass accumulations. Collard (1992) found that in some places in the Gulf of Mexico and North Atlantic food would be available for pelagic sea turtles in non-frontal zones. The Sea Turtle Research Unit (1995) of the Universiti Pertanian Malaysia has recently developed a technique to monitor movements of hatchlings at sea by miniaturization of radiotelemetry.

The epipelagic phase in green turtles has been estimated at little more than a year (Hughes 1974b), from 7 to 14 months (Carr et al. 1978), at least two years (Balazs et al. 1987), from 1 to 3 years (Ehrhart and Witherington 1992; Eckert and Honebrink 1992), and from 2 to 5 years (Aquirre et al. 1994b).

2.2.2 Juveniles, subadults, and adults

As mentioned in the preceding paragraphs, the epipelagic stage of hatchlings and juveniles may persist for a year or more. The meroplanktonic green turtles are commonly seen again when they enter shallow water near islands or the neritic habitat (see Fig. 8). At this stage they are chiefly herbivores, feeding on seagrasses and algae. The approximate sizes (carapace lengths) at which juvenile green turtles leave the epipelagic habitat and enter their shallow water feeding habitat, in the Pacific Ocean area, are: 30.5 cm, in Western Samoa (Witzell 1982); 35 cm, in the Hawaiian Islands (Balazs 1982a); 35 cm, at Johnston Atoll (Balazs 1985a); 36.8 cm, at Wuvulu Island in Papua New Guinea (Hirth et al. 1992); 36 cm, at Heron Reef, Australia (Limpus and Reed 1985a); 36 cm, at Crown Island in Papua New Guinea (Spring 1983); 40 cm, in Queensland, Australia (Limpus 1982a); and, 43.5 cm, in the Solomon Islands (Vaughan 1981). In the Atlantic Ocean and Mediterranean Sea area the smallest green turtles found in some benthic feeding habitats are: 21 cm, in Florida (Ehrhart 1983); 22-24 cm, in Turkey (Groombridge 1990); 22.2 cm in Texas (Coyne and Landry Jr. 1994); 23.6 cm, in Florida (Henwood and Ogren 1987); 24.6 cm, in Puerto Rico (Collazo et al. 1992); 25 cm, in the Bahama Islands (Bjorndal and Bolten 1988); 25 cm,

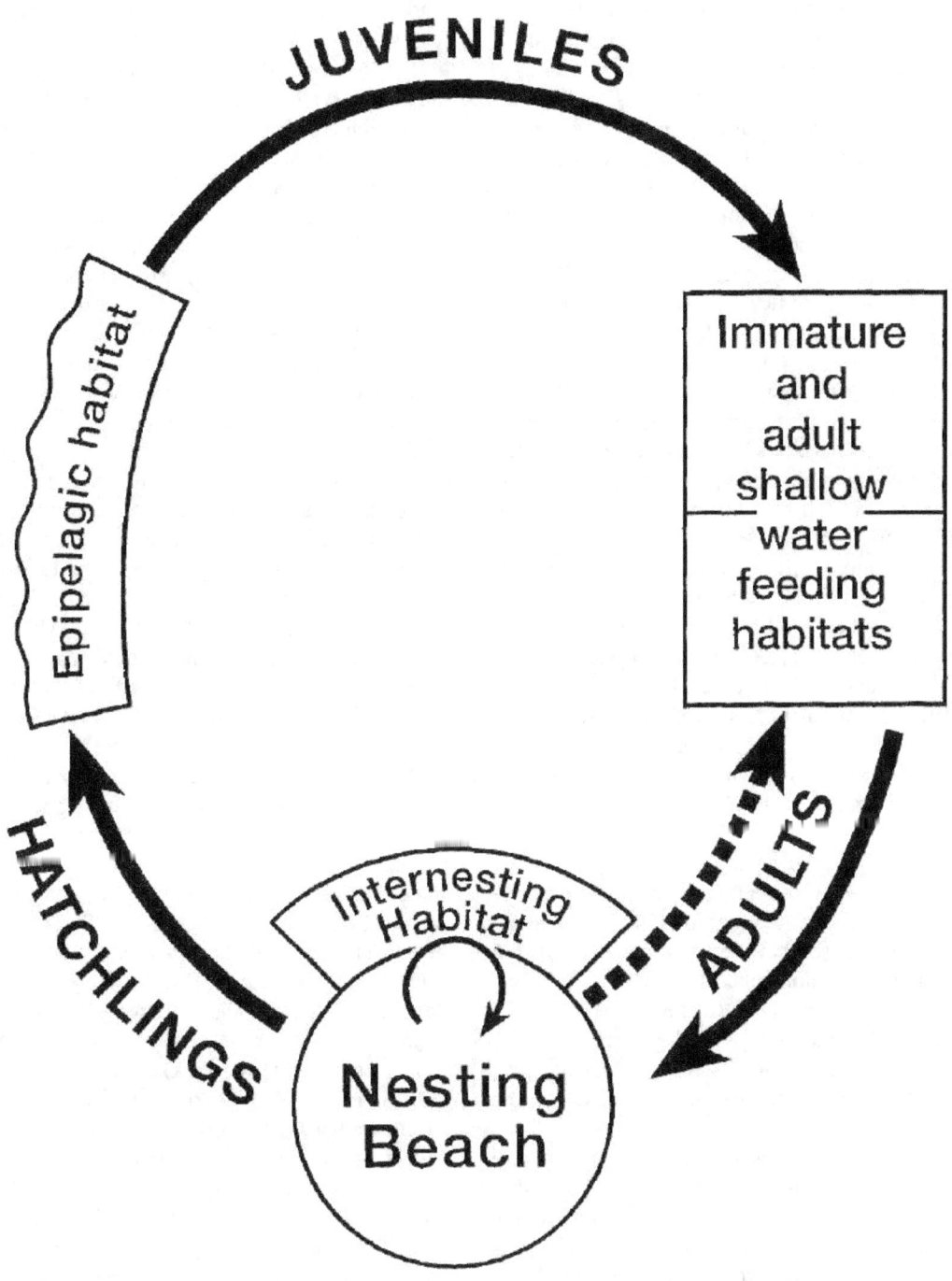

Fig. 8. Generalized life cycle of green turtles. The dashed line from the nesting beach to the feeding habitats indicates that the routes taken (i. e. direct or indirect) are generally unknown. (Figure modified from FAO, 1973).

in the U.S. Virgin Islands (Boulon and Frazer 1990); 26.6 cm, in Texas (Shaver 1994); 29.5 cm, in Florida (Mendonça 1981); 30 cm in Bermuda (Meylan et al. 1992a); and, about 31 cm in Brazil (da Costa 1969). Although the methodologies, objectives, and sample sizes in these studies were different, it appears that Pacific juvenile green turtles enter the nearshore feeding habitat at slightly larger sizes than their Atlantic counterparts.

Some green turtles may move through a series of "developmental" feeding habitats as they grow. For example, subadults are found in a feeding pasture off the west coast of Florida (Carr and Caldwell 1956) and juveniles and subadults are seen in the developmental habitats off the east coast of Florida (Mendonça and Ehrhart 1982; Ehrhart 1983; Wershoven and Wershoven 1992; Schmid 1995). Speaking about Florida turtles, Ehrhart and Witherington (1992) stated that "Juveniles 2-60 kg (4-130 lb) forage as herbivores in shallow coastal waters before abandoning this developmental habitat as sub-adults." The waters off the North Carolina coast may provide important developmental habitats for loggerhead, green and Kemp's ridley sea turtles (Epperly et al. 1995a, b). Bermuda, now, is strictly a developmental habitat (Meylan et al. 1992a). The evidence for a regular summering population of immatures in Nantucket Sound is problematical (Lazell 1980). Collazo et al. (1992) reported a juvenile and subadult feeding population in Puerto Rico. Evidence is accumulating that there is a green turtle developmental habitat off the Texas coast (Coyne and Landry Jr. 1994). Fortynine juvenile and subadult turtles have been captured there with straight line carapace lengths ranging from 22.2 to 81.5 cm. Possibly, there is an immature feeding population in Greece (Margaritoulis et al. 1992). Williams (1988) described the feeding behavior of an immature population in the U.S. Virgin Islands. Kaneohe Bay on Oahu, Hawaii, harbors a feeding population of about 500, mostly immature green turtles (Balazs et al. 1993). There is a foraging ground off southern Peru where 89% of 416 turtles in a sample were immatures (no hatchlings) (Brown and Brown 1982). On a map in Carr et al. (1982), well-known Carribbean green turtle developmental foraging habitats are plotted in Mexico, Nicaragua, Costa Rica, Panama, southern Bahamas, and in some places in the Lesser Antilles.

Lanyon et al. (1989) reviewed the Australian literature and stated that on the seagrass habitats of the Macarthur River Delta, Cleveland Bay, Shoalwater Bay, Repulse Bay and Moreton Bay, large immatures and adults predominate; but small-to-medium-sized immature turtles dominate the population structure in coral reef habitats off Heron Island, Cairns and eastern Torres Strait. The turtles feeding on Moreton Banks, Queensland, are mostly immature individuals, but this population may be in a state of recovery from past overharvesting (Limpus et al.

1994b).

Tagging projects now underway in some localities may eventually link developmental habitats with specific adult foraging habitats and with specific nesting beaches. Norman et al. (1993-94) briefly describe how genetic markers are being used to identify green turtle stocks in feeding grounds off eastern Australia. In a popular article, Bowen (1995) discusses how natural tags, e. g., mtDNA polymorphisms, can now be assayed to link a population's widely distant breeding and feeding sites.

On the other hand, some shallow water feeding grounds harbor aggregations of both immature and mature turtles: Brazil (da Costa 1969), Yemen (Hirth and Carr 1970), Nicaragua (Mortimer 1981), Oman (Ross 1985) and Turkey (Groombridge 1990). A resident population of immatures and adults may reside in Mussulo Bay, Angola (Carr and Carr 1991). On a map in Carr et al. (1982) well-known adult benthic foraging habitats of the Caribbean green turtles are depicted in Mexico, Nicaragua, Colombia, Venezuela and in some places in the Lesser Antilles.

The distribution of adults is determined to a large extent by the locations of their nesting beaches and feeding grounds. Nesting sites are shown in Figs. 9, 10, and 11, and nesting seasons are given in Table 1. All the major and minor nesting sites (except those in Turkey) are located between 30°N and 30°S latitudes. All nesting populations are important and need to be conserved.

A few pertinent comments on some well-known nesting beaches and adult distributions in the Pacific, Indian and Atlantic Oceans are given here. In addition to the Xisha Islands, Zhao and Adler (1993) list the occurrence of green turtles off the Chinese mainland provinces of Shandong, Jiangsu, Zhejiang, Fujian, Guangdong and Guangxi and off the islands of Taiwan and Hainan. The Ko Adang Group in Thailand is now part of the Tarutao National Park. A brief history of the Park and the sea turtle work is provided by Howlett (1982). The Sarawak Turtle Islands are Satang Besar, Talang Talang Besar and Talang Talang Kecil and the three principal nesting sites in the Sabah Turtle Islands (now incorporated into the Turtle Islands National Park) are Pulau Selingaan, Pulau Gulisaan and Pulau Bakkungan Kecil. According to Mortimer et al. (1993) important foraging areas for green turtles and hawksbills are found along the coasts of the States of Melaka and Negeri Sembilan in Malaysia. Liew and Chan (1993) state that the island of Pulau Redang, 45 km off the coast of Terengganu, provides nesting habitat for the largest concentration of green turtles in Peninsular Malaysia.

The major nesting sites in the Philippine Turtle Islands are Baguan Is., Taganak Is., Langaan Is., Great Bakkungaan Is., Lihiman Is., and Boaan Is. A small population of green turtles nests on several beaches on Wan-

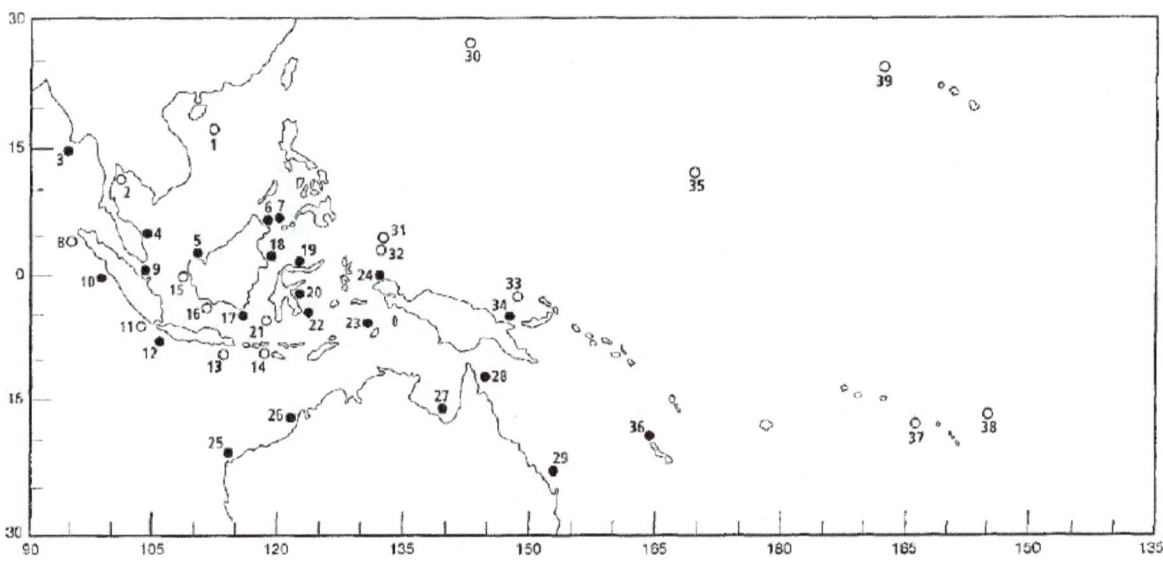

Fig. 9. Major nesting sites (solid circles; more than 500 nest annually, or an average of 500 if nesting is cyclic) and minor nesting sites (open circles; from 100 to 500 nest annually) of the green turtle. 1=Xisha Is. (Groombridge and Luxmoore 1989) 2=Ko Khram (Groombridge and Luxmoore 1989) 3=Thamihla Kyun (Groombridge and Luxmoore 1989) 4=Terengganu State (Groombridge and Luxmoore 1989) 5=Sarawak Turtle Islands (Hendrickson 1958; Groombridge and Luxmoore 1989) 6=Sabah Turtle Islands (de Silva 1982; Groombridge and Luxmoore 1989) 7=Philippine Turtle Islands (Trono 1991; Pawikan Conservation Project Staff 1993) 8=Aceh and North Sumatra Province (Salm 1984 in Groombridge and Luxmoore 1989) 9=Riau Province (Schulz 1987 in Groombridge and Luxmoore 1989) 10=West Sumatra Province (Salm 1984 in Groombridge and Luxmoore 1989) 11=South Sumatra Province (Schulz 1987 in Groombridge and Luxmoore 1989) 12=West Java Province (Salm 1984 and Schulz 1987 in Groombridge and Luxmoore 1989) 13=East Java Province (Schulz 1984 and 1987 in Groombridge and Luxmoore 1989) 14=West Nusa Tenggara Province (Schulz 1989 in Groombridge and Luxmoore 1989) 15=West Kalimantan Province (Schulz 1987 in Groombridge and Luxmoore 1989) 16=Central Kalimantan Province (Salm 1984 in Groombridge and Luxmoore 1989) 17=South Kalimantan Province (Schulz 1987 in Groombridge and Luxmoore 1989) 18=East Kalimantan Province (Schulz 1984 in Groombridge and Luxmoore 1989) 19=North Sulawesi Province (Salm 1984 in Groombridge and Luxmoore 1989) 20=Central Sulawesi Province (Salm 1984 in Groombridge and Luxmoore 1989) 21=South Sulawesi Province (Schulz 1989 in Groombridge and Luxmoore 1989) 22=Southeast Sulawesi Province (Salm 1984 in Groombridge and Luxmoore 1989) 23=Maluku Province (Schulz 1989 in Groombridge and Luxmoore 1989) 24=Irian Jaya Province (Salm 1984 in Groombridge and Luxmoore 1989) 25=Northwest Cape-Barrow Is. complex (Prince 1993; Limpus, pers. comm.) 26=Lacepede Is. complex (Prince 1993; Limpus, pers. comm.) 27=Wellesley group (Limpus 1982a) 28=Raine Is.-Moulter Cay complex (Limpus et al. 1993) 29=Capricorn-Bunker Group (Limpus 1980) 30=Ogasawara Is. (Suganuma 1985) 31=Merir Is. (Pritchard 1977; Johannes 1986) 32=Helen's Reef (Pritchard 1977; Johannes 1986) 33=Manus Province Is. (Spring 1982a) 34=Long Is. (Spring 1983) 35=Bikar Atoll (Fosberg 1969, 1990; Hendrickson 1972) 36=d'Entrecasteaux Reef system (Pritchard 1982a, 1987, Anon 1989) 37=Palmerston Atoll (Powell 1957; Groombridge and Luxmoore 1989) 38=Scilly Atoll (Lebeau 1985) 39=French Frigate Shoals (Anon. 1991a).

17

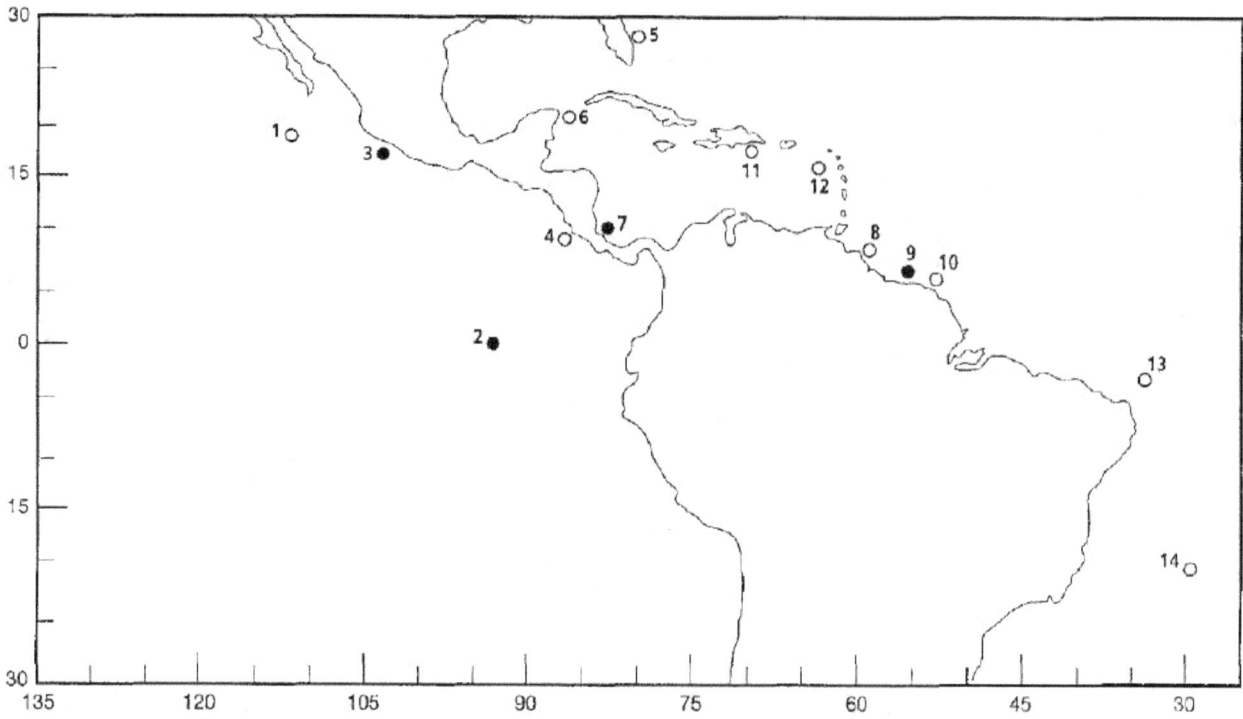

Fig.10. Major nesting sites (solid circles; more than 500 nest annually, or an average of 500 if nesting is cyclic) and minor nesting sites (open circles; from 100 to 500 nest annually) of the green turtle. 1=Islas Revillagigedo (Brattstrom 1982; Awbrey et al. 1984) 2=Galápagos Is. (Green 1983) 3=Colola and Maruata (Alvarado and Figueroa 1990) 4=Playa Naranjo (Cornelius 1976) 5=Southeast Florida (Ehrhart and Witherington 1992) 6=Yucatan Peninsula (Marquez in Ogren 1989) 7=Tortuguero (Carr et al 1982) 8=Shell Beach (Pritchard 1969) 9=Suriname (Schulz 1982) 10=French Guiana (Fretey 1984) 11=Dominican Republic (Ottenwalder 1981 in Groombridge and Luxmoore 1989) 12=Aves Is. (Medina and Sole in Ogren 1989) 13=Atol das Rocas (Bellini et al. 1996) 14=Ilha de Trindade (Moreira et al. 1995).

An Island, Peng-Hu Archipelago, Taiwan (Chen and Cheng 1995). Green turtles are known to nest on islands in the Ryukyu Archipelago (Kikukawa et al. 1996). The Indonesian nesting sites include several beaches. It is estimated that between 25,000 and 35,000 females nest annually in Indonesia (Groombridge and Luxmoore 1989). There is some nesting by green turtles on Inggresau Beach, Yapen Island, Irian Jaya Province in Indonesia (Maturbongs et al. 1993). Villagers here say the nesting season is April to July.

There are five major nesting concentrations in Australia. Limpus (1982a) states that the annual nesting population in the Wellesley group (including Bountiful and Pisonia Islands) is usually thousands. Limpus et al. (1993) declare that the Raine Is. - Moulter Cay complex (including Bramble Cay, and No. 7 and No. 8 Sandbanks) is the largest green turtle nesting aggregation in the world. The annual nesting population varies between a few hundred to tens of thousands. Low (1985) reported that 11,467 turtles were on Raine Is. at one time. Limpus (1987) describes how Raine Is. has probably been a nesting ground

for the past 1,130 years. In addition to these well-known nesting sites, Miller and Limpus (1991) list several islands off northeast Australia where several dozen turtles were recorded in the breeding season. About 5,000 nest annually in the Capricorn - Bunker group (Limpus and Fleay 1983). Lithou Cays, Magdeline Cays, Diamond Islets and Willis Islets are green turtle nesting sites of undetermined density, off Queensland, and should be investigated (Limpus 1980).

Pritchard (1977) estimated that several dozen nested on a good night on Merir Is. and Helen's Reef. The peak nesting season appears to be in the northern hemisphere summer. Wilson (1976) reported that a foreign fishing vessel had illegally caught over 214 green turtles in ten days at Helen's Reef. Rodda et al. (1991) list the green turtle as occurring on Cocos, Guam, Rota, Tinian and Saipan in the Mariana Islands. The annual nesting population in the Ogasawara Islands was estimated at between 43 and 162 between 1985 and 1993 (Horikoshi et al. 1994). In a September, 1988, survey of Pikaar Atoll (=Bikar), Jemo Island and Adkup Atoll, 176, 53 and 49 sets of turtle

18

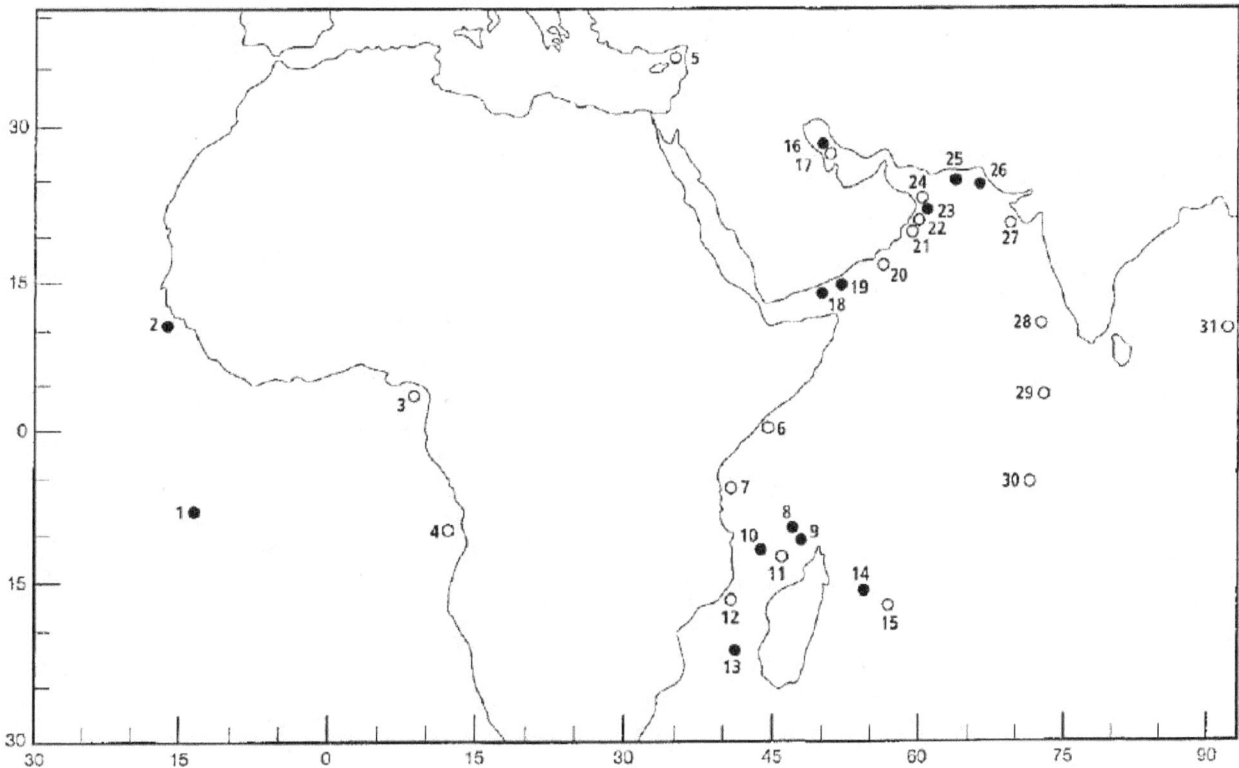

Fig. 11. Major nesting sites (solid circles; more than 500 nest annually, or an average of 500 if nesting is cyclic) and minor nesting sites (open circles; from 100 to 500 nest annually) of the green turtle. 1=Ascension Is. (Mortimer and Carr 1987) 2=Bijagos Archipelago (Limoges 1991 in Agardy 1991) 3=Bioko Is. (Adada, pers. comm; Butynski, pers. comm.) 4=Angola (Carr and Carr 1991) 5=Southeast Turkey (Groombridge 1990; Baran et al 1991; Coley and Smart 1992; Society for Protection of Nature 1992) 6=Southern Somalia (Goodwin 1971) 7=Maziwi Is. (Frazier 1982a) 8=Aldabra Atoll (Seabrook 1991) 9=Assumption, Astove and Cosmoledo Islands (Mortimer 1984) 10=Moheli Is. (Frazier 1985) 11=Mayotte Is. (Frazier 1985) 12=Primeiras Is. (Hughes 1974a) 13=Europa Is, (LeGall et al 1986) 14=Tromelin Is. (LeGall et al. 1986) 15=St. Brandon (Hughes 1974a, 1976) 16=Karan Is. (Miller 1989) 17=Jana Is. (Miller 1989) 18=Shihr and Shuhair (Hirth and Carr 1970) 19=Sharma and Ithmun (Hirth and Carr 1970) 20=Ras al Madrakah and Salalah (Ross and Barwani 1982) 21=Masirah Is. (Ross 1985) 22=Al Ashkara and Ras Jibsh (Ross and Barwani 1982) 23=Ras al Hadd (Ross and Barwani 1982) 24=Damanyat Is. (Ross and Barwani 1982) 25=Makran Coast (Groombridge et al. 1988) 26=Hawkes Bay and Sandspit (Kabraji and Firdous 1984 in Groombridge and Luxmoore 1989) 27=Gujarat State (Bhaskar 1984 in Groombridge and Luxmoore 1989) 28=Lakshadweep (Kar and Bhaskar 1982) 29=Maldives (Frazier 1990) 30=Chagos Archipelago (Frazier 1990) 31=Andaman and Nicobar Is. (Bhaskar 1979; Bhaskar 1984 in Groombridge and Luxmoore 1989).

tracks respectively were counted (Maragos 1994). A few green turtles have been seen in the lagoon on Caroline Atoll, Southern Line Islands, and a few may nest on the Atoll (Kepler et al. 1994).

There is scattered nesting in many areas of Papua New Guinea. Spring (1982a) mentions Mussau Is. in New Ireland Province and several islands in Milne Bay Province where an undetermined number of green turtles nest. In New Caledonia, the d'Entrecasteaux Reef system includes the Islands of Surprise, Leizour, Fabre and Huon. Pritchard (1994) and his associates tagged 149 green

turtles on Huon on 11 December 1991 and counted 1,800 tracks there. They also counted 572 tracks on Ile Fabre and 310 crawls on Ile Surprise. The nesting population on Scilly Atoll in the mid-1980's was estimated at between 300 and 400 (Lebeau 1985). Balazs et al. (1995) estimated a similar number of turtles nested there in 1991. Up to fifty adult turtles of both sexes are consumed annually under special governmental permission. Considerable incentive exists for poaching because an adult green turtle can be illegally sold in Tahiti for about US $1000 (Balazs et al. 1995). The nesting population in nearby

Table 1. Nesting locations and nesting seasons of green turtles. Parentheses indicate peak nesting months.

Location	J	F	M	A	M	J	J	A	S	O	N	D	Reference
Western Pacific Ocean													
China													
Nine Dragon's Beach						J	J	A	S	O			Morton (1992)
Xisha Is				A	(M	J	J)	A	S	O	N	D	Huang Chu-Chien (1982)
Thailand													
Ko Khram	J	F	(M	A	M	J	J	A	S)	O	N	D	Penyapol (1958)
Ko Adang	J	F	M	A							N	D	Polunin (1975)
Malaysia													
Peninsula, east coast	J	F	M	A	(M	J	J	A)	S	O	N	D	Leong and Siow 1984 in Groombridge and Luxmoore (1989)
Sarawak	J	F	M	A	M	J	(J	A)	S	O	N	D	Hendrickson (1958), Chin (1970)
Sabah	J	F	M	A	M	J	(J	A	S	O)	N	D	deSilva (1970)
Indonesia													
South Natuna Is.								A	S	O			Schulz 1987 in Groombridge and Luxmoore (1989)
Tambelan Arch.					M	J	J	A					Schulz 1987 in Groombridge and Luxmoore (1989)
Berau Is.	J	F	M	A	M	J	(J	A	S	O	N)	D	Schulz 1984 in Groombridge and Luxmoore (1989)
Aru Is.	J	F	M	A	M	J	J	A	S	O	N	D	Compost 1980 in Groombridge and Luxmoore (1989)
Sambas-Paloh	J	F	M	A	M	J	(J	A)	S	O	N	D	Schulz 1987 in Groombridge and Luxmoore (1989)
Pangumbahan	J	F	M	A	M	J	J	A	S	O	N	D	Schulz 1984, 1987 in Groombridge and Luxmoore (1989)
Sukamade	J	F	M)	A	M	J	J	A	S	O	N	(D	Suwelo (1975)
Al-Ketapang				A	M	J	J						Nuitja and Lazell (1982)
Mubrani-Jonsoribo				A	M								Adipati and Patay (1983)
Philippine Turtle Is.	J	F	M	A	(M	J	J	A	S)	O	N	D	Domantay (1952-53)
Taiwan, Wan-An Is.						J	(J	A)	S	O			Chen and Cheng (1995)
Ogasawara Is.					M	(J	J)	A					Suganuma (1985)
Merir Is. and Helen's Reef	J	F	M	A	M	(J	J)	A	S	O	N	D	Pritchard (1977)
Papua New Guinea													
Manus Province					M	J	J	A	S				Spring (1982a)
Long Is.	J	F	M	A	(M	J	J	A)	S	O	N	D	Spring (1983)
Milne Bay			M	A									Spring (1982a)
Eastern Australia	J)	F	M							O	N	(D	Bustard (1974), Kowarsky (1978), Stoddart et al. (1981)
Caroline Is.			M	A	M	J	J	A	S				McCoy (1982)
Solomon Is.	J	F	M)	A	M	J	J	A	(S	O	N	D	Vaughan (1981)
Vanuatu	J								S	O	N	D	Pritchard (1982a)
d'Entrecasteaux Reef	J	F									N	D	Pritchard (1987), Anon (1989)
Central And Eastern Pacific Ocean													
Bikar Atoll						J	J	A					Fosberg (1969), Hendrickson (1972), Pritchard (1982b)
Phoenix Is.	J	F	M	A	M	J	J	A	S	(O	N)	D	Balazs (1975)
Fiji	J	F									N	D	Pritchard (1982a)
Tokelau Is.									S	O	N		Balazs (1983b)

Table 1. Continued.

Location	J	F	M	A	M	J	J	A	S	O	N	D	Reference
Rose Atoll								A	S	O	N		Hirth (1971a), Tuato'o-Bartley (1993)
Tonga	J	F									N	D	Hirth (1971a)
French Frigate Shoals					M	(J	J)	A	S				Balazs (1980)
Scilly Atoll	J	F								O	N	D	Lebeau (1985)
Society Is.	J	F)	M	A	M	J	J	A	(S	O	N	D	Hirth (1971a), Pritchard (1982a), Lebeau (1985)
Islas Revillagigedos			M	A	M	J	J	A	S	O	N		Brattstrom (1982)
Galápagos Is.	J	(F	M)	A	M	J						D	Green (1983)
Mexico, Colola and Maruata									S	(O	N)	D	Alvarado and Figueroa (1990)
Guatemala									S	O			Kihn in Cornelius (1982)
El Salvador							J	A	S	O	N	D	Rosales and Benitez in Cornelius (1982)
Costa Rica, Playa Naranjo	J	F	M)	A	M	J	J	A	S	(O	N	D	Cornelius (1976, 1986)
Panama					M	J	J	A	S	O	N	D	Real in Cornelius (1982)
Ecuador	J	(F)	M	A	M							D	Green and Ortiz-Crespo (1982)
Western Atlantic Ocean													
USA, Southeast Florida						J	(J	A)	S				Withcrington and Ehrhart (1989a)
Eastern Mexico					M	(J	J	A)	S				Marquez (1990)
Mexico, Contoy Is.						J	J	A	S	O			Nájera (1991)
Mexico, El Cuyo						J	J	A	S	O			Rodriguez and Zambrano (1991)
Belize						J	J	A					Miller et al. (1984), Moll (1985)
Honduras								A	S				Cruz and Espinal 1987 in Groombridge and Luxmoore (1989)
Costa Rica, Tortuguero						J	(J	A	S)	O			Carr et al. (1978)
Panama						J	J	A					Carr et al. (1982)
Colombia					M	J	J	A					Mast 1986 in Groombridge and Luxmoore (1989)
Venezuela					M	J	J	A	S				Medina et al. 1987 in Groombridge and Luxmoore (1989)
Guyana, Shell Beach			M	A	M	J	J	A					Pritchard (1969)
Suriname		F	M	(A	M)	J	J						Schulz (1975)
French Guiana				A	M	J	J	A					Fretey (1984)
Brazil													
Mainland	J	F	M						S	O	N	D	Marcovaldi in Groombridge and Luxmoore (1989)
Praia do Forte	J	F								O	N	D	D'Amato and Marczwski (1993)
Atol das Rocas	J	F	(M	A)	M							D	Bellini et al. (1996)
Trindade and													
Fernando de Noronha Is.	J	F	M	A								D	Marcovaldi in Groombridge and Luxmoore (1989)
Bahamas						J	J	A	S				Carr et al. (1982)
Turks and Caicos Is.				A	M	J	J	A					Fletemeyer (1984b)
Cuba				A	M	J	J	A					Ottenwalder and Ross (1992)
Haiti					M	J	J	A					Kavanaght (1984)
Dominican Republic							J	(A	S)	O	N	D	Ottenwalder 1981 in Groombridge and Luxmoore (1989)
Puerto Rico					M	J	J	A	S				Gonzalez (1984)
British Virgin Is.						J	J	A	S	O			Fletemeyer (1984a)
U. S. Virgin Is.					M	J	J	A	S	O			Boulon (1984)

Table 1. Continued.

Location	J	F	M	A	M	J	J	A	S	O	N	D	Reference
													Month
St. Kitts—Nevis			M	A	M	J	J	A	S	O			Wilkins and Meylan (1984)
Barbuda					M	J	J	A	S	O	N		Joseph et al. (1984)
Antigua						J	J						Joseph et al. (1984)
Guadeloupe				A	M	J	J	A	S				Carr et al. (1982)
Aves Is.						(J	J	A)					Rainey (1971)
Dominica						J	J	A	S	O			Carr et al. (1982)
Martinique					M	J	J	(A	S)	O	N		Dropsy 1987 in Groombridge and Luxmoore (1989)
St. Lucia					M	J	J	A	S				Murray (1984)
St. Vincent Grenadines				A	M	J	J	A					Morris (1984)
Grenada				A	M	J	J	A	S				Finley (1984)
Trinidad				A	M	J	J	A					Cheong (1984)
Eastern Atlantic Ocean and Mediterranean Sea													
Ascension Is.	J	(F	M	A)	M							D	Mortimer and Carr (1987)
Mauritania						J							Maigret (1983)
Senegal	J	F	M				J	A	S	O			Dupuy (1986)
Equatorial Guinea, Bioko Is.	J	F)	M	A					S	O	N	(D	Adada, pers. comm., Butynski, pers. comm., Eisentraut (1964)
Angola	J										N	D	Carr and Carr (1991)
Turkey, southeast coast						J	J	A					Baran et al. (1991)
Israel				A	M	J	J						Sella (1982)
Cyprus						J	J	A	S				Demetropoulos and Hadjichristophorou (1982), Godley and Broderick (1993)
Western Indian Ocean and Red Sea													
Dahlak Arch.			M										Urban (1970)
Somalia									S	O	N		Karaani, pers. comm.
Maziwi Is.	J	F	M	A	M	J	J	A	S	O			Frazier (1984b)
Primeiras Is.	J	F										D	Hughes (1971)
Aldabra Atoll	J	F	M	A)	M	J	J	A	S	O	(N	D	Seabrook (1989a)
Assumption Is.		F	M	A	M	J	J	A	S	O	N	D	Frazier (1984b)
Cosmoledo Atoll		F	M	A	M								Frazier (1984b)
Astove Atoll	J	F	M	A	M	J	J						Frazier (1984b)
Moheli Is.	J	F	M	A	M	(J)	J						Frazier (1985)
Mayotte Is.		F	M	A	M	J	J						Frazier (1985)
Iles Glorieuses					(M	J	J)						Vergonzanne in Groombridge and Luxmoore (1989)
Europa Is.	J	F)	M	A	M	J	J	A	S	(O	N	D	Servan (1976)
Tromelin Is.	J)	F	M	A	M	J	J	A	S	O	(N	D	Hughes (1974a), LeGall et al. (1986)
St. Brandon Is.	J	F)	M	A	M	J	J	A	S	O	(N	D	Hughes (1974a, 1976)
Saudi Arabia													
Ras Bairdi					M	J	J	A	S				Miller (1989)
Karan Is.						J	(J)	A	S				Miller (1989)
Yemen													
Abdul Wadi	J	F	M	A	M	J	J	A	S	(O	N	D)	Hirth and Carr (1970)
Shuhair										(O	N)		Hirth and Carr (1970)
Shihr										(O	N)		Hirth and Carr (1970)
Sharma	J	F	M	A	M	J	J	A	S	(O	N)	D	Hirth and Carr (1970), FAO (1973)
Ithmun	J	F	M	A	M	J	J	A	S	O	N	D	Hirth and Carr (1970), FAO (1973)

Table 1. Continued.

Location	J	F	M	A	M	J	J	A	S	O	N	D	Reference
Oman													
Masirah Is.	J					J	J	A	(S	O	N)	D	Ross and Barwani (1982)
Ras al Hadd	J	F	M	A	M	J	J	(A	S	O	N	D)	Ross and Barwani (1982)
Northern and Eastern Indian Ocean													
Pakistan													
Makran coast	J	F	M						S	O	N	D	Groombridge et al. (1988)
Hawkes Bay and Sandspit	J	F	M	A	M	J	J	A	(S	O	N)	D	Kabraji and Firdous 1984 in Groombridge and Luxmoore (1989)
India													
Gujarat	J						J	A	S	O	N	D	Bhaskar 1984 in Groombridge and Luxmoore (1989)
Lakshadweep						J	J	A	S				Kar and Bhaskar (1982)
Andaman and Nicobar Is.	J	F	M	A	(M	J	J	A	S)	O	N	D	Bhaskar (1979)
Maldives	J	F	M	A	M	J	J	A	S	O	N	D	Frazier and Frazier 1987 in Groombridge and Luxmoore (1989)
Chagos Arch.						J	J	A	S				Frazier (1990)
Sri Lanka, Kosgoda	J	F	M	(A	M)	J	J	A	S	O	N	D	Dattatri and Samarajiva 1983 in Groombridge and Luxmoore (1989)
Bangladesh	J	F								O	N	D	Khan 1985 in Groombridge and Luxmoore (1989)
Burma, Thamihla Kyun	J	F	M	A	M	J	(J	A	S	O	N)	D	Kar and Bhaskar (1982)
Western Australia	J	F									N	D	Prince (1993)

Mopelia Atoll should be investigated since Sachet (1983) was informed by plantation workers that they take about 200 green turtles annually on Mopelia. Green turtles are reported to nest on Nukutipipi Atoll, in the Tuamotu Archipelago (Salvat and Salvat 1992). Apparently, green turtles lay eggs on the few beaches on Henderson Island (Quayle 1922 in Fosberg et al 1983). Based upon observations made in 1991-1992, a little nesting (about ten females per season with peak nesting January-March) occurs on Henderson Island (Brooke 1995). Weisler (1995) documents that nesting green turtles and their eggs were taken by prehistoric humans on Henderson Is.

Between 1,200 and 3,500 females nest annually in the Galápagos Is. (Green 1983). Most nesting, as far as is known, takes place on Isabela, Baltra, Santa Cruz and Santiago Islands. In 1989-90 an estimated 1,280 turtles nested in Michoacan State, Mexico, with about 967 of these at Colola and Maruata beaches (Alvarado and Figueroa 1990). Nesting activity continues on Playa Naranjo, Costa Rica. Between October 1989 and January 1993, 848 green turtle tracks were counted (Arauz-Almengor and Morera-Avila 1994). There is low-level, sporadic nesting year-around on the Osa Peninsula, Costa Rica (Drake 1996).

In southeast Florida, the greatest nesting concentrations are on Melbourne Beach, Hutchinson Island and Jupiter Island. Whether or not the numbers of green turtles in Florida are slowly increasing is a moot issue (Dodd 1982a, 1995; Thompson 1988, 1991; Magnuson et al. 1990; Dodd and Byles 1991; Ehrhart and Witherington 1992). When finalized, the Archie Carr National Wildlife Refuge in south Brevard and north Indian River counties will encompass about 40% of the green turtle nesting area (Ehrhart and Witherington 1992). In 1992, 12,754 loggerhead and a record high of 686 green turtle nests were laid in the Refuge (Anon 1993b). Johnson and Ehrhart (1995) stated that the proposed Archie Carr National Wildlife Refuge "may very well produce more Florida green turtle hatchlings annually than any other beach in the state."

23

Ogren (1989) calculated about 283 to 420 females nest annually on Mexico's Gulf of Mexico and Caribbean beaches and most of the nesting is probably on the Yucatan Peninsula and nearby islands.

The Tortuguero, Costa Rica, nesting beach is 35 km long and extends between the mouths of the Tortuguero and Parismina Rivers. The most concentrated nesting is about midway between these two river mouths. The estimated number of females nesting annually between 1971 and 1981 ranged between 5,178 and 52,046 (Carr et al. 1982). The nesting population at Tortuguero is now in its fortieth consecutive year of study. The major Suriname beaches are near Galibi, Matapica and Krofajapasi. It is estimated that between about 1,000 to 3,000 green turtles nested in Suriname annually from 1968 to 1979 (Schulz 1982) and between 1,464 and 2,160 annually between 1983 and 1987 (Mohadin in Ogren 1989). Some of the better known nesting sites in French Guiana are: Awara, Farez Kawana, Les Hattes and Pointe Isere (Fretey 1984). In the Dominican Republic there is scattered nesting on many beaches along the coast, with several dozen nesting in the Pedernales and La Altagracia Provinces. The 1980 nesting population in the country was estimated at between 160 and 360 (Ottenwalder 1981 in Groombridge and Luxmoore 1989). The annual average number of nesting females in the mid-1980's on Aves Is. was about 376 (Medina and Sole in Ogren 1989).

Atol das Rocas, in Brazil, is a minor nesting beach. It is estimated that about 20 green turtles nest annually on nearby Fernando de Noronha (Wells 1987) but more detailed nesting surveys are currently being conducted in the Archipelago (T. Sanches, pers. comm.). According to the literature references cited in Groombridge and Luxmoore (1989) the degree of nesting on the mainland of Brazil is debatable and needs reevaluation. D'Amato and Marczwski (1993) discovered that a few green turtles nested at Praia do Forte on the coast in the State of Bahia but the vast majority of nesters here were loggerheads. A total of 23 green turtle nests were made at Praia do Forte between 1987 and 1993 and the overall nesting season was from August to April (Marcovaldi and Laurent 1996). Based upon current information, Ilhe de Trindade is the main nesting site for green turtles in Brazil (Moreira et al. 1995). About 1,800 nests are made annually on the Island and the peak nesting season is from January through March.

Ascension Island is a major nesting site. About 1,650-3,000 nested annually in the late 1970's (Mortimer and Carr 1987). There is a dearth of confirmed major and minor nesting beaches on the west coast of Africa. However, Brongersma (1982) was of the opinion that "from the list of records it is clear that *C. mydas* breeds in many places: perhaps in southernmost Morocco, but definitely in Mauritania, Senegal, Sierra Leone, Liberia, Ghana,

Fernando Poo, São Thomé, Principe, Rolas, Congo, Zaire, Angola, and on rare occasions on St. Helena." Needless to say these nesting locales, if still extant, need to be accurately censused. According to Graff (1995) green turtles nest on several beaches in Saõ Tomé with peak nesting probably between November and January. Green turtles have been reported nesting in Gabon (Fretey and Girardin 1989). Green turtles are still somewhat common in the foraging pastures off Mauritania and Senegal (Maigret 1983 and Dupuy 1986, respectively) and some nesting is reported there. Green turtles have been reported as breeding in the Cape Verde Islands (Parsons 1962) but Brongersma (1982) suggested that the species may have been misidentified and he recommended verification. Sandys-Winsch and Harris (1994) mention only loggerheads and hawksbills as breeding on the sandy beaches in Cape Verde Islands, and these two species are hunted for their eggs and meat.

The southeast Turkey beaches, especially the beaches at Kazanli, Akyatan and Samandagi, harbor the largest green turtle nesting aggregation in the Mediterranean Sea. It is estimated that several hundred nest here annually. Groombridge (1990) estimated that about 75 females nest annually in Cyprus, about 25 and 50 on the south and north coasts, respectively. Godley and Broderick (1994) estimated that 154 green turtles nested on the beaches of Northern Cyprus in 1994 (compared to about 29 and 107 in 1992 and 1993 respectively). Some important nesting beaches in Cyprus are near Alagadi, Chelones Bay, Akdeniz, Esentepe and the Karpaz Peninsula. According to Demetropoulos and Hadjichristophorou (1995) "It is assumed that the green turtle population nesting in Cyprus does not exceed 200 turtles, the north and east coast beaches combined." Recent observations in Eritrea reported by Hillman and Gebremariam (1995) indicate that green turtles may nest there in April, May and June, in addition to the nesting noted there in March by Urban (1970). Aldabra Atoll is a major nesting site and in 1982 it was designated a World Heritage Site. Accounts of the ecology and geology of the Atoll are in Stoddart (1967, 1971). The estimated annual nesting population on Moheli is 1,800 (Frazier 1985). Maziwi Island, Tanzania, is reported to have been washed over by the sea (Anon. 1982). A legend about Maziwi told by the Arabs along the Tanzania coast is that if Maziwi Island should ever disappear beneath the sea the world will come to an end (Anon. 1969). Green turtles nest at some sites along the northeast and west coasts of Madagascar, between October and January, but the current sizes of the nesting populations need to be determined (Rakotonirina and Cooke 1994). Miller (1989) estimated that 1,350 turtles nested on Karan Is., Arabian Gulf, in 1986 and 450 in 1987. Jana Is., nearby, is a minor nesting site. Other islands in the Saudi Arabian sector of the Gulf of Arabia where nesting occurs are Kurayn Is., Harqis Is., and Jurayd Is. On the Saudi Arabian side of the Red Sea some nesting occurs in the vicinity of Tiran Is., the Wejh Bank, along the coast north of Yanbu, on the offshore islands south of Qunfadah, and on the islands off the Farasan Bank. The largest single nesting site is at Ras Bairdi, just north of Yanbu where between 50 and 100 green turtles nest from May through September (Miller 1989). Ross and Barwani (1982) estimate that 6,000 green turtles nest annually at Ras al Hadd in Oman. Salm and Salm (1991) estimate that up to 20,000 green turtles nest annually in Oman, with most nesting along a 45 km stretch of coast from Ras al Hadd south to Ras al Khabbah. Didi (1993) summarizes some of the current information about sea turtles in the Maldives. During a February-May, 1991, nesting beach survey of six islands in the southern Nicobars, Tiwari (1994) saw twelve green turtle crawls and six body pits but the vast majority of nesting was by leatherbacks (433 nests).

Current accurate surveys should be conducted at some sites that were censused decades ago. Nesting is reported at other sites around the tropics but quantitative data are lacking.

The internesting habitat (see Fig. 8) needs more study since some individuals may spend up to three months here as they renest at about thirteen day intervals. Most mating takes place in, or near, this habitat (but there are exceptions). Little is known about the duration of males in the internesting habitat. Ecologically, this habitat may be quite different from the shallow water feeding habitat. Characteristics of the internesting habitat may provide cues to homing turtles. The internesting habitat, along with the nesting beach, can be an area of intense human contact, directly or indirectly (e.g., recreational use, fishing, run-off pollution).

Dizon and Balazs (1982) found that the internesting habitat of females (and males) at French Frigate Shoals, Hawaii, was in close proximity to the nesting and basking islands where the turtles were captured. At Tortuguero, Meylan (1982a) found that the internesting turtles travelled parallel to shore, within the 24 meter contour line, and that the maximum longshore distance moved from site of nesting was 10 km. At Ascension Is., Mortimer and Portier (1989) tracked a few individuals and found that after oviposition most of them moved to a shallow area off the northwest coast of the island. Alvarado and Figueroa (1990) conducted preliminary studies on turtles in the internesting habitat off the Pacific coast of Mexico. A nesting female at Maruata Beach was fitted with a radio transmitter and over the next seven days she remained in Maruata Bay. Another nester from Colola Beach was radio-tracked as she moved 10 km east of the nesting beach over two days. Liew and Chan (1993) found that three Malaysian females tracked by means of radio and ultrasonic telemetry remained within 1 km of the coast during their internesting period of 10-11 days. They state that "they hardly ventured away from the vicinity of their nesting beach except turtle T2 which moved longshore 6 km south from her nesting site. She later returned to the vicinity of her nesting site a few days prior to renesting." Liew and Chan (1993) also found that the turtles spent the majority of their time resting on the seafloor at a mean depth of 10 m; that none of the turtles were observed foraging; and that one was seen mating during the internesting period.

2.3 Determinants of Distributional Changes

Green turtles are commonly found in warm tropical seas with major concentrations in their feeding pastures and at their nesting beaches.

Distribution of hatchlings and posthatchlings may be affected by changes in ocean currents, gyres and strong El-Niño years (section 2.2.1). Factors affecting reproduction and mortality can affect distribution (sections 4.3.2 and 4.4.2). The distribution of green turtles was certainly more extensive before human interference and exploitation.

2.4 Hybridization

Turtles hatched from a clutch of Suriname eggs appeared to be hybrids of *Chelonia mydas* and *Eretmochelys imbricata* and all the hybrids were males (Wood et al. 1983a). These hybrids, raised in the Cayman Turtle Farm, had high mortality and were more susceptible to lung infection than captive green turtles but at least one male hybrid survived to maturity, had motile sperm, and was observed mating with resident female green turtles (Wood in Karl et al 1995).

Karl et al. (1995) employed molecular genetic assays to document the natural occurrences of interspecific hybrids between a male green turtle and a female loggerhead (N=4 hatchling clutch-mates collected in Brazil) and between a female green turtle and a male hawksbill (N=1 individual collected in Suriname). The species involved in these hybridizations represent evolutionary lineages thought to have separated about 50 million years ago and thus may be among the oldest vertebrate lineages capable of producing viable hybrids in nature (Karl et al. 1995).

Some potential problems of intraspecific hybridization, as a consequence of manipulative management practices, are discussed by Carr and Dodd (1983). The F_2 green turtle hatchlings produced on the Cayman Turtle Farm are most likely intraspecific hybrids (see section 7).

3. BIONOMICS AND LIFE HISTORY
3.1 Reproduction

3.1.1 Sexuality
Green turtles are bisexual but sexual dimorphism is ex-

ternally apparent only in large subadults and adults. Adult males have a much thicker and longer tail than females. The male's tail extends well beyond the posterior margin of the carapace and it is somewhat prehensile. Mature males have longer claws on the foreflippers than do females. Adult males are sometimes viewed as having a more elongate carapace than females, especially in east Pacific populations (Carr 1952; Stebbins 1985). In a small sample (11m8f) of adult green turtles caught off Michoacan, Mexico, males had soft plastra while females exhibited well-cornified plastra (Wibbels et al. 1991). Mature females sometimes possess a "mating notch" in the shoulder regions of the carapace, produced by the gripping of the male's claws during copulation.

Evidence is slowly accumulating that mature males are smaller (i. e. shorter carapace length) than mature females in the same population: Witzell (1982) measured a few foraging adult turtles off Western Samoa and found males (mean straight carapace length=92.2 cm, range=86.5-102 cm, N=5) were smaller than adult females (mean straight carapace length = 96.9 cm, range=91.5-109 cm, N=9); Frazier (1984b) found breeding males (MCCL [mean curved carapace length] =ca. 102 cm, range ca. 94-116 cm, N=84) were smaller than breeding females (MCCL=ca. 108 cm, range=ca. 97-120 cm, N=54) in the Aldabra Atoll population; Limpus and Reed (1985a) stated that adult males (MCCL=98 cm, range=90.5-105.5 cm, N=24) in a feeding population off Heron Island, Australia, were significantly smaller than adult females (MCCL=103 cm, range=91.5-109.5 cm, N=16); Limpus and Reed (1985b) recorded that adult males (MCCL=98.4 cm, range 92.5-104.5 cm, N=9) in a feeding population in the Gulf of Carpentaria, Australia, were significantly shorter than adult females (MCCL=107.6 cm, range 98-123.5 cm, N=18); Miller (1989) said adult males (MCCL=94.7 cm, range=87-103 cm, N=14) were signficantly smaller than adult females (MCCL=100.6 cm, range=94-113 cm, N=21) in a feeding pasture at Dawhat Abu Ali, Saudi Arabia; Miller (1989) found breeding males (MCCL=91.3 cm, range=84-96 cm, N=21) to be significantly smaller than mature females (MCCL=98.8 cm, range=81.5-108.5 cm, N=43) in a nesting population at Karan Island, Saudi Arabia; and Limpus (1993b) stated that breeding males (MCCL=100.6 cm, range=89.5-114.5 cm, N=361) in the southern Great Barrier Reef population were smaller than mature females (MCCL=107 cm, range=91-124 cm, N=1942) in the same population.

The sex of hatchlings, juveniles and small subadults can be determined by dissection, histological examination, radioimmunological assays or by laparoscopy (Owens 1982; Wood et al. 1983b; Van der Heiden et al. 1985; Jackson et al. 1987; Wibbels et al. 1993). Wellins (1987) suggested that an H-Y antigen serological assay may be useful in determining the sex of immature sea turtles.

3.1.2 Maturity

The age at sexual maturity may vary among individuals of the same population and among individuals of different populations. The age at maturity has been estimated at more than 30 years in Australia (Limpus and Walter 1980); 25 to 30 years in Florida (Mendonça 1981); about 27 years in Bermuda (Burnett-Herkes et al. 1984); 18 to 27 years in Florida (Frazer and Ehrhart 1985); 40 to 50 years in Hawaii (Zug and Balazs 1985); 12 to 26 years in Costa Rica, 17 to 35 years at Ascension Island, 27 to 33 years in the Virgin Islands, and 24 to 36 years in Suriname (Frazer and Ladner 1986); about average of 25 years in Hawaii (Anon 1991a); 19 to 24 years in the western central Atlantic Ocean (Ehrhardt and Witham 1992); and, at least 36 years in the Galápagos Islands (Green 1993). These estimates are much longer than some of the earlier estimates cited in Hirth (1971b). The mean age of nesting on the Cayman Turtle Farm is 16 years (Wood and Wood 1993a).

Carr and Carr (1970b) discussed the variation in maturation size in the Tortuguero nesting colony. There is much information available on the sizes (carapace lengths) of nesting turtles (Table 2) and some information on the weights of nesters (Table 3). As mentioned in the preceding section, evidence is accumulating that mature males are smaller than mature females in some populations.

3.1.3 Mating

Most mating takes place in the vicinity of the nesting beach, but there are exceptions. Ross (1984) noted occasional mating on a feeding pasture near Masirah Island. Meylan et al. (1992b) reported that some Tortuguero Beach-bound turtles mate approximately 240 km distant in Panama. In the southern Great Barrier Reef system, Limpus (1993b) observed that mated females dispersed from the courtship area to beaches within 92 km, without necessarily nesting on the closest nesting beach to the courtship area. A female tagged while mating off one atoll in Yap State subsequently nested at another site 101 km distant from the mating event (Kolinski 1995).

It is unknown whether the males accompany the females from the feeding pastures to the nesting beach or whether they make synchronized rendezvous with females off the beach.

Evidence is accumulating to indicate that sperm produced during the copulations, usually at the beginning of the nesting season, is used only for the current season's ovulations (Booth and Peters 1972; Owens 1980; Wood and Wood 1980; Owens and Morris 1985). Green turtles in the Caribbean appear to follow a pre-nuptial pattern of spermatogenesis: i. e., testicular recrudescence and active spermiation precede mating (Engstrom 1994). Mul-

26

Table 2. Carapace lengths (straight line, cm) of nesting green turtles. *curved carapace length, **method not given, ca *(circa/approximately)*.

Location	Mean	Range	N	Reference
Pacific Ocean				
Ko Khram, Thailand		75-105**		Penyapol (1958)
Sarawak	ca 97.5**	ca 84-110	200	Hendrickson (1958)
Sukumade, Indonesia	99.7	85-120		Nuitja (1993-4); pers. comm.
Baguan Is, Philippines	99.5*			Trono (1991)
Wan-An Is., Taiwan	96.6	87-110.5	14	Chen and Cheng (1995)
Long Is, Papua New Guinea	94.7	84-106.4	268	Spring (1983)
Long Is, Papua New Guinea	97.5		16	Pritchard (1979a)
Solomon Is.	85	78-89	4	McKeown (1977)
Solomon Is.	110*		1	Vaughan (1981)
Bramble Cay, Australia	99.7		9	Kowarsky (1978)
Raine Is., Australia	100.2		4	Kowarsky (1978)
Raine Is., Australia	109*	90-122	124	Stoddart et al. (1981)
Heron Is., Australia	ca 106*	ca 89-127	1,192	Bustard (1972)
Heron Is., Australia	107*	91-124	451	Limpus (1980)
Ile Huon, New Caledonia	107.6*	94-122	70	Anon (1989)
Ile Surprise, New Caledonia	105.8*	100-112	6	Anon (1989)
Western Samoa	96.9[a]	91.5-109	9	Witzell (1982)
Scilly Atoll, French Polynesia	95.6**	80-109	338	Doumenge (1973)
Scilly Atoll, French Polynesia	96.3	83-105	38	Lebeau (1985)
French Frigate Shoals, Hawaii	92.2	80.8-106.2	379	Balazs (1980)
Colola and Maruata, Mexico	82*	60-102	718	Alvarado and Figueroa (1990)
Playa Naranjo, Costa Rica	82.9	73-97	73	Cornelius (1976)
Galápagos Is.	ca 81.3	72.4-94	88	Pritchard (1971)
Galápagos Is.	81.4	66.7-106.6		Green (1994)
Atlantic Ocean and				
Mediterranean Sea				
Kennedy Space Center, Florida	100.5	88-109.1	14	Ehrhart (1979b)
Cape Canaveral and				Witherington and Ehrhart
Melbourne, Florida	101.5	83.2-116.7	90	(1989a)
Melbourne, Florida	110	102-121	12	Bjorndal et al. (1983)
Hutchinson Is., Florida	101.1	95.3-111.8	4	Gallagher et al., (1972)
Contoy Is., Mexico	99	87-114	41	Nájera (1991)
El Cuyo, Mexico	108*	102-120	10	Rodriguez and Zambrano (1991)
Tortuguero, Costa Rica	ca 100.3[b]	ca 81.9-112.4	362	Carr and Giovannoli (1957)
Tortuguero, Costa Rica	100.1[b]	69.2-117.5	1,146	Carr and Ogren (1960)
Tortuguero, Costa Rica	100.3[b]	83.2-117.5	200	Carr and Hirth (1962)
Aves Is.	107.7	99.6-118.9	16	Rainey (1971)
Shell Beach, Guyana	103.9	96.5-106.7	22	Pritchard (1969)
Bigi Santi, Suriname	111.8	100.3-121.9	60	Pritchard (1969)
Suriname	109[b]	97-125	291	Schulz (1975)
Trindade, Brazil	116.8*	101-143	465	Moreira et al. (1995)
Praia do Forte, Brazil	123.3*	SD0.04	4	Marcovaldi and Laurent (1996)
Atol das Rocas, Brazil	118.6*	100-134	1,188	Bellini et al. (1996)
Ascension Is.	108.1	83.8-141	200	Carr and Hirth (1962)
Ascension Is.	ca 116.8*	101.6-131.5	738	Simon and Parkes (1976)
Alagadi, Cyprus	92*	SD7.9	30	Godley and Broderick (1993)
Kazanli, Turkey	ca 96	87-102	6	Baran et al. (1991)
Kazanli, Turkey	96*		5	Coley and Smart (1992)
Indian Ocean				
Maziwi Is.	113*	ca 100-125	110	Frazier (1984b)
Europa Is.	106.5	95.5-120.5	29	Hughes (1974a)
Europa Is.	108.9	91-125	294	Servan (1976)
Mayotte Is.	110.8*	102.5-121	43	Frazier (1985)
Moheli Is.	112.3*	102.5-122	51	Frazier (1985)

Table 2. Continued.

Location	Mean	Range	N	Reference
Aldabra Atoll	100.8	96.5-106.7	5	Hirth and Carr (1970)
Aldabra Atoll	103	ca 95-115	54	Frazier (1971)
Assumption Is.	102.2	100.3-104.1	2	Hirth and Carr (1970)
Assumption Is.	ca 109*	ca 97-120	42	Frazier (1984b)
Tromelin Is.	104.1	95.9-112	28	Hughes (1974a)
Ras Bairdi, Saudi Arabia	105.2*	92-114	15	Miller (1989)
Karan Is. Saudi Arabia	98*	89.5-108.5	102	Miller (1989)
Sharma, Yemen	96	78.7-114.3	225	Hirth and Carr (1970)
Sharma, Yemen	94.2	77-117	57	FAO (1973)
Masirah Is., Oman	93.2		90	Ross and Barwani (1982)
Ras al Hadd, Oman	97.1		62	Ross and Barwani (1982)

a Non-nesting adult females
b Total straight line carapace length

Table 3. Weights (kg) of nesting green turtles (after laying or presumably after laying).

Location	Mean	Range	N	Reference
Pacific Ocean				
Sarawak	111	89-126	10	Hendrickson (1958)
Long Is., Papua New Guinea	112.7	81-169	100	Spring (1983)
Scilly Atoll, French Polynesia	126.7	75-205	255	Doumenge (1973)
French Frigate Shoals, Hawaii	110	68-148	69	Kridler and Olsen in Balazs (1980)
Galápagos Is.	81.9	45.5-172.7		Green (1994)
Atlantic Ocean				
Kennedy Space Center, Florida	139.7	121.5-176.9	10	Ehrhart (1979b)
Cape Canaveral and Melbourne, Florida	136.1	104.3-176.8	15	Witherington and Ehrhart (1989a)
Tortuguero, Costa Rica	136	113-151	6	Carr and Hirth (1962)
Aves Is.	171	124-235	16	Rainey (1971)
Bigi Santi, Suriname	170	120-222	22	Pritchard (1969)
Suriname	182	130-235	50	Schulz (1975)
Ascension Is.	189	140-225	9	Carr and Hirth (1962)
Indian Ocean				
Europa Is.	166.9	124.8-208.8	30	Hughes (1974a)
Europa Is.	175	130-250	19	Servan (1976)
Tromelin Is.	159.8	127.1-183.9	29	Hughes (1974a)
Ras Bairdi, Saudi Arabia	126	94-152	13	Miller (1989)
Karan Is., Saudi Arabia	103.3	74-144	69	Miller (1989)
Hawkes Bay, Pakistan	136.5	123-150	2	Minton (1966)

tiple matings of females during a nesting season have been reported (Alvarado and Figueroa 1990, 1991; Rostal et al. 1990) and this behavior, and its significance, deserves more attention. Peare et al. (1994) stated that the prevalent mating system in the Tortuguero population is promiscuity—i. e., females mate with multiple males to fertilize each clutch. Evidence for this came from using multilocus minisattelite DNA fingerprinting which established that some females were using sperm from two to four males to fertilize their eggs. The authors also very briefly discuss how mating systems (e. g., promiscuous vs. monogamous) can influence both the effective population size and the level of genetic variability.

The diminution of observed mating activity offshore of Tortuguero nesting beach, after about the middle of the nesting season, may indicate that males leave the nesting area before females, or that they are just less visible in some other area of the internesting habitat (Carr et al. 1978). Speaking of sea turtles, Owens and Morris (1985) stated "It appears that mating aggregations peak just prior to the beginning of the nesting season, and that males subsequently leave the nesting area." In the southern Great Barrier Reef region, males are sexually active for about a month (Limpus 1993b). During this time it is not uncommon to see a male mounted on several different females. At the end of the mating period the majority of breeding males, here, disperse and presumably return to their feeding habitats.

Booth (in Booth and Peters 1972) swam with green turtles off Fairfax Island, Australia, was gradually accepted by them, and subsequently described their mating behavior (with excellent underwater photographs). Booth determined that the female is completely in control of whether mating occurs or not. Female behavior patterns to avoid copulation included carefully folding hind limbs together, swimming away from the male, facing the male and biting him on the head or neck if he got too close, assuming the "refusal" position (vertical position with plastron toward male and all limbs widespread) and resting in a sanctuary area. If the female was caught in water too shallow to assume the vertical "refusal" position she would often beach herself. Sexually aroused males would pursue any large swimming object in the water, including humans. The male turtles would usually respond to the "refusal" position of a human. A male turtle under "attack" by another male would attempt to escape by frantic splashing and swimming away. No male turtle was observed to use the "refusal" position. The longest continuous copulation observed was six hours, and copulation had already begun when the pair was first observed. Males engaged in multiple copulations. At Fairfax Is., copulating pairs may be accompanied by one to five "escort" males. These escorts may attempt to dislodge the copulating male, who holds on tenaciously to the female's carapace. Occasionally an escort will bite the tail or other parts of the mating male in attempts to dislodge him. Bustard (1972) observed courtship behavior off Bountiful Island, Australia, and, in general, the behavior was similar to that described by Booth and Peters (1972). Alvarado and Figueroa (1990) described the courting behavior of turtles off the Pacific coast of Mexico. Here the behavior can be divided into the following stages: males search for potential mate; males examine females, visually; male's physical contact with female; female accepts or rejects male; and, mounting. A female's rejection repertoire includes the face-to-face and "refusal" positions described by Booth and Peters (1972).

Hughes (1974b) observed that females beach themselves on Tromelin Island to escape the attention of males. Balazs (1980), Miller (1989) and Alvarado and Figueroa (1990) reported that escort males in Hawaii, Saudi Arabia and Mexico, respectively, also attempt to dislodge a mating male by biting the flippers and tail. Miller (1989) noted that the time interval between the sighting of a mounted pair and the first nesting attempt by the female averaged 15 days (range 1-38 days, N=10). Green (1983) noted that coupling lasts up to six hours in the Galápagos. Here a mating pair is accompanied by 1 to 6 escort males, but occasionally the escorts are females. Mating off the Sabah Turtle Islands was observed by de Silva (1969). Here, in most instances, a single female is escorted by several males. He observed that sometimes a mounted male will dismount, swim vigorously toward escort males, driving them away, and then return to the female. Limpus (1993b) observed that males missing the claw on one or both front flippers were usually unsuccessful in copulation because they could not firmly grip the female's carapace.

Comuzzie and Owens (1990) described courtship behavior of captive turtles on the Cayman Turtle Farm. Components of the courtship included gular rubbing, biting or nipping, cloacal checking, circling, chasing and mounting. Wood and Wood (1980) reported a mounting episode endured for 119 hours on the Cayman Turtle Farm.

3.1.4 Fertilization
Fertilization is internal.

3.1.5 Gonads
Miller and Limpus (1981) used several criteria for determining the sex of gonads including a gonadal ridge with tubular medulla and squamous epithelium in male gonads (dense medulla and columnar epithelium in females) and a degenerate Mullerian duct in males (developed Mullerian duct with lumen in females). The gonadal ridge of intersexes had a tubular medulla with tubes in contact with the epithelium and a partially developed Mullerian duct with the lumen nearly closed. Illustrations of male, female and intersex gonads are provided. Spotila et al. (1983) described some histological distinctions between the gonads of male and female hatchlings and included illustrations of male, female and intersex gonads. Van der Heiden et al. (1985) stated that it was possible to determine the sex of gonads by gross morphology. The male gonad exhibits a distinct overall granular pattern which is associated with the convolutions of the seminiferous tubules. The female gonad shows typical serrations of the lateral borders. Illustrations are provided. On the other hand, Jackson et al. (1987) had difficulty in sexing gonads using the Van der Heiden et al. (1985) technique.

As already mentioned (section 1.3.1) the ovary is a membranous organ with a relatively short attached border resulting in distinct folding (Aitken et al. 1976). Follicles occur on both surfaces. Illustrations in Aitken et al.

(1976) include an ovary with compact cortical layer and stromal space. Rainey (1981) illustrates the gonads of two immature males (with carapace lengths of 49 and 64 cm) two immature females (with carapace lengths of 61.5 and 68.5 cm) and one adult female (carapace length 86 cm).

3.1.6 Nesting process

Nesting behavior is an important aspect of a green turtle's life history because it relates directly to fitness.

There is a large amount of information available on the nesting behavior of green turtles. Much of the information is covered in several reviews (Hirth 1971b; Ehrenfeld 1979; Ehrhart 1982; Hendrickson 1982). It is believed, but not proven, that females nest on the beach where they hatched. Renestings during a nesting season are usually on the same sector of beach. Most females tend to return to the same nesting area on their reproductive migrations. Most nesting takes place at night (reflecting adaptations to diurnal predators and heat stress) on an elevated beach platform (berm). The turtles nest on beaches that vary markedly in terms of sand texture, mineral composition and color (Hirth and Carr 1970; Mortimer 1990). Green turtles have deposited eggs on man-made beaches (e.g., Cayman Turtle Farm) and on nourished beaches in Florida (Witham 1990). But this does not mean that bargeloads of sand can be randomly imported to restore green turtle nesting beaches. The sand should be of the same type as that on the natural nesting beaches in the area.

Carr and Ogren (1960) divided the nesting behavior into eleven stages (several of these stages are combined by other investigators): 1. stranding, testing of stranding site, and emergence from wave wash 2. selecting of course and crawling from surf to nest site 3. selecting of nest site 4. clearing of nest premises 5. excavating of body pit 6. excavating of nest hole 7. oviposition 8. filling, covering, and packing of nest hole 9. filling of body pit and concealing of site of nesting 10. selecting of course, and locomotion back to the sea 11. re-entering of wave wash and traversal of the surf.

Data in Table 1 indicate that there is year-around nesting (but with seasonal peaks) at some sites while at other locales shorter seasonal nesting prevails.

Green turtles spend about two and one-half hours on the beach for nesting (Hirth 1980c); about two hours in the actual construction and camouflaging of the nest (Hirth and Samson 1987). At Tortuguero, green turtles spend about 23 minutes in digging the body pit, about 23 minutes in digging the egg chamber, approximately 15 minutes in laying eggs, about 12 minutes in filling the egg chamber, and, approximately 43 minutes in filling the body pit and camouflaging the nest site. Inexperienced and experienced nesters at Tortuguero exhibit similar patterns of nesting and data indicate strong natural selection for a fixed nesting behavior in green turtles (Hirth and Samson 1987).

On Ascension Island, nest site selection seems to involve cues provided by an uneven beach topography—i. e., turtles usually attempted to nest only after they had crawled into the uneven beach zone above the spring high water line (Hays et al. 1995a).

3.1.7 Eggs

Freshly laid green turtle eggs are spherical and white with flexible shells. Using scanning electron microscopy, Baird and Solomon (1979) showed that the structure of the calcified layer of egg shells from farm-reared and wild turtles was somewhat different. Egg shells from farmed turtles contained distinct regions of blocks of calcite and spherulites of aragonite. The egg shells from feral populations consisted only of the spherulites. Shells with the more open calcitic framework are more susceptible to fungal invasion, *Aspergillus* sp. being one kind (Solomon and Baird 1980). The hyphae may impair gas exchange and also may create a calcium deficiency. Gas exchange between eggs and their ambient environment is discussed in section 3.4.4.

The average clutch size varies widely (Table 4) but there is a relationship between clutch size and carapace length (Fig. 12). The females nesting at Colola and Maruata (Pacific Mexico), Playa Naranjo (Pacific Costa Rica) and in the Galápagos Islands are among the smallest and they deposit the fewest eggs per clutch. The nesters in Suriname, Brazil, Europa Island and Maziwi Island are among the largest green turtles and they lay large clutches. The diameter of green turtle eggs, from 18 localities, ranged from 33.8 to 58.7 mm, with an overall average of about 45 mm (N=28 samples) (Table 5). The weight of eggs, from 16 localities, ranged from about 21 to 66 g, with an overall mean of about 47 g (N=20 samples) (Table 6).

The number of clutches laid in one nesting season can range from 1 to 9 in some nesting colonies but the overall average is about 3.3 (N=21 samples) (Table 7). Green turtles renest at about 13 day intervals (Table 8) and they occupy an internesting habitat (see section 2.2.2) between nesting episodes. Remigration intervals at different nesting colonies are provided in Table 9.

Several researchers have reported a positive relationship between size of nesting female and clutch within a nesting population: Hornell (1927) on Aldabra Atoll; Bustard (1972) on Heron Island; Simon and Parkes (1976) and Hays et al. (1993) on Ascension Island; Balazs (1980) on French Frigate Shoals; Hirth (1988) and Bjorndal and Carr (1989) at Tortuguero; Witherington and Ehrhart (1989a) in Florida; and, Chen and Cheng in Taiwan (1995). On the other hand, Hughes (1974a) found no correlation between size of female and clutch size on Europa Island, nor did Miller (1989) find a correlation on Karan Island. Alvarado and Figueroa (1990) found no correlation be-

Table 4. Clutch sizes of green turtles.

Location	Mean	Range	N	Reference
Pacific Ocean				
Xisha Is., China	ca 133			Huang Chu-Chien (1982)
Ko Khram, Thailand		70-130		Penyapol (1958)
Sarawak	104.7	3-184	8,147	Hendrickson (1958)
Sabah		3-190		de Silva (1970)
Pangumbahan, Indonesia	107			Suwelo and Kuntjoro (1969)
Sukumade, Indonesia	113			Nuitja (1993-4)
Pulau Berhala, Indonesia	118	48-175	22	Mohr (1927)
Baguan Is., Philippines	95.6		146	Trono (1991)
Wan-An Is., Taiwan	113	64-172	63	Chen and Cheng (1995)
Ogasawara Is.	103.8	70-150		Fukada (1965)
Long Is., Papua New Guinea	107.3	71-165	126	Spring (1983)
Solomon Is.	84.6	45-156	5	McKeown (1977)
Solomon Is.	97.3	37-143	8	Vaughan (1981)
Bramble Cay, Australia	103.4		8	Kowarsky (1978)
Raine Is., Australia	105.8		6	Kowarsky (1978)
Heron Is., Australia	ca 110	50-200		Bustard (1972)
Heron Is., Australia	112	61-153	35	Limpus (1980)
Scilly Atoll, French Polynesia	97.8	37-152	12	Lebeau (1985)
French Frigate Shoals, Hawaii	104	38-145	50	Balazs (1980)
Michoacan, Mexico	66			Marquez et al (1982)
Colola and Maruata, Mexico	76	11-146	397	Alvarado et al (1985)
Colola and Maruata, Mexico	69.2	5-136	636	Alvarado and Figueroa(1986)
Colola and Maruata, Mexico	65.1	1-130	916	Alvarado and Figueroa (1990)
Playa Naranjo, Costa Rica	87	65-107	10	Cornelius (1976)
Galápagos Is., James Bay	89.9	48-131	15	Pritchard (1971)
Galápagos Is., Indefatigable	71.4	19-116	27	Pritchard (1971)
Galápagos Is.	84	26-144		Green (1994)
Atlantic Ocean and				
Mediterranean Sea				
Canaveral National				
Seashore, Florida	127.5		7	Bryant (1986)
Cape Canaveral and	136	90-199	130	Witherington and
Melbourne, Florida				Ehrhart (1989a)
Hutchinson Is., Florida	134	94-180	18	Gallagher et al. (1972)
Broward County, Florida	120.3	58-164	25	Broward County Erosion
				Prevention Dist. (1987)
Contoy Is., Mexico	114	73-163	47	Nájera (1991)
El Cuyo, Mexico	113	36-169	19	Rodriguez and Zambrano
				(1991)
Tortuguero, Costa Rica	110	18-193	406	Carr and Hirth (1962)
Tortuguero, Costa Rica	104.1	7-178	188	Fowler (1979)
Tortuguero, Costa Rica	112.2	3-219	2,544	Bjorndal and Carr (1989)
Shell Beach, Guyana		106-138	6	Pritchard (1969)
Eilanti, Suriname	141.9	?-226	248	Pritchard (1969)
Bigi Santi, Suriname	142.8	87-174	20	Pritchard (1969)
Suriname	138	12-226	566	Schulz (1975)
Praia do Forte, Brazil	132.5	72-171	10	D'Amato and Marczwski
				(1993)
Praia do Forte, Brazil	127.8	SD28.2	25	Marcovaldi and Laurent (1996)
Ascension Is.	115.5	53-181	140	Carr and Hirth (1962)
Ascension Is. (1973)	116.3	51-190	169	Simon and Parkes
(1974)	127	31-180	163	(1976)
Ascension Is.	127.5	83-170	46	Hays et al (1993)
Ascension Is.	120.9		548	Mortimer and Carr (1987)
Alagadi, Cyprus	112.6	33-190	36	Godley and Broderick (1993)

Table 4. Continued.

Location	Mean	Range	N	Reference
Kazanli, Turkey	ca 126		43	Baran et al (1991)
Kazanli, Turkey	122		7	Coley and Smart (1992)
Indian Ocean				
Maziwi Is.	138			Frazier (1984b)
Primeiras Is.	115	100-130	2	Hughes (1974a)
Europa Is.	152	115-197	28	Hughes (1974a)
Europa Is.	142	75-238	27	Hughes (1974b)
Europa Is.	147			Servan (1976)
Mayotte Is.	121.6	104-139	5	Frazier (1985)
Moheli Is.	122.4	85-158	7	Frazier (1985)
Aldabra Atoll		150-200		Hornell (1927)
Aldabra Atoll	90+			Frazier (1971)
Tromelin Is.	129	81-173	10	Hughes (1974a)
Tromelin Is.	124.6	79-230	30	Hughes (1974b)
Karan Is., Saudi Arabia	88.5	60-136	59	Miller (1989)
Sharma, Yemen	106	70-130	30	Hirth and Carr (1970)
Sharma, Yemen	122.4	67-179	5	FAO (1973)
Masirah Is. Oman	97		16	Ross and Barwani (1982)
Ras al Hadd, Oman	103.5		58	Ross and Barwani (1982)
Hawkes Bay, Pakistan	108.5	81-125	4	Minton (1966)

Table 5. Diameters (mm) of green turtle eggs.

Location	Mean	Range	Clutches	Eggs	Reference
Pacific Ocean					
Xisha Is., China		ca 40-44			Huang Chu-Chien (1982)
Sarawak	ca 40				Hendrickson (1958)
Pangumbahan, Indonesia	45				Suwelo and Kuntjoro (1969)
Wan-An Is., Taiwan	45.1	41.4-47.7		35	Chen and Cheng (1995)
Ogasawara Is.	46				Fukada (1965)
Heron Is., Australia	ca 46				Bustard and Greenham (1969)
Heron Is., Australia	ca 46				Bustard (1972)
Heron Is., Australia	44.6	38.9-46.9	22	220	Limpus (1980)
French Frigate Shoals, Hawaii	44	43-46	1	99	Balazs (1980)
Atlantic Ocean					
Kennedy Space Center, Florida	47.5				Ehrhart (1979a)
Hutchinson Is., Florida	46	41-50	18		Gallagher et al. (1972)
Tortuguero, Costa Rica	45.7	41.1-50.1	20	400	Carr and Hirth (1962)
Tortuguero, Costa Rica	43.1	39-48	20	400	Hirth (1988)
Tortuguero, Costa Rica	44.4	39.1-48.4	97		Bjorndal and Carr (1989)
Aves Is.	44.4	42.6-47	1	48	Rainey (1971)
Shell Beach, Guyana	ca 48	47-48		4	Pritchard (1969)
Suriname	45	40-50			Schulz (1975)
Ascension Is.	54.6	49-58.7	5	100	Carr and Hirth (1962)
Ascension Is.	45.5	41-48.5	47	ca 470	Hays et al. (1993)
Indian Ocean					
Primeiras Is.	43.8	42.7-47.5	2	40	Hughes (1974a)
Europa Is.	44.7	41.6-47.2	28	280	Hughes (1974a)
Europa Is.	42.3	35-50		137	Servan (1976)
Mayotte Is.	ca 43.4	34-48	4	40	Frazier (1985)
Moheli Is.	ca 43.8	42-45	2	20	Frazier (1985)
Aldabra Atoll	46.3				Frazier (1971)
Tromelin Is.	44.6	42.5-46.1	10	200	Hughes (1974a)

Table 5. Continued.

Location	Mean	Range	Clutches	Eggs	Reference
Karan Is., Saudi Arabia	43.2	33.8-49	58	580	Miller (1989)
Abdul Wadi, Yemen	42.5	40-45	1	100	Hirth and Carr (1970)
Sharma, Yemen	45.5	41-48	5		FAO (1973)
Hawkes Bay, Pakistan		50-55			Minton (1966)

Table 6. Weights (g) of green turtle eggs.

Location	Mean	Range	Clutches	Eggs	Reference
Pacific Ocean					
Sarawak	36	28.6-44.7	3	30	Hendrickson (1958)
Sabah	ca 40.3				de Silva (1970)
Wan-An Is., Taiwan	53.2	44-65		35	Chen and Cheng (1995)
Long Is., Papua New Guinea	41.2	33-46.9		95	Spring (1983)
Heron Is., Australia	51.9	44.7-60.4	20		Bustard and Greenham (1969)
Heron Is., Australia	ca 51.6	44-60.4			Bustard (1972)
Heron Is., Australia	50	33.5-58.3	11	110	Limpus (1980)
French Frigate Shoals, Hawaii	50	45-54	1	99	Balazs (1980)
Atlantic Ocean					
Kennedy Space Center, Florida	60.1	55.8-63.8	1		Ehrhart (1979a)
Tortuguero, Costa Rica	48.8	35-66	20	400	Hirth (1988)
Aves Is.	45.1	40.5-49.4	1	48	Rainey (1971)
Indian Ocean					
Maziwi Is.		35-48.7			Frazier (1984b)
Primeiras Is.	44.9	41.3-49.7	2	40	Hughes (1974a)
Europa Is.	47.9	38.1-58.6	28	280	Hughes (1974a)
Europa Is.	45.8	40-50			Servan (1976)
Mayotte Is.	ca 46.3	21-60	4	40	Frazier (1985)
Tromelin Is.	48	41.8-53	10	200	Hughes (1974a)
Karan Is., Saudi Arabia	44.1	33.2-56.3	48	480	Miller (1989)
Abdul Wadi, Yemen	40.4	30-44	1	100	Hirth and Carr (1970)
Sharma, Yemen	42.3	37.5-47.5	1	50	Hirth and Carr (1970)
Sharma, Yemen	44.8	35-55	5		FAO (1973)

Table 7. Number of clutches of green turtles per nesting season.

Location	Mean	Range	N	Reference
Pacific Ocean				
Xisha Is., China	ca 3			Huang Chu-Chien (1982)
Sarawak	4.1	1-9	447	Hendrickson (1958)
Sukumade, Indonesia		2-4		Nuitja (1993-4)
Ogasawara Is.		1-5		Fukada (1965)
Ogasawara Is.	3.9			Horikoshi, pers. comm. in Mortimer and Carr (1987)
Heron Is. Australia	ca 4.5	3-6		Bustard (1972)
Heron Is. Australia	ca 5.5			Limpus (1980)
French Frigate Shoals, Hawaii	1.8	1-6	208	Balazs (1980)
Michoacan, Mexico	4			Marquez et al (1982)
Colola and Maruata, Mexico	2.8	1-9	379	Alvarado et al (1985)
Colola and Maruata, Mexico	3.5	1-9	100	Alvarado and Figueroa (1986)
Colola and Maruata, Mexico	2.5	1-7		Alvarado and Figueroa (1990)
Playa Naranjo, Costa Rica	ca 2	2-4	32	Cornelius (1976)
Galápagos Is.	ca 3	1-7		Green (1994)

33

Table 7. Continued.

Location	Mean	Range	N	Reference
Atlantic Ocean				
Cape Canaveral and				Witherington and
Melbourne, Florida	$\underline{ca}$ 2-3			Ehrhart (1989a)
Tortuguero, Costa Rica	$\underline{ca}$ 4-5			Carr and Carr (1970a)
Tortuguero, Costa Rica	2.8	1-8		Carr et al (1978)
Suriname	2.9	1-9	602	Schulz (1975)
Ascension Is.	$\underline{ca}$ 3		78	Mortimer and Carr (1987)
Indian Ocean				
Europa and Tromelin Is.	$\underline{ca}$ 3			Bonnet et al. (1985a)
Aldabra Atoll	$\underline{ca}$ 3			Hornell (1927)
Aldabra Atoll	$\underline{ca}$ 3			Frazier (1971)
Karan Is., Saudi Arabia	4			Miller (1989)

Table 8. Renesting intervals (days) of green turtles.

Location	Mean	Range	N	Reference
Pacific Ocean				
Xisha Is., China	$\underline{ca}$ 14			Huang Chu-Chien (1982)
Sarawak	10.5	8-17	4,493	Hendrickson (1958)
Sukumade, Indonesia		9-16		Nuitja (1993-4)
Baguan Is., Philippines	14.5		74	Trono (1991)
Wan-An Is., Taiwan	14.9	12-17	40	Chen and Cheng (1995)
Long Is., Papua New Guinea		10-16	35	Spring (1983)
Heron Is., Australia	14.5	9-21		Bustard (1972)
Heron Is., Australia	13.5	10-21	253	Limpus (1980)
French Frigate Shoals, Hawaii	13.2	11-18	89	Balazs (1980)
Michoacan, Mexico	14			Marquez et al (1982)
Colola and Maruata, Mexico	$\underline{ca}$ 12-14	1-51	916	Alvarado and Figueroa (1986, 1990)
Playa Naranjo, Costa Rica	$\underline{ca}$ 12.5		42	Cornelius (1976)
Galápagos Is.	15	8-27		Green (1994)
Atlantic Ocean and				
Mediterranean Sea				
Cape Canaveral and				Witherington and
Melbourne, Florida	14			Ehrhart (1989a)
Hutchinson Is., Florida	14		2	Gallagher et al. 1972
Tortuguero, Costa Rica		$\underline{ca}$ 10-14	$\underline{ca}$ 21	Carr and Giovannoli (1957)
Tortuguero, Costa Rica	12.5	$\underline{ca}$ 12-14	104	Carr and Ogren (1960)
Tortuguero, Costa Rica	12.6	9-16	48	Carr and Hirth (1962)
Tortuguero, Costa Rica	12.1	6-51	5,300	Carr et al (1978)
Shell Beach, Guyana	13		1	Pritchard (1969)
Bigi Santi, Suriname	13-14			Pritchard (1969)
Suriname	13.4	11-16	465	Schulz (1975)
Ascension Is.	14.5	10-17	76	Carr and Hirth (1962)
Ascension Is.	$\underline{ca}$ 11-14	9-26	75	Simon and Parkes (1976)
Ascension Is.	13.9	7-92	840	Mortimer and Carr (1987)
Alagadi, Cyprus	13	10-15	7	Godley and Broderick (1993)
Indian Ocean				
Europa Is.	12	10-15	56	Servan (1976)
Europa and Tromelin Is.	$\underline{ca}$ 13			Bonnet et al (1985a)
Aldabra Atoll	$\underline{ca}$ 13-15			Hornell (1927)

Table 8. Continued.

Location	Mean	Range	N	Reference
Aldabra Atoll	ca 13-15			Frazier (1971)
Karan Is., Saudi Arabia	12.3	9-15		Miller (1989)
Sharma, Yemen	9.6	7-13	5	Hirth and Carr (1970)

Table 9. Remigration intervals (years) of green turtles.

Location	Predominant or Mean	Range	N	Reference
Pacific Ocean				
Sarawak	3			Hendrickson (1958)
Sabah	3	2-4	102+	de Silva (1982)
Baguan Is., Philippines	2.5		24	Trono (1991)
Ogasawara Is.		2-4	7	Kurata, undated, in Groombridge and Luxmoore (1989)
Ogasawara Is.	4	2-7		Suganuma (1989)
Raine Is., Australia	5			Limpus et al. (1993)
Heron Is., Australia	4			Bustard (1972)
Heron Is., Australia	4.65	2-7	31	Limpus (1993b)
French Frigate Shoals, Hawaii	2	2-6	21	Balazs (1980)
French Frigate Shoals, Hawaii	2-3	1-8	130	Balazs (1983a)
Michoacan, Mexico	1.8			Marquez et al. (1982)
Colola and Maruata, Mexico	3	1-5	261	Alvarado and Figueroa (1990)
Galápagos Is.	3	2-6	85	Green (1994)
Atlantic Ocean				
Cape Canaveral and Melbourne, Florida	2			Witherington and Ehrhart (1989a)
Melbourne, Florida	2			Bjorndal et al. (1983)
Tortuguero, Costa Rica	3			Carr and Ogren (1960)
Tortuguero, Costa Rica	3	2-3	46	Carr and Hirth (1962)
Tortuguero, Costa Rica	3	2-9	117	Carr and Carr (1970a)
Tortuguero, Costa Rica	3	1-4+	1,412	Carr et al (1978)
Suriname	2.3	1-4	599	Schulz (1975)
Ascension Is.	3-4	2-9	69	Mortimer and Carr (1987)
Indian Ocean				
Europa and Tromelin Is.	3			Bonnet et al (1985a)
North West Cape and Muiron Is., Western Australia		2-5	4	Prince (1993)
Barrow Is., Western Australia		2-5	17	Prince (1993)
Lacepede Is., Western Australia		2-5	228	Prince (1993)

tween body size and clutch size (in 1986, 1987, 1989) nor between body size and overall seasonal fecundity (in 1987, 1988) in Michoacan turtles. However, they did find a positive correlation between carapace length and overall seasonal fecundity in 1985 (Alvarado and Figueroa 1986).

Carr and Hirth (1962), Mortimer and Carr (1987) and Hays et al. (1993) reported a tendency for earlier clutches to be larger than later clutches on Ascension Island. At

Tortuguero, Fowler (1979) and Bjorndal and Carr (1989) found no significant trend in clutch size, at the individual level, over a season. Alvarado and Figueroa (1990) detected no significant increase or decrease in clutch size over the course of a season at Michoacan.

At Tortuguero, recruits lay an average of 2.7 clutches with a mean clutch size of 111.4 eggs while remigrants lay an average of 3.4 clutches and their mean clutch size is 116.8 eggs (Carr et al. 1978; Bjorndal 1980b).

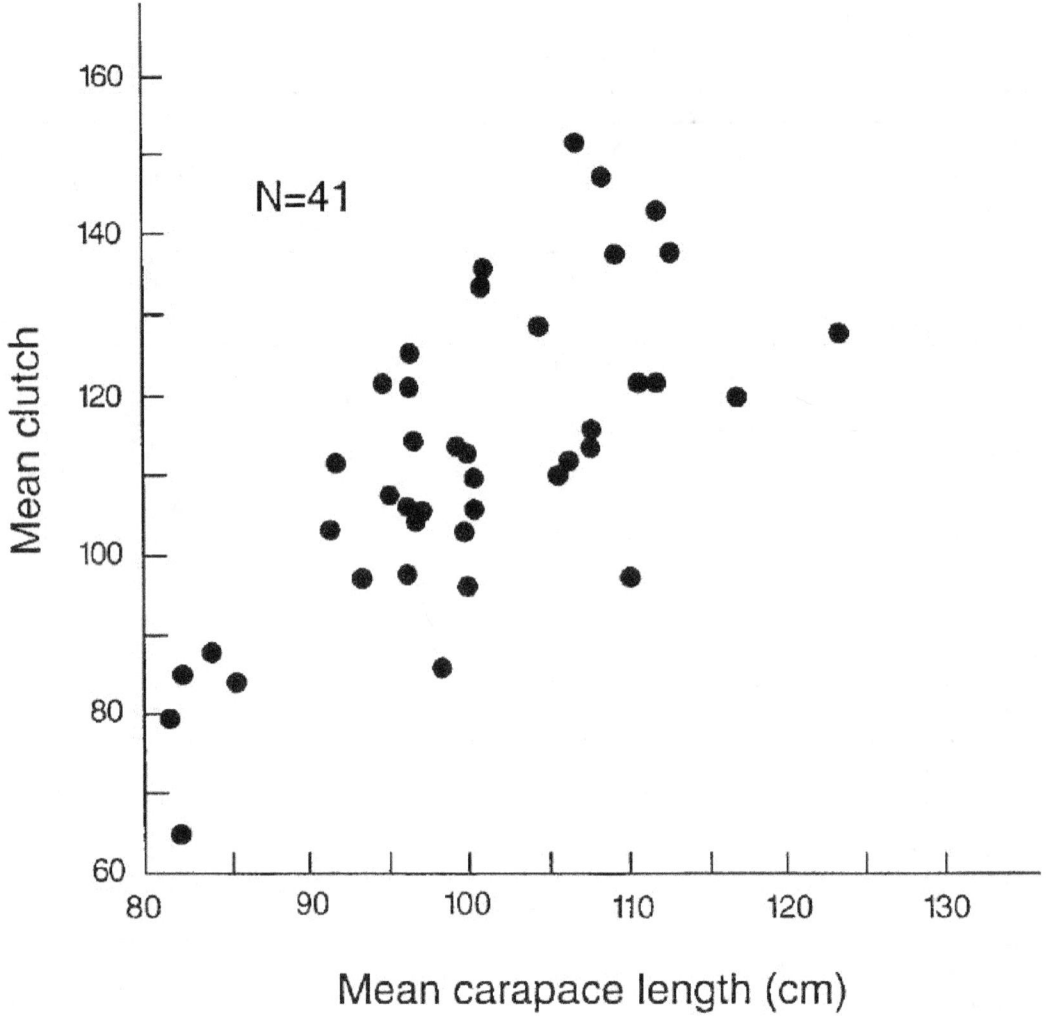

Fig. 12. Mean clutch sizes and average carapace lengths of nesting green turtles from around the world (data from Tables 2 and 4). Statistical significance was not tested because the turtles were measured in several different ways and because sample sizes were very different—but the trend is obvious.

Hays et al. (1993) discovered that the sizes (diameters) of eggs within a clutch were variable on Ascension Island. Larger eggs are laid at the start of a clutch and smaller eggs at the end. This decline in egg size between the beginning and end of a clutch averaged 1.21 mm.

Van Buskirk and Crowder (1994) found a significant trade-off between clutch size and egg size among the seven species of marine turtles.

Natural incubation periods as well as length of incubation in some egg hatcheries are listed in Table 10. The overall average is about 57 days.

Average incubation times are about twenty days longer in the wet season than in the dry season in Sarawak (Hendrickson 1958). Servan (1976) stated that on Europa Island, incubation time ranges from 50 days in the summer to 99 days in the winter.

Predators of green turtle eggs include crabs, insects, lizards, coatis, raccoons, foxes, jackals, dogs, pigs and birds (in already partially depredated nests) (section 3.3.4).

Hatching success at a number of beaches bordering the Pacific, Atlantic and Indian Oceans are provided in Table 11. The mean and range listed for Sarawak (Groombridge and Luxmoore 1989) in the Table are the overall average and the overall range of averages for the years 1970 through 1985. Likewise, the mean and range given for Sabah (de Silva 1982) are the overall average and overall range of averages for the years 1966 through 1978. Leh (1994) reported that mean hatch rates in the egg hatcheries on the Sarawak Turtle Islands, between 1970-1990, varied between 53 and 96%, with higher percentages of hatching in the drier months and lower hatching success in the wet monsoon months (November to April).

Table 10. Natural incubation periods (days) of green turtle eggs (from oviposition to emergence of hatchlings on the surface) *hatchery.

Location	Mean	Range	N	Reference
Pacific Ocean				
Xisha Is., China		ca 40-50		Huang Chu-Chien (1982)
Ko Khram, Thailand		45-50		Penyapol (1958)
Sarawak	54 (dry) *		328	Hendrickson (1958)
	70 (wet) *			
Sabah		49-73 *		de Silva (1970)
Pangumbahan, Indonesia	50.6	49-52	10	Suwelo and Kuntjoro (1969)
Baguan Is., Philippines	54.3		146	Trono (1991)
Wan-An Is., Taiwan	49.3	46-52	50	Chen and Cheng (1995)
Ogasawara Is.	ca 63			Fukada (1965)
Solomon Is.	60	57-63	5	McKeown (1977)
Heron Is., Australia	56	42-77		Bustard (1972)
French Frigate Shoals, Hawaii	64.5	54-88	38	Balazs (1980)
Michoacan, Mexico		45-55		Marquez et al (1982)
Galápagos Is.	55	45-75		Green (1994)
Atlantic Ocean				
Cape Canaveral and	54	SD3.2	20	Witherington and
Melbourne, Florida				Ehrhart (1989a)
El Cuyo, Mexico	59	53-66	10	Rodriguez and Zambrano (1991)
Tortuguero, Costa Rica	57.5[a]	48-70	117	Carr and Ogren (1960)
Tortuguero, Costa Rica	55.6*	48-70	217	Carr and Hirth (1962)
Tortuguero, Costa Rica	61.9	53-81	125	Fowler (1979)
Bigi Santi, Suriname	58.3	47-64	40	Pritchard (1969)
Suriname	56.4	49-65	259	Schulz (1975)
Praia do Forte, Brazil	50	48-55	8	D'Amato and Marczwski (1993)
Atol das Rocas, Brazil	61	51-74	153	Bellini et al. (1996)
Ascension Is.	59.5	58-62	10	Carr and Hirth (1962)
Indian Ocean				
Maziwi Is.		ca 52-64		Frazier (1984b)
Europa Is.		50-99		Servan (1976)
Aldabra Atoll	ca 47			Hornell (1927)
Aldabra Atoll	ca 69			Frazier (1971)
Karan Is., Saudi Arabia	62.5	56-68	4	Miller (1989)
Abdul Wadi, Yemen	49		1	Hirth and Carr (1970)

[a] Natural and hatchery

The data in Table 11 indicate that hatching success in the Galápagos can vary from about 2 to 78%. The low emergence rate on Quinta Playa is due mostly to egg predation by a beetle (*Trox suberosus*) and nest destruction by feral pigs. The extremely poor hatching success on Espumilla is due to feral pigs (Green and Ortiz-Crespo 1982). There is about a 20% higher hatching rate in the natural nests on Colola and Maruata (Pacific Mexico) than in hatchery nests, 83% versus 64%. The 64% rate is an average for the hatcheries at Colola and Maruata in 1989.

For five years the egg hatchery at Colola has had a higher percentage hatch than the one at Maruata and this is believed due to the higher moisture content of the sand at Colola (Alvarado and Figueroa 1990). In 64 green turtle nests in an egg hatchery in Sri Lanka, Hewavisenthi (1994a) found a negative correlation between clutch size and percentage of live hatchlings. Most mortality was in the late embryonic and early hatching stages. The reduced oxygen supply, in nests with large clutches, during the late stages of development may play a role in these

Table 11. Percentage emergence of hatchlings from natural nests. *hatchery ?unknown.

Location	Mean	Range	Nests	Eggs	Reference
Pacific Ocean					
Sarawak	73.3*	47.1-96.0		450,450	Groombridge and Luxmoore (1989)
Sarawak	47.1*		354		Hendrickson (1958)
Sabah	67.3*	54.5-90.6		2,705,903	de Silva (1982)
Baguan Is., Philippines	85.7		146		Trono (1991)
Ogasawara Is.	54.6* (1982)			13,265	Suganuma (1985)
	83.1* (1983)			13,953	
	77.5* (1984)			27,878	
Long Is., Papua New Guinea	89		1		Spring (1983)
Solomon Is.	68.4?	42-93	5		McKeown (1977)
Solomon Is.	78.9?	30-95	8		Vaughan (1981)
Raine Is. Australia	75-80				Limpus et al (1993)
Heron Is., Australia	88 (1966-7)		26		Bustard (1972)
	85 (1967-8)		40		
	67 (1965-6)*			29,948	
	65 (1966-7)*			17,112	
	52 (1967-8)*			29,997	
French Frigate Shoals, Hawaii	70.8	0-97.6	40		Balazs (1980)
Colola and Maruata, Mexico	83		344	22,360	Alvarado and Figueroa (1990)
Colola and Maruata, Mexico	64*		1,888	123,959	Alvarado and Figueroa (1990)
Las Bachas, Galápagos Is.	78.4		22	1,687	Green and Ortiz-Crespo (1982)
Bahia Barahona, Galápagos Is.	72.9		69	5,643	
Las Salinas, Galápagos Is.	64.8		175	15,062	
Bartolome, Galápagos Is.	47.2		15	1,142	
Quinta Playa, Galápagos Is.	41.7		328	26,417	
Espumilla, Galápagos Is.	1.9		122	9,709	
Atlantic Ocean and					
Mediterranean Sea					
Melbourne, Florida	61.6	SD33.9	25		Witherington and Ehrhart (1989a)
Broward County, Florida	61.8		12	1,420	Broward County Erosion
	64.6*		16	1,921	Prevention District (1987)
El Cuyo, Mexico	86.5		15	1,638	Rodriguez and Zambrano (1991)
Tortuguero, Costa Rica	50.7* (1959)			12,000	Carr and Hirth (1962)
	50.8* (1960)			30,484	
Tortuguero, Costa Rica	83.1		134	14,272	Fowler (1979)
Tortuguero, Costa Rica	46.3 (shaded)		32		Horikoshi (1989)
	57.3 (open)		42		
Suriname	84	ca 5-95	57		Schulz (1975)
	58*	ca 5-95	100		
Krofajapasi, Suriname	80.4	1.5 SE	80		Whitmore and Dutton (1985)
Ascension Is.	54.4			1,208	Carr and Hirth (1962)
Cyprus	ca 75*				Demetropoulos and Lambert (1986)
Alagadi, Cyprus	85.3		34		Godley and Broderick (1993)
Indian Ocean					
Maziwi Is.	78?				Frazier (1984b)
Europa Is.	77.6?				Hughes (1974b)
Europa Is.	84	71-96	5		Servan (1976)
	54*	26-70	6		
Tromelin Is.	69.8?				Hughes (1974b)
Karan Is., Saudi Arabia	81.7	60.9-95	4		Miller (1989)
Abdul Wadi, Yemen	48		1		Hirth and Carr (1970)

findings (Hewavisenthi 1994a).

In Suriname, Schulz (1975) reported a successful hatch of about 86% in styrofoam boxes but he also noted that incubation time in boxes was longer than that in natural nests and this was probably due to lower temperatures. We now know that this practice probably produced more male hatchlings. Whitmore and Dutton (1985) noted an average of 72.9% hatch of Suriname eggs in boxes.

Carr (1984) discussed how the number of eggs laid by a green turtle at each oviposition has adaptive value. Some of these advantages include escape from some predation by swamping the predators on the beach and in the littoral zone; metabolic heating of the nest by a mass of eggs; social facilitation in the climb to the sand surface; and, group orientation in the crawl to the sea.

3.2 Embryonic and Hatchling Phase

3.2.1 Embryonic phase

Miller (1985) reviewed the earlier literature on embryology and provided a composite account, with photographs, of the embryology of six species of sea turtles, including *Chelonia mydas*. He divided the embryology into 31 stages of development (5 preovipositional and 26 postovipositional stages). Stages 1 - 5 are preovipositional cleavage stages. Stages immediately following oviposition (6 - 10) were defined by changes in the shape of the blastopore and by differentiation of the notochord, neural folds and head folds. The number of somites and the differentiation of the heart and pharyngeal clefts primarily defined stages 11 - 18. Stages 19 to hatching were determined by modifications in the limbs, formation of the shell and development of scales and pigmentation. The frequency of occurrence of abnormal embryos among marine turtles is low (reviewed in Miller 1985). Lewis et al. (1992) briefly review some reports of twinning and they describe in some detail the histopathologic and anatomic relations of one case of omphalopagus twins. Improper handling of eggs at any time during their development reduces hatching success.

Ackerman (1981b) found that green turtle embryos grow slowly during the first half of their incubation and rapidly during the second half. The rapid phase slows prior to hatching resulting in a sigmoid-shaped overall growth process.

3.2.2 Hatchling phase

Sexual differentiation in the green turtle, as in other sea turtles, is determined by the substrate temperature (other environmental factors may be involved) during incubation. This is commonly referred to as TSD (temperature-dependent sex determination) or ESD (environmental-dependent sex determination). The middle trimester of incubation appears to be the critical period in which temperature directly affects the gonadal differentiation of embryos. Warmer temperatures produce females and cooler temperatures, males. TSD in sea turtles and in reptiles has been the subject of two reviews (respectively, Standora and Spotila 1985, and Janzen and Paukstis 1991). The proceedings of a recent symposium (Lance 1994) on environmental sex determination in reptiles includes twelve papers on the subject (some specific papers are cited in this section of the synopsis). Spotila et al. (1983) have written a manual describing methodology for studying TSD. For measuring incubation temperatures on sea turtle beaches, Godfrey and Mrosovsky (1994) recommend using a module that memorizes maximum and minimum temperatures. They report that for beach temperatures at marine turtle nest depth, the average of the maximum and minimum temperatures over a 24 hr interval is very close to the mean based on more frequent readings. The relatively inexpensive unit also provides flexibility in choice of recording site.

The adaptive significance of TSD in reptiles is unclear but is discussed by Bull and Charnov (1989), Ewert and Nelson (1991), Janzen and Paukstis (1991) Burke (1993) and Ewert et al. (1994). On the other hand, what was adaptive when TSD evolved may no longer be pertinent. Davenport (1989) and Mrosovsky and Provancha (1992) have discussed some possible effects of global warming (the greenhouse effect) on sex determination in sea turtles. Based on his empirical research with hatchling painted turtles, *Chrysemys picta,* in their shallow nests in Illinois, Janzen (1994) found that annual offspring sex ratio was highly correlated with mean July air temperature (July corresponds to the developmental period when embryonic sex is determined). He calculated that an increase in the mean July temperature of 4°C would effectively eliminate production of males in this population. He concluded by stating "populations of species with temperature-dependent sex determination may act as bellwethers for the impending disruption to biological systems posed by global temperature change." The possible physiological and molecular bases for TSD in reptiles have recently been discussed by Wibbels et al. (1994) and Spotila et al. (1994), respectively.

Mrosovsky and Pieau (1991) recommend standardization of terms used in describing sexual determination especially in view of the fact that the subject is now of great interest to a wide range of people, including geneticists, evolutionary ecologists and conservationists. They recommend the following terms and definitions: transitional range of temperature—that range between male and female producing temperatures, within which both sexes may differentiate among individuals of a population; masculinizing and feminizing limit temperatures—those temperatures delimiting the transitional range, below, or above, which masculinization, or feminization, are maximum; pivotal temperature—that temperature within the transitional range giving 50% of each sex in experiments in which eggs are incubated at constant temperatures. Pivotal temperatures can be determined for a number of clutches or for a particular clutch or for a sample from a clutch. Mrosovsky and Provancha (1992) discuss some of the precautions to take in the collection and in the analysis of data pertaining to reptilian sex ratios, especially those of sea turtles. Vogt (1994) describes how some conservation managers' attempts to produce equal numbers of females and males (by incubating eggs at the pivotal temperature) may not be in the best interests of turtles. He argues that, in some cases, it may be more useful to produce more females than males in order to enhance the reproductive output of the population, and that incubation of eggs near the pivotal temperature has a higher probability of producing intersexes. However, Mrosovsky and Godfrey (1995) caution that careful planning is necessary before wildlife managers manipulate sex ratios. Lovich (1996) continues the cautious approach of Mrosovsky and Godfrey (1995) and discusses how knowledge of natural sex ratio variation, multiple paternity and sperm competition, fertility factors and intersexual and intrasexual competition is needed before "jump-starting" declining turtle populations by manipulating sex ratios.

Miller and Limpus (1981) found that in a clutch of eggs from Heron Island, incubation at 26°C resulted in 85.7% males, 0% females and 14.3% intersexes; incubation at 29°C resulted in 0% males, 90.2% females and 9.8% intersexes; and incubation at 33°C produced 0% males, 85.7% females and 14.3% intersexes. Limpus et al. (1983) reported that the sex ratios of green turtles hatched on the warmer side of Heron Island differed from that on the cooler side. Hays et al. (1995b) found that inter-beach thermal variation on Ascension Island was large—with the darkest beach (albedo, 0.16) being 4.2° C warmer than the lightest colored beach (albedo, 0.73)—and they show how these temperature data could be used to calculate hatchling sex ratios here. Limpus et al. (1993-94) briefly summarized results of constant temperature incubation studies of green, loggerhead and flatback turtles in eastern Australia with the statement "The timing of the breeding season and the location of the rookeries used by a stock appear to be selected to provide a range of nest temperatures above and below the pivotal temperature rather than temperatures coinciding with the pivotal temperature."

On the Tortuguero nesting beach Spotila et al. (1987) found that temperatures >30.3°C during the middle third of incubation produced females and temperatures <28.5°C produced males. Thus, the pivotal temperature for Tortuguero green turtles is between 28.5 - 30.3°C. They estimated that the sex ratio produced on the Tortuguero nesting beach, which has sunny and shaded nesting sites, in one season, was 67% female and 33% male. In Tortuguero nests at the pivotal temperature, eggs near the center of the nest produced females and those at the periphery, males, and this may have been due to metabolic heating (Standora et al. 1982a). Horikoshi (1992), working on Tortuguero Beach, estimated pivotal temperature at between 28.5 and 29.0°C and he calculated an overall sex ratio, in one season, of about 40% female. Bjorndal and Bolten (1992) predicted that the primary sex ratio in the Tortuguero colony will vary from year to year because the nesting sites of individuals are not consistent.

In Suriname, Mrosovsky et al. (1984) reported that more males were produced in the cooler, wetter months and more females during the warmer, drier months of the nesting season. The pivotal temperature was estimated at 28.8°C and the overall sex ratio was estimated at 53.9% female. Only 1.1% from the field sample were intersexes. Godfrey et al. (1996) estimated that 63.8% of the green turtle hatchlings produced on Matapica Beach, Suriname, in 1993, were females. They further estimated that over fourteen years the overall sex ratio on Matapica Beach averaged 68.4% females.

Using thermocouples along a beach transect, Alvarado and Figueroa (1990) estimated more females were produced at Colola and more males at Maruata but the overall sex ratio in the Michoacan area was about 50:50.

Eleven natural nests (1,089 eggs) were reburied in an egg hatchery in Sarawak and produced 81.3 - 91.3% females when temperatures during the middle third of the incubation period ranged between 29.5 - 30.3°C (Leh et al. 1985).

The natural sex ratio on Baguan Island in the Philippines was calculated at about 90% female and the sex ratio in a partly shaded egg hatchery was computed at 38% female, 36% male, and 26% intersexes (Trono 1991).

Mrosovsky (1994) reviewed the available literature and concluded that pivotal temperatures for sea turtles are clustered close to 29°C. He also described how SSPPs (seasonal sex production profiles) can show how similar overall sex ratios can be achieved in dissimilar ways.

Many factors probably affect TSD of green turtles including nest site, depth of body pit, depth of clutch, position of egg in the clutch, weather during the incubation period, sand color and beach topography.

Needless to say, serious thought must be given to resulting sex ratios when any manipulative project is undertaken, such as egg transplanting and artificial incubation. For example, Mrosovsky (1982) reported on the masculinization of hatchlings incubated in styrofoam boxes. Morreale et al. (1982) cautioned that the incubation of eggs in central beach hatcheries or in hatcheries aboveground should only be attemped after the appropriate TSD is defined. The taking of eggs by humans for sustenance on easily accessible parts of the beach or at certain times of the nesting season could affect overall sex ratios in the nesting colony. Predators can affect natural sex ratios by taking eggs laid in more shallow nests under shrubs. Even with our knowledge of TSD, the least manipulative management strategies are preferred by the author of this synopsis (see section 6.2).

The hatchling cuts through its eggshell with the aid of a horny protuberance, sometimes called the egg caruncle, or egg tooth, on the tip of its snout. This caruncle disappears after a few days. The histological structure of the egg tooth is interesting for the arrangement of its collagenous fibers of dermis and for its thick stratum corneum (Bons and Bonaric 1971).

Over the course of several days, and in a synchronous manner, the hatchlings climb to the surface. Emergence on the surface is synchronized with a certain sand threshold temperature or, more likely, with a sand temperature gradient. Emergence is predominantly at night, usually as a single unit, but sometimes a few individuals may precede or follow nest exit of the main group. Nocturnal emergence is adaptive in that it eliminates exposure to diurnal predators and it eliminates exposure to hot sand surface temperatures which could be lethal or which could slow down the hatchling in its crawl to the sea and thus lengthen its exposure time to predators. Details of the aforementioned hatchling behavior can be found in: Hendrickson (1958), Carr and Hirth (1961), Bustard (1967), Mrosovsky (1968, 1980), Hirth (1971b), and Gyuris (1993).

Hatchlings crawl along the sand surface using their four flippers in typical reptilian fashion (front member moved in conjunction with hind member on opposite side), while adults on shore heave themselves along using sometimes only the front flippers simultaneously but usually all four flippers simultaneously. Hatchling green turtles may exhibit optokinetic responses as early as 30 minutes after leaving the nest (Ireland 1979). Experiments with hatchlings kept in tanks for several days and then released crawled slower down the beach than fresh hatchlings and they had difficulty entering the sea against incoming waves (Hewavisenthi 1994b).

The hatchling's orientation to the sea is based primarily on visual cues. In the 1960's, Archie Carr and his colleagues set the agenda for much of the hatchling behavioral work that would ensue for the next three decades. Carr and Ogren (1960) conducted a series of tests on the Tortuguero, Costa Rica, beach and concluded that the hatchlings' fundamental goal sense involved visual stimuli and that the response was a modified phototaxis. The "openness of outlook" of a sea-sky horizon was important and would even draw the hatchlings away from a moon or sun where either was over land. Later, several investigators described the crawl to the sea in terms of a positive phototropotaxis and they explained how this behavior would be successful under almost all natural con-

ditions (Ehrenfeld 1968; Mrosovsky and Shettleworth 1968; Mrosovsky 1970, 1972, 1978b; Mrosovsky et al. 1979; Mrosovsky and Kingsmill 1985). Mrosovsky (1978a) also demonstrated how hatchlings integrate brightness information over time in their sea-finding behavior. That is, a flashing light did not influence a turtle's behavior as much as a continuous light, so a hatchling should not be influenced by lightning flashes over a beach. However, Van Rhijn's (1979) experiments with hatchlings pointed to a redundant system of orienting mechanisms that has both optic and non-optic components. Based on laboratory experiments, Van Rhijn and Van Gorkom (1983) concluded that hatchlings primarily orient visually but a photic system may take over under conditions that still have to be explained. Mrosovsky and Kingsmill (1985) rejected, as unlikely, the possibility of a system redundant to a complex phototropotactic system.

The sea-finding ability of hatchlings, as well as adult females, was further examined on the Tortuguero beach by Ehrenfeld and Carr (1967) and Ehrenfeld (1968). Spectacles containing special filters were fitted to the heads of adults, and hatchlings were tested in a circular arena where the view of the horizon was unobstructed or where it was blocked by a low wall. They substantiated the claim of others that the water-finding orientation is primarily a visual process (based on brightness rather than color), that it involves an appraisal of beach topography, and that depolarizing filters did not affect orientation. They also concluded that there was no innate compass direction based on celestial cues, although Fischer (1964) did find a fixed direction preference related to the position of the sun in hatchlings tested in a water arena.

Mrosovsky and Carr (1967) examined light preferences of hatchlings in a simple apparatus on the natural nesting beach and discovered that when given a two-choice situation, they prefer blue and green stimuli over red. Light preferences were analyzed further by Mrosovsky (1967) and by Mrosovsky and Shettleworth (1968) and it was found that while wavelength preferences of hatchlings are controlled primarily by brightness, the existence of some color preference cannot be ruled out. In the laboratory, using a V-maze, Witherington and Bjorndal (1991) found that hatchlings oriented toward near-ultraviolet (360 nm), violet (400 nm) and blue-green (500 nm) and chose a standard light source over an adjustable light source.

Salmon et al. (1992) described the behavior of hatchlings in an arena where manipulation of visual and slope stimuli was possible. Hatchlings oriented toward the more intensely illuminated sections of the arena and they also oriented away from dark silhouettes which simulated an elevated horizon, typical of the view toward land. When hatchlings were presented simultaneously with silhouette and photic cues, at eye level, in different directions, they oriented away from the silhouette cues. Responses of green turtles to slope cues, under near normal nocturnal light conditions, were weak. The authors conclude that green turtle hatchlings usually find the sea by orienting away from elevated silhouettes and that, ecologically, this is a reliable cue for nesters on continental beaches. On some relatively flat, island beaches photic cues may play a more important role. Working on a Suriname beach, where green turtle eggs laid below the high tide line are reburied on safer ground, Godfrey and Barreto (1995) demonstrated that when reburied in dense vegetation the subsequent hatchlings showed no significant orientation to the sea. Thus, they advise caution in the selection of relocation sites.

Lab-reared yearlings retain the ability to find the sea and even cross complex terrain to reach it, and adult males evidently possess the same ability, although once reaching the surf as hatchlings, they never normally return to a terrestrial environment, except at those few locations where terrestrial basking occurs (Carr and Hirth 1962). After conducting a variety of experiments with green turtles in the Gulf of California, Caldwell and Caldwell (1962) concluded that the sea approach ability is present in both sexes of all ages.

When arriving at the wet, wave-washed sand, the hatchlings appear to crawl faster and immediately after entering the surf their swimming behavior is commonly described as a frenzy. The swim frenzy is strongly adaptive in all sea turtle species in that it takes the hatchlings quickly away from the predator-rich shallow water out to deeper waters and into current systems where food and shelter exist. But, as already mentioned (section 2.2.1), the flatback turtle may lack a pelagic phase.

In a laboratory study, Wyneken and Salmon (1992) compared the swim frenzy of green, loggerhead and leatherback hatchlings from beaches in southeast Florida. All species swam almost continuously during their first 24 hours and then there was a decrease in swimming as they became less active at night. The species differed in levels of nocturnal activity, this being highest in leatherbacks and lowest in loggerheads.

It has been shown that hatchling green, loggerhead and leatherback turtles can maintain a constant compass course in shallow water by using waves as an orientation cue (Salmon and Lohmann 1989; Wyneken et al. 1990; Lohmann et al. 1990; Lohman 1992; Lohmann and Lohmann 1992). After entering the sea, hatchlings swim into the waves and this could take them directly to the open ocean. In a laboratory setting, Lohmann et al. (1995) demonstrated that hatchling green and loggerhead turtles can determine the propagation direction of ocean waves by monitoring the circular movements that occur as waves pass over them.

Lohmann et al. (1990) found that a crawl across the beach was not necessary for normal orientation in shal-low water (cf. Frick, 1976). Lohmann et al. (1990) concluded that hatchlings sequentially employ two different orientation systems: visual cues are used to crawl from the nest to the surf and, then, in the ocean, hatchlings orient by swimming into waves.

Lohmann (1991, 1992) and Lohmann and Lohmann (1993) found that loggerhead and leatherback hatchlings have a magnetic sense and this sense may complement, or supplant, wave orientation in deep water. Laboratory experiments with loggerhead hatchlings demonstrated that visual cues available on land set the preferred direction of magnetic orientation (Lohmann and Lohmann 1994a). Light et al. (1992, 1993) discovered that loggerhead hatchlings respond to inclination, but not polarity, of the earth's geomagnetic field, and, since inclination changes with latitude, sea turtles may use inclination as one component of the "map sense". In laboratory experiments, Lohmann and Lohmann (1994b) demonstrated that loggerhead hatchlings can distinguish between different magnetic inclination angles and perhaps derive from them an approximation of latitude. They also hypothesized how this ability to recognize specific inclination angles could help explain how adult sea turtles can identify their natal beaches after years at sea. In later experiments, Lohmann and Lohmann (1996a) demonstrated that loggerhead hatchlings can also distinguish between different magnetic field intensities found along their migratory route. Possessing abilities to distinguish between different field intensities and different magnetic inclination angles, loggerhead hatchlings (and presumably green turtle hatchlings) have the abilities necessary to assess global position using a bicoordinate magnetic map.

Perry et al. (1985) found magnetic remanence in the head region (the greatest concentration in the anterior part of the dura mater) of nine green turtles (four hatchlings, three juveniles and two adults).

The sizes and weights of hatchlings are provided in Tables 12 and 13, respectively.

The eggs and hatchlings of twenty recruits at Tortuguero were analyzed and it was found that at their first oviposition large recruits lay more eggs and produce more hatchlings than do smaller recruits and that the hatchlings of the larger nesters were slightly smaller than the hatchlings of the smaller nesters (Hirth 1988). Pinckney (1990) found an inverse relationship between clutch size and hatchling length in loggerheads on Kiawah Island, South Carolina. Chen and Cheng (1995) found a statistically significant relationship between straight carapace length of nester and straight carapace length of the hatchling ($r^2=0.13$, N=6). Hatchling size may be influenced by maternal and genetic factors. Environmental factors such as hydric, thermal and respiratory variables within the egg chamber may also affect the size of hatchlings. In a laboratory setting, McGehee (1990) found

Table 12. Carapace lengths (mm) of hatchling green turtles.

Location	Mean	Range	Nests	Hatchlings	Reference
Pacific Ocean					
Xisha Is., China	ca 40				Huang Chu-Chien (1982)
Sabah	49	46-51		10	de Silva (1970)
Wan-An Is., Taiwan	46.9	41.4-52.4		327	Chen and Cheng (1995)
Ogasawara Is.	ca 32				Fukada (1965)
Long Is., Papua New Guinea	46.3		1	10	Spring (1983)
Solomon Is.	49	45-52			McKeown (1977)
Heron Is., Australia	ca 50				Bustard (1972)
Heron Is., Australia	49.7	40.2-51.9	11	110	Limpus (1980)
French Frigate Shoals, Hawaii	53	48-59		556	Balazs (1980)
Playa Naranjo, Costa Rica	51.2	50-52	1	5	Cornelius (1976)
Galápagos Is.	46.2	41-49.5		29	Pritchard (1971)
Atlantic Ocean and					
Mediterranean Sea					
El Cuyo, Mexico	51.4	48.5-53.6	6	60	Rodriguez and Zambrano (1991)
Tortuguero, Costa Rica	49.7	46-56		100	Carr and Hirth (1962)
Tortuguero, Costa Rica	51.5	47-56	20	400	Hirth (1988)
Aves Is.	54.6	52.8-56.5	1	24	Rainey (1971)
Bigi Santi, Suriname	53.5	51-55	1	169	Pritchard (1969)
Suriname	51	48-53			Schulz (1975)
Ascension Is.	51.7	49.1-55		100	Carr and Hirth (1962)
Alagadi, Cyprus	47	S.D. 0.4		48	Godley and Broderick (1993)
Indian Ocean					
Maziwi Is.	48				Frazier (1984b)
Europa Is.	48.5	45.8-51.4	20	50	Hughes (1974a)
Europa Is.	50.9	35-54		131	Servan (1976)
Moheli Is.	49.2	47-52	4	36	Frazier (1985)
Aldabra Atoll	50.1	ca 45-53	4	184	Frazier (1971)
Tromelin Is.	48.6	45.2-51.9	17	50	Hughes (1974a)
Karan Is., Saudi Arabia	48	45-52.1	12	120	Miller (1989)
Abdul Wadi, Yemen	46.9	44-48.4	1	20	Hirth and Carr (1970)
Hawkes Bay, Pakistan		48-53		8	Minton (1966)

that loggerhead hatchlings' carapace lengths were strongly correlated with sand moisture content, and Broadwell (1992) showed that larger loggerhead hatchlings were produced on Florida beaches containing more moisture and greater pore spacing. Good reviews on this subject are Packard and Packard (1988), Wilbur and Morin (1988) and Stearns (1992). Packard et al. (1992) review some methods for measuring water potential in subterranean nests and they recommend using thermocouple psychrometry.

Virtually nothing is known about the survival rates of green turtle hatchlings once they enter the sea. Larger hatchlings may climb to the sand surface quicker, crawl to the sea faster, be better swimmers, experience faster growth rates and have fewer predators than smaller hatchlings, but all of this needs investigation.

Green turtle hatchlings appear to be faster swimmers and to use their foreflippers more than either ridleys or loggerheads and unlike other sea turtle hatchlings who employ a foreflipper beat or a hindflipper action as the dominant slow swimming stroke, green turtles use the dog-paddle (Davenport and Pearson 1994). Twelve hatchling green turtles observed in captivity by Davenport and Pearson (1994) had difficulty diving at first but all were able to dive and exhibited neutral or negative buoyancy by the time they weighed between 100 and 150 g. Laboratory studies show that young green turtles, weighing between 200 and 1,200 g, are excellent swimmers who use their foreflippers like wings rather than oars (Davenport et al. 1984).

3.3 Juvenile, Subadult, and Adult Phase

3.3.1 Longevity

Little is known about the longevity of green turtles. At Tortuguero, Costa Rica, there are records of a female nesting over a 19-year span, and of two others for over 17 years (Carr et al. 1978). In 1985, the author of this syn-

Table 13. Weights (g) of hatchling green turtles.

Location	Mean	Range	Nests	Hatchlings	Reference
Pacific Ocean					
Sarawak	21.2	17.7-23.0	4	20	Harrisson (1955)
Sabah	22.1	17.9-24.4		10	de Silva (1970)
Wan-An Is., Taiwan	22.7	16.5-32		327	Chen and Cheng (1995)
Solomon Is.	22.6	17-26			McKeown (1977)
Heron Is., Australia	ca 21				Bustard (1972)
Heron Is., Australia	24.8	19.8-28.4	11	110	Limpus (1980)
French Frigate Shoals, Hawaii	31	25-35		120	Balazs (1980)
Atlantic Ocean					
Kennedy Space Center, Florida	31.1	26.1-34.1	1		Ehrhart (1979a)
Southeast Florida	ca 30				Ehrhart and Witherington (1992)
Tortuguero, Costa Rica	25.9	15-31	20	400	Hirth (1988)
Aves Is.	27	25.1-28.9	1	24	Rainey (1971)
Indian Ocean					
Maziwi Is.	25				Frazier (1984b)
Europa Is.	22.9	18.4-26.2	20	50	Hughes (1974a)
Europa Is.	27.6	18-31		245	Servan (1976)
Moheli Is.	21.7	19-22.6		8	Frazier (1985)
Aldabra Atoll	28.2			64	Frazier (1971)
Tromelin Is.	24	19.8-29.4	17	50	Hughes (1974a)
Karan Is., Saudi Arabia	22	18.2-25	12	120	Miller (1989)
Abdul Wadi, Yemen	23	20-28	1	20	Hirth and Carr (1970)

opsis found a turtle nesting on Tortuguero Beach that had been tagged there in 1962, representing a reproductive life of at least 23 years. If we assume turtles in the Costa Rica population reach maturity in 12 to 26 years (Frazer and Ladner 1986) then the turtles mentioned above may have been between 29 and 49 years of age. The present maximum reproductive lifespan of female green turtles at Heron Island, Australia, is about 22 years and one male green turtle here has been recorded over an 18 year reproductive lifespan (Fitzsimmons et al. 1995b). Frazer (1983) estimated a maximum reproductive life span of 32 years for Georgia loggerheads. Some factors affecting longevity are described in sections 3.3.4 and 4.4.2.

3.3.2 Hardiness

In 1976, Felger et al. published a paper on the dormant, partially buried green turtles overwintering on the sea bottom in the Gulf of California. Here, the Seri Indians harpooned the turtles buried at water depths of from 4 to 8 m, and Mexican fishermen caught dormant turtles at depths of from 10 to 15 m. The green turtle is dormant at water temperatures below approximately 15°C in the Gulf of California. Owens (1993-94) reported that at about 15°C environmental temperature, *C. mydas* became quiescent and at 10°C they are quiescent, do not feed and appear to be hibernating. In retrospect, Carr (1982) noted that some of the immature green turtles off the west coast of Florida went into winter dormancy in the mud.

Schwartz (1989) stated that sea turtles do not hibernate and that muddying (digging) in is a response by the turtle to keep from floating upwards. Gregory (1982) has written a comprehensive review of reptilian hibernation and Penny (1987) has reviewed the major physiological mechanisms involved in the overwintering strategies of frogs and turtles.

Witherington and Ehrhart (1989b) reported on several hypothermic stunning episodes that occurred in Mosquito Lagoon, Florida, between 1977 and 1986. Average water depth here is only about 1.5 m. Of 342 green turtles collected, there was an 11.5% mortality. Cloacal temperatures of 22 living turtles averaged 6.1°C. Morning surface water temperatures during these cold-stunning events generally were below 8°C. Schroeder et al. (1990) reported that 246 green turtles were recovered cold-stunned in the Mosquito Lagoon area in December 1989; 67 were dead or died within 12 hours. Minimum water temperature was below 10°C during the episode. A few cold-stunned juvenile green turtles have been collected in New York waters (Morreale et al. 1992). Schwartz (1978) stated that the lethal temperature for *Chelonia mydas* is about 5 - 6.5°C. Ogren and McVeay (1982) compared the apparent hibernation and hypothermic stunning of green and loggerhead turtles.

The body temperatures (thermoprobe inserted about 15 cm into the cloaca) of fifty immature turtles with an average curved carapace length of 55.7 cm (range 42.1-85.1

cm) were taken in Moreton Bay, Australia. The body temperatures did not deviate significantly from water temperatures throughout seasonal fluctuations in water temperatures in the range of 15 to 22.7°C (Read et al. 1996). The authors raise the possibility that immature green turtles in Moreton Bay are more tolerant of cold water than individuals in some other populations.

On the other end of the thermal spectrum, it has been found that when a hatchling's body temperature reaches about 36°C, it starts seeking shade (Bustard 1970) and that sea turtles may extend their normal ranges in response to warmer water temperatures (Radovich 1961).

The normal resting and active body temperatures of green turtles are discussed in section 3.4.4.

As far as is known, the green turtle is the only sea turtle that spends time on land for non-nesting purposes. This behavior has been observed in Australia (Garnett et al. 1985a), Hawaiian Archipelago (Balazs 1980; Whittow and Balazs 1982), Socorro Island and Galápagos Islands (Fritts 1981; Snell and Fritts 1983) and in Namibia (Tarr 1987). Non-nesting emergences of both sexes have been seen in daytime and at night and involve some small but mostly large individuals. In the Wellesley Group, Australia, basking solitary turtles or sometimes groups of up to 400 in a small embayment (made up mostly of internesting females and some adult males) can periodically be seen (Limpus et al. 1994a). Hawaiian green turtles of all sizes regularly "bask" in captivity (Balazs and Ross 1974; Kam 1984). Garnett et al. (1985a) review some of the reasons for nonnesting emergences, including avoidance of courting males by females, synthesis of vitamin D, acceleration of digestion, egg maturation, avoidance of predation by sharks and energy conservation. Congdon (1989) reviews the basking habit of turtles and in addition to the aforementioned possible reasons for non-nesting emergences, he cites elimination of ectoparasites and epizoic algae and drying of integument to reduce bacterial and fungal infections.

The green turtles' sensitivities to parasites and diseases are discussed in section 3.3.5. The fact that green turtles can be raised and kept in captivity for years, albeit not without major problems, attests to their hardiness. There is some nipping and biting between males and between males and females in the courtship and mating repertoire (see section 3.1.3).

Evidently because of the lack of food, little feeding occurs off nesting beaches (but see section 3.4.1). Some long-range oceanic migrations during which adult turtles are presumed not to feed are described in section 3.5.1.

Stabenau et al. (1993) review the suggested methods for resuscitation of comatose sea turtles (compression of plastron, electrical stimulation of pectoral region, insertion of plastic tube into trachea followed by blowing into the tube) and they recommend a method that has been used successfully with Kemp's ridley turtles. The field method involves maintaining the turtle in a prone position, intubation with an endotracheal tube fitted with a low-pressure cuff, and ventilating with a manual resuscitator.

The current method being used to treat carapace injuries at Sea World in Florida is a transparent wound dressing known as tegaderm (Walsh et al. 1994). The healing sequence in these types of wounds starts with granulation of healthy tissue, followed by re-epithelization and pigmentation, and then calcification.

Campbell (1996) describes rehabilitation of injured and sick sea turtles. Some of the common broad-spectrum antibiotics used are chloramphenicol succinate, enrofloxin and trimethoprin-sulfadiazine.

3.3.3 Competitors

Heinsohn et al. (1977) briefly describe how, in some Australian waters, food (seagrasses) competition between green turtles and dugongs is reduced by the former's reliance also on algae while the latter's primary food sources are seagrasses. In the Torres Strait where much seagrass is eaten by dugongs, Garnett et al. (1985b) found that the most common plants consumed by green turtles were five genera of algae and the seagrass *Thalassia*.

In the Caribbean grass meadows, sea urchins and certain fishes are the main competitors of green turtles. Three species of sea urchins that graze extensively on seagrass are *Diadema antillarum*, *Tripneustes ventricosus* and *Lytechinus variegatus*. The sea urchins tend to graze the distal portions of the grass blades. The bucktooth parrotfish, *Sparisoma radians*, feeds primarily on *Thalassia testudinum*. Several other species of parrotfish and surgeonfish feed on seagrasses, especially on the epiphytized tips of the blades (Zieman et al. 1984). Along with *C. mydas*, grazers in the tropical western Atlantic seagrass communities include gammarid amphipods, gastropods, echinoids and fish (references in Dawes et al. 1991).

In the Arabian region, dugongs are among the larger grazers of seagrasses. The smaller grazers include the urchin *(Tripneustes gratilla)*, surgeonfish *(Zebrasoma xanthurum* and *Ctenochaetus striatus)* and rabbitfish *(Siganus rivulatus)*. In a quantitative study, urchin consumption was equivalent to about 33% of the total seagrass growth and consumption by fish amounted to less that 5% of the total plant growth (references in Sheppard et al. 1992).

Intraspecific density-dependent nest destruction may prevail on beaches, usually small island beaches, where nesting space is limited (Bustard and Tognetti 1969). Monk seals with pups sometimes compete with green turtles for choice basking spaces on French Frigate Shoals (Balazs 1980).

Humans sometimes compete with marine turtles for beaches. An example is the drive to acquire beachfront for the Archie Carr National Wildlife Refuge, in Florida, in face of pressure to develop the beach for humans (Anon 1993b; Owen et al. 1994).

3.3.4 Predators

Significant predators of eggs are various species of crabs and mammals (Table 14). Some crabs burrow into nests and may provide routes for secondary predators, such as a variety of insects. On several beaches, ants and fly larvae are associated with rotting eggs. Feral dogs are major predators on some beaches. The elaborate camouflaging of the nest site must have been naturally selected to counter some egg predation. On the Tortuguero Beach, Costa Rica, in 1977, between 24% and 38% of the nests were destroyed by predators, mainly dogs, coatis and vultures (Fowler 1979). In July 1993, about 63.8% of the green turtle nests on Akyatan Beach, Turkey, were preyed upon by either red fox (*Vulpes vulpes*) or golden jackal (*Canis aureus*) (Brown and Macdonald 1995). About 66% of the eggs were consumed in the vicinity of the predated nests. The tracks of the canids indicated that the predators were systematically searching for turtle nests. Predation here occurred over at least four weeks of incubation. Hatching success was only 10.8% and hatchlings were preyed upon at seven of ten nests.

Significant predators of hatchlings are crabs, including at least six species of *Ocypode*, fishes and birds. Shallow water predation by fishes is assumed to be high. The nocturnal emergence of hatchlings on the beach, usually but not always in one large mass, their innate orientation to visual cues on the beach, their swim frenzy, and their countershading may be viewed as adaptations to predator pressure.

Gyuris (1994) quantified hatchling predation rates by tethering them on a 10m monofilament line and following them as they swam across the water's edge to the reef crest on Heron Island, Australia. Predation rates under different combinations of environmental variables (tide, moonphase, time of day) varied from 0 to 85% with a mean of 31%. Predation was lower during high tide than during low tide. The most common predators were fishes of the family Serranidae, followed by Lutjanidae and Labridae. Small sharks, lethrinids and eels occasionally preyed on the hatchlings. Most attacks were sudden rushes by the predators and no hatchlings took evasive action to avoid the predators. Gyuris (1994) stated that "for the green turtle populations breeding in eastern Australia, most first year mortality is caused by predation while crossing the reef within the first hour of entering the sea."

Wyneken et al. (1994) observed that hatchling green turtles, as well as loggerhead and leatherback hatchlings, in nearshore Florida waters, dove in response to overhead threats. They also found that green turtle hatchlings encountered fewer aquatic threats than the loggerhead and leatherback hatchlings and they attributed this to the protective coloration provided by the countershading of the green turtles. Most green and leatherback hatchlings ignored fish threats and when a response occurred it was frequently a change in course. Unlike some loggerheads, green hatchlings did not become immobile when threatened.

Sharks are major predators of large green turtles. Hendrickson (1958) estimated that 4% of the adult females on the Malaysian beaches showed signs of assumed shark attack — amputated flippers and missing pieces of shell. In agreement with some of the islanders, he was of the opinion that sharks do apparently congregate in large numbers around the Sarawak Turtle Islands during the peak breeding season. Witzell (1987) reviewed some of the literature and reported that tiger sharks, *Galeocerdo cuvier*, prey on large marine turtles, including green turtles, around the world.

Autar (1994) recorded 82 nesting green turtles being killed by jaguars (*Panthera onca*) on the beaches in Suriname between 1963 and 1973. Thirteen green turtles were killed in 1980 and more were still being killed by jaguars as recently as 1994 in Suriname.

Stancyk (1982) reviewed some of the older literature on marine turtle predation and he describes some predator control methods including chemical control, shooting and trapping, nest transplants and egg hatcheries.

3.3.5 Parasites, commensals and diseases

There are several hundred scientific papers dealing directly or indirectly with the parasites, commensals and diseases of green turtles. Some of the more recent and significant papers are cited in Table 15. Species from the five kingdoms occur as symbionts with *Chelonia mydas*. Some bacterial symbionts in the gut of the green turtle are associated with degradation of cellulose (see section 3.4.1).

The turtle barnacle, *Chelonibia testudinaria*, was found on the carapaces of 52.9% of 814 turtles on a feeding pasture off Queensland, Australia (mean count of 2.6 barnacles per turtle) (Limpus et al. 1994b). *Platylepus decorata* occurred in appreciable numbers on the skin of almost every turtle. Other barnacles on individuals in this population were *Tubicinella cheloniae*, *Stomatolepas transversa* and *Stephanolepas muricata*. Ozobranchid leeches, *Ozobranchus margoi*, and/or their eggs also occurred on almost every turtle in this feeding population

Brock et al. (1976) described an outbreak of tuberculosis in captive turtles in Hawaii caused by tubercle bacilli of the *Mycobacterium avium* complex. Glazebrook et al. (1993) describe a serious disease complex (ulcerative stomatitis-obstructive rhinitis-pneumonia) in captive hatchlings and juveniles in Australia. Three bacteria (*Vibrio alginolyticus, Aeromonas hydrophila* and *Flavobacterium sp.*) and four genera of fungi (*Paecilomyces sp., Penicillium sp., Aspergillus sp.,* and *Fusarium sp.*)

Table 14. Representative predators of green turtles.

Predator	Location	Reference
	EGGS	
Crabs		
Birgus latro	Aldabra Atoll	Honegger (1967)
Brachyura sp.	Aldabra Atoll	Honegger (1967)
Ocypode quadrata	Suriname	Schulz (1975)
Ocypode quadrata	Costa Rica	Fowler (1979)
Ocypode sp.	Yemen	Hirth and Carr (1970)
crabs	Karan Is.	Miller (1989)
Insects		
Trox suberosus	Galápagos Is.	Green and Ortiz-Crespo (1982)
beetles	Karan Is.	Miller (1989)
Reptiles		
Varanus sp.	East Indies	Raven (1946)
Varanus sp.	Pakistan	Minton (1966)
Mammals		
Canis aureus	Turkey	Brown and Macdonald (1995)
Herpestes auropunctatus	U. S. Virgin Is.	Henry 1993 in Mackay (1994)
Nasua narica	Costa Rica	Fowler (1979)
Procyon lotor	Florida	Bryant (1986)
Vulpes vulpes	Turkey	Brown and Macdonald (1995)
dogs	Pakistan	Minton (1966)
dogs	Yemen	Hirth and Carr (1970)
dogs	Suriname	Schulz (1975)
dogs	Costa Rica	Fowler (1979)
dogs	Comoros	Frazier (1985)
fox	Yemen	Hirth and Carr (1970)
jackal	Pakistan	Minton (1966)
pigs	East Indies	Raven (1946)
pigs	Galápagos Is.	Green and Ortiz-Crespo (1982)
Birds		
Cathartes aura	Costa Rica	Fowler (1979)
Coragyps atratus	Costa Rica	Fowler (1979)
crows	Pakistan	Minton (1966)
	HATCHLINGS	
Crabs		
Birgus latro	Gielop Is.	Kolinski (1994b)
Coenobita cavipes	Europa Is.	Hughes (1974b)
Coenobita cavipes	Tromelin Is.	Hughes (1974b)
Coenobita compressus	Galápagos Is.	Green (1983)
Coenobita perlata	Bikar Atoll	Fosberg (1969)
Coenobita rugosus	Europa Is.	Hughes (1974b)
Coenobita rugosus	Tromelin Is.	Hughes (1974b)
Coenobita sp.	Karan Is.	Miller (1989)
Eriphia sebana	Karan Is.	Miller (1989)
Grapsus grapsus	Trindade Is.	Moreira et al. (1995)
Grapsus lagostoma	Trindade Is.	Moreira et al. (1995)
Grapsus tenuicrustatus	Karan Is.	Miller (1989)
Grapsus sp.	Europa Is.	Hughes (1974b)
Grapsus sp.	Tromelin Is.	Hughes (1974b)
Ocypode ceratopthalmus	Cocos-Keeling Is.	Gibson-Hill (1950)
Ocypode ceratopthalmus	Malaysia	Hendrickson (1958)
Ocypode ceratopthalmus	Heron Is.	Bustard (1966)

47

Table 14. Continued.

Predator	Location	Reference
Ocypode ceratopthalmus	Aldabra Atoll	Frith (1975)
Ocypode ceratopthalmus	Hawaii	Balazs (1980)
Ocypode ceratopthalmus	Comoros	Frazier (1985)
Ocypode gaudichaudi	Galápagos Is.	Green (1983)
Ocypode laevis	Hawaii	Balazs (1980)
Ocypode madagascariensis	Comoros	Frazier (1985)
Ocypode quadrata	Suriname	Schulz (1975)
Ocypode quadrata	Costa Rica	Fowler (1979)
Ocypode saratan	Karan Is.	Miller (1989)
Ocypode sp.	Yemen	Hirth and Carr (1970)
crabs	Trindade Is.	Olson (1981)
Fishes		
Caranx ignobilis	Aldabra Atoll	Honegger (1967)
Caranx lugubrix	Trindade Is.	Moreira et al. (1995)
Carcharinus spallanzani	Heron Is.	Bustard (1966)
Choerodon cyanodus	Heron Is.	Gyuris (1995)
Coryphaena hippurus	Florida	Witham (1974)
Cromileptes altivelis	Heron Is.	Gyuris (1994)
Echidnae sp.	Europa Is.	Hughes (1974b)
Echidnae sp.	Tromelin Is.	Hughes (1974b)
Epinephelus labriformis	Galápagos Is.	Pritchard (1971)
Epinephelus sp.	Heron Is.	Gyuris (1994)
Epinephelus sp.	Yemen	Hirth and Carr (1970)
Epinephelus sp.	Trindade Is.	Moreira et al. (1995)
Eulamia spallanzani	Fairfax Is.	Booth and Peters (1972)
Germo albacora	Europa Is.	Hughes (1974b)
Hynnis cubensis	Trindade Is.	Moreira et al. (1995)
Lutianus argentimaculatus	Europa Is.	Hughes (1974b)
Lutianus bohar	Aldabra Atoll	Honegger (1967)
Lutianus sp.	Heron Is.	Gyuris (1994)
Mycteroperca sp.	Trindade Is.	Moreira et al. (1995)
Sphyrraena barracuda	Trindade Is.	Moreira et al. (1995)
black tip reef shark	Heron Is.	Gyuris (1994)
sharks	Ascension Is.	Carr and Hirth (1962)
sharks	Aldabra	Honegger (1967)
sharks	Yemen	Hirth and Carr (1970)
sharks	Suriname	Schulz (1975)
sharks	Galápagos Is.	Green (1983)
Reptiles		
Boiga dendrophila	Malaysia	Hendrickson (1958)
Masticophis anthonyi	Islas Revillagigedo	Brattstrom (1982)
Python reticulatus	Malaysia	Hendrickson (1958)
Varanus sp.	Malaysia	Hendrickson (1958)
Mammals		
Mus musculus	Karan Is.	Miller (1989)
Nasua narica	Costa Rica	Fowler (1979)
Rattus exulans	Bikar Atoll	Fosberg (1969)
cats	Ascension Is.	Carr and Hirth (1962)
cats	Galápagos Is.	Green (1983)
cats	Aldabra Atoll	Seabrook (1989b)
dogs	Suriname	Schulz (1975)
dogs	Costa Rica	Fowler (1979)
gray fox	Florida	Broward County Erosion Prevention District (1987)

Table 14. Continued.

Predator	Location	Reference
rats	Malaysia	Hendrickson (1958)
rats	Galápagos Is.	Green (1983)
Birds		
Ardea cinerea	Aldabra Atoll	Honegger (1967)
Cathartes aura	Costa Rica	Fowler (1979)
Coragyps atratus	Suriname	Schulz (1975)
Coragyps atratus	Costa Rica	Fowler (1979)
Corvus albus	Aldabra Atoll	Honegger (1967)
Corvus albus	Europa Is.	Hughes (1974b)
Corvus albus	Comoros	Frazier (1985)
Corvus corax	Islas Revillagigedos	Awbrey et al. (1984)
Dryolimnas cuvieri	Aldabra Atoll	Frith (1975)
Fregata ariel	Aldabra Atoll	Honegger (1967)
Fregata minor	Aldabra Atoll	Honegger (1967)
Fregata minor	Europa Is.	Hughes (1974b)
Fregata minor	Tromelin Is.	Hughes (1974b)
Larus novaehollandiae	Heron Is.	Bustard (1966)
Milvus migrans	Comoros	Frazier (1985)
Nyctanassa violacea	Galápagos Is.	Green (1983)
Nycticorax caledonicus	Raine Is.	Limpus et al. (1993)
Phoenicopterus ruber	Aldabra Atoll	Honegger (1967)
Sterna anaethetus	Karan Is.	Miller (1989)
Threskiornis aethiopica	Aldabra Atoll	Frith (1975)
burrowing owl	Islas Revillagigedo	Brattstrom (1982)

IMMATURES AND ADULTS

Fishes		
Carcharhinus longimanus	South Africa	Hughes (1974b)
Epinephelus tauvina	Hawaii	Balazs (1980)
Galeocerdo cuvier	Worldwide	Witzell (1987)
Promicrops lanceolatus	Tonga	Witzell (1981)
Reptile		
Crocodylus porosus	Ponape Is.	Allen (1974)
Mammal		
Panthera onca	Suriname	Autar (1994)

Table 15. Some symbionts (parasites, commensals, mutualists) of green turtles. Complete geographic locations of some symbionts and their host are provided in the references.

Species	Location	Reference
Monera		
Aeromonas hydrophila	Captive (Australia)	Glazebrook and Campbell (1990a), Glazebrook et al. (1993)
Arizona hinshairi	Captive (Australia)	Glazebrook and Campbell (1990a)
Escherichia coli	Captive (Australia)	Glazebrook and Campbell (1990a)
Flavobacterium sp.	Captive (Australia)	Glazebrook and Campbell (1990a), Glazebrook et al. (1993)
Mycobacterium sp.	Captive (Australia)	Glazebrook and Campbell (1990a)
Mycobacterium avium	Captive (Hawaii)	Brock et al. (1976)

Table 15. Continued.

Species	Location	Reference
Pseudomonas aeruginosa	Captive (Australia)	Glazebrook and Campbell (1990a)
Pseudomonas fluorescens	Captive (Australia)	Glazebrook and Campbell (1990a)
Salmonella enteritidis	Captive (Australia)	Glazebrook and Campbell (1990a)
Streptococcus sp.	Captive (Australia)	Glazebrook and Campbell (1990a)
Vibrio alginolyticus	Captive (Australia)	Glazebrook and Campbell (1990a), Glazebrook et al. (1993)
Unidentified	Nicaragua	Fenchel et al. (1979)
Protista		
Achnanthes sp.	Captive (USA)	Schwartz (1992)
Balantidium bacteriophorus	Caribbean	Fenchel (1980)
Caryospora cheloniae	Captive (Grand Cayman)	Leibovitz et al. (1978)
Caryospora cheloniae	Australia	Gordon et al. (1993)
Entamoeba invadens	Captive	Frank et al. (1976)
Lichmorpha ehrenbergii	Captive (USA)	Schwartz (1992)
Octomitus sp.	Caribbean	Fenchel (1980)
Nitshia sp.	Captive (USA)	Schwartz (1992)
Trypanosoma testundinis	Not stated	Ernst and Ernst (1979)
Fungi		
Aspergillus sp.	Captive (Australia)	Glazebrook et al. (1993)
Cladosporium sp.	Captive (Grand Cayman)	Jacobson et al. (1979)
Fusarium sp.	Captive (Australia)	Glazebrook et al. (1993)
Paecilomyces sp.	Captive (Grand Cayman)	Jacobson et al. (1979)
Paecilomyces sp.	Captive (Australia)	Glazebrook and Campbell (1990a)
Paecilomyces sp	Captive (Australia)	Glazebrook et al. (1993)
Penicillium sp	Captive (Australia)	Glazebrook et al. (1993)
Sporotrichium sp.	Captive (Grand Cayman)	Jacobson et al. (1979)
Plantae		
Acrochaetium sp.	Johnston Atoll	Balazs (1985a)
Acrochaetium gracile	Hawaii	Balazs (1980)
Chadophora sp.	Johnston Atoll	Balazs (1985a)
Ectocarpus indicus	Hawaii	Balazs (1980)
Enteromorpha clathrata	Hawaii	Balazs (1980)
Falkenbergia rufolanosa	Hawaii	Balazs (1980)
Lyngbya cinerescens	Hawaii	Balazs (1980)
Lyngbya majuscula	Hawaii	Balazs (1980)
Lyngbya semiplens	Johnston Atoll	Balazs (1985a)
Melobesia sp.	Hawaii	Balazs (1980)
Oscillatoria sp.	Hawaii	Balazs (1980)
Pilina sp.	Johnston Atoll	Balazs (1985a)
Polysiphonia dotyi	Hawaii	Balazs (1980)
Polysiphonia tsudana	Hawaii	Balazs (1980)
Polysiphonia tsudana	Johnston Atoll	Balazs (1985a)
Sphacelaria furcigeria	Hawaii	Balazs (1980)
Sphacelaria novae-hollandiae	Hawaii	Balazs (1980)
Sphacelaria tribuloides	Johnston Atoll	Balazs (1985a)
Ulva fasciata	Brazil	Frazier et al. (1992)
Urospora sp.	Johnston Atoll	Balazs (1985a)
Animalia		
Cnidaria		
Hydrozoa		
Tubularia sp.	Brazil	Frazier et al. (1992)
Platyhelminthes		
Trematoda		
Adenogaster serialis	Mexico	Ernst and Ernst (1977)
Amphiorchis amphiorchis	Not stated	Smith (1972)

Table 15. Continued.

Species	Location	Reference
Angiodictyum longum	Australia	Blair (1986)
Angiodictyum longum	Hawaii	Dailey et al. (1993)
Angiodictyum parallelum	Puerto Rico	Dyer et al. (1991)
Angiodictyum parallelum	Egypt	Sey (1977)
Angiodictyum posterovitellatum	Australia	Blair (1986)
Angiodictyum sp.	Australia	Glazebrook and Campbell (1990b)
Calycodes anthos	Egypt	Ernst and Ernst (1977)
Carettacola hawaiiensis	Hawaii	Dailey et al. (1993)
Charaxicephalus robustus	Egypt	Sey (1977)
Cricocephalus albus	Trinidad	Gupta (1961)
Cricocephalus megastomus	Taiwan	Ernst and Ernst (1977)
Cricocephalus resectus	Egypt	Sey (1977)
Cricocephalus ruber	Australia	Ernst and Ernst (1977)
Cricocephalus sp.	Captive (Australia)	Glazebrook and Campbell (1990a, b)
Cymatocarpus solearis	Not stated	Ernst and Ernst (1977)
Desmogonius desmogonius	Taiwan	Ernst and Ernst (1977)
Desmogonius sp.	Australia	Glazebrook and Campbell (1990b)
Deuterobarus chelonei	Trinidad	Gupta (1961)
Deuterobarus proteus	Egypt	Sey (1977)
Deuterobarus proteus	Puerto Rico	Dyer et al (1991)
Deuterobarus viridis	Not stated	Ernst and Barbour (1972)
Diaschistorchis lateralis	Japan	Ernst and Ernst (1977)
Diaschistorchis pandus	Australia	Ernst and Ernst (1977)
Distoma testudinis	Not stated	Ernst and Ernst (1977)
Distomum constrictum	Not stated	Ernst and Barbour (1972)
Enodiotrema megachondrus	Egypt	Ernst and Ernst (1977)
Glyphicephalus lobatus	Puerto Rico	Dyer et al. (1991)
Glyphicephalus solidus	Brazil	Ernst and Ernst (1977)
Haemoxenicon chelonenecon	Not stated	Smith (1972)
Haemoxenicon stunkardi	Panama	Ernst and Ernst (1977)
Hapalotrema dorsopora	Hawaii	Dailey et al. (1993)
Hapalotrema loossi	Egypt	Ernst and Ernst (1977)
Hapalotrema pambanensis	India	Gupta and Mehrotra (1981)
Hapalotrema postorchis	Hawaii	Dailey et al. (1993)
Hapalotrema sp.	Australia	Glazebrook and Campbell (1990b)
Hapalotrema sp.	Captive (Australia)	Glazebrook and Campbell (1990b)
Learedius europaeus	Not stated	Ernst and Ernst (1977)
Learedius learedi	Panama	Ernst and Ernst (1977)
Learedius learedi	Captive (Grand Cayman)	Greiner et al. (1980)
Learedius learedi	Bermuda	Rand and Wiles (1985)
Learedius learedi	Puerto Rico	Dyer et al. (1991)
Learedius learedi	Hawaii	Dailey et al. (1993)
Learedius loochooensis	Japan	Ernst and Ernst (1977)
Learedius orientalis	Pakistan	Ernst and Ernst (1977)
Learedius orientalis	Puerto Rico	Dyer et al. (1995)
Learedius similis	Not stated	Smith (1972)
Learedius sp.	Australia	Glazebrook and Campbell (1990b)
Medioporus cheloniae	Japan	Ernst and Ernst (1977)
Metacetabulum invaginatum	Brazil	Ernst and Ernst (1977)
Microscaphidium aberrans	Egypt	Sey (1977)
Microscaphidium aberrans	Australia	Blair (1986)
Microscaphidium reticulare	Egypt	Sey (1977)
Microscaphidium reticulare	Puerto Rico	Dyer et al. (1995)
Microscaphidium reticulare	Australia	Blair (1986)
Microscaphidium warui	Australia	Blair (1986)

51

Table 15. Continued.

Species	Location	Reference
Monostoma pseudamphistomum	Not stated	Ernst and Ernst (1977)
Monticellius indicum	Pakistan	Ernst and Ernst (1977)
Neoctangium travassosi	Trinidad	Gupta (1961)
Neospirorchis schistosomatoides	Not stated	Smith (1972)
Neospirorchis schistosomatoides	Bermuda	Rand and Wiles (1985)
Octangium hasta	Egypt	Ernst and Ernst (1977)
Octangium hyphalum	Australia	Blair (1987)
Octangium sagitta	Egypt	Sey (1977)
Octangium sagitta	Australia	Blair (1987)
Octangium sagitta	Puerto Rico	Dyer et al. (1991)
Octangium takonoi	Malaya	Ernst and Ernst (1977)
Octangium sp.	Australia	Glazebrook and Campbell (1990b)
Orchidasma amphiorchis	Mexico	Caballero y Caballero (1962)
Pachypsolus irroratus	France	Ernst and Ernst (1977)
Paralepoderma acariaeum	Puerto Rico	Dyer et al. (1995)
Phyllodistomum cymbiforme	Not stated	Ernst and Barbour (1972)
Pleurogonius bilobus	Egypt	Ernst and Ernst (1977)
Pleurogonius chelonii	Pakistan	Ernst and Ernst (1977)
Pleurogonius linearis	Brazil	Ernst and Ernst (1977)
Pleurogonius longiusculus	Egypt	Ernst and Ernst (1977)
Pleurogonius mehrai	Trinidad	Gupta (1961)
Pleurogonius mehrai	Captive (Grand Cayman)	Greiner et al. (1980)
Pleurogonius minutissimus	Egypt	Ernst and Ernst (1977)
Polyangium linguatula	Egypt	Sey (1977)
Polyangium linguatula	Puerto Rico	Dyer et al. (1991)
Polyangium linguatula	Hawaii	Dailey et al. (1993)
Polyangium miyajimai	Malaya	Ernst and Ernst (1977)
Polyangium sp.	Australia	Glazebrook and Campbell (1990b)
Polygorgyra cholados	Australia	Blair (1986)
Polystoma mydae	Not stated	Ernst and Barbour (1972)
Pronocephalus obliguus	Brazil	Ernst and Ernst (1977)
Pyelosoma cochlear	Hawaii	Dailey et al. (1993)
Pyelosomum cochlear	Puerto Rico	Dyer et al. (1991)
Rhytidodes gelatinosus	Egypt	Ernst and Ernst (1977)
Rhytidodes sp.	Australia	Glazebrook and Campbell (1990b)
Rhytidodoides intestinalis	Captive (USA)	Price (1939)
Rhytidodoides similis	Captive (USA)	Price (1939)
Schizamphistomoides chelonei	Trinidad	Gupta (1961)
Schizamphistomoides spinulosum	Brazil	Ernst and Ernst (1977)
Schizamphistomum erratum	Australia	Blair (1983)
Schizamphistomum sceloporum	Australia	Blair (1983)
Schizamphistomum sp.	Australia	Glazebrook and Campbell (1990b)
Schizamphistomum sp.	Puerto Rico	Dyer et al. (1995)
Spirorchis parvum	Not stated	Ernst and Ernst (1977)
Squaroacetabulum solus	India	Simha and Chattopadhyaya (1970)
Cestoda		
Ancistrocephalus imbricatus	Not stated	Ernst and Ernst (1977)
Tentacularia coryphaenae	Not stated	Ernst and Ernst (1977)
Nematoda		
Angusticaecum holoptera	Europe	Ernst and Ernst (1977)
Anisakis sp.	Captive (Australia)	Burke and Rodgers (1982)
Anisakis sp.	Captive (Australia)	Glazebrook and Campbell (1990a)
Porrocaecum sulcatum	USA	Allison et al. (1973)
Sulcascaris sulcata	Not stated	Sprent (1977)
Tonaudia tonaudia	Ceylon	Ernst and Ernst (1977)

Table 15. Continued.

Species	Location	Reference
Mollusca		
Mytilus edulis platencis	Brazil	Frazier et al. (1992)
Pleuroploca princeps	Galápagos	Frazier et al (1985)
Bryozoa		
Electra sp.	Pakistan	Frazier et al. (1992)
Unidentified	Brazil	Frazier et al. (1992)
Annelida		
Hirudinea		
Ozobranchus branchiatus	USA	Nigrelli and Smith (1943)
Ozobranchus branchiatus	Malaysia	Hendrickson (1958)
Ozobranchus branchiatus	Costa Rica	Sawyer et al. (1975)
Ozobranchus branchiatus	Hawaii	Balazs (1980)
Ozobranchus margoi	Captive (USA)	Schwartz (1974)
Ozobranchus margoi	Captive (Hawaii)	Balazs (1980)
Ozobranchus sp.	Comoros	Frazier (1985)
Ozobranchus sp.	India	Frazier (1989)
Arthropoda		
Arachnida		
Unidentified mites	Australia	Glazebrook and Campbell (1990b)
Cirripedia		
Chelonibia testudinaria	Malaysia	Hendrickson (1958)
Chelonibia testudinaria	Aldabra	Frazier (1971)
Chelonibia testudinaria	Hawaii	Balazs (1980)
Chelonibia testudinaria	Peru	Brown and Brown (1982)
Chelonibia testudinaria	Comoros	Frazier (1985)
Chelonibia testudinaria	India	Frazier (1989)
Chelonibia sp.	Europa	Hughes (1974b)
Chelonibia sp.	Tromelin	Hughes (1974b)
Chelonibia sp.	Papua New Guinea	Spring (1983)
Chelonibia sp.	Australia	Glazebrook and Campbell (1990b)
Lepas sp.	Peru	Brown and Brown (1982)
Platylepas hexastylos	USA	Schwartz (1960)
Platylepas hexastylos	Aldabra	Frazier (1971)
Platylepas hexastylos	Hawaii	Balazs (1980)
Platylepas hexastylos	Comoros	Frazier (1985)
Platylepas hexastylos	Johnston Atoll	Balazs (1985a)
Platylepas hexastylos	India	Frazier (1989)
Platylepas sp.	Papua New Guinea	Spring (1983)
Platylepas sp.	Australia	Glazebrook and Campbell (1990b)
Stephanolepus muricata	Malaysia	Hendrickson (1958)
Stephanolepus muricata	Hawaii	Balazs (1980)
Stephanolepus sp.	Europa	Hughes (1974b)
Stomatolepus elegans	Not stated	Ernst and Barbour (1972)
Amphipoda		
Hyachelia tortugae	Hawaii	Balazs (1980)
Hyachelia tortugae	Johnston Atoll	Balazs (1985a)
Isopoda		
Eurydice sp.	Malaysia	Hendrickson (1958)
Decapoda		
Planes cyaneus	Peru	Brown and Brown (1982)
Insecta		
Eumacronychia sternalis	Mexico	Alvarado and Figueroa (1990)

are implicated and a method of treatment is suggested. Haines (1988) summarized what is known about gray patch disease in cultured green turtles. The cause of the disease is a herpes-type virus and the result is a maceration and erosion of the skin and carapace. Stress factors and water temperatures appear to play important roles since crowding and increased temperatures increase occurrence of the infections. Treatment with metabolic inhibitors is available. Jacobson et al. (1986) suggested that a herpesvirus was involved in the pathogenesis of LETD (lung, eye and trachea disease) in captive green turtles. LETD is a respiratory disease characterized by gasping, buoyancy abnormalities and inability to dive properly. The eyes are often covered with caseous exudate, which is also seen around the glottis and within the trachea. The systemic diseases of farmed animals, including diseases of the integumentary, sensory, skeletal, muscular, digestive, respiratory, cardiovascular and excretory systems, are discussed by Glazebrook and Campbell (1990a, b).

Sindermann (1988) briefly summarized coccidian disease in farmed green turtles. Gordon et al. (1993) reported on a recent epizootic of coccidiosis among green turtles off the coast of Queensland, Australia. Clinically the most consistent signs were pronounced weakness and depression. They speculated that a heavy concentration of infective stages on the feeding grounds may have precipitated the epizootic. Mycotic pneumonia has been diagnosed in captive juvenile turtles (Jacobson et al. 1979).

Green turtles are parasitized by a wide variety of trematodes, including six species of *Pleurogonius*, at least five species of *Learedius*, and at least four species of *Cricocephalus*, *Hapalotrema*, and *Octangium*.

Glazebrook et al. (1989) found the incidence of cardiovascular flukes and/or their eggs (*Haplotrema spp.* and *Learedius spp.*) in marine turtles from northeast Queensland to be 4.8% (5 of 104 from turtle farms), 33.3% (5 of 15 from an oceanarium) and 77.3% (17 of 22 wild turtles). Of the 27 turtles infected, 23 were green turtles and 4 were hawksbills. The average number of flukes per host was 47. Gross pathological changes associated with the presence of flukes in some individuals included thickening of arterial walls, thrombus formation and an excess of pericardial fluid. Microscopically, the essential change was that of chronic inflammation.

The source of infection of *Anisakis sp.* in the captive turtles in the Torres Strait appeared to be raw sardines (Burke and Rodgers 1982).

Remoras *(Echenesis sp.)* have been seen attached to green turtles in a wide variety of locales.

Fibropapillomatosis is a debilitating and life-threatening disease of green turtles. Fibropapillomas of various sizes can be found on several body sites, including the skin, eyes and surrounding tissue, mouth and viscera. In severe cases, turtles have reduced vision and difficulty in eating and swimming. Affected individuals are also anemic compared to normal animals.

Turtles with fibropapillomatosis have been reported from such widely scattered places as the Caribbean (Puerto Rico, U. S. Virgin Islands, Cayman Islands, Dominican Republic, Antigua, Barbados, Trinidad, Netherlands Antilles, Bahamas, Mexico, Belize, Panama, Colombia, Venezuela), Florida, California, Hawaiian Islands, Japan, Malaysia, Indonesia and Australia (Jacobson 1990; Williams et al. 1994). Fibropapillomas were seen on at least two nesting green turtles in Yap State, Federated States of Micronesia, in 1992 (Kolinski 1994a). The appearance of fibropapillomas on some San Diego Bay green turtles is presumed to be a recent occurrence (McDonald and Dutton 1990). Some fishermen informed Guada et al. (1991) that green turtles with fibropapillomas are commonly caught, eaten and sold illegally in some parts of Venezuela. The epizootic of fibropapillomas in the Caribbean has occurred since the mid-1980s, about five years later than similar epizootics in Florida and Hawaii, and all may be part of a panzootic (Williams et al. 1994). Of 166 green turtles recaptured around the Cayman Islands, after being released as hatchlings or yearlings from the Cayman Turtle Farm, 66% were infected with cutaneous fibropapillomas. Seventy-two percent of the individuals retaken within less than one year from release did not exhibit any fibropapillomas while only 26% of the turtles recaptured after more than a year after release lacked fibropapillomas (Wood and Wood 1993b). Sixty-nine percent of 26 immature green turtles captured in Florida Bay, Florida, in 1991, exhibited fibropapilloma (Schroeder and Foley 1995). The prevalence of fibropapilloma in the Indian River, Florida, green turtle population varied from 40 to 60% between 1982 and 1992. In 1993 its prevalence was 20% (Ehrhart and Redfoot 1995). About half of the turtles in Kaneohe Bay, Hawaii, now have tumors and up to 10% of the nesting females on French Frigate Shoals, Hawaii, possess fibropapillomas (respectively, Balazs et al. 1993 and Dailey et al. 1992). Fibropapillomas were recorded on 62 (7.9%) of 784 green turtles at a feeding site on Moreton Banks, Queensland, Australia (Limpus et al. 1994b).

The etiology of fibropapilloma is unknown, although there are several hypotheses linking viruses, parasites, pollutants, or combinations of these agents to the disease.

Jacobson et al. (1989) described fibropapillomas in six juvenile Florida green turtles. The cutaneous fibropapillomas were characterized by papillary proliferation of the epidermis on broad fibrovascular stalks. No trematode eggs were seen in any of the biopsy (N=28) specimens. Brooks et al. (1994) examining, histologically, the eyes of three stranded juvenile turtles from Florida found ocular fibropapillomas composed of an overlying hyperplastic epithelium, a well-vascularized collagenous stroma and a population of reactive fibroblasts. A herpesvirus was found in cutaneous fibropapillomas in two juvenile turtles from Florida (Jacobson et al. 1991). In preliminary experiments on the transmission of fibropapillomatosis, Herbst et al. (1994a) concluded that it is unlikely that trematode eggs are a primary cause of the disease. In more recent transmission experiments, Herbst et al. (1994b; 1995) have shown that fibropapillomatosis can be experimentally transferred to disease free recipient turtles. Latency to tumor development is about four months. The experiments suggested that fibropapillomatosis is caused by a subcellular agent and most likely is a virus. Although several field studies suggest that high green turtle fibropapillomatosis is associated with near-shore marine habitats that have been impacted by human activities, Herbst and Klein (1995a) caution that the role of environmental cofactors in fibropapillomatosis will require careful scientific study.

Ten Hawaiian turtles with fibropapillomas were examined by Dailey et al. (1992) and were found infected with 232 worms comprising seven species of digenetic trematodes. Examining tumors from Hawaiian green turtles, Dailey and Morris (1995) found that all tumors examined (N=61) contained spirorchid eggs and they feel that the information suggests a direct link between fibropapillomas and spirorchid trematode infections. Working with Florida green turtles, Greiner (1995) stated that there is a possibility that trematode eggs are indirectly or directly involved with fibropapillomas. All the tumors (N=39) from Caribbean green turtles that Williams et al. (1994) examined histologically had spirorchid eggs, and the leech, *Ozobranchus branchiatus*, was associated with three diseased individuals. Aguirre et al. (1994b) evaluated Hawaiian green turtles for potential pathogens associated with fibropapillomas but were unable to isolate the etiologic agent. Selected tissues from juvenile Hawaiian green turtles afflicted with fibropapillomas did not contain any of the selected organochlorines, polychlorinated biphenyls, organophosphates, or carbamate insecticides in concentrations above stated methods of detection limits (Aguirre et al. 1994a, c).

Aguirre et al. (1995) determined that subadult Hawaiian turtles with fibropapillomas were immunosuppressed and chronically stressed prior to being subjected to capture stress. This determination was based upon raised corticosterone concentrations and a positive correlation with heterophil/lymphocyte ratios.

A flow cytometric DNA content analysis indicated that fibropapillomas and visceral tumors have normal cell cycles (Papadi et al. 1995).

Normal and tumor-bearing immature turtles were monitored with ultrasonic transmitters in Kaneohe Bay, Oahu,

Hawaii (Brill et al. 1995). The presence of the tumors had no obvious effect on habitat use or movements of the turtles.

The tumors occasionally occur on loggerheads and possibly hawksbills and other sea turtles (Williams et al. 1994). The use of cryosurgery in the treatment of the disease shows promise (Morris and Balazs 1994).

A review of fibropapillomatosis with pertinent references, is by Balazs and Pooley (1991). Herbst and Jacobson (1995) briefly review the diseases of captive and wild marine turtles under categories of viral, bacterial, endoparasites, ectoparasites and neoplastic. Useful reviews of the diseases of reptiles are those of Cooper and Jackson (1981a, b) and Hoff et al. (1984).

Parasitic infestations of green turtles to some extent depend upon such factors as host heterogeneity, age and sex as well as on the dynamic processes of the parasites themselves. Indeed, one possible advantage of individual heterogeneity within a population may be to keep the parasites "off-balance."

3.4 Nutrition and Growth

3.4.1 Feeding

Like other animals, green turtles allocate assimilated energy into growth, maintenance and reproduction. It is generally assumed that hatchling green turtles, like other marine turtles, are chiefly carnivorous, but this needs validation. Large juveniles, subadults and adults are predominantly herbivorous.

As already mentioned (section 2.2.1), hatchlings and post-hatchlings feed in the epipelagic zone and immature and mature individuals graze in developmental or resident feeding habitats. In some regions, turtles feed on route between grazing pastures and the nesting beach (Meylan 1982b). Evidently, because of the scarcity of food, little feeding takes place off the nesting beaches. However, Balazs (1980) found that turtles do feed off the French Frigate Shoals nesting site. Juvenile and adult green turtles have been recorded feeding at all hours of the diel cycle, but daytime records predominate.

Two hatchlings at Heron Island, Australia, were tethered on a nylon cord and kept up to 4-1/2 months while their feeding behavior in the sea was observed (Booth and Peters 1972). They caught and ate ctenophores and pelagic tunicates. When these invertebrates were not available, they dove and attempted to bite pieces out of the oral discs of sea anemones.

In captivity, Davenport and Oxford (1984) observed that hatchlings readily consumed sea lettuce *(Ulva lactuca)* along with purse sponge *(Grantia compressa)*, sea anemone *(Sargartia elegans)*, shrimp *(Crangon vulgaris)* and fish *(Gobiusculus flavescens)* and this suggested an omnivorous opportunistic feeding habit. The hatchlings also appeared to have a cellulose degrading gut microflora. Green turtles not only change their diet during their ontogeny but their gut proportions are also modified. The large intestine of post-hatchlings is about half the length of the small intestine while that of adults is more than twice the length of the small intestine. These changes in gut proportions are correlated with a shift from a carnivorous, or omnivorous, to a herbivorous diet (Davenport et al. 1989). Herbivory is associated with a voluminous large intestine — a place where food spends a long time. Bels and Renous (1992) analyzed films of the feeding behavior of captive, juvenile green turtles and stated that the protraction-retraction cycle of the forelimb is clearly associated with the gape cycle.

The adaptations of the Caribbean green turtle to a diet chiefly of seagrass, *Thalassia testudinum*, which is high in cellulose content and thus low in quality, are hindgut microbial fermentation and selective grazing (Bjorndal 1982b). Bjorndal (1979) has shown how cellulose is digested through microbial fermentation as efficiently in the green turtle as it is in dugongs and ruminants, and, Bjorndal (1980a) found that green turtles on a *T. testudinum* grazing pasture in the Bahamas maintained grazing plots of young leaves by constant recropping. The young leaves are higher in protein and lower in lignin than older leaves. Zieman et al. (1984) hypothesized that the foraging behavior of green turtles evolved to avoid the epiphytic carbonate of the upper regions of seagrass leaves. On the other hand, Williams (1988) observed that green turtles ate all accessible *T. testudinum* in a stressed pasture in the Virgin Islands.

Vicente and Tallevast (1995) surveyed green turtle foraging pastures around six islands in the Commonwealth of Puerto Rico and the U. S. Virgin Islands. Among their findings were that green turtles graze more frequently along extensive continuous or discontinuous bands between deep coral reef habitats or barren mud bottom and dense grass beds; on extensive seagrass beds, green turtle grazing was always limited to the deeper zones of the bed; when several species of seagrasses occur together, the turtles do not discriminate among the species; and, juvenile turtles graze on shallow (1m) and on deep (15.2m) grass beds and on both exposed and protected beds.

Green turtles at a *Thalassia testudinum* site in the Bahamas consume the equivalent of about 0.24% to 0.33% of their body weight each day (Bjorndal 1980a). The carrying capacity of a *T. testudinum* feeding pasture in the Caribbean was estimated at one turtle per 72 m^2 (Bjorndal 1982b). In a stressed *T. testudinum* pasture in the Caribbean, Williams (1988) estimated a carrying capacity of one turtle per 669 - 3,946 m^2.

Garnett et al (1985b) found that green turtles in the Torres Strait eat both algae and seagrass and their review of the literature indicates that algae are not nutritionally superior to seagrass. Bjorndal et al. (1991) state that "Ani-

mals consistently ingesting a mixed diet would almost certainly develop a microflora capable of degrading the various complex carbohydrates." Lanyon et al. (1989) describe how seasonal fluctuations in total seagrass nutrients may have important consequences for the nutritional status and life history of green turtles. Limpus and Nicholls (1988) have demonstrated a linkage between the ENSO (El Niño Southern Oscillation) and the number of green turtles that breed on eastern Australian beaches two years later. They suggest that the ENSO may regulate nesting numbers via a nutritional pathway. Philander (1990) describes some of the research going on regarding the southern oscillation. J.R. Wood and F.E. Wood (1977) and F.E. Wood and J.R. Wood (1977) have determined the quantitative requirements of hatchlings for lysine, tryptophan, methionine, valine, leucine, isoleucine and phenylalanine. Wood and Wood (1981) found that young captive turtles fed on rations containing 35% protein grew faster than turtles fed on rations with 30% and 25% protein. In captive green turtles on the Cayman Turtle Farm, feed conversion varies from 1.2 to 6.5 units of diet to unit of body weight, increasing with size of the individual (Wood 1991). Bjorndal (1985) has reviewed the literature on nutrient digestibility for organic matter, cellulose, nitrogen and carbon and she points out the significant difference in some digestibility values between farm-reared and wild turtles.

3.4.2 Food

The most comprehensive studies of the food of green turtles have primarily come from examinations of stomach contents of large individuals. Representative plants eaten by green turtles in the Pacific, Atlantic and Indian Ocean regions are given in Table 16. It is interesting to note that at least nine species of *Gracilaria* and at least eight species of *Sargassum* are eaten. At least eight species of *Caulerpa* and six species of *Codium* are ingested, with some species of each eaten in the Pacific, Atlantic and Indian Ocean regions. Some species of the seagrasses *Halophila* and *Syringodium* are also eaten in the three large ocean regions.

Thirty-four species of algae were recorded from the stomachs of three adult and one subadult turtle from the Ogasawara Islands (Kurata et al 1978). Brown algae formed the greatest bulk of the diet and was represented by 19 species. Some hydrozoa were found in the stomachs, as well as a piece of plastic.

Garnett et al. (1985b) examined the stomach contents of 44 turtles from Torres Strait, 34 of which were adult females, and found that six genera contributed 73.5% of the total dry matter weight: *Hypnea* (27.7%), *Laurencia* (11.9%), *Caulerpa* (9.8%), *Vidalia* (9.8%), *Sargassum* (5.9%), and the seagrass *Thalassia* (8.8%). Red algae made up the bulk of most stomach contents; large amounts of brown or green algae were eaten by a few individuals.

Table 16. Representative plant food of mostly subadult and adult green turtles. With few exceptions, animal food is eaten only in small amounts by wild, large green turtles and is discussed in the text.

Food	Location	Reference
Chlorophyta		
Anadyomene sp.	Torres Strait	Garnett et al. (1985b)
Avrainvillea riukiuensis	Ogasawara Is.	Kurata et al. (1978)
Avrainvillea sp.	Brazil	Ferreira (1968)
Bryopsis pennata	Johnston Atoll	Balazs (1985a)
Caulerpa brachypus	Torres Strait	Garnett et al. (1985b)
Caulerpa cupressoides	Brazil	Ferreira (1968)
Caulerpa cupressoides	Torres Strait	Garnett et al. (1985b)
Caulerpa lentillifera	Torres Strait	Garnett et al. (1985b)
Caulerpa mexicana	Brazil	Ferreira (1968)
Caulerpa mexicana	Comoros	Frazier (1985)
Caulerpa prolifera	Brazil	Ferreira (1968)
Caulerpa prolifera	Nicaragua	Mortimer (1981)
Caulerpa racemosa	Hawaii	Balazs (1980)
Caulerpa racemosa	Johnston Atoll	Balazs (1985a)
Caulerpa racemosa	Torres Strait	Garnett et al. (1985b)
Caulerpa sertularioides	Brazil	Ferreira (1968)
Caulerpa sertularioides	Nicaragua	Mortimer (1981)
Caulerpa sertularioides	Torres Strait	Garnett et al. (1985b)
Caulerpa urvilliana	Torres Strait	Garnett et al. (1985b)
Caulerpa sp.	Torres Strait	Garnett et al. (1985b)
Caulerpa sp.	Aldabra Atoll	Frazier (1971)
Chaetomorpha area	Oman	Ross (1985)
Chaetomorpha sp.	Comoros	Frazier (1985)
Chaetomorpha sp.	Torres Strait	Garnett et al. (1985b)
Cladophora sp.	Comoros	Frazier (1985)
Codium adhaerens	Ogasawara Is.	Kurata et al. (1978)
Codium arabicum	Hawaii	Balazs (1980)
Codium edule	Hawaii	Balazs (1980)
Codium isthmocladum	Brazil	Ferreira (1968)
Codium isthmocladum	Nicaragua	Mortimer (1981)
Codium phasmaticum	Hawaii	Balazs (1980)
Codium tomentosum	Ogasawara Is.	Kurata et al. (1978)
Codium sp.	Aldabra Atoll	Frazier (1971)
Codium sp.	Torres Strait	Garnett et al. (1985b)
Dictyosphaeria cavernosa	Ogasawara Is.	Kurata et al. (1978)
Dictyosphaeria versluysii	Ogasawara Is.	Kurata et al. (1978)
Enteromorpha flexuosa	Comoros	Frazier (1985)
Halimeda gracilis	Comoros	Frazier (1985)
Halimeda tuna	Comoros	Frazier (1985)
Halimeda sp.	Nicaragua	Mortimer (1981)
Halimeda sp.	Torres Strait	Garnett et al. (1985b)
Monostroma oxyspermum	Brazil	Ferreira (1968)
Penicillus capitatus	Nicaragua	Mortimer (1981)
Rhizoclonium sp.	Torres Strait	Garnett et al. (1985b)
Udotea flabellum	Nicaragua	Mortimer (1981)
Udotea sp.	Torres Strait	Garnett et al. (1985b)
Ulva fasciata	Brazil	Ferreira (1968)
Ulva fasciata	Ogasawara Is.	Kurata et al. (1978)
Ulva fasciata	Hawaii	Balazs (1980)
Ulva lactuca	Oman	Ross (1985)
Ulva lactuca	Comoros	Frazier (1985)
Ulva pertusa	Ogasawara Is.	Kurata et al. (1978)
Valonia aegagropila	Tokelau	Balazs (1983b)

Table 16. Continued.

Food	Location	Reference
Phaeophyta		
Chlanidophora repens	Ogasawara Is.	Kurata et al. (1978)
Chnoospora implexa	Torres Strait	Garnett et al. (1985b)
Cystoseira prolifera	Ogasawara Is.	Kurata et al. (1978)
Cystoseira sp.	Torres Strait	Garnett et al. (1985b)
Dictyopteris delicatula	Brazil	Ferreira (1968)
Dictyopteris delicatula	Nicaragua	Mortimer (1981)
Dictyopteris delicatula	Comoros	Frazier (1985)
Dictyopteris undulata	Ogasawara Is.	Kurata et al. (1978)
Dictyota dichotoma	Brazil	Ferreira (1968)
Dictyota sp.	Torres Strait	Garnett et al. (1985b)
Endarachne binghamiae	Ogasawara Is.	Kurata et al. (1978)
Giffordia mitchellae	Comoros	Frazier (1985)
Halothrix ambigua	Ogasawara Is.	Kurata et al. (1978)
Homoeostrichus flabellatus	Ogasawara Is.	Kurata et al. (1978)
Hydroclathrus clathratus	Torres Strait	Garnett et al. (1985b)
Padina australis	Torres Strait	Garnett et al. (1985b)
Padina commersonii	Ogasawara Is.	Kurata et al. (1978)
Padina minor	Ogasawara Is.	Kurata et al. (1978)
Padina pavonia	Oman	Ross (1985)
Petalonia fascia	Ogasawara Is.	Kurata et al. (1978)
Pocockiella variegata	Brazil	Ferreira (1968)
Sargassum cymosum	Brazil	Ferreira (1968)
Sargassum duplicatum	Ogasawara Is.	Kurata et al. (1978)
Sargassum filipendula	Nicaragua	Mortimer (1981)
Sargassum hystrix	Nicaragua	Mortimer (1981)
Sargassum illicifolium	Oman	Ross (1985)
Sargassum micracanthum	Ogasawara Is.	Kurata et al. (1978)
Sargassum tosaense	Ogasawara Is.	Kurata et al. (1978)
Sargassum vulgare	Brazil	Ferreira (1968)
Sargassum vulgare	Nicaragua	Mortimer (1981)
Sargassum sp.	Torres Strait	Garnett et al. (1985b)
Spatoplossum schroederi	Brazil	Ferreira (1968)
Sphacelaria sp.	Torres Strait	Garnett et al. (1985b)
Sporochnus pedunculatus	Nicaragua	Mortimer (1981)
Trichogloea requienii	Ogasawara Is.	Kurata et al. (1978)
Turbinaria ornata	Ogasawara Is.	Kurata et al (1978)
Turbinaria ornata	Hawaii	Balazs (1980)
Turbinaria ornata	Tokelau	Balazs (1983b)
Turbinaria sp.	Torres Strait	Garnett et al. (1985b)
Zonaria stipitata	Ogasawara Is.	Kurata et al. (1978)
Rhodophyta		
Acanthophora spicifera	Brazil	Ferreira (1968)
Acanthophora spicifera	Torres Strait	Garnett et al. (1985b)
Acanthophora sp.	Torres Strait	Garnett et al. (1985b)
Agardhiella tenera	Brazil	Ferreira (1968)
Amansia glomerata	Hawaii	Balazs (1980)
Amansia glomerata	Torres Strait	Garnett et al. (1985b)
Amansia glomerata	Comoros	Frazier (1985)
Amansia multifida	Brazil	Ferreira (1968)
Amansia multifida	Nicaragua	Mortimer (1981)
Amansia sp.	Torres Strait	Garnett et al. (1985b)
Botryocladia sp.	Torres Strait	Garnett et al. (1985b)
Bryothamnion seaforthii	Brazil	Ferreira (1968)

Table 16. Continued.

Food	Location	Reference
Bryothamnion triquetrum	Brazil	Ferreira (1968)
Caulacanthus sp.	Torres Strait	Garnett et al. (1985b)
Centroceras clavulatum	Ogasawara Is.	Kurata et al. (1978)
Centroceras clavulatum	Comoros	Frazier (1985)
Ceramium sp.	Torres Strait	Garnett et al. (1985b)
Champia parvula	Comoros	Frazier (1985)
Champia sp.	Torres Strait	Garnett et al. (1985b)
Chondria sp.	Torres Strait	Garnett et al. (1985b)
Coelothrix indica	Comoros	Frazier (1985)
Coelothrix sp.	Torres Strait	Garnett et al. (1985b)
Corallina cubensis	Nicaragua	Mortimer (1981)
Corallina mediterranea	Ogasawara Is.	Kurata et al. (1978)
Cryptonemia crenulata	Brazil	Ferreira (1968)
Cryptonemia crenulata	Nicaragua	Mortimer (1981)
Cryptonemia luxurians	Brazil	Ferreira (1968)
Dasya sp.	Torres Strait	Garnett et al. (1985b)
Enantiocladia duperryi	Brazil	Ferreira (1968)
Enantiocladia duperryi	Nicaragua	Mortimer (1981)
Eucheuma muricatum	Torres Strait	Garnett et al. (1985b)
Eucheuma sp.	Brazil	Ferreira (1968)
Eucheuma sp.	Torres Strait	Garnett et al. (1985b)
Galaxaura obtusata	Brazil	Ferreira (1968)
Galaxaura veprecula	Comoros	Frazier (1985)
Galaxaura sp.	Ogasawara Is.	Kurata et al. (1978)
Galaxaura sp.	Torres Strait	Garnett et al. (1985b)
Gelidiella acerosa	Brazil	Ferreira (1968)
Gelidiella acerosa	Torres Strait	Garnett et al. (1985b)
Gelidiella trinitatensis	Brazil	Ferreira (1968)
Gelidiopsis acrocarpa	Torres Strait	Garnett et al. (1985b)
Gelidiopsis gracilis	Brazil	Ferreira (1968)
Gelidiopsis variabilis	Torres Strait	Garnett et al. (1985b)
Gelidium corneum	Brazil	Ferreira (1968)
Gelidium sp.	Aldabra Atoll	Frazier (1971)
Gelidium sp.	Oman	Ross (1985)
Gigartina sp.	Peru	Brown and Brown (1982)
Gracilaria cervicornis	Brazil	Ferreira (1968)
Gracilaria crassa	Torres Strait	Garnett et al. (1985b)
Gracilaria cuneata	Brazil	Ferreira (1968)
Gracilaria cylindrica	Nicaragua	Mortimer (1981)
Gracilaria domingensis	Brazil	Ferreira (1968)
Gracilaria ferox	Brazil	Ferreira (1968)
Gracilaria foliifera	Brazil	Ferreira (1968)
Gracilaria mammillaris	Nicaragua	Mortimer (1981)
Gracilaria verrucosa	Nicaragua	Mortimer (1981)
Gracilaria sp.	Nicaragua	Mortimer (1981)
Gracilaria sp.	Torres Strait	Garnett et al. (1985b)
Gracilariopsis sjoestedtii	Brazil	Ferreira (1968)
Griffithsia sp.	Torres Strait	Garnett et al. (1985b)
Haloplegma duperreyi	Brazil	Ferreira (1968)
Halymenia floresia	Brazil	Ferreira (1968)
Halymenia floresia	Nicaragua	Mortimer (1981)
Halymenia sp.	Torres Strait	Garnett et al. (1985b)
Heterosiphonia sp.	Torres Strait	Garnett et al. (1985b)
Hypnea cervicornis	Brazil	Ferreira (1968)

Table 16. Continued.

Food	Location	Reference
Hypnea musciformis	Brazil	Ferreira (1968)
Hypnea musciformis	Nicaragua	Mortimer (1981)
Hypnea sp.	Torres Strait	Garnett et al. (1985b)
Hypnea sp.	Oman	Ross (1985)
Hypoglossum sp.	Torres Strait	Garnett et al. (1985b)
Jania niponica	Ogasawara Is.	Kurata et al. (1978)
Jania sp.	Comoros	Frazier (1985)
Laurencia brongniartii	Torres Strait	Garnett et al. (1985b)
Laurencia sp.	Brazil	Ferreira (1968)
Laurencia sp.	Aldabra Atoll	Frazier (1971)
Laurencia sp.	Torres Strait	Garnett et al. (1985b)
Lenormandiopsis lorentzii	Torres Strait	Garnett et al. (1985b)
Lenormandiopsis sp.	Torres Strait	Garnett et al. (1985b)
Leveilla jungermannioides	Torres Strait	Garnett et al. (1985b)
Liagora setchellii	Ogasawara Is.	Kurata et al. (1978)
Platysiphonia sp.	Torres Strait	Garnett et al. (1985b)
Plenosporium pusillum	Ogasawara Is.	Kurata et al. (1978)
Polysiphonia denudata	Comoros	Frazier (1985)
Polysiphonia sp.	Torres Strait	Garnett et al. (1985b)
Prionites obtusa	Torres Strait	Garnett et al. (1985b)
Protokuetzingia schottii	Brazil	Ferreira (1968)
Pterocladia capillacea	Hawaii	Balazs (1980)
Rhodochorton howei	Ogasawara Is.	Kurata et al. (1978)
Rhodopeltis borealis	Ogasawara Is.	Kurata et al. (1978)
Rhodymenia intricata	Ogasawara Is.	Kurata et al. (1978)
Rhodymenia sp.	Peru	Brown and Brown (1982)
Scinaia sp.	Torres Strait	Garnett et al. (1985b)
Spyridia filamentosa	Hawaii	Balazs (1980)
Spyridia filamentosa	Nicaragua	Mortimer (1981)
Spyridia filamentosa	Torres Strait	Garnett et al. (1985b)
Tolypiocladia glomerulata	Torres Strait	Garnett et al. (1985b)
Vidalia obtusiloba	Brazil	Ferreira (1968)
Vidalia obtusiloba	Nicaragua	Mortimer (1981)
Vidalia sp.	Torres Strait	Garnett et al. (1985b)

Helobiae

Food	Location	Reference
Cymodocea serrulata	Yemen	Hirth et al. (1973)
Cymodocea sp.	Torres Strait	Garnett et al. (1985b)
Cymodocea sp.	Aldabra Atoll	Frazier (1971)
Cymodocea (or Thalassia)	Comoros	Frazier (1985)
Halodule uninervis	Yemen	Hirth and Carr (1970)
Halodule uninervis	Oman	Ross (1985)
Halodule wrightii	Brazil	Ferreira (1968)
Halodule wrightii	Nicaragua	Mortimer (1981)
Halophila baillonis	Nicaragua	Mortimer (1981)
Halophila ovalis	Tonga	Hirth (1971a)
Halophila ovalis	Oman	Ross (1985)
Halophila spinulosa	Torres Strait	Garnett et al. (1985b)
Syringodium filiforme	Nicaragua	Mortimer (1981)
Syringodium isoetifolium	Fiji	Hirth (1971a)
Syringodium isoetifolium	Tonga	Hirth (1971a)
Syringodium isoetifolium	Yemen	Hirth et al. (1973)
Thalassia hemprichi	Torres Strait	Garnett et al. (1985b)
Thalassia testudinum	Nicaragua	Mortimer (1981)
Thalassodendron ciliatum	Comoros	Frazier (1985)

No differences in diet were detected between the sexes. Of the animal food identified, sponges were predominant, but apart from shell, no animal material contributed more than 5% to any one stomach.

The most common mouth contents of a largely immature feeding population off Queensland, Australia, were in order of frequency of occurrence, the seagrasses *Halophila ovalis, Halodule uninervis, Zostera capricorni and Halophila spinulosa,* and algae, *Hypnea cervicornis.* Individuals in this population also occasionally were seen feeding on jellyfish, *Catostylus mosaicus* (Limpus et al. 1994b).

The stomach contents of 518 green turtles feeding on algae on the reef around Heron Is, Australia, were retrieved by gastric lavage (Forbes 1994). The sample included juveniles, subadults, adults, females, males and individuals of undetermined sex. The pooled diets of all turtles contained 38 species of Rhodophyta, 21 species of Chlorophyta and 10 species of Phaeophyta. Animal matter, present in some samples, typically represented less than 1% of the diet volume.

Green turtles in the Hawaiian Archipelago eat 56 species of algae (out of approximately 400 species present in the Archipelago), 1 marine grass, and 9 kinds of invertebrates. However, nine species of algae are the principal foods (Balazs 1980). *Codium* and *Ulva* are the principal foods of juveniles, subadults and adults. Juveniles and subadults have been observed feeding on *Physalia, Velella* and *Janthina* that occasionally drift into the coastal areas. A small, black sponge, *Chondrosia chucalla,* is also sometimes eaten. Hawaiian green turtles, of all sizes, generally bite off only small pieces of algae while foraging. The serrated edges of the beak appear well adapted to this purpose (Balazs 1980). Russell and Balazs (1994) document how just three years after being introduced into Hawaii (from Florida) the red alga, *Hypnea musciformis,* was being eaten by green turtles.

Galápagos green turtles feed on at least 30 species of algae including *Callithamnion, Gelidium, Gracilaria, Padina* and *Ulva* (Green 1994).

Brown and Brown (1982) recorded the stomach contents of 39 subadult and adult green turtles in Peru and found, in addition to algae, a significant amount of animal matter (molluscs, polychaetes, jellyfish, amphipods, sardines and anchovies).

Mortimer (1981) found that the most important item in the diet of subadult and adult turtles in the feeding pastures off Nicaragua is turtle grass, *Thalassia testudinum,* which accounted for about 79% of the total dry weight of the samples (N=243). Other seagrasses and algae accounted for, respectively, 9.7% and 8.2% dry weight of the samples. Red algae made up most of the algae by dry weight, and brown algae the least. No differences were found in food preferences of the two sexes. Animal mat-

ter constituted only about 1.4% of the dry weight of the samples. The major kinds of animals, in decreasing order of abundance, were sponges, tunicates, soft corals, epiphytic animal matter and non-epiphytic hydrozoans.

Ferreira (1968) examined the stomach contents of 94 immature and mature turtles caught on the feeding pastures off Ceará, Brazil. Marine benthic algae (in order of importance, Rhodophyceae, Chlorophyceae, Phaeophyceae) was the primary food and occurred in 88.3% of the stomachs. *Gracilariopsis sjoestedtii* and *Gracilaria domingensis* were especially common foods, occurring in, respectively, 46.8% and 40.4% of the stomachs. The seagrass *Halodule wrightii* was found in 20.2% of the stomachs. Molluscs and ascidians occurred in 7.4% of the stomachs, and sponges, bryozoans, crustaceans and echinoderms in less than 5% of the stomachs. Gut contents of four immature green turtles caught off the State of São Paulo, Brazil, consisted mainly of red and brown algae (Sazima and Sazima 1983). Moll (1983) hypothesized how sea level drops during the Pleistocene glacial periods could have forced Brazilian green turtles into scarce and relatively small feeding pastures. Contraction and expansion of feeding pastures could have occurred several times during the Pleistocene. Bowen (1993-94) hypothesized that the feeding pastures off Brazil may serve as a refuge for green turtles or as a source of colonizers.

In the stomachs of nine individuals from Oman, the bulk of the food was seagrasses and algae (Ross 1985). Three turtles in this sample ate bulk amounts of both seagrass and algae.

One adult female found stranded in the Gulf of Kutch, India, had 13 species of algae in the stomach with the 4 most prevalent species being *Caulerpa scalpelliformis, Gelidiella acerosa, Ulva lactuca* and *Laurencia pedicularoides* (Frazier 1989). In the Cocos (Keeling) Islands three species of seagrasses *(Thalassia hemprichii, Syringodium isoetifolium* and *Thalassodendron ciliatum)* appear to be grazed by green turtles, but quantitative data are lacking (Williams 1994).

The following reviews list some of the older, or regional, accounts of food preferences of green turtles: Hirth 1971b, 1993; Mortimer 1982b; Bjorndal 1985; Márquez 1990. C. den Hartog (1970) has written an interesting monograph on the seagrasses of the world and Mukai (1993) has updated the biogeography of seagrasses in the western Pacific Ocean. In many instances the distribution of green turtles coincides with the distribution of seagrasses, and certainly a century ago the fit was even closer.

Turtles from different nesting populations sometimes mix on the same feeding pasture. Particularly well-revealed mixed assemblages are those off the coast of Brazil (Meylan 1982b), in the Caribbean (Meylan et al. 1990; Solé 1994) and those in the Australian region (Limpus et al. 1992).

Mortimer (1982b) and Garnett et al. (1985b) briefly review the literature describing how some traditional turtle hunters can detect differences in the flavor of the meat between turtles feeding on seagrasses and those eating algae, with the seagrass-eating turtles being more tasty.

Samples of a turtle's diet can be retrieved by stomach flushing. Forbes and Limpus (1993) describe a method that has been used successfully on green turtles between 35 and 118 cm in carapace length. The technique, modified from previous described methods, can be performed in less than ten minutes and involves use of a pry bar, water-injection tube, retrieval tube and collection bag.

3.4.3 Growth rate

Many factors affect a green turtle's growth rate, including individual physiology, age, sex, diet and geographical location of the feeding habitat with its attendant water quality and temperature.

As far as is known, there are no data on growth rates of wild hatchlings, based upon marked and recaptured individuals. Twelve posthatchlings varied considerably in growth rates over 176 days when fed satiation rations (trout pellets) in captivity, but individuals had constant specific growth rates (Davenport and Scott 1993a). Growth rate was predominately controlled by efficiency of assimilation of nutrients, rather than by size of appetite or metabolic level (Davenport and Scott 1993b). Hadjichristophorou and Grove (1983) observed the feeding behavior of captive one-year old turtles feeding on floating trout pellets. They found that diets containing 40-50% protein and 4.2-5 kcal/g were assimilated with efficiencies of 76% ± 6SD and 86% ± 6SD for energy and protein nitrogen, respectively. Fourteen hatchling Mexican green turtles raised in captivity for one year and fed a 1:1 mixture of fresh fish and commercial dry pellet food (38% protein) attained an average weight of 2,000 g and a mean curved carapace length of 26 cm (Godinez-Dominguez et al. 1993). This rate of growth was greater than some other captive hatchling growth studies although the feeding regimes in the studies did vary.

Growth rates for different size wild green turtles are given in Table 17. The data show that growth is slow and that there is some geographic variability in growth. Samples from the Bahamas, Florida, Galápagos, Texas and the Virgin Islands exhibit a trend toward decreasing growth rate with increasing size. A sample from the Bahamas indicates that immature females and males grow at similar rates (Bolten et al. 1992).

The mean rates of growth of immature Hawaiian turtles, at seven sites, ranged from 0.08 to 0.44 cm/month in straight carapace length (Balazs 1982a). Growth rates at two sites in the main islands were greater than growth rates at five sites in the northwestern segment of the Archipelago.

In the sea off Queensland, Limpus (1993b) determined that the mean growth rate of 25 adult males was 0.046 cm/year.

It is generally assumed that growth in wild and captive green turtles, of both sexes, is negligible, or sharply reduced, once sexual maturity is reached (Carr and Goodman 1970; Bjorndal 1980b; LeGall et al. 1985; Limpus 1993b; Wood and Wood 1980, 1993a). Statistically significant carapace length-weight relationships were described for adult females and males at several nesting sites and feeding pastures (Hirth 1982).

Mean growth rate for captive-reared yearlings released and recaptured in the sea around the Cayman Islands was 8.3 cm/year, for the 30 - 40 cm size class (Wood and Wood 1993b). In captive green turtles, the logistic growth equation best describes the growth (Wood and Wood 1993a).

Bjorndal and Bolten (1995) and Bjorndal et al. (1995) demonstrated how length-frequency analysis shows promise as a method for the study of growth in marine turtles. The method may be especially useful for populations of immature turtles, in sea turtle tagging studies with low recapture rates, and for work that involves terminal sampling.

3.4.4 Metabolism

Ackerman (1980) found that sea turtle eggs exchange respiratory gases with the surrounding substrate as their metabolic activity increases throughout the incubation period and that growth rate and mortality of the embryos is related to respiratory gas exchange. The pattern of oxygen uptake in eggs over the incubation period was sigmoidal (Ackerman 1981a). Ackerman et al. (1985) also described how the exchanges of respiratory gases, heat and water between the egg clutch and its surroundings were interactive. They viewed an egg clutch as a very large egg which is much less sensitive to the hydric environment than a single, smaller egg. Booth and Thompson (1991) reviewed and compared the gaseous environment of sea turtle nests with that of other reptiles.

Baldwin et al. (1989) demonstrated that Heron Island hatchlings utilize anaerobic metabolism during their digging out from the nest, crawling across the beach, and while swimming through offshore shallow water.

Davenport et al. (1982) found that the heart rate of yearlings in the laboratory during gentle activity was 46 - 48 beats per minute and that this rose to 64 - 68 beats per minute during vigorous activity and slowed to 25 - 28 beats per minute during a ten-minute dive.

Smith et al. (1986) discovered an uncoupling of heart rate and temperature- dependent metabolic requirements during cooling of green turtles in thermoregulation experiments.

During the course of feeding experiments on young turtles in the laboratory, Lutz (1990) determined that the metabolic rates ranged from 47.9 to 73.8 ml/kg/h.

Table 17. Growth rates of wild green turtles, expressed as changes in length of carapace (straight line measurements, except curved measurement for Australian sample).

Carapace length cm	Mean growth cm/yr	Location	Reference
20-30	6.9	Virgin Is.	Boulon and Frazer (1990)
20-30	3.6	Puerto Rico	Collazo et al. (1992)
20-30	9.0	Texas	Shaver (1994)
30-40	5.3	Florida	Mendonça (1981)
30-40	8.8	Bahamas	Bjorndal and Bolten (1988)
30-40	5.0	Virgin Is.	Boulon and Frazer (1990)
30-40	5.1	Puerto Rico	Collazo et al. (1992)
30-40	8.9	Texas	Shaver (1994)
40-50	0.8	Australia	Limpus and Walter (1980)
40-50	4.9	Bahamas	Bjorndal and Bolten (1988)
40-50	4.7	Virgin Is.	Boulon and Frazer (1990)
40-50	6.0	Puerto Rico	Collazo et al. (1992)
40-50	0.4	Galápagos	Green (1993)
50-60	1.0	Australia	Limpus and Walter (1980)
50-60	3.1	Florida	Mendonça (1981)
50-60	3.1	Bahamas	Bjorndal and Bolten (1988)
50-60	3.5	Virgin Is.	Boulon and Frazer (1990)
50-60	3.8	Puerto Rico	Collazo et al. (1992)
50-60	0.5	Galápagos	Green (1993)
50-60	6.6	Texas	Shaver (1994)
60-70	1.4	Australia	Limpus and Walter (1980)
60-70	2.8	Florida	Mendonça (1981)
60-70	1.8	Bahamas	Bjorndal and Bolten (1988)
60-70	1.9	Virgin Is.	Boulon and Frazer (1990)
60-70	3.9	Puerto Rico	Collazo et al. (1992)
60-70	0.2	Galápagos	Green (1993)
70-80	1.5	Australia	Limpus and Walter (1980)
70-80	2.2	Florida	Mendonça (1981)
70-80	1.2	Bahamas	Bjorndal and Bolten (1988)
70-80	0.1	Galápagos	Green (1993)
80-90	1.1	Australia	Limpus and Walter (1980)
80-90	0.1	Galápagos	Green (1993)

Studying adult females on the Tortuguero nesting beach, Jackson and Prange (1979) found that active metabolism, averaging 0.23 l/kg•h, was about ten times the standard resting level. Most of the active metabolism is aerobic. Berkson (1966) has shown that green turtles are tolerant of anoxia while diving. The respiratory physiology of diving in sea turtles was reviewed by Lutz and Bentley (1985) and they concluded that most dives appear to be aerobic with the lung serving as the principal oxygen store. Gatz et al. (1987) described several cardiopulmonary characteristics in *C. mydas* adaptive to diving, including a large tidal volume relative to functional residual capacity and a concomitant rise of pulmonary blood flow and oxygen uptake with temperature. The former trait promotes fast exchange of alveolar gas when the turtle surfaces for breathing and the latter aids oxygen transport regardless of wide temperature variations encountered during migrations. Kooyman (1989) compared some aspects of the green turtle's diving physiology with that of other vertebrates. The cardiovascular changes associated with intermittent ventilation at rest and with sustained swimming were determined by West et al. (1992). Prange (1976) estimated that adult turtles making the round-trip breeding migration between Brazil and Ascension Island (about 4,600 km) would require the equivalent of about 21% of their body weight in fat stores to account for the energetic cost of swimming. As already mentioned (section 1.3.3) the energy required for migrations may come from sub-carapace depot fat. Butler et al. (1984) determined that green turtles can maintain high swimming speeds (at least 0.6 m s^{-1}) and metabolize aerobically with little or no resort to anaerobiosis.

Six juvenile green turtles off the east coast of Florida, fitted with radio and sonic tags and with a PIT tag, were at the surface an average of 7.4% and submerged 92.6% of the time, during a one week study period (Nelson 1994). Working with nine immature turtles, fitted with radio and sonic transmitters, at a jettied pass in Texas in July, August and September, Renaud et al. (1995) found that 99% of all the turtle submergence times were <20 min. Brill et al. (1995) used depth-sensitive ultrasonic transmitters to monitor the movements of twelve immature turtles in Kaneohe Bay, Oahu, Hawaii. All turtles remained within a small portion of the Bay where patch reefs and algae were common. Over 90% of the submergence intervals were 33 min. or less.

Jackson (1985) reviewed some of the earlier literature and described how the respiratory system of the green turtle is well adapted to meet its diverse requirements, such as vigorous swimming and deep diving and nesting activities. Two of the special traits of the green turtle's respiratory system include rapid emptying of the lungs and a high capacity for oxygen exchange.

Internal body temperatures of green turtles on land have been recorded under a variety of conditions, in a variety of ways, and the sample sizes have differed, but all the means have registered between 27.4°C and 33.2°C (Hirth 1962; Mrosvsky and Pritchard 1971; Brattstrom and Collins 1972; Whittow and Balazs 1982; Standora et al. 1982b; Snell and Fritts 1983).

Using biotelemetry, Standora et al. (1982b) found an actively swimming green turtle had an internal body temperature (pectoral region) of 37.1°C in water at 29.1°C and they found that even when the turtles are inactive their metabolism is sufficient to keep the body temperature as much as 2°C above the water and air temperatures. Standora et al. (1982b) posited that heat is produced in the metabolically active tissues and then is slowly distributed to the rest of the body, i.e., the green turtle is a regional endotherm.

Prange (1985) reviewed some of the pertinent literature on sea turtle post-orbital salt glands — the primary means by which marine turtles secrete excess monovalent salts — and he reported how the concentrations of the secretions from the salt glands can be twice that of seawater.

Nicolson and Lutz (1989) demonstrated that the salt gland secretion of juvenile turtles was free of protein and was mainly composed of chloride and sodium ions, in similar relative concentrations to those of sea water, but that there were also substantial amounts of potassium and magnesium ions and lesser quantities of urea and bicarbonate. As other investigators reported, they found that the tear flow from the two eyes frequently did not function in synchrony.

According to Marshall and Cooper (1988), the lachrymal salt glands of hatchlings are functional upon emergence from the nest and the hatchlings have the potential to obtain osmotically free water immediately on entering the sea by a combination of drinking seawater and salt excretion by the salt gland. Using X-ray microanalysis, Marshall (1989) discovered that, in salt glands of hatchlings, during secretion, intracellular Na^+ concentration in the principal cells increased while Cl^- and K^+ concentrations remained unchanged. The change in Na^+ and the high Cl^- concentration suggested similarities with the elasmobranch rectal gland.

Marshall and Saddlier (1989) studied the duct system of the lachrymal gland and showed that the duct comprises central canals, secondary ducts and a sac-like main duct and it was suggested that the duct system is unlikely to be merely a passive conduit, but that it may have a role in the modification of the fluid secreted by the gland.

The possible role of a salt gland, along with other attributes, in the evolution of marine reptiles from estuarine predecessors is discussed by Dunson and Mazzotti (1989) and Kinneary (1996).

In a comparative study of western Atlantic turtles, Bjorndal (1982b) explained how a Tortuguero-nesting green turtle, feeding on seagrasses in the internesting years, channels approximately 10% of its annual energy budget into reproduction while a Suriname-nesting turtle, feeding on algae in the internesting years, allocates about 24% of its annual energy budget to reproduction.

3.5 Behavior

3.5.1 Migrations and local movements

Adult turtles make gametic migrations between their feeding pastures and nesting beaches, and some of these migrations may encompass thousands of km. Fig. 13 illustrate some long-range movements and provide an idea of the total range of at least some members of the population.

The dispersal of fifty female turtles tagged in western Australia is depicted in Fig. 13a. One turtle was recovered in the Aru Islands, Indonesia (Prince 1993). Two hundred and seventy three recoveries have been made of green turtles nesting in eastern Australia (Limpus et al. 1992). International recoveries encompass New Caledonia, Vanuatu, Papua New Guinea and Indonesia.

Four females were tracked by the Argos satellite during their post-reproductive migration from Pulau Redang, Malaysia, and three reached their feeding grounds (in Sabah, Indonesia and Philippines) some 923-1,616 km distant, in between 27 and 29 days (Luschi et al. 1996).

Eleven green turtles tagged in the Sabah Turtle Islands have been retaken in the Philippines and two were recaptured in Indonesia (de Silva 1986). The most distant recovery was from Bakkungan Kecil to Kai Kechil, Indonesia, a distance of 1,556 km. A female marked in the

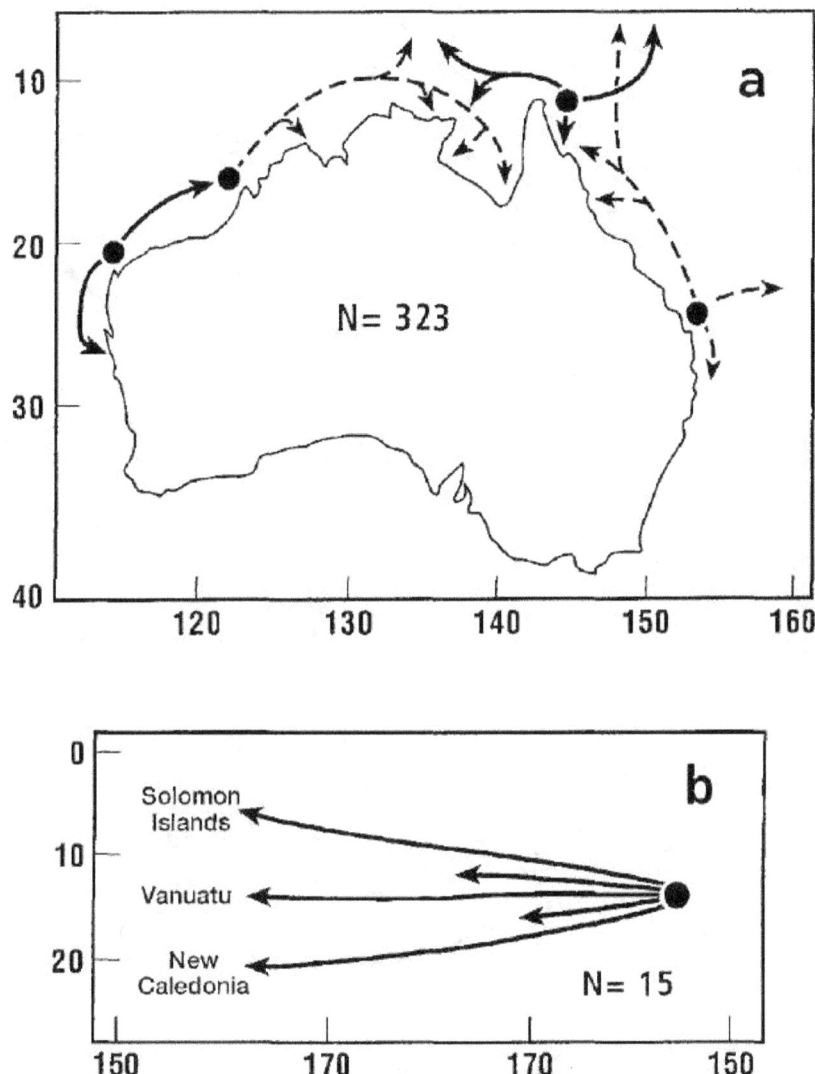

Fig. 13. Long distance recoveries of green turtles. Arrows indicate spread from the nesting beach, or tagging area, and are not intended to suggest routes. a—the tagging sites are North West Cape and Barrow Island (solid lines) and Lacepede Islands (dashed lines) in western Australia (schematic adapted from Prince 1993); in eastern Australia, tagging sites are Raine Island-Pandora Cay Group (solid lines) and the Capricorn-Bunker Group (dashed lines) (schematic adapted from Bustard 1976, Limpus and Parmenter 1986, and Limpus et al. 1992). b—the tagging locale is Scilly Atoll in French Polynesia and the three most distant recovery sites are indicated. Other, less distant recoveries, are identified in the text (schematic adapted from Hirth 1993).

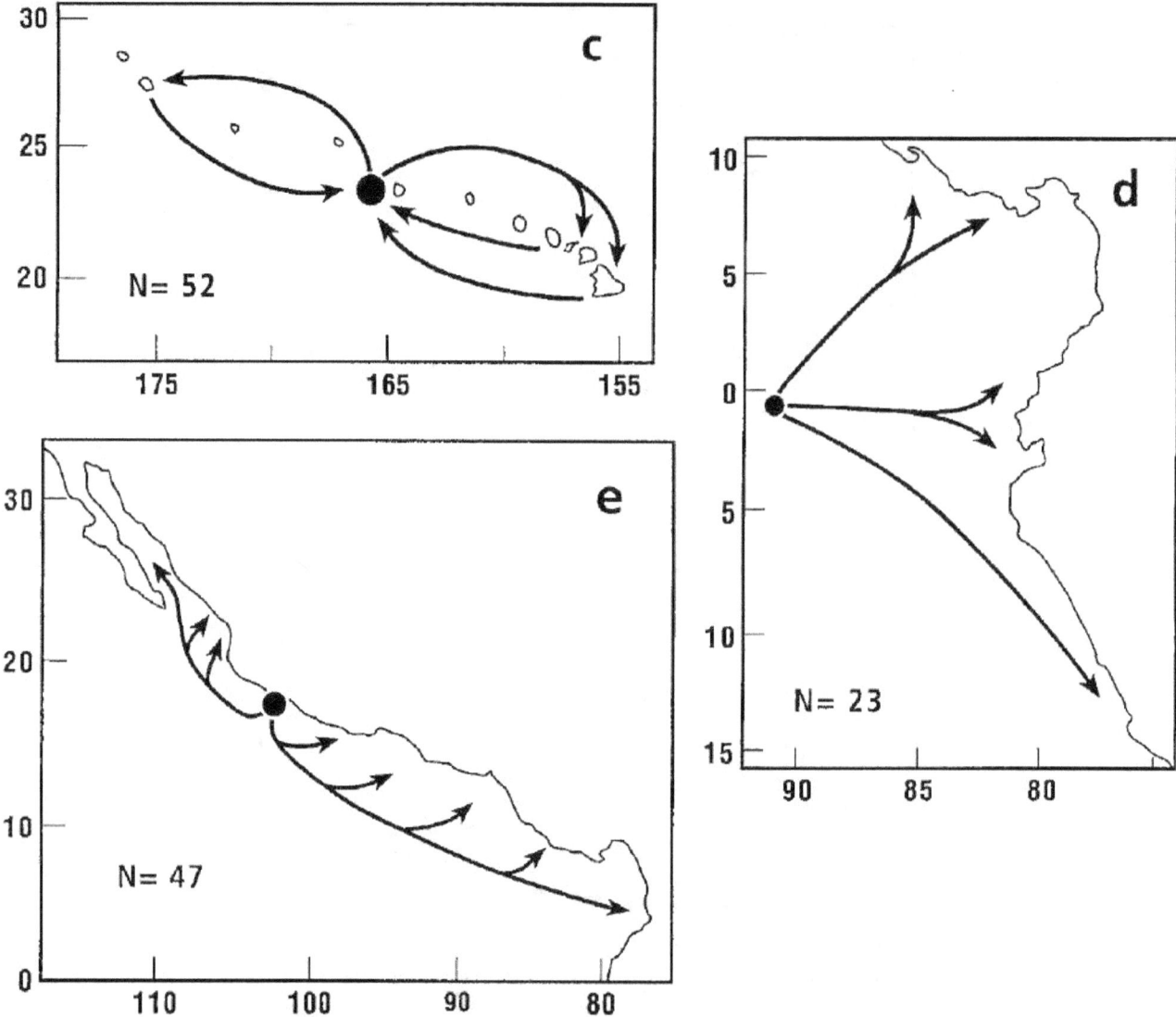

Fig. 13. Long distance recoveries of green turtles. Arrows indicate spread from the nesting beach, or tagging area, and are not intended to suggest routes. c—the nesting site is French Frigate Shoals, in the middle of the Hawaiian Archipelago (schematic adapted from Balazs 1980). d—tagging sites are eleven nesting and foraging grounds in the Galápagos Islands (schematic adapted from Green 1984). e—tagging sites are Colola and Maruata, Mexico (schematic adapted from Alvarado and Figueroa 1992) f—tagging site is Tortuguero, Costa Rica (schematic adapted from Carr 1984). g—tagging beaches are in eastern Suriname and western French Guiana (schematic adapted from Pritchard 1976). h—tagging beach is Aves Island (schematic adapted from Bainbridge 1991 and Solé 1994). i—tagging beach is Ascension Island (schematic adapted from Carr 1984). j—tagging sites are Ras al Hadd and Masirah Island, Oman (solid lines) and Musa and Sharma beaches, Yemen (dashed lines) (schematic adapted from, respectively, Ross 1987; and Hirth and Carr, 1970, FAO, 1973, and updated by Hirth). k—tagging sites are Tromelin Island (solid lines) and Europa Island (dashed lines) (schematic adapted from Hughes 1982 and Le Gall and Hughes 1987).

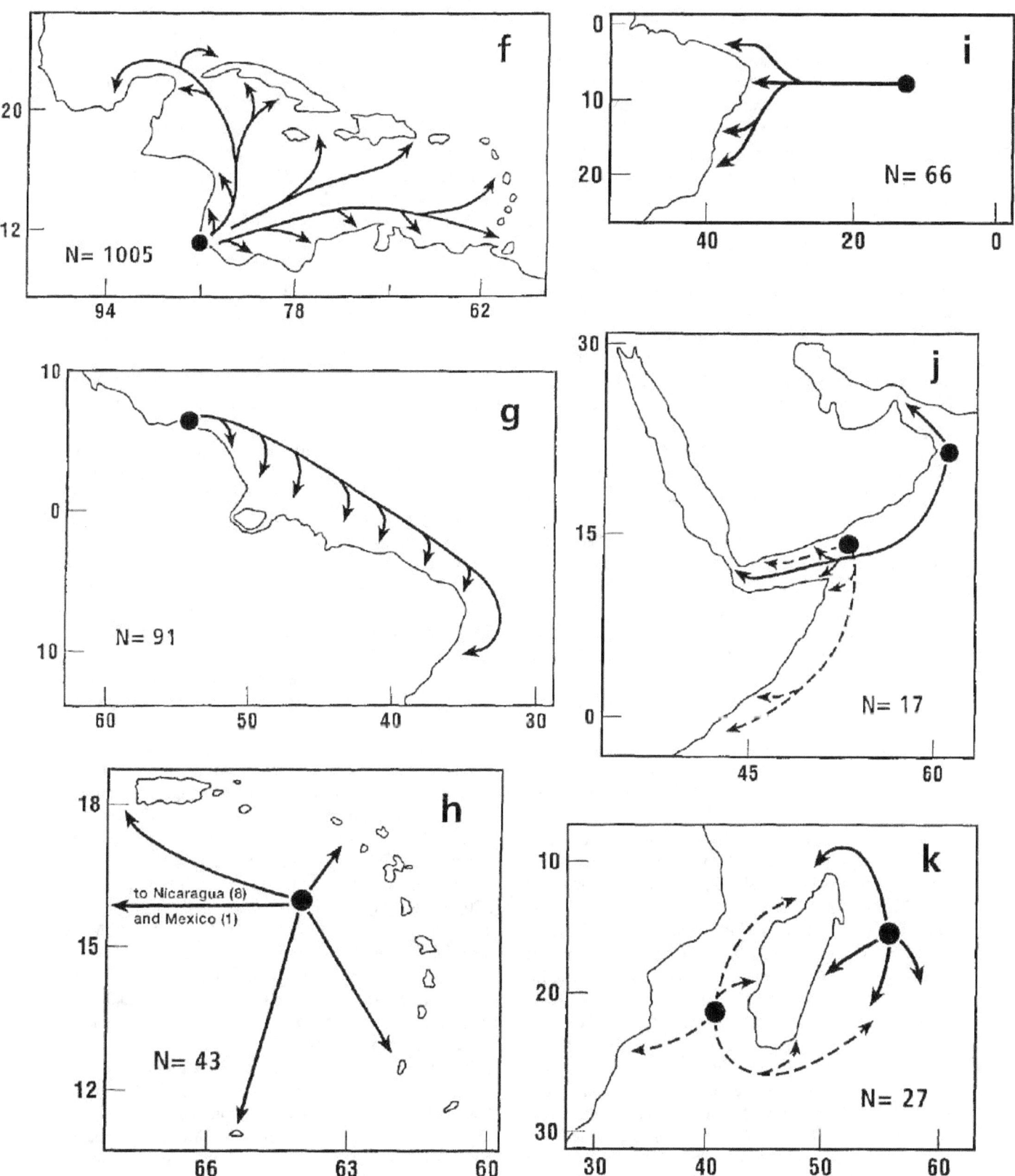

Sarawak Turtle Islands was found 800 km away in North Borneo (Harrisson 1960). Five turtles nesting on Long Island, Papua New Guinea, were taken later in Irian Jaya, Indonesia (Spring 1983).

A nester tagged on Gielop, Yap, Federated States of Micronesia, on 11 May 1991 was incidentally caught in fishing gear in Langob, Philippines on 17 January 1992. Yap and Langob are separated by about 1,472 km. Green turtles tagged in the Philippine Turtle Islands have been recaptured in the Sabah Turtle Islands and vice versa (Ramirez de Veyra 1994a).

Four females tagged while nesting on Gielop Island, Yap State, Federated States of Micronesia, and one male tagged while mating off Gielop Is., were subsequently recovered in the Philippines to the west, between approximately 1,550 and 1,950 km distant from the tagging site, and from 139 to 530 days after tagging. However, it is noteworthy that one individual tagged while nesting on Gielop Island was recovered at Majuro Island in the Marshall Islands, about 3,410 km to the east, after less than 239 days at large. Two individuals marked while nesting on Ngulu Atoll, Yap State, were recovered in the Philippines, from 1,690 to 2,020 km distant, between 84 and less than 217 days after tagging. Of two females tagged on Elato Atoll, Yap State, one was retaken in the Philippines, 2,760 km distant, after 384 days at sea; and, the other was retaken while feeding off Kavieng, Papua New Guinea, about 1,270 km southeast of the tagging site, and after 171 days at sea (Kolinski 1995).

Turtles tagged in the Ogasawara Islands have been recovered at various sites in the Japanese Archipelago (Kurata et al. 1978). After two decades of tagging nesters in the Ogasawara Islands it is concluded that these females are migrating to feeding grounds off the main islands of Japan (Tachikawa et al. 1994). One nester seen on Oroluk Atoll in the Caroline Islands on 2 June 1986 was seen in Taiwan on 18 April 1987 (Edson and Curren 1987).

Turtles tagged on Scilly Atoll in French Polynesia (Fig. 13b) have been recovered as far west as New Caledonia, Vanuatu and the Solomon Islands, distances of about 4,000 km. Other recapture sites have included Tonga, Fiji, Wallis and Futuna and the Cook Islands (Hirth 1993). Tuato'o-Bartley et al. (1993) reported that two green turtles tagged on Rose Atoll in American Samoa were recovered in Fiji, also a westward movement. Three turtles on Rose Atoll were fitted with satellite transmitters in November 1993 and were recovered 1,600 km to the west in Fiji between 34 and 45 days later (Craig 1994). However, one nesting green turtle fitted with a satellite transmitter swam from Rose Atoll to the vicinity of Tahiti, a southeast direction, over a period of 36 days (Craig and Balazs 1995).

Long distance recoveries of 52 female and male turtles in the Hawaiian Archipelago are shown in Fig. 13c. The tag recoveries demonstrate that the breeders at French Frigate Shoals, in the middle of the Archipelago, are recruited from both ends of the island chain. The longest distance between recovery points was about 1,100 km (Balazs 1980).

Twenty-three turtles have been retaken from a total of 5,844 individuals tagged in the Galápagos Islands (Green 1984). Recovery sites include Peru, Ecuador, Colombia, Panama and Costa Rica (Fig. 13d). The approximate maximum distance was 2,163 km, from Bahia Barahona, Isabela Island to San Andres, Peru.

Of 5,176 green turtles tagged at Colola and Maruata, Mexico, there have been 47 recoveries more than 100 km from the nesting beaches (Fig. 13e). International recoveries are from El Salvador, Guatemala, Nicaragua, Costa Rica and Colombia (Alvarado and Figueroa 1992). Five nesters at Colola, Mexico, were fitted with transmitters and tracked via the Tiros-Argos satellite system in 1991. Results revealed that at least some of the turtles swam hundreds of kilometers away from land in very deep water (Byles et al. 1995).

Most of the Tortuguero, Costa Rica international tag recoveries (N=1,005) have come from Nicaragua, especially from the Miskito Cays region, where extensive seagrass pastures are located. Numerous recoveries have also been made in Mexico, Panama, Colombia and Venezuela (Fig. 13f). One important result of the Tortuguero tagging work, now in its fortieth year and with over 55,000 turtles tagged (Anon 1991b), is that turtles tagged at the Tortuguero nesting beach have not been seen renesting anywhere else than at Tortuguero.

Long-distance recoveries of females tagged on their nesting beaches have ranged between 0.4% (Galápagos) and 9.3% (Tortuguero) (Alvarado and Figueroa 1992).

Of 91 green turtles retaken after being tagged on nesting beaches in eastern Suriname and western French Guiana, all but one were from Brazil (Fig. 13g). Sixty-two were taken off the coastal state of Ceará (Pritchard 1976). These turtles mingle with turtles from Ascension Island on the Brazilian algal feeding pastures.

Aves Island, in the eastern Caribbean Sea, is only about 500 m in length, about 120 m wide at the widest point, and approximately 3.3 m at its highest elevation. More than 4,000 green turtles have been tagged at Aves Island and 43 have been recaptured (Fig. 13h) (Solé 1994). One tagged turtle was recorded nesting on Mona Island, Puerto Rico; the rest were recaptured at sea. Recaptures have been made from 12 islands in the Caribbean Sea and 5 continental nations bordering the Caribbean Sea and Atlantic Ocean. Most of the recaptures (37.2%) were off the coasts of Nicaragua and the Dominican Republic. The most distant recapture was made in Maranhao, Brazil, about 2,870 km from Aves Island. This turtle swam an average of 23 km daily over a period of 125 days.

About 3,384 green turtles have been tagged on Ascension Island and there have been 66 recoveries, all from the coast of Brazil (Mortimer and Carr 1987), about 2,300 km distant (Fig. 13i). The shortest recovery interval was 56 days.

Six green turtles tagged at Ras al Hadd and at Masirah Island, Oman, have been recovered in Saudi Arabia, United Arab Emirates, Yemen, Eritrea and Somalia (Ross 1987). Nine green turtles tagged on Musa and Sharma beaches, Yemen, have been retaken off the east coast of Somalia, and two more were captured on the feeding pastures within Yemen (Hirth and Carr 1970; FAO 1973; Hirth, updated) (Fig. 13j).

Out of 4,843 and 3,766 females tagged on Europa and Tromelin Islands there have been, respectively, 15 and 12 international recoveries (Fig. 13k). Maximum distance between site of tagging (Europa) and site of recapture (Maurice) was about 2,250 km (LeGall and Hughes 1987). Some of the green turtles taken by fishermen around the Toliara (Madagascar) coral reef feeding grounds may be migrants from Europa Island (Rakotonirina and Cooke 1994).

Two turtles tagged on Karan Island, Saudi Arabia, were recovered in Kuwait, approximately 250 km away (Miller 1989).

One green turtle tagged in Cyprus was recaptured in the Gulf of Gabé in Tunisia (Laurent et al. 1990).

Minimum average swimming speeds for migrating green turtles have ranged between about 20 and 90 km/day (Meylan 1982b).

Information on migrations of males is accumulating slowly. In the Hawaiian Archipelago, nine males have been recorded migrating between French Frigate Shoals and Pearl and Hermes Reef, Oahu and Lisianski (Balazs 1983a). Green (1984) reported that two males tagged in the Galápagos Islands were recaptured in Peru and another marked in the Galápagos was retaken in Costa Rica. The longest distance traveled, to Peru, was 2,150 km. Two males tagged on Scilly Atoll in French Polynesia were recaptured in Fiji, almost 3,000 km distant (Galenon 1979 in Green 1984). Twenty-five breeding males tagged in the Capricorn and Bunker Groups of the southern Great Barrier Reef were recaptured at various feeding areas: 21 within the Capricorn Group, 3 elsewhere in Queensland, and 1 in New Caledonia. These recapture sites ranged from <10 km to 1,443 km from the tagging area (Limpus 1993b).

Some information is available on the local and long-range movements of immature green turtles. In some localities, at least some immature individuals have a tendency to remain in the vicinity of, or to return to, their foraging area (Schmidt 1916; Carr and Caldwell 1956; Ireland 1980; Balazs 1982a; Williams 1988; Manzella et al. 1990; Hirth et al. 1992; Renaud et al. 1994; McDonald

and Dutton 1995). Several recent, long-range movements have been recorded: Guseman and Ehrhart (1992) report that two juveniles were tagged in Mosquito Lagoon, Florida, and one was recovered in Cuba and the other in Nicaragua; and, Hirth et al. (1992) reported how one immature was tagged on Wuvulu Island, Papua New Guinea on 1 July 1989 and was retaken on 1 October, 1989, in northeastern Irian Jaya, Indonesia. In the latter example, the shortest straight line distance between points of contact was 305 km. Head-started green turtles, released in Florida, have been recorded along the Atlantic coast of the U.S. as far north as New York, the eastern Atlantic Ocean (Azores, Madeiria and Mauritania) and South America (Colombia, Venezuela, Guyana, Brazil) (Witham 1991). Of 399 captive-reared turtles that were released when 2 to 3 years of age from Puerto Morelos, Mexico, 4 were recaptured in Cuban waters when they were between 7 and 9 years of age (Zurita et al. 1994). A fifth turtle from this captive-reared cohort was retaken in Mexico, about 45 km from the site of release, when it was 11 years old. It was placed in a pen, extending from the beach out 50m into the sea, and it nested four times on the beach.

Green (1993) cites several older papers describing long-distance movements of wild- and captive-reared juvenile green turtles of from 2,300 to 5,600 km.

A green turtle's migrations are an important and integral part of its life history strategy. The vast majority of migrating, adult, female green turtles exhibit philopatry (regional homing) and strong nest site fixation in their renesting episodes. However, the short- and long-range orienting and navigating mechanisms remain largely unknown. The genetic, hormonal and environmental variables influencing migration are just beginning to be unraveled. Furthermore, there must be some individual behavioral plasticity in response to changing environmental conditions affecting oriented travel and more information at this individual level is sorely needed. Telemetric monitoring of individuals will certainly help in this regard.

Adult and hatchling green turtles probably have similar sensory modalities and some of the behavioral research with hatchlings, especially their seaward orientation in shallow water off the nesting beach, and their magnetic detection abilities, may be applicable to the long-distance migrations of adults (see section 3.2.2). It is possible that adults use wave propagation and a geomagnetic sense, along with other cues, in their long-range oceanic navigation.

Carr (1965) considered celestial navigation as a possible guidance mechanism in the long-range travels of the green turtle, but this hypothesis was untested after Ehrenfeld and Koch (1967) found the Atlantic green turtle to be extremely myopic when its eyes are out of water.

However, it has now been shown that the eyes of *Chelonia mydas* are approximately emmetropic in air and this would allow them to view celestial objects with greater clarity than was previously thought possible (Northmore and Granda 1991).

Carr and Coleman (1974) postulated that the Ascension Island - Brazil migration may have evolved gradually over 70 million years as the South Atlantic Ocean widened via plate tectonic movements. But, based on mtDNA analysis, Bowen et al. (1989) stated that the colonization of Ascension has been evolutionarily recent. LeGall (1989) elaborated on the possible link between plate tectonics and other long-range green turtle migrations. The widening Gulf of Aden was mentioned as a possible link to the evolution of the Yemen - Somalia migration (FAO 1973). The evolution of the Gulf of Aden is described by Courtillot and Vink (1983) and by Girdler (1984).

Other ultimate factors that may be involved in long-range migrations of sea turtles include evolution along a behavioral continuum (Hirth 1978) and glaciation-associated sea level fluctuations (Moll 1983). It has recently been reported (Wuethrich 1993) that leatherback turtles may follow contours of underwater mountain ranges and continental slopes in their migrations away from Costa Rica.

Koch et al. (1969) hypothesized that olfactory cues emanating from Ascension Island could be recognized by turtles off the Brazilian coast and this, in combination with other cues, could play a part in the island-finding navigation. Carr (1972a) elaborated on the dual olfaction and sun-compass guidance mechanisms that might help explain the Brazil - Ascension migration. Brown (1990), however, concluded that the employment of the chemosensory component of the navigation hypothesis to Ascension is doubtful given the existence of the South Equatorial Countercurrent. Lohmann and Lohmann (1996a, b) hypothesize how an adult green turtle could accurately migrate between Ascension Is. and Brazil using a bicoordinate magnetic map (see section 3.2.2).

As already mentioned, adult females show strong nest site fidelity in their renestings and this fact, along with others, has given rise to the hypothesis that adult green turtles return to their natal beach to nest. This natal homing hypothesis is based on the idea that the turtles are imprinted, chemically, to the beach during a sensitive period in the nest and/or as hatchlings crawling down the beach and swimming through the shallow water. Each nesting beach and neighboring internesting habitat may have their own unique chemical make-up, augmented over the years by millions of disintegrating green turtle eggs. Many years later in the turtle's life, these imprinting cues are used to locate the natal beach. Although it may not be conventional thinking, hatchlings may be imprinted to a variety of cues, over a period of weeks, as they move away from their natal beach.

Using operant conditioning techniques, Manton et al. (1972a, b) established that small green turtles are capable of underwater chemoreception and they discuss use of this ability for navigation purposes. Owens et al. (1986) reviewed some of the pertinent literature and research on chemoreception in amphibians and reptiles and concluded that sea turtles can orient to specific chemical cues learned early in their lives. In a laboratory setting, Grassman and Owens (1987) found that the chemosensory environment of nestling and hatchling green turtles affected their subsequent behavior, and more recently, Grassman (1993) has provided a general review of sea turtle chemical imprinting.

Owens et al. (1982) proposed a social facilitation model that might also explain the nest site selection process. Under this model first-time nesters encounter and follow experienced adults to the nesting beach which they learn by olfactory and other navigational processes. They hypothesize that the ability of adults to learn and remember the location of a suitable nesting beach is a more parsimonious hypothesis than hatchling imprinting. Memory cues, for example, would have to persist for only 1-4 years whereas an imprinted hatchling would have to remember cues for 15-45 years.

However, Meylan et al. (1990) reported that geographical distribution of mtDNA genotypes, in the Caribbean region, supported the natal homing hypothesis and indicated that social facilitation to non-natal sites is rare. Using restriction-fragment-length polymorphisms of mtDNA, Bowen et al. (1992) identified significant differences among several green turtle colonies in the Atlantic and Pacific Oceans thus giving support for the natal homing hypothesis. Using mtDNA sequences of the control region, Allard et al. (1994) provided further support for natal homing by showing how the Tortuguero and Florida nesting populations were structured differently along maternal lineages. After analyzing mtDNA control region sequences of nesters from nine green turtle colonies, Encalada (1994) concluded that "the population genetic structure of green turtles in the Atlantic is indeed shaped by natal homing." Or, put another way, and based on their research with genetic assays, Bowen and Avise (1996) stated "Although a predisposition to utilize environmental cues must surely have a genetic basis in marine turtles, the positional information essential for navigation to a particular locality probably is learned (imprinted) rather than inherited." While supporting the natal homing hypothesis, at least at the regional level, Limpus et al. (1992) discuss how some Australian turtles display a site-fixity to their feeding area. They state "Fidelity to the feeding area requires an additional imprinting of the turtle to an underwater habitat to occur during adult or near-adult life.

If this can occur, it is not unreasonable to admit the possibility of a later imprinting of a turtle during its first breeding season to the nesting beach it chooses from within the natal-rookery region." This idea is reiterated in Limpus and Miller (1993).

This brief review indicates that the behavioral mechanisms underlying the short-and long-range movements of adult green turtles, especially, still remain largely unknown. What are needed are more experiments to determine the turtle's umwelt. Then, armed with this information, scientists can test hypotheses concerning coordinated oceanic travel. It is most likely that turtle navigation and homing is a composite process employing different senses, based on a multiplicity of cues, and related hierarchically.

The use of satellites for monitoring the long-range travel of green turtles has great potential and several examples have already been given in this section. Byles (1989) describes the use of the Argos System for tracking free-ranging sea turtles which includes a method for recording dives and water temperature. Byles and Keinath (1990) outline the use of the Tiros-Argos System and they discuss various aspects of transmitter attachment including weight, hydrodynamics, color and fouling. Beavers et al. (1992) describe their experiences in attaching PTTs (Platform Transmitter Terminals) to hard shell turtles. They chose a dental compound over fiberglass/resin and epoxy for tagging turtles at sea. Renaud et al. (1993a) discuss some of the problems associated with transmitter attachment to wild green turtles and they describe a method of fiberglassing transmitters to a sea turtle's carapace. Three adult green turtles at French Frigate Shoals were fitted with Argos satellite system transmitters and within four weeks two had reached Oahu and one swam directly to Johnston Atoll. The turtles' routes were over deep water where no known navigational cues exist (National Marine Fisheries Service, 1993). The Argos satellite system was used to track a turtle between Pulau Redang, Malaysia, across the South China Sea to Pulau Natuna Besar, Indonesia (Anon 1994a; Papi et al. 1995). A PTT was attached to the turtle after her last nesting of the season on 23 September 1993 and over the next 13 days she swam 750 km (average about 58 km per day) to Pulau Natuna Besar, where she remained for the next couple weeks (presumably the feeding ground). The final segment of this journey, over about 470 km, was almost straight and was made in the absence of any landmarks. A magnetic compass, as part of a navigational system, was proposed to explain this open sea migration. Three adult female green turtles were fitted with Argos satellite transmitters after nesting in the Archie Carr Wildlife Refuge in Florida in July 1994 (Anon 1994b). The preliminary result based on this tracking study is that Florida green turtles utilize reefs and seagrass meadows around the Florida Keys as their primary feeding grounds

(Anon 1995a).

Two adult male green turtles were fitted with satellite transmitters at Bocas del Toro, Panama in July 1995 and tracking data are now being analyzed (Anon 1995b).

Papi and Luschi (1996) review some of the current literature on satellite tracking of sea turtles and albatrosses and point out how, in spite of different ecological and physiological constraints, these oceanic navigators may share some navigational abilities.

It is apparent that many interesting things remain to be learned about the oceanic movements of green turtles.

3.5.2 Schooling

As far as is known, green turtles do not school in the classical sense of aquatic organisms. Large numbers of turtles are seen in some feeding habitats and off and on some nesting beaches, but whether they arrive or depart from these places in schools is unknown.

As mentioned in the preceding section, Meylan (1982b) reported minimum average travel speeds of between 20 and 90 km/day. She also referred to the possibility of group migration. The evidence most commonly cited for this activity is the simultaneous recovery in a distant habitat of two or more individuals which were tagged while nesting together.

3.5.3 Responses to stimuli

Green turtles' responses to stimuli can be gleaned from almost every behavioral section in this synopsis; sexual stimuli involved in mating behavior (section 3.1.3), natural visual cues in hatchlings' crawl to the sea and wave cues in shallow water (section 3.2.2), imprinting and navigational stimuli (section 3.5.1), disorientation of hatchlings due to photopollution (section 4.4.2) and ingestion of artifical food items (section 4.4.2).

Mrosovsky (1980) wrote an interesting paper on the responses of sea turtles to temperature stimuli. This included the effect of temperature on sexual differentiation of embryos, emergence from the nest, growth, hibernation and survival.

The responses of green turtles to humans in the sea can vary. Cousteau (1971) stated that large turtles off Europa Island showed no fear of divers. Divers were able to touch and even handle the turtles without difficulty. After many hours of her presence in the water with them off Fairfax Island, Australia, many turtles gradually accepted Booth (Booth and Peters 1972) and she was able to approach mated pairs and single individuals. Balazs et al. (1987) noted that when encountered by divers in their resting habitat, Hawaiian turtles had a tendency to swim toward deeper water. The current tameness to humans of green turtles in shallow water off Punalu'u on Hawaii, along with their shift from nighttime to daytime foraging, are believed to be the result of reduced hunting pressure

(Balazs et al. 1994b). Williams (1988) reported that grazing subadults in the Virgin Islands were not disturbed by observers. Hirth et al. (1992) noted that on night dives in Papua New Guinea, when a light was shone on a swimming or resting immature turtle, the turtle's behavior was unpredictable. Some individuals swam off into deep water and some were attracted to the light. There are numerous anecdotal accounts of divers photographing juvenile, subadult and adult green turtles in their marine habitat. Responses of nesting turtles to humans are discussed in section 4.3.2.

4. POPULATION
4.1 Structure

4.1.1 Sex ratio
The sex ratios of hatchlings on some beaches have been discussed in section 3.2.2, and as pointed out in that section, a number of temporal and ecological factors can affect natural, hatchling sex ratios.

The sex ratio of a largely immature population (N=197) inhabiting the feeding grounds around Heron Reef was equivalent to 1:1 (Limpus and Reed 1985a). Of 784 individuals, mostly immature, sampled on the Moreton Banks, Queensland, Australia feeding area, 65.6% were females (Limpus et al. 1994b). The sex ratio of 56 immature turtles on the Bermuda foraging grounds was not significantly different from 1:1 (Meylan et al. 1992a). Of 120 immature turtles sampled on a feeding ground in the Bahamas, 46 were males, 65 were females and the sex of 9 was undetermined. The sex ratio is not statistically different from 1:1 (Bolten et al. 1992). Sixty six immature turtles that died during a cold-stunning episode in a developmental habitat in east central Florida were necropsied. Of these, 42 and 24 were females and males respectively—a significantly female biased ratio (Schroeder and Owens 1994). The sex ratio of a pooled sample (N=66) of immature Hawaiian turtles caught in their feeding habitats did not differ significantly from 1:1 (Wibbels et al. 1993).

On the feeding pastures in Oman, Ross (1984) determined a 1:1 adult sex ratio (N=242). However, in commercial catches of mostly subadult and adult turtles elsewhere, females have usually outnumbered males: Nicaragua (Carr and Giovannoli 1957; Mortimer 1981), Baja California (Caldwell 1962b), Yemen (Hirth and Carr 1970) and South Africa and St. Brandon (Hughes 1974a).

The optimal male: female sex ratio in the breeding herd in the Cayman Turtle Farm is about 1:4 (Wood 1991).

4.1.2 Age composition
No complete age-sex pyramid has been constructed for any green turtle population. The epipelagic phase of the green turtle, and hence the turtle's age, has been estimated to last for one to five years (see section 2.2.1). Estimates of growth rates and age at maturity are provided in sections 3.1.2 and 3.4.3 and Table 17.

4.1.3 Size composition
Information on the size composition of green turtle populations is presented in section 2.2.2 which describes the sizes of green turtles when they enter their nearshore feeding habitats and the size classes seen on some developmental and adult feeding pastures.

4.2 Abundance and Density

4.2.1 Average abundance and density
The numbers of nesters on some of the well-known nesting beaches are given in section 2.2.2 and in Figs. 9, 10 and 11. Natural fluctuations in numbers of nesters have been recorded on several beaches (see following section). Without historical records, it is impossible to determine if small nesting populations are inherently small, or if they are remnants of a once larger nesting population, or if they are incipient colonizers. King (1982) has reviewed the decline and extirpation of green turtles in several locales, especially in places where commercial exploitation replaced subsistence take. As far as is known, no extirpated nesting colony has been, or is being, recolonized. As Avise and Bowen (1994) point out in their discussion of the mtDNA research, green turtle nesting sites tend to be strongly isolated from one another over ecological timescales because of the propensity for natal homing by females (but weakly differentiated over evolutionary timescales because of mistakes in natal homing), so that decline or loss of a specific nesting site is not likely to be compensated by natural recruitment of females hatched elsewhere—at least over timescales germane to human interests.

Aerial surveys are sometimes used to obtain crude estimates of mating aggregations or nesting activity and offer the advantages of checking beaches on isolated atolls and can cover much territory in a short time. But such estimates always need to be verified by ground-truth observations preferably over a number of consecutive days. Hirth and Ogren (1987) have described how the visible aspects of a sea turtle nest can change significantly over time.

Long range, demographic studies on nesting sites are important and can provide, among other things, information on aging, phenotypic plasticity, remigrations, nest site selection and population cycles.

4.2.2 Changes in abundance and density
The density of nesting can fluctuate dramatically from year to year on some beaches. Limpus (1980) reported a nesting population of about 1,100 on Heron Island in 1974-75 and then about 50 the following nesting season. On Raine Island in the peak nesting season of 1974-75 over

11,000 nesting turtles were ashore on one night on the 1.7 km long beach yet the following year only about 100 turtles nested on Raine nightly (Limpus 1982a).

At Tortuguero, it was estimated that 31,211 green turtles nested in 1978, 5,178 in 1979, 52,046 in 1980 and 8,430 in 1981 (Carr et al. 1982). Over a fifteen year period (1971-1985) on the regularly censused 8 km study beach at Tortuguero, the number of nesters ranged from 413 in 1979 to 3,022 in 1980 (Anon 1987).

Schulz (1982) cited some significant fluctuations in the number of nests on Suriname beaches: there were 3,610 nests in 1975 and 8,080 in 1976.

The nesting density at Ras al Hadd changes from year to year (Ross 1987). During the August through December peak of nesting in 1983 about 340 turtles nested nightly. During the same peak months in 1984, 1985 and 1986, about 185, 750 and 740, respectively, nested nightly. Le Gall et al. (1986) recorded fluctuations in the nesting population on Europa Island. Estimations of nesters range between 2,000 and 11,000 during the peak nesting months.

In Michoacan, Alvarado and Figueroa (1990) estimated that the numbers of females nesting annually from 1981 through 1989 were approximately: 5,586; 4,483; 1,000; 940; 1,200; 3,334; 1,993; 570 and 1,300.

4.3 Natality and Recruitment

4.3.1 Reproduction rates

Green turtles are characterized by slow growth, delayed sexual maturity, high fecundity, iteroparity, relatively high predation rates on eggs and hatchlings and a relatively long reproductive life. All of these parameters affect their reproductive rates

Numerous data concerning reproductive strategies are given in Tables 4, 7, 9, and 11. Using these data one can calculate the number of eggs and hatchlings that a nester, and nesting population, can produce over one or many nesting seasons. There are a lack of data on the reproductive lifespan of green turtles, but Frazer (1983) calculated a maximum reproductive life span of 32 years for female loggerheads in the Georgia population.

Carr and Carr (1970a) have shown how a few Tortuguero turtles have shifted from a 3 to a 2 year remigration cycle and vice versa, and they postulated that this may be a reflection of feeding regimes.

In contrast to the abundant data on female remigration intervals (Table 9), little is known about the migratory cycles of males. Research at three localities does indicate that males have shorter remigration intervals than females at the same sites. Balazs (1983a) found that of 52 recaptures of males at French Frigate Shoals, 42.3% returned after 1 year, 32.7% after 2 years, and 25% after 3 years. Of 130 females at the same site, 36.2% exhibited a 2 year cycle, 43.1% a 3 year cycle, 7.7% a 4 year

cycle and 12.2% migrated at intervals from 5 to 8 years. One female nested after an interval of 1 year. The average remigration interval of males in the Capricorn and Bunker Groups of the southern Great Barrier Reef is 2.08 years (range 1-5, N = 24). This is shorter than that recorded for females on Heron Island where the mean remigration cycle is 4.65 years (range 2-7, N = 31) (Limpus 1993b). Males, in the Galápagos Is. most commonly remigrate annually while females here exhibit a predominately three year cycle (Green 1994).

4.3.2 Factors affecting reproduction

Many factors affect reproduction and they have been discussed in specific sections. Some differences in hatching success of eggs and temperature dependent sex determination are described in sections 3.1.7 and 3.2.2, respectively. When nests are constructed in the shade of condominiums the natural sex ratios may be altered, as Mrosovsky et al. (1994) surmised for loggerheads on a Florida beach. A male's fitness, at least during one reproductive season, may be determined by whether he succeeds in copulation or is relegated to a role of "escort" (section 3.1.3). Natural sex ratios in some populations are now being reported (section 4.1.1). Because individuals from different nesting beaches sometimes overlap on foraging grounds and in migrational corridors, mortality of turtles in these areas could decimate multiple nesting populations simultaneously (discussed by Avise and Bowen 1994).

Storms, tides, erosion and accretion are some of the natural forces affecting the foreshore and backshore and hence the quality of a nesting beach. For instance, wave motion sometimes produces a beach scarp over which turtles are unable to crawl (FAO 1973). In such cases, turtles may crawl along the foreshore a few meters to locate a more negotiable scarp, or reenter the sea and emerge later at another site, or lay their eggs at the base of the scarp. Eggs laid at the base of the scarp are usually lost because of flooding/suffocation. In Turkey, Van Piggelen and Strijbosch (1993) observed that some clutches on the nesting beach are flooded by a fluctuating ground water table.

Fowler (1979) determined that beach erosion destroyed 20 or 5.7% of the clutches laid on a section of Tortuguero Beach, Costa Rica, in 1977. Dutton and Whitmore (1983) estimated that 119 of 567 clutches laid by green turtles on Krofajapasi Beach, Suriname, in 1982, were laid below the spring high tide level, and were considered "doomed".

Agardy (1990) reported how Hurricane Hugo in the Caribbean region in 1989 caused some erosion on nesting beaches and decimated some seagrass beds, and how Hurricane Gilbert in the preceding year destroyed all the clutches in an egg hatchery in Mexico. As pointed out by

73

Milton et al. (1994) hurricanes can adversely affect sea turtle populations by, among other things, washing-out nests completely, flooding nests and suffocating/drowning eggs and hatchlings, removing some sand from tops of nests, depositing extra sand over nests, mixing and changing beach particle size, and depositing debris on the nesting beach. Radically altered beach topography and beach chemistry may affect the natal beach homing hypothesis since the altered beach may have little resemblance to the female's natal beach.

Limpus (1993a) very briefly mentions how climate change and sea level rise in the South Pacific region could affect sex ratios of incubating eggs, erode some existing nesting sites and affect the frequency of ENSO episodes which, in turn, could affect green turtle breeding cycles.

Daniels et al. (1993) have discussed how rising sea levels, due to the greenhouse effect, could reduce loggerhead turtle nesting habitat in South Carolina. Their methodologies and scenarios are applicable to green turtle nesting on other coasts.

It goes without saying, that mining beach sand can have devastating affects on green turtle nesting. Sella (1982) described such a situation in Israel.

Nesting green turtles avoid artificial lights at Tortuguero (Carr and Carr 1972; Witherington 1992) and on Ascension Island (Mortimer 1982a). Witherington (1992) has shown, where beach lighting is essential, that the use of yellow, low pressure sodium vapor luminaires has no significant effect on nesting but white, mercury vapor luminaires significantly reduces the number of green turtles emerging and nesting. The sodium vapor luminaires emit light near the peak of spectral sensitivity for green turtles (Granda and O'Shea 1972) and the light may represent an inane color to nesters.

It is well known that reckless use of lights (e. g. flashlights, flash photography) and excessive human movements and barking dogs can cause emerging green turtles to return to the sea. Green turtles are especially sensitive to lights and movements up until oviposition. While some human interference (tagging, measuring, checking epibionts, counting eggs, photographing, etc.) may not cause a green turtle to abandon its nest after oviposition has begun, it has been shown that some harassed turtles will complete the nest covering and camouflaging process in a hurried or desultory manner (Hirth and Samson 1987; Campbell 1994). Such less-than-normal nests may be subject to more predation and clutches may suffer from abnormal temperature, moisture and gas exchange regimes. It is recommended that turtles be allowed to complete their entire nesting repertoire under as natural conditions as possible. Ecotourists should cooperate with guides when they are informed of these matters.

Jacobson and Lopez (1994) conducted a study on the effect of tourists on green turtle nesting activity on Tortuguero Beach, Costa Rica, in 1990. They found that the presence and behavior of tourists resulted in disturbance of nesters. Tourists visitation was concentrated on weekends, correlating with the times that one third fewer turtles came to the beach. A pilot training course and guide program involving Tortuguero residents was successful in helping to mitigate the impact of tourists by controlling the number of people on the nesting beach at night and by controlling the use of flashlights and flash photography (Jacobson and Robles 1992).

Witham (1982) discussed the affect of human activities on sea turtle nesting beaches, including impact from artificial lights, physical barriers such as sea walls, groins and jetties, and vehicular traffic, with an emphasis on Florida beaches. Coston-Clements and Hoss (1983) reviewed some of the literature on the impact of humans on sea turtle beaches and cite several papers dealing with other species of turtles but whose conclusions are applicable to green turtles.

Compaction of sand by human and vehicular traffic and beach nourishment may act to impair natural gas exchange, which Ackerman (1980) found could lower the effectiveness of incubation.

Use of vehicles on beaches by sea turtle researchers should be discouraged. Of all people, turtle researchers should walk gently on the beach. Transporting tourists in vehicles along the beach is also discouraged.

Crain et al. (1995) briefly review some of the sea turtle factors which should be considered in beach nourishment schemes including escarpments which can impede the crawl of nesters onto the beach; beach compaction which can alter egg chamber architecture; and, changes in the gaseous, hydric and thermal microclimate of the nesting arena which may affect hatchling embryology and survivorship.

Rimkus and Ackerman (1995) assessed the impact of beach renourishment on the hydric microclimate of nesting beaches on the east coast of Florida and found that renourished beaches are wetter than natural beaches; that egg-water exchange due to water potential differences is probably not affected; and, that the thermal conductivity of renourished beaches is likely to be higher than natural beaches and that this may influence the nest/egg water exchange.

Oolitic aragonite sand from the Bahama Islands is under consideration as a source of fill for some Florida beach nourishment projects even though Florida beaches are composed primarily of silicate sand (Shaw et al. 1995b). Aragonite sand was about 2°C cooler than Florida silicate on a loggerhead beach in Florida and extended the incubation period by five days and possibly altered natural loggerhead sex ratios. The same may be true for Florida green turtle clutches in aragonite sand.

Ryder (1995) found that loggerhead nesting and

hatchling success on a renourished beach and a control beach on the east coast of Florida were similar although there were differences in compaction and sand temperatures between the two beaches. These findings may be applicable to green turtles which nest in the same area.

Large or heavy litter that has been washed up on the beach over a clutch of eggs can interfere with hatchling emergence. Sharp objects can cut flippers. Weathering of tar balls and human debris on the beach may affect the nest-site selection process. Litter of all kinds on the beach impedes the crawl of hatchlings to the sea (Hirth 1987). Anthropogenic debris on some beaches of Karan Island interferes with turtles nesting there (Miller 1989).

4.3.3 Recruitment

Recruitment is the influx of new members into a population by reproduction or immigration. Crude hatchling recruitment rates can be computed for certain populations by referring to Tables 4, 7 and 11. Recruitment rates for juvenile and subadult size classes are unknown. Recruitment into nesting populations is better known. For example, at Tortuguero, from 1969 to 1974, recruits accounted for 80.4 to 90.0% of the total number of turtles seen each year. From 1975 to 1978, recruits comprised 62.5 to 80.7% of the turtles seen. Whether this change reflected a decrease in recruitment or an increase in adult survivorship was not clear (Bjorndal 1980b). Remigrants accounted for 15.8% of the nesting population at Tortuguero in 1968 and 8.7% of the population in 1969 (Carr and Carr 1970b).

Relevant survivorship data are in section 4.5.

4.4 Mortality

4.4.1 Mortality rates

Bjorndal (1980b) estimated instantaneous death rates of between 0.2929 and 0.5538 for fourteen cohorts (1959-1972) of adult females at Tortuguero. The estimates were made during a time period when the colony was heavily exploited. See section 4.5 for discussion of survivorship rates.

4.4.2 Factors causing or affecting mortality

There are many factors affecting mortality and they have been referred to in specific sections. For example, growth rate and mortality of embryos is related to respiratory gas exchange (section 3.4.4). Eggs are taken by a number of predators with various species of crabs and mammals taking significant numbers. Major predators on hatchlings include crabs, fishes and birds. Sharks prey upon large individuals (section 3.3.4). Survivorship may be related to growth rates in the sense that faster growing individuals are subject to less predation (section 3.4.3). Hypothermic stunning episodes have been reported (section 3.3.2). Green turtles are host to a number of parasites and diseases including tuberculosis, pneumonia, coccidiosis and fibropapillomatosis (section 3.3.5). Long distance migrations may be more hazardous than short migrations although data are lacking on this subject. Green turtles, and other species of marine turtles, may be accidentally speared by billfishes (Frazier et al. 1994). Collisions with coral and rock, especially at the entrance to nesting beaches, sometimes result in injuries.

Factors that reduce the green turtles' ability to survive need to be studied in a quantitative fashion. Such studies should include biomagnification of pollutants in the food chain, synergistic effects of environmental pollutants and chemical pollution in the algae/seagrass feeding pastures. For example, Abdellatif (1993) identified pesticide runoff (from locust spraying on the coastal plain) as probably the most serious threat to the Red Sea environment off the Sudanese coast.

During a six-week study on Europa Island, it was observed that 50 green turtles perished by falling into reef crevices on their return to the sea after nesting (Hughes 1974b). Heat exhaustion killed many turtles on Raine Island when, due to the high numbers of nesters, some individuals resorted to nesting in the daytime (Low 1985). In 1984, the storm surge of Cyclone Kathy stranded over 1,000 green turtles in Australia. It is estimated that more than 500 would have died on the mudflats without human aid (Limpus and Reed 1985b).

Green turtles are impacted by humans, directly or indirectly, in all of their critical habitats: on the nesting beach and in the internesting habitat; in the epipelagic habitat; on the developmental and adult foraging habitats; and, in the migrating routes between these habitats. Some of the marine impacts are complicated by the fact that mitigation will require international cooperation.

It was found that green turtle eggs collected on Ascension Island contained DDE and PCB residues (Thompson et al. 1974). Low levels of DDE and DDT were detected in green turtle eggs in Florida (Clark and Krynitsky 1980). McKim and Johnson (1983) analyzed polychlorinated residues in the muscle and liver of juvenile green turtles collected on the east coast of Florida, finding only low concentrations. In the muscle and liver, DDE residues were less than 1 ppb and less than 10 ppb, respectively. Total PCB levels ranged from 5.9-9.4 ppb in muscle and from 43-80 ppb in the liver.

Green turtle hatchlings are disoriented by photopollution on the hatching beach (literature reviewed in Verheijen 1985). Raymond (1984) reviewed the problem of hatchlings' disorientation on beaches due to a variety of man-made lights, including building lights, streetlights, vehicular lights and flashlights. He recommended a number of solutions ranging from eliminating the problem lights to preventing direct lights on the beach to reducing the intensity of the lights.

Chan and Liew (1988) reviewed some of the literature on the effects of oil pollution on sea turtles. They quoted some reports showing that fresh oil can induce embryonic mortality, that hatchlings associated with pelagic drift lines are extremely vulnerable to the effects of oil and that dermopathologic changes were seen in subadults exposed to oil. Several green turtle deaths in the Gulf of Mexico were associated with an oil spill (Shabica 1982). Berger (1991) examined the potential environmental impact of offshore oil spills in the vicinity of Palawan, Philippines. The oil spill trajectories would be dependent upon spill location and time of the year. Depending on these circumstances the green and hawksbill nesting sites on Palawan and the Calamian Islands would be at risk.

Based upon gas chromatographic analysis of oil residues scraped from four species of marine turtles, including green turtles, stranded in the Gulf of Mexico region, Van Vleet and Pauly (1987) concluded that the turtles were impacted by oil originating from tanker discharge.

Miller (1989) discussed the direct and indirect affects of oil spills on turtles in the Gulf of Arabia. He said that the effect of the NOWRUZ oil spill (1983) was probably severe—contributing to the death of numerous turtles and impacting seagrass foraging areas and nesting beaches. According to Miller (1989) the major threats to the survival of green turtles in the Arabian Gulf are oil pollution, habitat destruction and to a lesser extent fishing. The 1991 Gulf War oil spill severely impacted the sandy beaches on Karan and Jana Islands. On Karan contractors removed 14,000 m^3 of tar and oil sediment from the sandy beaches. Clean marine sand was used to re-establish the original configuration of the beaches. Marine turtles continue to nest in apparently normal numbers. In 1991, 164 hawksbills and about 1,100 green turtles nested on Karan and Jana Islands. In 1992, 150 hawksbills and 700 greens nested on the two islands (Krupp and Jones 1993). The five coral islands of Harqus, Karan, Kurayn, Jana and Jurayd form part of a proposed marine sanctuary (Krupp and Jones 1993). Three species of sea grasses (*Halodule uninervis, Halophila ovalis* and *H. stipulacea*) in the northwestern Gulf have not suffered acute or longterm degradation as a result of the 1991 Gulf War oil spill (Kenworthy et al. 1993; Durako et al. 1993).

Mosier (1994) describes how use of GIS (Geographical Information System — a system of hardware and software which is designed to analyze spatially referenced data) can aid in such marine turtle research as the relationships between oil spills and sea grass beds and nest sites. GIS can also help relate turtle strandings and geographic data to spatial patterns of turtle mortality.

There is circumstantial evidence to suggest that green turtles, like other sea turtles, can suffer from underwater explosions used to remove oil platforms (Klima et al. 1988).

Quantitative studies are needed on the interactions of humans and green turtles in the internesting habitat. Studies which come to mind include the numbers of turtles taken by harpoons and nets while copulating offshore; the number of collisions with, and injuries caused by, boats; and the degree of disruption of internesting movements caused by jetties, water pollution and divers.

The ingestion of tar balls and plastics by green turtles, their entanglement in oceanic debris, and the effects of these factors on morbidity and mortality have been discussed by Balazs (1985b). Turtles may be attracted to debris because it resembles natural food in size or shape or color, or the debris itself may be appealing to turtles. The debris may be ingested incidentally with natural food items. The stage of appetite must also influence feeding behavior. The effects of ingested debris may be related to the amount and kind ingested and possibly could range from mechanical blockage of the gut to subtle interference with the turtle's metabolism. Entanglement can interfere with all aspects of a turtle's behavior. Bjorndal et al. (1994) noted that anthropogenic debris was found in the digestive tracts of 24 of 43 juvenile green turtle carcasses that washed ashore in Florida. The death of two turtles was attributed to ingestion of debris. Plastics were the most commonly ingested debris and fishing line, fish hooks, rubber, aluminum foil and tar were also swallowed.

Thirteen of 784 turtles in a feeding population off Queensland, Australia, displayed evidence of having been impacted by anthropogenic activities (e. g. entanglement in fishing line or rope; boat or propeller injuries) (Limpus et al. 1994b).

The Center for Environmental Education (1987) has published an illuminating report on the types, sources and impacts of nondegradable plastics in the marine ecosystem, with emphasis on U. S. waters.

Carr (1987b) described how the post-hatchlings and young turtles may eat plastic scraps and other buoyant debris as they occupy the same driftlines in the epipelagic habitat. Plotkin and Amoss (1990) found that 7 of 15 green turtles stranded on the south Texas coast from 1986 through 1988 had ingested marine debris. Uchida (1990) concluded that most of the sea turtles found in waters adjacent to Japan show evidence of plastic ingestion.

In laboratory experiments, Lutz (1990) stated that low levels of plastic ingestion had no significant effect on gut function, metabolic rate, blood chemistry, liver function or salt balance in young green turtles. Further studies with latex indicated the sojourn of the latex material in the gut ranged from a few days to four months. Later, studying four, captive immature turtles, Schulman and Lutz (1995) concluded that "Even small amounts of plastic may remain in the gut for months, causing a disturbance in gut function, lipid metabolism and resulting in excessive gas accumulation in the gut."

Murphy and Hopkins-Murphy (1989) reviewed the relevant literature and estimated that up to 300 green turtles (10,000 loggerheads, 800 ridleys) may be drowned annually in U. S. waters as a result of shrimp trawling activities. The Sea Turtle Stranding and Salvage Network (STSSN) publishes regular reports on the numbers of stranded sea turtles from Maine to Texas and in parts of the U. S. Caribbean. Although exact causes of death or morbidity are frequently undetermined, many strandings can be linked to incidental capture in fishing activities. In 1990, 1991, 1992 and 1993 respectively, 329, 248, 225 and 207 green turtles were reported stranded (Teas 1992a, b, 1993, 1994). Thirty-eight green turtles were recorded stranded in the northwestern Gulf of Mexico between 1986 and 1989 and during the same interval 515 loggerheads and 357 Kemp's ridleys were stranded. Strong circumstantial evidence suggests a linkage between strandings and shrimping (Caillouet et al. 1991). The recently organized Caribbean Stranding Network, with participants from nine Caribbean countries, has the stated primary objectives of uniting stranding efforts throughout the Caribbean region and coordinating assessments of marine vertebrate deaths (Pinto-Rodríquez et al. 1995). The projects of this network include mortality assessments, rescue and rehabilitation, and education.

Magnuson et al. (1990) reviewed the data linking shrimp trawling and sea turtle mortality (mostly loggerheads and Kemp's ridleys, some green turtles) in U. S. waters and they concluded that shrimp trawling was the primary agent for sea turtle mortality caused by humans. They recommended the use of TEDs (Turtle Excluder Devices) (see section 6.2)

Two immature green turtles, 1 hawksbill, 30 Kemp's ridleys and 50 loggerheads were verified caught in the summer flounder *(Paralichthys dentatus)* trawl fishery off North Carolina between November 1991 and February 1992 and because a total of 1,063 turtles was estimated to have been caught (and 89-181 estimated to have died as a result of the trawl fishery) Epperly et al. (1995c) recommended that sea turtle regulations are needed for this fishery.

Chester et al. (1994) describe how sea surface temperature imagery derived from the U. S. A.'s polar orbiting satellite is being used, along with other data, to help reduce the impact of commercial trawl fishing on sea turtles off the east coast of the U. S. A.

Green turtles, along with flatbacks, loggerheads and ridleys, are incidentally taken in Australia's prawn fishery, but the impact of trawl-induced drownings on the turtle populations there is probably not of such proportions as to create immediate concern according to Poiner et al. (1990). Approximately 5,295 sea turtles are caught annually in the trawling fishery of Queensland, Australia,

with about 30% of these being green turtles (Robins 1995). It is estimated that 1% of these drown in the nets and if all comatose turtles are assumed to die then up to 6.8% of all trawl caught turtles die. The observed mortality rate for the Queensland coast trawl fishery is lower than other trawl fisheries and this is believed due to the short tow durations (<80 min).

It was estimated that 245 and 100 green turtles, respectively, were incidentally caught in 1984 and 1985 in trawl nets and drift/gill nets off Terengganu, Malaysia (Chan et al. 1988).

The estimated bycatch of the Japanese large-mesh driftnet fishery in the North Pacific Ocean in 1990-1991 was 1,501 turtles, of which 248 were estimated to be green turtles (Wetherall et al. 1993). It was further speculated by the aforementioned authors that of the 248 green turtles entangled the minimum mortality was 74 turtles, mostly juveniles and subadults, and that the likely sources of the green turtles would include the nesting colonies in the Ogasawara Islands and French Frigate Shoals.

The incidental take of sea turtles during dredging operations has been documented for the Cape Canaveral Entrance Channel in Florida and the King's Bay Entrance Channel in Georgia (Dickerson et al. 1992). There were 16 incidents in the Canaveral Entrance and 1 incident in the King's Bay Entrance between 1980 and 1991.

Wershoven and Wershoven (1992) stated that since 1986 propeller injuries were cited in 34 of 56 stranding deaths of Florida juvenile and subadult turtles, and that fishing hooks and lines were responsible for another 7 deaths. One male (curved carapace length, 78 cm) and one female (curved carapace length, 70 cm) were caught in the tuna longline fishery off Costa Rica in the Pacific Ocean (Segura and Arauz 1995). One was hooked in the mouth and the other on a flipper. Squid, herring and sail fish were the bait. Both survived.

Between 1981 and 1990 an average of 14 green turtles was caught annually in shark nets off Natal, South Africa, and 35% were subsequently released (Dudley and Cliff 1993).

The loss of green turtles to "ghost fishing" (lost or discarded fishing gear continues to catch and drown/kill sea turtles) should be addressed especially in view of the large amounts and numerous types of fishing gear now in use and their construction from durable material.

4.5 Dynamics of Populations

A green turtle survivorship curve is roughly concave indicating high egg and hatchling mortality (under natural conditions).

After examining fourteen cohorts of adult females from Tortuguero, Bjorndal (1980b) computed that for the Tortuguero population to maintain itself, one out of every 245.5 eggs, or one out of every 97.2 hatchlings reaching the sand surface, must live to sexual maturity and reproduce. Working with data available at the time, Hirth and Schaffer (1974) estimated a range of 0.22 to 1% for hatchling survival rates necessary to maintain a stable population. Frazer (1986) reviewed some of the earlier work dealing with gross survivorship from egg to maturity in four species of sea turtles. He calculated that the proportion of eggs surviving to adulthood ranges between 0.0009 and 0.0018 in a declining population of loggerheads.

Iverson (1991) reviewed the literature on survivorship schedules of turtles and he cited the following annualized survivorship for green turtles from egg to hatching: 0.86 in Australia, 0.767 in Hawaii, 0.69 in Suriname, 0.558 in the Galápagos, and 0.396 at Tortuguero (0.607 for adult females at Tortuguero).

Bustard and Tognetti (1969) produced a model showing how nest destruction is dependent on population density and how this provides a mechanism to regulate population size.

Wilbur and Morin (1988) briefly point out how different kinds and levels of human predation, from little disturbance to high predation on eggs and to high predation on eggs and adults, could influence life histories of isolated green turtle populations. Dunham et al. (1988) discuss how reliable life tables for turtles are much needed and how sound management programs for commercially valuable or endangered species can be derived from life tables. Although not dealing specifically with sea turtles, Soulé (1987) discusses some of the minimum conditions (population size and range) necessary for the long-term viability of natural populations and metapopulations.

One of the best sea turtle population models so far developed is one formulated for loggerheads. Using demographic data from the southeastern U. S. loggerhead population, Crouse et al. (1987) developed a stage-based population model showing that survival in the juvenile and subadult stages has the largest effect on population growth. In this model, annual survivorship of hatchlings (<1 year age), small juveniles (1-7 years age), large juveniles (8-15 years age), subadults (16-21 years age), and breeders (22-54 years age) were estimated at, respectively, 0.67, 0.79, 0.68, 0.74 and 0.81. Green turtle populations which portray demographic parameters similar to these loggerheads, may exhibit similar survivorship patterns. Congdon et al. (1993) briefly discuss how sea turtles have some life history traits similar to Blanding's turtles (Emydoidea blandingii) and how "the suite of life history traits that coevolve with longevity results in populations that are severely limited in their ability to respond to chronic increases in mortality of neonates and even less so to increased mortality of juveniles and adults." They concluded that the protection of all life stages is important for the conservation of long-lived organisms. They reached the

same conclusion after a long-term study of common snapping turtles (Chelydra serpentina) (Congdon et al. 1994).

Using a stage-class matrix model, Siddeek and Baldwin (1996) assessed the Oman green turtle stock and found that (1) juveniles (1-29 years of age) dominated the stable stage-class population vector (2) a maximum hunting quota of about 143 females maintained a stable population (3) in addition to protecting eggs and hatchlings, reduction in juvenile mortality significantly increased the population growth rate and (4) simulated reduction in the current annual 4,280 female fishing deaths to 268 produced a positive population growth rate within feasible stock parameter values.

Using a series of deterministic matrix models for yellow mud turtles (Kinosternon flavescens) and Kemp's ridleys (Lepidochelys kempi), Heppell et al. (1996) argued that management efforts focused exclusively on improving survival in the first year of life are unlikely to be effective for long-lived turtles; that population projections for both species predict that headstarting can augment increasing populations when adult survival is maintained at high levels; and, if subadult and adult survival is reduced, headstarting cannot compensate for losses in later stages.

In view of these aforementioned demographic studies, the best conservation strategy for green turtles, at the present time, is the one that provides protection for all critical stages in the turtles' life cycle.

Many population models are based on the number and fecundity of tagged migrants and untagged recruits that are observed nesting. Consequently the problem of tag loss has significant implications in studies of population dynamics (assuming complete beach coverage). Nesters are tagged on the trailing edges of each front flipper with self-piercing strap tags made of various metals—monel, titanium or inconel, or with plastic tags. Based on long-term multiple tagging studies in eastern Australia, Limpus (1992) determined that titanium tags outlasted monel tags and that the best place for a flipper tag was through, or immediately adjacent to, the most proximal large scale on the trailing edge of the front limb. Alvarado et al. (1993) found that plastic tags were retained better than monel tags on Mexican turtles, regardless of the flipper tagged. Plastic tags were also retained longer than monel tags on Galápagos turtles (Green 1979).

A passive integrated transponder (PIT) tag has been used on Kemp's ridley turtles. This basically is a pre-programmed microchip capable of receiving and transmitting specific radio signals and it shows promise as a potential life-long tag for sea turtles (Fontaine et al. 1987). Camper and Dixon (1988) evaluated a PIT marking system for some amphibians and reptiles, including loggerhead and Kemp's ridley turtles. Parmenter (1993a) found that there was only an 8% loss of PIT tags in adult female flatback turtles over a two year period, and that this retention rate compared very favorably with traditional tagging. These 11.5 x 2.0 mm tags were implanted into the right shoulder of the flatback. The major disadvantage of PITs is that tagged individuals cannot be visually identified.

Other innovative tagging methods have been described but have not been widely used: internal magnetized wire tag (Schwartz 1981); tissue grafting (Hendrickson and Hendrickson 1981); Ir markers (Umezu et al. 1991); and engraving carapacial scutes (Balazs 1995).

4.6 The Population in the Community and the Ecosystem

Green turtles occupy a series of habitats throughout their lives (Fig. 8) and in former days, before their overexploitation by humans, their role in the habitats may have been very substantial.

Posthatchlings and small juveniles are carnivorous or omnivorous and thus occupy the second, third or higher tropic levels in simple predator food chains. Subadults and adults are chiefly herbivorous and therefore are constituents of the second trophic level in simple grazing food chains. Trophic level changes associated with ontogenetic habitat shifts are discussed in sections 3.4.1 and 3.4.2.

Adult green turtles are one of the few macroherbivores that graze on seagrass blades. Other large herbivores are sea urchins, fishes and sirenians (see section 3.3.3). Today, on a global scale, most of the energy in a seagrass ecosystem is channeled through the detritus food chain.

Thayer et al. (1984) reviewed some of the pertinent literature and described how the feeding behavior of green turtles can have profound effects on the seagrass ecosystem. Two notable effects are the establishment of distinct grazing plots in the seagrass meadow and the interruption of nitrogen cycling.

Quantitative studies are needed on how the foraging of green turtles decreases the effectiveness of the seagrass beds in stabilizing the seabed against erosional forces and how their grazing reduces the effectiveness of the pastures in serving as nursery areas for resident and migrating fauna. The effect of green turtle grazing on biodiversity may be substantial due to the fact that seagrass blades serve as substrate for diverse epiphytic communities. On the other hand, the physical-chemical changes produced by the grazing turtles may create new niches that can be colonized by a different suite of organisms. The role of green turtles in maintaining productive seagrass beds and their role in recycling nutrients are discussed in sections 3.4.1 and 3.4.2. Satellite imagery can be used as a research tool to map the distribution and changes in some seagrass beds.

Rogers (1989) described how green turtle crawls and nest digging behavior disturbs beach vegetation on Heron Island. It was estimated that up to 20% of the eastern portion of the Island has been subject to turtle disturbance in recent years.

Green turtle faeces (composed of partially digested algae, *Codium edule* and *Amansia glomerata*) washed ashore in large amounts on a beach in Oahu, Hawaii, in 1989, causing a temporary closure of the beach to public use (Balazs et al. 1993). The reason for this phenomenon was not determined, but several possible explanations were given.

Green turtles and their eggs are food for a variety of organisms (section 3.3.4). Unhatched eggs add nutrients to the beach.

At Fairfax Island, Australia, green turtles are groomed by cleaner fish: *Abudefduf sexfasciatus* were observed eating algae on a turtle's head and *Thalassoma lunare* were seen picking at small barnacles on the neck (Booth and Peters 1972). At French Frigate Shoals, Hawaii, Balazs (1980) identified certain underwater sites where green turtles regularly position themselves while surgeonfish and wrasses feed on epizootics. At a cleaning station near Waikiki Beach, Hawaii, several species of fish commonly graze on algae and on small barnacles growing on the skin and carapace of mainly subadult green turtles (Balazs et al. 1994a). Losey et al. (1994) reported on a cleaning symbiosis between green turtles and the carnivorous wrasse, *Thalassoma duperry*, in Kaneohe Bay, Hawaii. Five of 15 wrasses captured at the cleaning stations apparently specialized on the parasitic turtle barnacles, *Platylepas hexastylos*, occurring on the skin. The turtles exhibited a solicitation posture which included the cessation of swimming; fully extended flippers drooped downward; the neck, often fully extended, arched upward or downward; and, the bites of the fish resulted in the feeding site being more fully exposed.

Floating turtles may serve as passive fish aggregators.

5. EXPLOITATION

5.1 Fishing Equipment and Methods

Green turtles are taken in a variety of ways, including swimming or diving after them and capturing by hand, noosing, gaffing, harpooning, trapping, netting, use of seines, spearguns, decoys and suckerfish, and "turning turtle" on the nesting beaches. No special equipment is needed to locate and dig up the eggs on the beach, although a straight stick to probe for the clutch is useful.

Some general accounts of fishing equipment and methods of fishing in widely scattered geographic areas are described by Parsons (1962), Hirth (1971b) and Groombridge and Luxmoore (1989).

Some regional accounts of subsistence and traditional hunting methods are: Southwest Pacific (Kowarsky 1982; Spring 1982b; Polunin 1985; Nietschmann 1989; Bradley 1991), South and Central Pacific (Hirth 1971a; Balazs

1980), Western Pacific (McCoy 1982; Johannes 1986), Pacific Mexico (Cliffton et al. 1982; Felger and Moser 1985), Caribbean (Nietschmann 1982; Pritchard and Trebbau 1984), and Indian Ocean (Frazier 1980, 1982b). Fishing methods and "turning turtle" on beaches are also noted on some specific feeding pastures and nesting sites (section 2.2.2 for references).

Suckerfish or remora *(Echeneis sp.)* have been used to capture turtles in such widely scattered places as the South China Sea, northern Australia, east coast of Africa and the Caribbean. Parsons (1962) gives a vivid account of this extraordinary, but now seldom used, method of capturing turtles.

Recent archaeological work reveals that early Polynesians relied heavily on sea turtles (green, hawksbill, and to a lesser extent, loggerhead) for food on some islands (Dye and Steadman 1990).

In general, traditional labor-intensive fishing methods are being replaced by motorized boats and use of synthetic nets.

5.2 Fishing Areas

Most green turtles are taken on their feeding pastures, in shallow water just off the nesting beaches (part of their internesting habitat) and on the nesting beaches (see section 2). Some are incidentally caught in other fishing operations (section 4.4.2).

5.3 Fishing Seasons

In some places, green turtles are taken opportunistically at any time where regulations are lacking or where rules are not enforced. Regulations pertaining to the taking of turtles and/or eggs and to open and closed fishing seasons vary widely among nations (section 6.1).

5.4 Fishing Operations and Results

Green turtles have had a long history of human exploitation. In many parts of the world, green turtle flesh and eggs have been eaten for centuries. Calipee (cartilaginous material) is used in soup manufacture and the skin is processed into leather goods. In the past, dried calipee was a significant export product. The oil is used for medicinal and cosmetic purposes. The carapace is used for a variety of utilitarian purposes at the village level (e.g., as baby cradles, to patch holes in huts, as windbreaks) and polished shells are sold to tourists. Thick scutes are sometimes carved into trinkets and the more typical thin scutes are sometimes used in veneering and inlaying. Green turtles of all sizes are sometimes stuffed for the tourist souvenir trade. Fortunately, international trade in many green turtle products is now being reduced as more countries join and abide by CITES.

Depending upon the area, local customs, and regulations, green turtle eggs are harvested in several ways: by local people on a subsistence basis, through village cooperatives, or by government license. Where the government controls the licensing, a certain percentage of the eggs are usually incubated in hatcheries and the hatchlings released into the sea. Where mechanized boats or roads and vehicles are available, eggs are now being transported to larger towns and cities, which may be some distance from the nesting beaches. The eggs' alleged aphrodisiac qualities adds to their popularity. In some regions, even though turtles and/or eggs are available, the flesh and eggs are not eaten because of religious or cultural reasons. However, local workers may be employed in capturing turtles for export.

In general, the plight of green turtles is now exacerbated by human population growth (and the concomitant alteration of natural habitats and the desire for animal protein), the trend toward regional and global market economies, and by the lack of enforced, long-range conservation strategies. Traits of green turtles which render them particularly susceptible to overexploitation by humans are their large size, proclivity for colonial nesting on certain beaches, and their docility on the beach.

Some global and regional exploitation patterns are described in Parsons (1962), Hirth (1971b, 1993), Rebel (1974), King (1982), Mack et al. (1982), Sternberg (1982) and Groombridge and Luxmoore (1989).

A list of countries with regulations pertaining to the take of green turtles and/or their eggs, and hence an idea of the level of harvesting, is given in section 6.1.

King (1982) described the overexploitation of the Cayman turtle fishery and stated that the Cayman nesting population was extinct by 1900. He also described the demise of the Bermuda and Dry Tortugas (Florida) nesting populations. Little is known about the former numbers of green turtles nesting in the Florida Keys National Wildlife Refuge although an active turtle fishery in the Florida Keys did take an unknown number of adult green turtles (Wilmers 1994). In any case, it appears that only 3 or 4 breeders now comprise the entire green turtle nesting population in the Refuge. Nesting colonies have been extirpated, mostly by overexploitation, on Mauritius, Rodrigues and Réunion (reviewed in Groombridge and Luxmoore 1989). The green turtle population that formerly nested on Bali has been extirpated (Schulz 1984 in Groombridge and Luxmoore 1989), but thousands of green turtles are brought into Bali each year (21,000 in 1990), where they are butchered for meat (Barr 1992). In vivid, pictorial essays, Lindsay (1995, 1996) describes how and why green turtles are collected and killed for Balinese ceremonies and rituals. The remaining nesting populations of green turtles in the Fiji Islands, Kingdom of Tonga and Western Samoa are described in terms of critical, bleak and probably extinct, respectively (Zann 1994). Horikoshi et al. (1994) briefly described the decline of the green turtle population in the Ogasawara Islands from 1880 when about 1,800 adult turtles were harvested to the mid-1920's when fewer than 250 were caught annually to an annual harvest of between 45 and 225 between 1973 and 1993. Green turtles continue to be taken by netting off the Peruvian coast where there is a great demand for meat (Vargas et al. 1994). Pritchard (1982c) reports that the Europa Island population, once probably heavily exploited but protected since 1933, may be an example of a recovered nesting population. The Environmental Investigation Agency (1995) generally describes the current exploitation of sea turtles in Sri Lanka and the Maldive Islands, with emphasis on the tortoiseshell trade. A useful, 150-entry bibliography of marine turtle work in Sri Lanka, from 1700-1993, was prepared by Hewavisenthi (1994c).

Harvesting of green turtles in Australia is by Aboriginal and Torres Strait Islanders. Turtles are taken for subsistence purposes and the total annual catch in Australian waters was estimated at between 7,500 and 10,500 (Kowarsky 1982). The most common method of capturing turtle is by harpoon from a boat. Today there is widespread use of motorized aluminum boats in contrast to the traditional dugout canoes powered by paddles or sail. Compared to the exploitation of green turtles for meat, the consumption of eggs in Australia appears to have an insignificant impact on natural populations (Kowarsky 1982). Also, Kowarsky (1982) was of the opinion that hunting pressure on turtles in the past was at least as great, if not greater, than today, and that future levels of hunting pressure will depend on the socio-economic goals of the Aboriginal people. Limpus and Fleay (1983) and Limpus and Parmenter (1986) were of the opinion that turtles in the Torres Strait region were being overharvested. Daley (1990) reported an estimate of 10,000 adult green turtles are harvested annually in the Torres Strait with about 4,000 of these taken by Torres Strait Islanders and about 6,000 by Papua New Guineans for sale in their coastal markets. Marketing patterns of green turtles in the main market of Port Moresby were monitored by Hirth and Rohovit (1992). Parmenter (1993b) provides a brief review of Australian green turtle exploitation, conservation and current research projects.

Excessive egg exploitation has been documented in several areas. The egg production on Thamihla Kyun (Burma) in the early 1980s was about 200,000 annually. This represents a 90% reduction from over the preceding 80 years (Groombridge and Luxmore 1989). Polunin and Nuitja (1982) showed that there was an overall decline in egg yields on the nesting beaches of Ko Khram and Phangnga (Thailand) and Berau, Pangumbahan and Sukamade (Indonesia) from about 1960 to 1975. In Indonesia, eggs are eaten throughout the country but meat is consumed in only certain areas. Available evidence indicates that egg har-

vests and turtle catches (on the nesting beach and at sea) are far in excess of sustainable levels (Polunin 1983; Groombridge and Luxmoore 1989; Barr 1992).

There has been an 88% decline in green turtle eggs laid in the Philippine Turtle Islands between 1959 and 1992. The decline is due to the overharvesting of eggs by residents (Pawikan Conservation Project Staff, 1993). However, the collection of eggs is now regulated and of an estimated egg production of 9,022,553 between 1984 and 1992, 65% were conserved. The Pawikan Conservation Project was created in 1979 to address the decline of marine turtles in the Philippines and it has been effective in promoting conservation and scientific management of the turtle resources although much still needs to be done (Ramirez-deVeyra 1994b).

The majority of Malaysians do not eat turtle meat, but eggs have been collected for many decades. Mortimer (1992) described the decline in number of eggs laid in Terengganu (on Peninsular Malaysia) from 928,900 in 1956 to between 107,135 and 417,981 annually from 1984 to 1989. Most of the decline is due to decades of overharvesting of eggs, but turtles now also suffer from habitat destruction and incidental capture in fishing gear. In 1989 in Peninsular Malaysia, about 17.5% of the eggs laid by green turtles (and olive ridleys and hawksbills) were placed in egg hatcheries and the hatchlings released (Mortimer 1992).

Although advising that egg yield data must be viewed with caution, Groombridge and Luxmoore (1989) estimated that egg production in the Sabah Turtle Islands has declined about 45% in the last two decades. Groombridge and Luxmoore (1989) also document a long-term decline in the number of eggs laid on the Sarawak Turtle Islands, from a high of about 3,000,000 in the mid-1930s to between 138,741 and 309,800 annually between 1975 and 1985.

In Middle America, Cornelius (1982) observed that "Nesting turtles are rarely killed by coastal residents of the Pacific, as most do not consider the meat very good. In general, the Pacific coast populace do not have a strong marine component of their culture, except for the consumption of turtle eggs. This contrasts sharply with the Caribbean side of the isthmus, where sea turtles have traditionally been an important dietary item." Zurita et al. (1992) describe the history of the turtle fishery in Quintana Roo, Mexico. The turtle fishery and the consumption of sea turtles on the Guajira Peninsula, Colombia, are discussed by Rueda-Almonacid et al. (1992).

Chelonia mydas, as well as other species of sea turtles, have been implicated in several cases of turtle poisoning (chelonitoxication). One case of poisoning, resulting in 14 fatalities in the Philippines in 1917, was supposedly due to a green turtle (de Celis 1982). Silas and Fernando (1984) cited three instances (in 1840, 1977 and 1983) of green turtle chelonitoxication in Sri Lanka and India which resulted in 27 deaths. Halstead (1988) and Halstead et al. (1990) list the green turtle as being sometimes poisonous to eat in some localities. Most sea turtle chelonitoxications have occurred in the Indo-West Pacific region. The origin of the turtle poison is unknown, but most likely is derived from the food chain. Turtle poisoning may result from ingestion of fat, flesh, viscera or blood. The symptoms vary with the amount ingested and the person, and symptoms develop within a few hours to several days after eating. Initial symptoms include nausea and vertigo, followed by lethargy, then, in severe cases, somnolence (Halstead, 1988). There are no known antidotes. There are no reliable external characteristics which differentiate a poisonous sea turtle from a harmless one.

6. PROTECTION AND MANAGEMENT

6.1 Regulatory Measures

Possibly one of the first conservation laws passed to protect green turtles was enacted in 1620 in the Bermuda Islands. The law prohibited the killing of turtles less than eighteen inches in breadth or diameter within five leagues of the land—the penalty for each offense being the forfeiture of fifteen pounds of tobacco (Garman 1884 in Carr 1952).

Several international agreements are now in existence wherein *Chelonia mydas* are afforded protection. Green turtles are listed in Appendix I of CITES (The Convention on International Trade in Endangered Species of Wild Fauna and Flora) and as such, international trade in the species and their products and derivatives is prohibited except under exceptional circumstances. Wells and Barzdo (1991) discuss how marine turtles have benefited from CITES controls. All marine turtles are listed in Class A of the Annex to the African Convention (The African Convention on the Conservation of Nature and Natural Resources), which means that sea turtles are totally protected throughout the territories of the Parties and take is allowed only in special circumstances. All sea turtles are listed in Appendix I or II of the Bonn Convention (The Convention on the Conservation of Migratory Species of Wild Animals) which provides the framework for the conservation of migratory species. In addition to according full protection for endangered species, Parties to the Bonn Convention are obliged to prohibit the taking of endangered species during their migrations, beyond national jurisdiction, on the high seas (Hykle 1992).

Under the United Nations Convention on the Law of the Sea signatory coastal states have control over natural resources within their 200 nautical mile exclusive economic zones. Since most green turtle feeding habitats are within 200 nautical miles of the coast, much international cooperation will be needed to manage green turtle populations that migrate between feeding habitats in one country's jurisdiction to nesting beaches in another (see Fig. 14). According to the U. N. Convention on the Law of the Sea, anadromous species on the high seas are the domain of nations that sustain them in their natal habitat (Van Dyke 1993). While not anadromous, this principle may also apply to green turtles. At least, it should give countries that host natal habitats some leverage over the high seas fishery.

The "Rio Summit" (United Nations Conference on Environment and Development, 1 - 12 June 1992, Rio de Janeiro) focused worldwide attention on global environmental issues and a convention on protecting biodiversity was signed by 153 nations. As mentioned in section 1.2.2, all green turtle populations are important because they represent genetic diversity and the population is the evolving unit in nature. Management plans and recovery plans should revolve around this independent nature of populations and metapopulations. The preservation of genetic diversity was one of the cornerstones of the I.U.C.N.'s (1980) "World Conservation Strategy", and the conservation of genetic, species and ecosystem diversities is promulgated in the successor "Caring for the Earth" (I.U.C.N./U.N.E.P./W.W.F. 1991).

Indirect protection of sea turtles is provided by such international agreements as the London Dumping Convention (The International Convention on the Prevention of Marine Pollution by Dumping of Wastes and Other Matter) and the MARPOL protocol (the International Convention for the Prevention of Pollution from Ships). There is a significant body of international and regional laws which prohibit the discharge of plastic debris into the oceans (Joyner and Frew 1991).

On a regional level, UNEP's (United Nations Environment Program) Regional Seas Program fosters regional cooperation of shared natural resources and seeks to control pollution. The regional programs are shaped according to the needs of the nations in the region. Two such programs are SPREP (The South Pacific Regional Environmental Programme) and the Cartagena Convention (The Convention for the Protection and Development of the Marine Environment of the Wider Caribbean Region).

Groombridge (1990) describes how the conservation of Mediterranean marine turtles is a regional problem, and he lists the international agreements that Mediterranean nations have ratified. All marine turtles in the Mediterranean Sea are listed in Appendix II of the Bern Convention (The Convention on the Conservation of European Wildlife and Natural Habitats), which requires contracting Parties to take measures to protect listed species. Demetropoulos and Hadjichristophorou (1995) have authored a beautifully illustrated manual that provides practical information for marine turtle conservation in the Mediterranean Sea. Miller et al. (1989) describe the critical habitats of marine turtles in Saudi Arabia and they

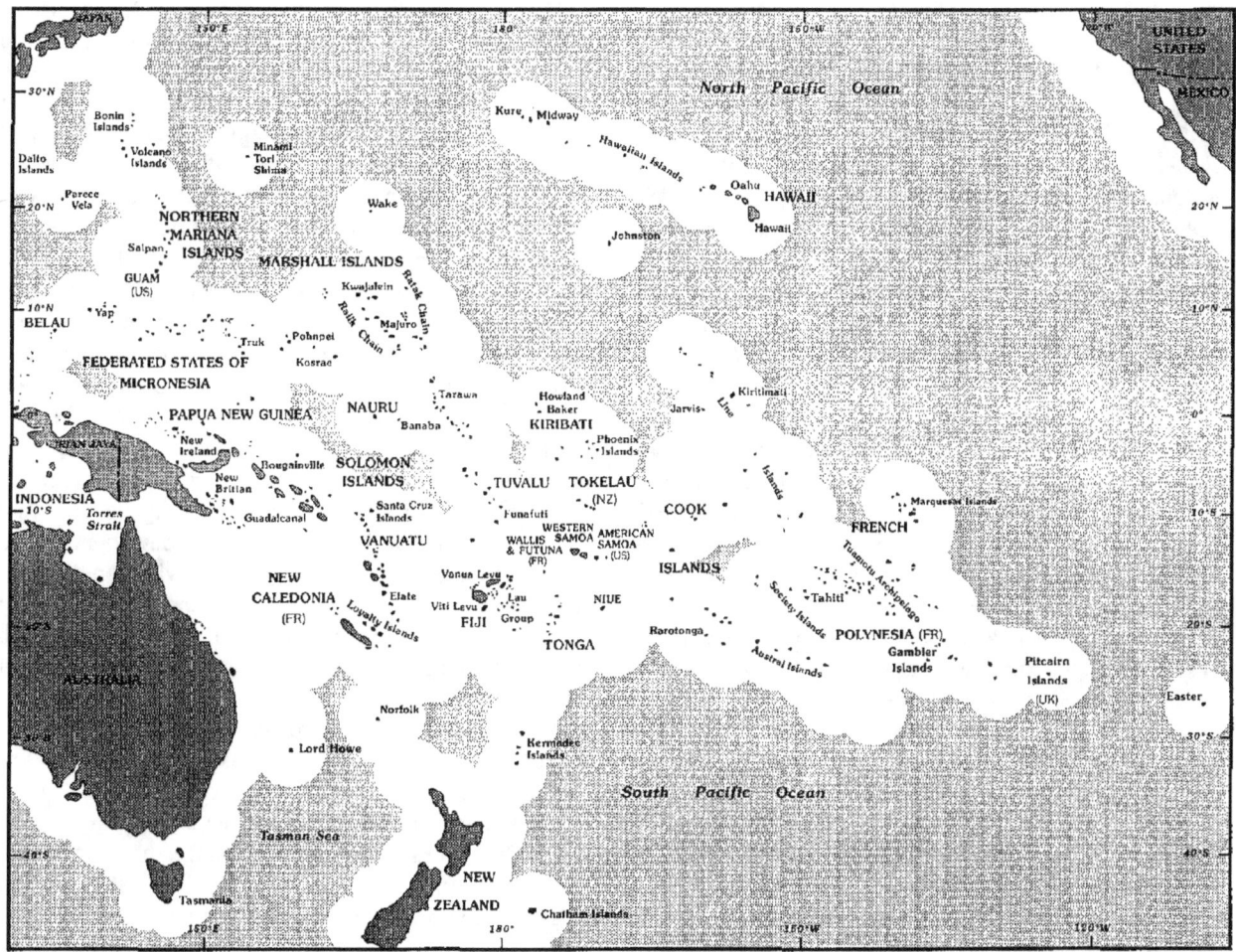

Fig. 14. Pacific islands exclusive economic zones, illustrating how regional cooperation here, and elsewhere, is necessary for the conservation of green turtles and other migratory fauna. From Shannon, S. and J. R. Morgan. 1993. Management of insular Pacific marine ecosystems. Pages 196-213 *in* E. M. Borgese, N. Ginsburg and J. R. Morgan (eds.), Ocean Yearbook 10. University of Chicago Press, Chicago. Copyright 1993 by The University of Chicago.

give recommendations for the conservation of turtles there.

There are many regulations pertaining to green turtles at the national level. The following list of countries and territories, where green turtles occur, have some form of regulations protecting sea turtles and/or their eggs (from Navid 1982; Groombridge and Luxmoore 1989; Hirth 1993; and updated as to CITES to June 1996). Some regulations do not refer to sea turtles as such but refer to testudines or reptiles or, in a few cases, products of fisheries. Also, a few countries listed do not have regulations pertaining to sea turtles or reptiles, but are listed because green turtles occur in their territories and they are signatories to CITES and thus have obligations for marine turtles (Note: as of 10 June 1996 there were 132 party countries to CITES not all of which, of course, harbor green turtles, but all have obligations on the trade in sea turtles). A signatory country, or association with a sig-

natory to CITES, is indicated by an asterisk in the following list. Needless to say, enforcement of regulations in many areas is difficult at best. The list of countries/territories: American Samoa*, Angola, Anguilla, Antigua and Barbuda, Argentina*, Aruba, Ascension and St. Helena*, Australia*, Bahamas*, Bangladesh*, Barbados*, Belize*, Benin*, Bermuda*, Brazil*, British Indian Ocean Territories*, British Virgin Islands*, Brunei Darussalem*, Burma, Cameroon*, Canada*, Canary Islands*, Cayman Islands*, Chile*, China*, Colombia*, Costa Rica*, Cuba*, Cyprus*, Djibouti*, Dominica*, Dominican Republic*, Ecuador*, Egypt*, El Salvador*, Equatorial Guinea*, Eritrea*, Federated States of Micronesia*, Fiji, French Guiana*, French Polynesia, Gabon*, Gambia*, Ghana*, Greece*, Grenada and the Grenadian Grenadines, Guadeloupe*, Guam*, Guatemala*, Guinea*, Guinea Bissau*, Guyana*, Haiti, Hawaii*, Honduras*, Hong

Kong*, India*, Indonesia*, Iran*, Israel*, Italy*, Ivory Coast, Jamaica, Japan*, Kenya*, Kiribati, Korea*, Liberia*, Madagascar*, Madeira and Azores*, Malaysia*, Maldives, Malta*, Marshall Islands*, Martinique*, Mauritania, Mauritius and dependencies*, Mayotte, Mexico*, Montserrat*, Mozambique*, Namibia*, Netherlands*, Netherlands Antilles, New Caledonia*, New Zealand*, Nicaragua*, Nigeria*, Northern Marianas*, Oman, Pakistan*, Palau*, Panama*, Papua New Guinea*, Peru*, Philippines*, Pitcairn Island*, Portugal*, Puerto Rico*, Reunion and Iles Eparses*, Senegal*, Seychelles*, Sierra Leone*, Singapore*, Solomon Islands, Somalia*, South Africa*, Spain*, Sri Lanka*, St. Kitts - Nevis, St. Lucia*, St. Vincent and the St. Vincent Grenadines*, Sudan*, Suriname*, Tanzania*, Thailand*, Togo*, Tokelau, Tonga, Trinidad and Tobago*, Tunisia*, Turkey, Turks and Caicos Islands, Tuvalu, United Arab Emirates*, United States of America*, U.S. Pacific Islands*, U.S. Virgin Islands*, Uruguay*, Vanuatu*, Venezuela*, Wallis and Futuna*, and Zaire*.

In the U.S.A., *Chelonia mydas* (including *agassizi*) was listed (under the Endangered Species Act of 1973) in 1978 as a threatened species, but the breeding populations in Florida and on the Pacific coast of Mexico were listed as endangered. Under this listing, it is unlawful for any person subject to the jurisdiction of the U.S. to possess, sell, import or export endangered or threatened species unless under special circumstances and with a permit. The U.S. National Marine Fisheries Service has jurisdiction for sea turtles while the turtles are in the sea, and the U.S. Fish and Wildlife Service has jurisdiction for sea turtles when they are on land. The Act provides means whereby the ecosystems upon which the endangered and threatened species depend can be conserved. Details of the listing and current regulations can be found in the Code of Federal Regulations (1992). This is one of the most significant pieces of conservation legislation ever enacted in the U.S.A.

In the U.S.A., marine turtles are afforded direct and indirect protection under such laws as the Marine Protection, Research and Sanctuaries Act, the Coastal Zone Management Act, the Clean Water Act, and the Oil Pollution Act.

6.2 Management Strategies

There are several management options applicable to green turtles. The author is of the opinion that the least manipulative strategies are the best (see also Ehrenfeld 1982). The strategies are covered under categories of habitat preservation and restoration; enforcement of international, regional and national regulations; education; recovery plans; reduction of incidental catch; and manipulative techniques. The relative importance of these strategies will vary geographically.

Habitat preservation and restoration: One of the best management strategies is to direct efforts to preserve the natural quality of the critical habitats of the species: the nesting beaches, internesting habitat, epipelagic habitat and the developmental and feeding habitats. This may include, among other things, gazetting nesting beaches and adjacent internesting habitat as nature reserves with complete protection for adults, eggs and hatchlings (eggs should be left in place to incubate and hatchlings should be allowed to crawl to the sea); cleaning-up anthropogenic debris on the beach; controlling human activity and lights on the beach during the nesting season; and mitigating effects of pollution in the feeding and epipelagic habitats (see sections 4.3.2 and 4.4.2 for factors affecting reproduction and survival). Conservation of any one green turtle population almost certainly will require regional cooperation. The protection of nesting beaches and internesting habitat is critical because development and urbanization of the coastal zone is growing rapidly. According to the World Resources Institute (1994) "Coastal urban populations are expected to increase globally, with the most dramatic increases expected in Asia, Africa and South America."

Visible effects of egg protection may not be seen for decades considering the time it takes for green turtles to attain reproductive maturity and assuming that they return to their natal beach. Even then the benefits may be difficult to access because of natural fluctuations in numbers of nesters.

Protected nesting colonies will attract ecotourists, and, when properly conducted with involvement of local people, ecotourism can be a potent force for conservation. Some aspects of Florida's turtle watch program, designed specifically for watching nesting loggerheads on Florida's beaches, are appropriate for other ecotourism programs (Johnson et al. 1996a, b). The Florida program includes guidelines for size of groups, positioning of group around nesting turtle, and prohibition of flash photography. Results of this program indicate that nesters being watched spend significantly less time camouflaging nest sites than control turtles, but that hatching success and hatchling emergence success were not significantly different between nests of watched and control turtles. Zurita et al. (1993) and Taft (1996) briefly describe some of the problems associated with increased tourism at sea turtle sites. Ecotourists are not only attracted to nesting turtles and hatchlings crawling to the sea. For some, scuba diving to observe and photograph turtles in their marine habitat is a main attraction. Jones and Shimlock (1994) briefly describe the popularity of diving off Sipadan Island (Malaysia) and Sangalakki Island (Indonesia) to observe green turtles. In some places where it is imperative to restrict access and preserve the nesting habitat (core area) and all nesters and eggs, preservation may be more easily achieved by establishing buffer zones around the core area where some human activity is allowed, as exemplified by the biosphere reserve concept of UNESCO. Under this concept the area managed for biodiversity extends beyond the core boundaries.

People living near the nesting beaches must be involved in the conservation strategies regarding the nesting population and eggs. The local people are the ultimate stewards of green turtle genetic diversity. Where complete protection of the nesters and eggs is not justified, long-range, sustainable yield programs, focused on local needs and customs, are warranted. The Wildlife Management Area (WMA) concept, as practiced in Papua New Guinea, is one model of this kind of stewardship. A WMA is an area where traditional owners of the land and offshore water control the conservation of the habitat and its natural resources (Kwapena 1982; Spring 1982c; Eaton 1988; Carew-Reid 1990). Long Island in Papua New Guinea has been designated a WMA, and it is designed to protect the marine turtles from overexploitation (Eaton 1985). There are numerous examples in Latin America and in the Caribbean area describing how local communities are involved in the management of protected areas and natural resources. One example is Tortuguero National Park, in Costa Rica, where park staff have begun a process of local community involvement which may lead to mutual partnership (Barzetti 1993). Local people can also be the most effective force in combating poaching. Tambiah (1995) has shown how a sea turtle conservation program should be integrated into the larger necessity of natural resource management. Such a strategy is being developed in Guyana. Brief accounts of sea turtle conservation in the national parks of Venezuela and the conservation efforts of the Brazilian TAMAR project are given by Guada and Vernet (1995) and Baptistotte (1995) respectively. References to other conservation practices are cited in section 5.

Nietschmann (1973, 1982) described the subsistence patterns of Miskito hunters in the Nicaraguan feeding habitats before and after commercialization, the conclusion being that, in general, exploitation of green turtles for subsistence is much less a threat to their survival than is market exploitation. The Caribbean Conservation Corporation's Miskito Coast Protected Area plan is laudable because it encompasses not only conservation of green turtle feeding habitat, but conservation of multispecies in the ecosystem (Anon 1993a).

Venizelos (1991) describes the efforts of MEDASSET (Mediterranean Association to Save the Sea Turtles), a non-government organization, in the conservation of Mediterranean marine turtles. Argano (1992) discusses some of the efforts to conserve marine turtles in Italian waters. Conservation efforts on the Kazanli Beach in Turkey include educating the local people on the general

biology and conservation of green turtles, beach clean-up campaigns and the rescue of hatchlings disoriented by nearby factory, village, campsite and car lights (Society for the Protection of Nature, 1992).

The conservation programs of Mexican sea turtles have been summarized by Márquez et al. (1990). Mexico operates about 10 sea turtle camps (not all for green turtle) on the Gulf of Mexico and Caribbean shores, and about 25 sea turtle camps on the Pacific coast for the study of and conservation of marine turtles (Gonzalez-de-la-Vega et al., 1993-94). In an essay on possible lines of future research on Mexican sea turtles, Benabib (1992) discusses the need for research on basic biologic parameters as well as on conservation and management programs. The Mexican Sea Turtle Information and Data Base Center (BITMAR) continuously inventories and updates the databases of its nesting sites and thus is a valuable source of information for turtle researchers and governmental policy makers (Briseño-Dueñas and Abreu-Grobois 1994).

Boza (1993) has described the history of the National Parks system in Costa Rica, including Tortuguero National Park (established in 1970). He reports on the current status of the parks, and he describes some plans for the future. Like some conservation leaders in other countries, he advocates fewer outside consultants and more support for environmental action at the grass-roots level.

Enforcement of international, regional and national regulations: There are a large number of regulations dealing with management and conservation of marine turtles (see preceding section). The problem is that many rules are not enforced. Education can help with this problem. Conservation agendas, with adequate funding and resolve, in the platform of political parties can also help. Realistic environmental impact statements and realistic recovery plans can aid enforcement.

Education: Public education, at all levels, promoting a conservation ethic can be a very effective management strategy. There is a rapidly-growing awareness among people everywhere of their responsibility in the stewardship of natural resources (Fig. 15).

Conservation education can take many forms: publications, formal instruction at all levels in schools, informal volunteerism programs, governmental and non-governmental conservation agencies, ecotourism, and media events. The education should emphasize long-term habitat conservation, importance of biodiversity, regional cooperation, and reasons for regulations. Where possible, hands-on learning experiences are recommended. Volunteers have proven valuable in monitoring nesting beaches in Florida (Hoffman and Conley 1987).

Conservation and education can be promoted with the issuing of postage stamps and currency depicting sea turtles. Linsley and Balazs (1994) mention that as of 1 January 1994, 90 countries and territories have issued 416

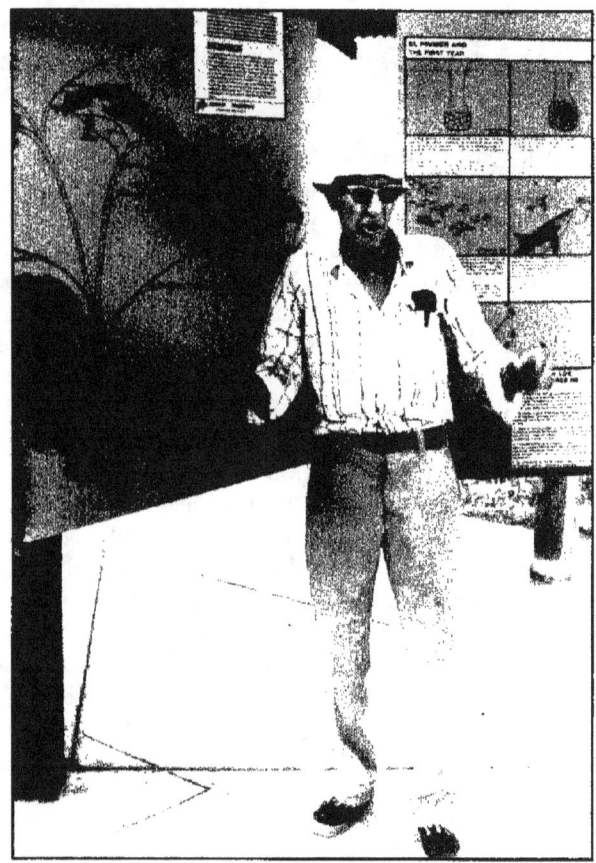

Fig. 15. Dr. Archie Carr (1909-1987) discussing migrations of the green turtle at the kiosk in Tortuguero National Park, Costa Rica, in 1983.

stamps portraying marine turtles. Green turtles are featured on 123 stamps.

Conservation alerts, as well as any other important, timely information, can now be transmitted to educators and scientists in many countries through electronic highways.

Recovery plans: Recovery plans focus attention on the critical areas of sea turtle recovery, but they must go further than providing only paper protection and recovery. Scientists, educators, legal officers, government and non-government personnel can help facilitate converting recovery plans into action plans.

The recovery plan for the United States populations of the Atlantic green turtle (National Marine Fisheries Service and U.S. Fish and Wildlife Service, 1991) recommends six major actions to achieve recovery: provide long-term protection on important nesting beaches; ensure at least 60 percent hatch on major nesting beaches; implement effective lighting ordinances on nesting beaches; determine distribution and seasonal movements for all life

stages in the marine environment; minimize mortality from commercial fisheries; and reduce threat to population and foraging habitat from marine pollution.

Comprehensive sea turtle recovery plans have been prepared for several countries: Antigua and Barbuda (Fuller et al. 1992); Barbados (Horrocks 1992); British Virgin Islands (Eckert et al. 1992); Netherlands Antilles (Sybesma 1992); St. Kitts and Nevis (Eckert and Honebrink 1992); Aruba (Barmes et al. 1993); Suriname (Reichart and Fretey 1993); and St. Vincent and the Grenadines (Scott and Horrocks 1993).

Reduction of incidental catch: Mortality from incidental take in shrimp trawls, gill nets, beach seines, trammel nets and longlines can be high in some places (section 4.4.2). Incidental capture of sea turtles on a global scale was reviewed by Hillestad et al. (1982). Andrew and Pepperell (1992) briefly review the design of fishing gear that allows by-catch, especially turtles and fin-fishes, to escape.

As mentioned in section 4.4.2, Magnuson et al. (1990) stated that in U.S. waters, shrimp trawling was the primary cause for sea turtle mortality caused by humans and they recommend the use of TEDs. All U.S. shrimp trawlers are required to use TEDs by December 1994 (Crouse 1993a). All Mexican shrimp trawlers operating in the Gulf of Mexico and the Caribbean are required to use TEDs commencing April 1993 (Crouse 1993b). Other countries operating commercial shrimp trawlers in the Gulf of Mexico, Caribbean and Western Atlantic now use, or are encouraged to use, TEDs (briefly reviewed by Gibbons-Fly et al. 1994; Steiner 1994; Steiner et al. 1995).

Crouse et al. (1992) summarized the current results of the use of TEDs in U.S. waters by illustrating how the 1990 and 1991 shrimp catch in the Gulf of Mexico and the 1991 shrimp catch off South Carolina were actually higher than in some previous years when TEDs were not required; that claims for gear loss and damage have declined since the advent of TEDs; that in 1990-1991 there were no reported injuries associated with TEDs; and strandings of drowned sea turtles have been dramatically lower during periods when TEDs were required. They state how the TED experience is a dramatic example of how balance can be achieved between the conservation of endangered/threatened sea turtles and the socioeconomics of the shrimping industry.

In a study conducted from March 1988 to August 1990 from North Carolina to Texas, investigators determined that there was no significant difference in shrimp CPUE (catch-per-unit-effort) between standard nets and nets equipped with Super Shooter TEDs with a funnel, but that there was a mean loss in shrimp CPUE of 3.6% and 13.6% with nets equipped with, respectively, Georgia TEDs with funnels and Georgia TEDs without funnels (Renaud et al. 1993b). In the northwestern Gulf of Mexico, Caillouet et al. (1996) found that TED regulations in force in 1990-1993 did not diminish the statistical relationship between sea turtle strandings (5 species combined, including green turtles, but mostly loggerheads and Kemp's ridleys) and shrimp fishing intensities, despite a reduction in total strandings. They offer several hypotheses to explain the continued statistical association including failure of TED's to eject turtles, turtle stress in passing through trawls, violations of TED regulations and nonshrimping causes of strandings. Mitchell et al. (1995) describe the latest advancements in TED technology, with emphasis on methods of improving TED performance for shrimp retention.

Magnuson et al. (1990) provide an annotated, chronological list of educational efforts on TED usage for fishermen by the U.S. National Marine Fisheries Service and by U.S. Sea Grant Institutions from 1977 to 1989.

Manipulative techniques: When or where eggs are subject to excessive erosion, predation, or poaching, the eggs may be carefully reburied in nearby sites or reburied in a central, protected hatchery. Each of these procedures has limitations (see Pritchard et al. 1983; Mortimer 1992). Special consideration must be given to the fact that transplanted eggs may produce unnatural sex ratios through TSD. Because the mechanisms of imprinting remain unknown, and because there may be sound, although unrecognized, ecological reasons for the absence of sea turtle nesting colonies in many areas, it is inadvisable at this time to attempt to establish new nesting colonies by mass transplanting of eggs. The problem of hybridization between translocated individuals and local individuals also needs to be taken into consideration (Carr and Dodd 1983).

Headstarting is the raising of hatchlings to a size at which they are presumed to have greater survivorship before releasing them into their natural habitat. Large-scale headstarting experiments are not recommended. A thirty-year headstart program in Florida has revealed some good information on survival and growth rates of captive-reared individuals (Witham 1980, 1991), but no more releases are planned until there is evidence of nesting by headstarted turtles (Huff 1989). The captive rearing part of the Kemp's ridley headstart project involving the U.S.A. and Mexico was terminated in 1993 (Byles 1993). Magnuson et al. (1990) recommend evaluating headstarting experiments along four criteria: survival and growth of headstarted turtles; nesting of headstarted turtles on a natural beach; nesting of enough turtles to contribute to the maintenance or recovery of the population; and demonstration that a headstarted turtle is more likely to survive and reproduce than one released as a hatchling. There is as yet no indication of success regarding the last three criteria in any headstart project. Frazer (1992) characterized headstarting as a form of "halfway technology" —i.e., an inappropriate technological response which does not address the real causes of sea turtle mortality. In a later article, Frazer (1994) discusses the roles of headstarting and egg hatcheries in terms of the goals of the management programs. Some population models which evaluate headstarting as a management tool are cited in section 4.5.

7. MARICULTURE

Ranching and farming are two types of green turtle mariculture. Ranching involves the raising of individuals in semi- or complete captivity for a period of time, after which they are slaughtered for meat and products (e. g., skin, polished shells). The sources of the stock are eggs or hatchlings from natural populations. Sometimes the eggs taken are so-called "doomed eggs" (those laid below the berm) and sometimes the hatchlings taken are from daytime emergences (supposedly subject to high bird predation). The take of wild stock is sometimes offset by releasing some captive-reared young turtles into the sea. The degree of sophistication of ranching can range from cottage-level husbandry to high technology, land-based factories. Bonnet et al. (1985a), LeGall (1985), Le Bourdiec (1987), Groombridge and Luxmoore (1989) and Derand (1994) describe the operation of the Réunion Island green turtle ranch. Evidently, commercial operations at the Reunion ranch are to be phased-out over the next five years (Patel 1995). At its meeting in Florida, USA, in November 1994, CITES approved a set of guidelines concerning proposals for ranching sea turtles (CITES Secretariat 1995). Major components of the guidelines include implementation of national and regional turtle management plans and strict requirements for control of the trade in sea turtles.

A sea turtle farm is a self perpetuating population in an artifical habitat. The only large farm in existence is Cayman Turtle Farm (1983) Ltd. on Grand Cayman Island, British West Indies. Aspects of the farm have been described by Wood and Wood (1980), Groombridge and Luxmoore (1989) and Wood (1991). Some of these aspects are: eggs are incubated in styrofoam boxes; turtles are fed a commercially-prepared pelleted diet and the turtles are moved through a series of tank sizes as they grow; turtles grow to a processing weight of about 24 kg after 3-4 years; and products of the farm are meat, skins, oil, soup products and shell. Wood and Wood (1990) reported that F_2 hatchlings have been produced on the farm. According to Schroeder (1995) this F_2 generation is almost certainly intraspecific hybrid. Some of the health-related problems at the Cayman Turtle Farm are addressed by Jacobson (1996).

Ranching and farming schemes have their proponents and opponents. In addition to the descriptions and activities of the ranch and farm referenced to in the preceding two paragraphs, Brongersma (1980) was of the opinion that turtle farms and well-controlled turtle ranches may lessen the pressure on wild populations. Reichert (1982) stated how captive rearing can benefit conservation by providing the economic incentive to protect wild populations (the sources of eggs or hatchlings for the schemes) and by incorporating headstart programs into the operational schemes a predetermined number of captive-reared animals are released into the sea at regular intervals. Hughes (1989) briefly described how the nesting grounds on Tromelin and Europa Islands are protected and how by taking hatchlings from daytime emergences for stock for the Réunion ranch that this is conservation operating in accord with the World Conservation Strategy. Groombridge and Luxmoore (1989) suggested that the transfer of local populations from CITES Appendix I to Appendix II for the purposes of ranching should be considered on the basis of individual proposals. But this suggestion was challenged by Ehrenfeld (1990). Mrosovsky (1983) was of the opinion that the issue of turtle farming has been much overemphasized.

Opponents of commercial turtle mariculture state how turtle farming is severely limited by the biology of the turtles themselves; that commercial aquaculture could stimulate global markets which in turn would stimulate proliferation of farms or ranches, or could provoke poaching of natural populations; how the business of turtle mariculture encourages the marketing of farmed and ranched products for the luxury trade which then undermines local conservation laws; how the business may lead to ill-conceived "conservation" activities; how headstarted animals do not substitute for wildstock taken because there is no evidence that they survive and reproduce in adequate numbers or that they join their natural populations; and, how the intentional or unintentional release of cultured turtles might lead to hybridization of green turtle populations (Ehrenfeld 1974, 1980, 1982; Dodd 1982b; Carr and Dodd 1983; Donnelly 1994).

In the preface to their book on the history of the Cayman Turtle Farm, Fosdick and Fosdick (1994) state "From the outset, our mission was to present a fair, accurate, and balanced discussion of this critical issue." Among the subjects they discuss are the establishment of the Farm, the philosophy behind "conservation through commerce," the conflict with some conservationists, and the current situation on the Farm.

8. REFERENCES

Abdellatif, E. M. 1993. Factors threatening the marine and coastal environment of the Red Sea in Sudan: a call for attention. Sudanese Environment Conservation Society, 31 pp., Office Business Co. Ltd. (OBCO), Khartoum, Sudan.

Ackerman, R. A. 1980. Physiological and ecological aspects of gas exchange by sea turtle eggs. Amer. Zool. 20(3): 575-583.

Ackerman, R. A. 1981a. Oxygen consumption by sea turtle (*Chelonia, Caretta*) eggs during development. Physiol. Zool. 54(3): 316-324.

Ackerman, R. A. 1981b. Growth and gas exchange of embryonic sea turtles (*Chelonia, Caretta*) Copeia 1981(4): 757-765.

Ackerman, R. A., R. C. Seagrave, R. Dmi'el and A. Ar. 1985. Water and heat exchange between parchment-shelled reptile eggs and their surroundings. Copeia 1985(3): 703-711.

Ackman, R. G., T. Takeuchi and G. H. Balazs. 1992. Fatty acids in depot fats of green turtles *Chelonia mydas* from the Hawaiian Islands and Johnston Atoll. Comp. Biochem. Physiol. 102B(4): 813-819.

Adipati, E. and M. Patay. 1983. Investigations on marine turtles and their nesting sites on beaches of the Kepala Burung, Irian Jaya. WWF/IUCN Conservation Programme in Irian Jaya, Project 1528: 1-13, Jayapura, Indonesia.

Agardy, M. T. 1990. Preliminary assessment of the impacts of Hurricane Hugo on sea turtle populations of the eastern Carribbean. Pages 63-65 *in* T. H. Richardson, J. I. Richardson and M. Donnelly (compilers), Proceedings of the tenth annual workshop on sea turtle biology and conservation. NOAA Tech. Memo. NMFS-SEFC-278, 286 pp.

Agardy, M. T. 1991. Conserving sea turtles while building an ecotourism industry in Guinea Bissau, West Africa. Pages 3-6 *in* M. Salmon and J. Wyneken (compilers). Proceedings eleventh annual workshop on sea turtle biology and conservation. NOAA Tech. Memo. NMFS-SEFSC-302, 195 pp.

Aguirre, A. A., G. H. Balazs, B. Zimmerman and F. D. Galey. 1994a. Organic contaminants and trace metals in the tissues of green turtles (*Chelonia mydas*) afflicted with fibropapillomas in the Hawaiian Islands. Marine Pollution Bull. 28(2); 109-114.

Aguirre, A. A., G. H. Balazs, B. Zimmerman and T. R. Spraker. 1994b. Evaluation of Hawaiian green turtles (*Chelonia mydas*) for potential pathogens associated with fibropapillomas. J. Wildlife Diseases 30(1): 8-15.

Aguirre, A., A., G. H. Balazs, B. Zimmerman and T. R. Spraker. 1994c. Fibropapillomas in the Hawaiian green turtle: research update. Page 2 *in* K. A. Bjorndal, A. B. Bolten, D. A. Johnson and P. J. Eliazar (compilers), Proceedings of the fourteenth annual symposium on sea turtle biology and conservation. NOAA Tech. Memo. NMFS-SEFSC-351, 323 pp.

Aguirre, A., A., G. H. Balazs, T. R. Spraker and T. S. Gross. 1995. Adrenal and hematological responses to stress in juvenile green turtles (*Chelonia mydas*) with and without fibropapillomas. Physiol. Zool. 68(5): 831-854.

Aitken, R. N. C. and S. E. Solomon. 1976. Observations on the ultrastructure of the oviduct of the Costa Rican green turtle (*Chelonia mydas* L.) J. Exp. Mar. Biol. Ecol. 21(1): 75-90.

Aitken, R. N. C., S. E. Solomon and E. C. Amoroso. 1976. Observations on the histology of the ovary of the Costa Rican green turtle, *Chelonia mydas* L. J. Exp. Mar. Biol. Ecol. 24(2): 189-204.

Albrecht, P. W. 1976. The cranial arteries of turtles and their evolutionary significance. J. Morphology 149(2): 159-182.

Allard, M. W., M. M. Miyamoto, K. A. Bjorndal, A. B. Bolten and B. W. Bowen. 1994. Support for natal homing in green turtles from mitochondrial DNA sequences. Copeia 1994(1): 34-41.

Allen, G. A. 1974. The marine crocodile, *Crocodylus porosus*, from Ponape, Eastern Caroline Islands, with notes on food habits of crocodiles from the Palau Archipelago. Copeia 1974(2): 553.

Allison, V. F., R. W. Webster, Jr., J. E. Ubelaker and J. M. Riddle. 1973. Redescription of *Porrocaecum sulcatum* (Rudolphi, 1819) from the sea turtle *Chelone mydas*. Trans. Amer. Micros. Soc. 92(2): 291-297.

Alvarado, J. and A. Figueroa. 1986. The ecological recovery of sea turtles of Michoacan, Mexico. Special Attention: the black turtle (*Chelonia agassizi*). Final report. U. S. Fish and Wildlife Service, Albuquerque, New Mexico, 51 pp.

Alvarado, J. and A. Figueroa. 1990. The ecological recovery of sea turtles of Michoacan, Mexico. Special attention: the black turtle *Chelonia agassizi*. Final report 1989-1990, U. S. Fish and Wildlife Service, Albuquerque, New Mexico, 97 pp.

Alvarado, J. and A. Figueroa. 1991. Comportamiento reproductivo de la tortuga negra *Chelonia agassizi*. Ciencia y Desarrollo 17(98):43-49.

Alvarado, J. and A. Figueroa. 1992. Recapturas post-anidatorias de hembras de tortuga marina negra (*Chelonia agassizi*) marcadas en Michoacan, Mexico. Biotropica 24(4): 560-566.

Alvarado, J., A. Figueroa and H. Gallardo. 1985. Ecologia y conservacion de las tortugas marinas de Michoacan, Mexico. Escuela de Biologia, Universidad Michoacana de San Nicolas de Hidalgo, Morelia, Michoacan, Mexico, 44 pp.

Alvarado, J., A. Figueroa, C. Delgado, M. T. Sanchez and E. Lopez. 1993. Differential retention of metal and plastic tags on the black sea turtle (*Chelonia agassizi*). Herp. Review 24(1): 23-24.

Andrew, N. L. and J. G. Pepperell. 1992. The by-catch of shrimp trawl fisheries. Pages 527-565 *in* M. Barnes, A. D. Ansell and R. N. Gibson (eds.), Oceanography and Marine Biology Annual Review, Vol. 30, University College London Press, U. K., 627 pp.

Anon. 1969. CAWM students survey coast. African Wildlife News 4(3): 9-10.

Anon. 1982. Lost island. Oryx 16(5): 400.

Anon. 1987. Yearly change in the composition and size of the assemblage of nesting female green turtles at Tortuguero. Page 4 *in* Velador: Newsletter of the Caribbean Conservation Corporation. Winter 1987. Caribbean Conservation Corporation, Gainesville, Florida, 6 pp.

Anon. 1989. Rapport mission d'observation: du 9 au 17 Janvier 1989, tortues marines et oiseaux de mer, Iles Surprise et Huon (Récifs de' Entrecasteaux). Assoc. Sauvegarde Nature Néo-Caledonienne, 20 pp.

Anon. 1991a. 17. Hawaiian green turtle. Pages 65-67 *in* R. Neal, S. Smith and L. Vlymen (eds.), Status of Pacific oceanic living marine resources of interest to the USA for 1991. U. S. Dept. of Commerce, NOAA Tech. Memo. NOAA-TM-NMFS-SWFSC-165, 78 pp.

Anon. 1991b. Tortuguero tag return summary. Page 4 *in* Velador: Newsletter of the Caribbean Conservation Corporation. Summer 1991. Caribbean Conservation Corporation, Gainesville, Florida, 4 pp.

Anon. 1993a. CCC and U. S. AID form a $1.3 million team to protect the Miskito Coast. Pages 1, 2 *in* Velador: News-letter of the Caribbean Conservation Corporation. Spring 1993. Caribbean Conservation Corporation, Gainesville, Florida, 8 pp.

Anon. 1993b. Coastal development threatens the Archie Carr National Wildlife Refuge. Pages 1, 3 *in* Velador: News-letter of the Caribbean Conservation Corporation . Spring 1993. Caribbean Conservation Corporation, Gainesville, Florida, 8 pp.

Anon. 1994a. Long distance migration of green sea turtles from Pulau Redang tracked by satellites. Marine Turtle Newsletter 66: 5-6.

Anon. 1994b. Transmitters keeping tabs on high-tech turtle trio. Pages 1, 12 *in* Velador: Newsletter of the Caribbean Conservation Corporation. Fall 1994. Caribbean Conservation Corporation, Gainesville, Florida, 12 pp.

Anon. 1995a. Solving the mystery: where do Florida green turtles migrate? Page 6 *in* Velador: Newsletter of the Caribbean Conservation Corporation. Fall 1995. Caribbean Conservation Corporation, Gainesville, Florida, 8 pp.

Anon. 1995b. Satellite technology offers first glimpse at the migratory patterns of Caribbean male turtles. Page 7 *in* Velador: Newsletter of the Caribbean Conservation Corporation. Fall 1995. Caribbean Conservation Corporation, Gainesville, Florida, 8 pp.

Arauz-Almengor, M. and R. Morera-Avila. 1994. Status of the marine turtles *Dermochelys coriacea, Chelonia agassizi* and *Lepidochelys olivacea* at Playa Naranjo, Parque Nacional Santa Rosa, Costa Rica. Page 175 *in* K. A. Bjorndal, A. B. Bolten, D. A. Johnson and P. J. Eliazar (compilers), Proceedings of the fourteenth annual symposium on sea turtle biology and conservation. NOAA Tech. Memo. NMFS-SEFSC-351, 323 pp.

Argano, R. 1992. Tartarughe marine e foca monaca nei mari Italiani: salvaguardia e prospettive. Boll. Mus. Ist. Biol. Univ. Genova 56-57: 113-135.

Autar, L. 1994. Sea turtles attacked and killed by jaguars in Suriname. Marine Turtle Newsletter 67: 11-12.

Avise, J. C. and B. W. Bowen. 1994. Investigating sea turtle migration using DNA markers. Current Opinion in Genetics and Development 4 (6): 882-886.

Avise, J. C., B. W. Bowen, T. Lamb, A. B. Meylan and E. Bermingham. 1992. Mitochondrial DNA evolution at a turtle's pace: evidence for low genetic variability and reduced microevolutionary rate in the Testudines. Molecular Biology and Evolution 9(3): 457-473.

Awbrey, F. T., S. Leatherwood, E. D. Mitchell and W. Rogers. 1984. Nesting green sea turtles (*Chelonia mydas*) on Isla Clarión, Islas Revillagigedos, Mexico. Bull. Southern Calif. Acad. Sci. 82 (2): 69-75.

Bachère, E. 1981. Le caryotype de la tortue verte, *Chelonia mydas* L. dans l' Océan Indien (Canal du Mozambique). Comptes Rendus Acad. Sci. Paris 292(21): 1129-1131.

Bacon, P. R., F. Berry, K. Bjorndal, H. Hirth, L. Ogren and M. Weber (eds.). 1984. Proceedings of the Western Atlantic Turtle Symposium. Vol. 3: The national reports. U. Miami Press, Miami, Florida, 514 pp.

Bainbridge, J. S., Jr. 1991. Five weeks on a magnet. Audubon 93(1): 72-81.

Baird, T. and S. E. Solomon. 1979. Calcite and aragonite in the egg shell of *Chelonia mydas* L. J. Exp. Mar. Biol. Ecol. 36(3): 295-303.

Balazs, G. H. 1975. Marine turtles in the Phoenix Islands. Atoll Res. Bull. 184: 1-7.

Balazs, G. H. 1980. Synopsis of biological data on the green turtle in the Hawaiian Islands. NOAA Tech. Memo. NMFS, Honolulu, Hawaii, 141 pp.

Balazs, G. H. 1982a. Growth rates of immature green turtles in the Hawaiian Archipelago. Pages 117-125 in K. A. Bjorndal (ed.), Biology and conservation of sea turtles. Smithsonian Institution Press, Washington, D. C., 583 pp.

Balazs, G. H. 1982b. Status of sea turtles in the Central Pacific Ocean. Pages 243-252 in K. A. Bjorndal (ed.), Biology and conservation of sea turtles. Smithsonian Institution Press, Washington, D. C., 583 pp.

Balazs, G. H. 1983a. Recovery records of adult green turtles observed or originally tagged at French Frigate Shoals, Northwestern Hawaiian Islands. NOAA-TM-NMFS-SWFC-36, 42 pp.

Balazs, G. H. 1983b. Sea turtles and their traditional usage in Tokelau. Atoll Res. Bull. 279: 1-30.

Balazs, G. H. 1985a. Status and ecology of marine turtles at Johnston Atoll. Atoll Res. Bull. 285: 1-46.

Balazs, G. H. 1985b. Impact of ocean debris on marine turtles: entanglement and ingestion. Pages 387-429 in R. S. Shomura and H. O. Yoshida (eds.), Proceedings of the workshop on the fate and impact of marine debris. NOAA Tech. Memo. NMFS-SWFC-54.

Balazs, G. H. 1986. Ontogenetic changes in the plastron pigmentation of hatchling Hawaiian green turtles. J. Herpetology 20(2): 280-282.

Balazs, G. H. 1995. Innovative techniques to facilitate field studies of the green turtle, Chelonia mydas. Pages 158-161 in J. I. Richardson and T. H. Richardson (compilers), Proceedings of the twelfth annual workshop on sea turtle biology and conservastion. NOAA Tech. Memo. NMFS-SEFSC-361, 274 pp.

Balazs, G. H., W. C. Dudley, L. E. Hallacher, J. P. Coney and S. K. Koga. 1994b. Ecology and cultural significance of sea turtles at Punalu'u, Hawaii. Pages 10-13 in K. A. Bjorndal, A. B. Bolten, D. A. Johnson and P. J. Eliazar (compilers), Proceedings of the fourteenth annual symposium on sea turtle biology and conservation. NOAA Tech. Memo. NMFS-SEFSC-351, 323 pp.

Balazs, G. H., R. G. Forsyth and A. K. H. Kam. 1987. Preliminary assessment of habitat utilization by Hawaiian green turtles in their resident foraging pastures. NOAA-TM-NMFS-SWFC-71, 107 pp.

Balazs, G. H., R. Fujioka and C. Fujioka 1993. Marine turtle faeces on Hawaiian beaches. Marine Pollution Bull. 26(7): 392-394.

Balazs, G. H., R. K. Miya and M. A. Finn. 1994a. Aspects of green turtles in their feeding, resting, and cleaning areas off Waikiki Beach. Pages 15-18 in B. A. Schroeder and B. E. Witherington (compilers), Proceedings of the thirteenth annual symposium on sea turtle biology and conservation. NOAA Tech. Memo. NMFS-SEFSC-341, 281 pp.

Balazs, G. H. and S. G. Pooley (eds.). 1991. Research plan for marine turtle fibropapilloma. NOAA Tech. Memo. NMFS-SWFSC-156, 113 pp.

Balazs, G. H. and E. Ross. 1974. Observations on the basking habit in the captive juvenile Pacific green turtle. Copeia 1974(2): 542-544.

Balazs, G. H., P. Siu and J.-P. Landret. 1995. Ecological aspects of green turtles nesting at Scilly Atoll in French Polynesia. Pages 7-10 in J. I. Richardson and T. H. Richardson (compilers), Proceedings of the twelfth annual workshop on sea turtle biology and conservation. NOAA Tech. Memo. NMFS-SEFSC-361, 274 pp.

Baldwin, J., E. Gyuris, K. Mortimer and A. Patak. 1989. Anaerobic metabolism during dispersal of green and loggerhead turtle hatchlings. Comp. Biochem. Physiol. 94A(4): 663-665.

Baptistotte, C. 1995. A clarification on the activities of Project TAMAR, Brazil. Chelonian Conservation and Biology 1(4): 328-329.

Baran, I., S. H. Durmus, and M. K. Atatür. 1991. On Chelonia mydas (L.) (Reptilia: Chelonia) population of Mersin-Kazanli region. Doga-Tr. J. Zoology 15: 185-194.

Barmes, T., K. L. Eckert and J. Sybesma. 1993. WIDECAST sea turtle recovery action plan for Aruba (K. L. Eckert ed.). CEP Tech. Report No. 25. UNEP Caribbean Environment Programme, Kingston, Jamaica, 58 pp.

Barr, C. 1992. Current status of trade and legal protection of sea turtles in Indonesia. Pages 11-13 in M. Salmon and J. Wyneken (compilers), Proceedings of the eleventh annual workshop on sea turtle biology and conservation. NOAA Tech. Memo. NMFS-SEFSC-302, 195 pp.

Barragán, A. R. 1994. Notes on the cardiovascular anatomy of a juvenile black turtle (Chelonia mydas agassizi). Pages 19-21 in B. A. Schroeder and B. E. Witherington (compilers), Proceedings of the thirteenth annual symposium on sea turtle biology and conservation. NOAA Tech. Memo. NMFS-SEFSC-341, 281 pp.

Barzetti, V. (ed.). 1993. Parks and progress: protected areas and economic development in Latin America and the Caribbean. IUCN-The World Conservation Union, Washington D. C., 240 pp.

Basso, R. 1992. Osservazioni e ricerche sulle tartarughe marine presenti nei mari italiani. Edizioni del GRIFO, Lecce, Italy, 72 pp.

Bauer, A. M. and J. V. Vindum. 1990. A checklist and key to the herpetofauna of New Caledonia, with remarks on biogeography. Proc. Calif. Acad. Sci. 47 (2): 17-45.

Beavers, S. C., E. R. Cassano and R. A. Byles. 1992. Stuck on turtles: preliminary results from adhesive studies with satellite transmitters. Pages 135-138 in M. Salmon and J. Wyneken (compilers), Proceedings of the eleventh annual workshop on sea turtle biology and conservation. NOAA Tech. Memo. NMFS-SEFSC-302, 195 pp.

Bellini, C., M. A. Marcovaldi, T. M. Sanches, A. Grossman, and G. Sales. 1996. Atol das Rocas biological reserve: second largest Chelonia rookery in Brazil. Marine Turtle Newsletter 72: 1-2.

Bels, V. L. and S. Renous. 1992. Kinematics of feeding in two marine turtles (Chelonia mydas and Dermochelys coriacea). Proc. Sixth Ord. Gen. Meet. S. E. H., Budapest 1991: 73-78.

Benabib, M. 1992. Posibles lineas de investigacion sobre tortugas marinas en Mexico. Pages 51-58 in M. Benabib and L. Sarti (eds.), Memorias del VI encuentro interuniversitario sobre tortugas marinas. Publ. Soc. Herpetologica Mexicana No. 1, 96 pp.

Berger, K. J. E. 1991. The impacts of South China Sea oil spills on the environment of Palawan. The Philippine Scientist 28 (1991): 27-54.

Berkson, H. 1966. Physiological adjustments to prolonged diving in the Pacific green turtle (Chelonia mydas agassizi). Comp. Biochem. Physiol. 18(1): 101-109.

Bhaskar, S. 1979. Sea turtle survey in the Andaman and

Nicobars. Hamadryad 4(3):2-26.

Bickham, J. W., K. A. Bjorndal, M. W. Haiduk and W. E. Rainey. 1980. The karyotype and chromosomal banding patterns of the green turtle (*Chelonia mydas*). Copeia 1980(3): 540-543.

Bjorndal, K. A. 1979. Cellulose digestion and volatile fatty acid production in the green turtle, *Chelonia mydas*. Comp. Biochem. Physiol. 63A: 127-133.

Bjorndal, K. A. 1980a. Nutrition and grazing behavior of the green turtle *Chelonia mydas*. Marine Biology 56: 147-154.

Bjorndal, K. A. 1980b. Demography of the breeding population of the green turtle, *Chelonia mydas*, at Tortuguero, Costa Rica. Copeia 1980(3): 525-530.

Bjorndal, K. A. (ed.), 1982a. Biology and conservation of sea turtles. Smithsonian Institution Press, Washington, D. C., 583 pp.

Bjorndal, K. A. 1982b. The consequences of herbivory for the life history pattern of the Caribbean green turtle, *Chelonia mydas*. Pages 111-116 *in* K. A. Bjorndal (ed.), Biology and conservation of sea turtles, Smithsonian Institution Press, Washington, D. C., 583 pp.

Bjorndal, K. A. 1985. Nutritional ecology of sea turtles. Copeia 1985(3): 736-751.

Bjorndal, K. A. and A. B. Bolten. 1988. Growth rates of immature green turtles, *Chelonia mydas*, on feeding grounds in the southern Bahamas. Copeia 1988(3): 555-564.

Bjorndal, K. A. and A. B. Bolten. 1992. Spatial distribution of green turtle (*Chelonia mydas*) nests at Tortuguero, Costa Rica. Copeia 1992(1): 45-53.

Bjorndal, K. A. and A. B. Bolten. 1995. Comparison of length-frequency analyses for estimation of growth parameters for a population of green turtles. Herpetologica 51(2): 160-167.

Bjorndal, K. A., A. B. Bolten and C. J. Lagueux. 1994. Ingestion of marine debris by juvenile sea turtles in coastal Florida habitats. Marine Pollution Bull. 28(3): 154-158.

Bjorndal, K. A. and A. B. Bolten, A. L. Coon Jr., and P. Kleiber. 1995. Estimation of green turtle (*Chelonia mydas*) growth rates from length-frequency analysis. Copeia 1995(1): 71-77.

Bjorndal, K. A. and A. Carr. 1989. Variation in clutch size and egg size in the green turtle nesting population at Tortuguero, Costa Rica. Herpetologia 45 (2): 181-189.

Bjorndal, K. A., A. B. Meylan and B. J. Turner 1983. Sea turtles nesting at Melbourne Beach, Florida, I. Size, growth and reproductive biology. Biol. Conserv. 26(1): 65-77.

Bjorndal, K. A., H. Suganuma and A. B. Bolten. 1991. Digestive fermentation in green turtles, *Chelonia mydas*, feeding on algae. Bull. Mar. Sci. 48(1): 166-171.

Blair, D. 1983. Paramphistomes (Digenea: Paramphistomidae) parasitic in marine turtles (Reptilia: Chelonia). Aust. J. Zool. 31: 851-867.

Blair, D. 1986. A revision of the subfamily Microscaphidiinae (Platyhelminthes: Digenea: Microscaphidiidae) parasitic in marine turtles (Reptilia: Chelonia). Aust. J. Zool. 34: 241-277.

Blair, D. 1987. A revision of the subfamily Octangiinae (Platyhelminthes: Digenea: Microscaphidiidae) parasitic in marine turtles (Reptilia: Chelonia). Aust. J. Zool. 35: 75-92.

Bocourt, M. F. 1868. Description de quelques chéloniens nouveaux appartenant à la faune mexicaine. Ann. Sci. Natur., Ser. 5, Zool. 10: 121-122.

Bolten, A. B. and K. A. Bjorndal. 1992. Blood profiles for a wild population of green turtles (*Chelonia mydas*) in the southern Bahamas: size-specific and sex-specific relationships. J. Wildlife Diseases 28(3): 407-413.

Bolten, A. B., K. A. Bjorndal, J. S. Grumbles and D. W. Owens. 1992. Sex ratio and sex-specific growth rates of immature green turtles, *Chelonia mydas*, in the southern Bahamas. Copeia 1992(4): 1098-1103.

Bonnet, B. (ed.) 1986. Les tortues marines daus les Iles du Sud-Ouest de l'Océan Indian. Rapport de l'Atelier Régional "Resources Biologiques Aquatiques de l'AIRDOI". Association des Institutions de Recherche et de Développement dans l'Océan Indien, St. Denis, Reunion, 69 pp.

Bonnet, B., J.-Y. Le Gall and G. Lebrun. 1985a. Tortues marines de la Reunion et des Iles Eparses. Universite de la Reunion, Institut Français de Recherches pour l' exploitation de la mer et Association pour le developpement de l'aquaculture, 24 pp.

Bonnet, B., P. Gendre and E. Bacherc. 1985b. Etude quantitative et ultrastructurale des thrombocytes de la tortue verte (*Chelonia midas* L.). C. R. Acad. Sci. Paris 301(3): 77-82.

Bons, J. and J. C. Bonaric. 1971. Description histologique de la "dent de l'eclosion" ou caroncule chez *Chelonia mydas* (L.). British J. Herp. 4(8): 202-206.

Booth, D. T. and M. B. Thompson. 1991. A comparison of reptilian eggs with those of megapode birds. Pages 325-344 *in* D. C. Deeming and M. W. J. Ferguson (eds.), Egg incubation: its effects on embryonic development in birds and reptiles. Cambridge Univ. Press, Cambridge, U. K., 448 pp.

Booth, J. and J. A. Peters. 1972. Behavioural studies on the green turtle (*Chelonia mydas*) in the sea. Anim. Behav. 20(4): 808-812.

Boulon Jr., R. 1984. The national report for the country of United States Virgin Islands. Pages 489-499 *in* P. Bacon, F. Berry, K. Bjorndal, H. Hirth, L. Ogren and M. Weber (eds.) Proc. Western Atlantic Turtle Symposium Vol 3, U. Miami Press, 514 pp.

Boulon, R. H., Jr., and N. B. Frazer. 1990. Growth of wild juvenile Caribbean green turtles. J. Herp. 24(4): 441-445.

Bourret,. R. 1941. Les tortues de l'Indochine. L'Institut Océanographique de L'Indochine. 235 pp.

Bowen, B. W. 1993-94. Evolutionary ecology and phylogeography of marine turtles. Second World Congress of Herpetology, Abstract, page 36, University of Adelaide, Adelaide, Australia.

Bowen, B. W. 1995. Tracking marine turtles with genetic markers. Bioscience 45(8): 528-534.

Bowen, B. W. and J. C. Avise. 1994. Tracking turtles through time. Natural History 103(12): 36-43.

Bowen, B. W. and J. C. Avise. 1996. Conservation genetics of marine turtles. Pages 190-237 *in* J. C. Avise and J. L. Hamrick (eds.), Conservation genetics: case histories from nature. Chapman and Hall, New York, 512 pp.

Bowen, B. W., A. B. Meylan and J. C. Avise. 1989. An odyssey of the green sea turtle: Ascension Island revisited. Proc. Natl. Acad. Sci. 86(2): 573-576.

Bowen, B. W., A. B. Meylan, J. P. Ross, C. J. Limpus, G. H. Balazs and J. C. Avise. 1992. Global population structure and natural history of the green turtle (*Chelonia mydas*) in terms of matriarchal phylogeny. Evolution 46(4): 865-881.

Bowen, B. W., W. S. Nelson and J. C. Avise. 1993. A molecular phylogeny for marine turtles: trait mapping, rate assessment, and conservation relevance. Proc. Nat. Acad. Sci. 90(12): 5574-5577.

Boza, M. A. 1993. Conservation in action: past, present, and future of the national park system of Costa Rica. Conservation Biology 7(2): 239-249.

Bradley, J. J. 1991. "Li-Maramaranja". Yanyuwa hunters of marine animals in the Sir Edward Pellew Group, Northern Territory. Records South Australia Museum. 25(1): 91-110.

Brattstrom, B. H. 1982. Breeding of the green sea turtle, *Chelonia mydas*, on the Islas Revillagigedo, Mexico. Herp. Review 13 (3): 71.

Brattstrom, B. H. and R. Collins. 1972. Thermoregulation. Int. Turtle and Tortoise Soc. J. 6(5): 15-19.

Brill, R. W., G. H. Balazs, K. N. Holland, R. K. C. Chang, S. Sullivan and J. C. George. 1995. Daily movements, habitat use, and submergence intervals of normal and tumor-bearing juvenile green turtles (*Chelonia mydas* L.) within a foraging area in the Hawaiian Islands. J. Exper. Mar. Biol. Ecol. 185(2): 203-218.

Briseño-Dueñas, R. and F. A. Abreu-Grobois. 1994. BITMAR's survey of sea turtle nesting beaches is part of new approaches to conservation in Mexico. Pages 198-201 *in* K. A. Bjorndal, A. B. Bolten, D. A. Johnson and P. J. Eliazar (compilers), Proceedings of the fourteenth annual symposium on sea turtle biology and conservation. NOAA Tech. Memo. NMFS-SEFSC-351, 323 pp.

Broadwell, A. L. 1992. Effects of beach renourishment on the survival of loggerhead sea turtle nests. Pages 21-23 *in* M. Salmon and J. Wyneken (compilers), Proceedings of the eleventh annual workshop on sea turtle biology and conservation. NOAA Tech. Memo. NMFS-SEFSC-302, 195 pp.

Brock, J. A., R. M. Nakamura, A. Y. Miyahara and E. M. L. Chang. 1976. Tuberculosis in Pacific green sea turtles, *Chelonia mydas*. Trans. Amer. Fish. Soc. 105(4): 564-566.

Brongersma, L. D. 1972. European Atlantic turtles. Zool. Verhand. Leiden, 121: 1-318.

Brongersma, L. D. 1980. Turtle farming and ranching. British Herpetological Soc. Bull. 2: 15-19.

Brongersma, L. D. 1982. Marine turtles of the eastern Atlantic Ocean. Pages 407-416 *in* K. A. Bjorndal (ed.) Biology and conservation of sea turtles. Smithsonian Institution Press, Washington, D. C., 583 pp.

Brongersma, L. D. and A. F. Carr. 1983. *Lepidochelys kempi* (Garman) from Malta. Proc. Konin. Neder. Akad. van Wetensch., Series C, 86(4): 445-454.

Brongniart, A. 1800. Essai d'une classification naturelle des reptiles. Bull. Sci. Soc. Philom. Paris 2(36): 89-91.

Brooke, Mde L. 1995. Seasonality and numbers of green turtles *Chelonia mydas* nesting on the Pitcairn Islands. Biological J. Linnean Soc. 56(1-2): 325-327.

Brooks, D. E., P. E. Ginn, T. R. Miller, L. Bramson and E. R. Jacobson. 1994. Ocular fibropapillomas of green turtles (*Chelonia mydas*). Vet. Pathol. 31: 335-339.

Broward County Erosion Prevention District. 1987. Sea turtle conservation project Broward County, Florida, 1987 Report. Broward County Environmental Quality Control Board, Ft. Lauderdale, Florida, 26 pp.

Brown, C. H. 1990. The significance of the South Atlantic Equatorial Countercurrent to the ecology of the green turtle breeding population of Ascension Island. J. Herpetology 24(1): 81-84.

Brown, C. H. and W. M. Brown. 1982. Status of sea turtles in the southeastern Pacific: emphasis on Peru. Pages 235-240 *in* K. A. Bjorndal (ed.), Biology and conservation of sea turtles, Smithsonian Institution Press, Washington, D. C., 583 pp.

Brown, L. and D. W. Macdonald. 1995. Predation on green turtle *Chelonia mydas* nests by wild canids at Akyatan Beach, Turkey. Biol. Conserv. 71(1): 55-60.

Bryant, R. M. 1986. 1985 marine turtle screening program at Canaveral National Seashore, Florida. CPSU Technical Report 20, Univ. of Georgia, Athens, Georgia, 17 pp.

Bull, J. J. and E. L. Charnov. 1989. Enigmatic reptilian sex ratios. Evolution 43(7): 1561-1566.

Burke, J. B. and L. J. Rodgers. 1982. Gastric ulceration associated with larval nematodes (*Anisakis sp.* Type 1) in pen reared green turtles (*Chelonia mydas*) from Torres Strait. J. Wildl. Diseases 18(1): 41-46.

Burke, R. L. 1993. Adaptive value of sex determination mode and hatchling sex ratio bias in reptiles. Copeia 1993 (3): 854-859.

Burnett-Herkes, J., H. C. Frick, D. C. Barwick and N. Chitty. 1984. Juvenile green turtles (*Chelonia mydas*) in Bermuda: movements, growth and maturity. Pages 250-251 *in* P. Bacon, F. Berry, K. Bjorndal, H. Hirth, L. Ogren and M. Weber (eds.), Proceedings of the Western Atlantic Turtle Symposium, Vol. 1, RSMAS Printing, Miami, Florida, 306 pp.

Bustard, H. R. 1966. Turtle biology at Heron Island. Australian Nat. Hist. 15 (8): 262-264.

Bustard, H. R. 1967. Mechanism of nocturnal emergence from the nest in green turtle hatchlings. Nature 214(5085): 217.

Bustard, H. R. 1970. The adaptive significance of coloration in hatchling green sea turtles. Herpetologica 26(2): 224-227.

Bustard, H. R. 1972. Sea turtles: Their natural history and conservation. W. Collins & Sons, London. 220 pp.

Bustard, R. 1973. Kay's turtles. Collins Sons Ltd., London, 128 pp.

Bustard, H. R. 1974. Barrier Reef sea turtle populations. Pages 227-234 *in* Proc. Second Int. Coral Reef Symposium 1. Great Barrier Reef Committee, Brisbane, Australia.

Bustard, H. R. 1976. Turtles of coral reefs and coral islands. Pages 343-368 *in* O. A. Jones and R. Endean (eds.), Biology and geology of coral reefs, Vol. 3, Biology 2, Academic Press, New York, 435 pp.

Bustard, H. R. and P. Greenham. 1969. Nesting behavior of the green sea turtle on a Great Barrier Reef island. Herpetologica 25(2): 93-102.

Bustard, H. R. and K. P. Tognetti. 1969. Green sea turtles: a discrete simulation of density-dependent population regulation. Science 163: 939-941.

Butler, P. J., W. K. Milsom and A. J. Woakes. 1984. Respiratory, cardiovascular and metabolic adjustments during steady state swimming in the green turtle, *Chelonia mydas*. J. Comp. Physiol. B (1984) 154: 167-174.

Byles, R. A. 1989. Development of a sea turtle satellite biotelemetry system. Page 311 *in* L. Ogren, F. Berry, K. Bjorndal, H. Kumpf, R. Mast, G. Medina, H. Reichart and R. Witham (eds.), Proceedings of the second western Atlantic turtle symposium. NOAA Tech. Memo. NMFS-SEFC-226, 401 pp.

Byles, R. 1993. Head-start experiment no longer rearing Kemp's ridleys. Marine Turtle Newsletter 63: 1-3.

Byles, R., J. Alvarado and D. Rostal. 1995. Preliminary analysis of post-mating movements of the black turtle *(Chelonia agassizi)* from Michoacan, Mexico. Pages 12-13 *in* J. I. Richardson and T. H. Richardson (compilers), Proceedings of the twelfth annual workshop on sea turtle biology and conservation. NOAA Tech. Memo. NMFS-SEFSC-361, 274 pp.

Byles, R. A. and J. A. Keinath. 1990. Satellite monitoring sea turtles. Pages 73-75 *in* T. H. Richardson, J. I. Richardson and M. Donnelly (compilers), Proceedings of the tenth annual workshop on sea turtle biology and conservation, NOAA Tech. Memo. NMFS-SEFC-278, 286 pp.

Caballero y Caballero, E. 1962. Trematodos de las tortugas de Mexico. X. Presencia de *Orchidasma amphiorchis* (Braun 1899) Looss, 1900 in una tortuga marina, *Chelone mydas,* de las costas del estado de Tamaulipas, Mexico. Anales del Instituto de Biologia (Univ. Mex.) 33(1-2): 47-55.

Caillouet, C. W. Jr., M. J. Duronslet, A. M. Landry Jr., D. B. Revera, D. J. Shaver, K. M. Stanley, R. W. Heinly and E. K. Stabenau. 1991. Sea turtle strandings and shrimp fishing effort in the northwestern Gulf of Mexico, 1986-89. Fish. Bull. 89(4): 712-718.

Caillouet, C. W. Jr., D. J. Shaver, W. G. Teas, J. M. Nance, D. B. Revera and A. C. Cannon. 1996. Relationship between sea turtle stranding rates and shrimp fishing intensities in the northwestern Gulf of Mexico: 1986-1989 versus 1990-1993. Fish. Bull. 94(2): 237-249.

Caldwell, D. K. 1962a. Sea turtles in Baja Californian waters (with special reference to those of the Gulf of California) and the description of a new subspecies of northeastern Pacific green turtle. Los Angeles Co. Mus. Contr. Sci. (61): 1-31.

Caldwell, D. K. 1962b. Carapace length-body weight relationship and size and sex ratio of the northeastern Pacific green sea turtle, *Chelonia mydas carrinegra.* Contrib. Sci. Los Angeles County Mus. 62: 3-10.

Caldwell, M. C. and D. K. Caldwell. 1962. Factors in the ability of the northeastern Pacific green turtle to orient toward the sea from the land, a possible coordinate in long-range navigation. Contrib. Sci. Los Angeles County Mus. 60: 1-27.

Campbell, C. L. 1994. The effects of flash photography on nesting behavior of green turtles *(Chelonia mydas)* at Tortuguero, Costa Rica. Pages 23-24 *in* K. A. Bjorndal, A. B. Bolten, D. A. Johnson and P. J. Eliazar (compilers), Proceedings of the fourteenth annual symposium or sea turtle biology and conservation. NOAA Tech. Memo. NMFS-SEFSC-351, 323 pp.

Campbell, T. W. 1996. Sea turtle rehabilitation. Pages 427-436 *in* D. R. Mader (ed.), Reptile medicine and surgery, W. B. Saunders Co., Philadelphia, 512 pp.

Camper, J. D. and J. R. Dixon. 1988. Evaluation of a microchip marking system for amphibians and reptiles. Texas Parks and Wildlife Dept., Research Publ. 7100-159, pp. 1-22.

Carew-Reid, J. 1990. Conservation and protected areas on South Pacific Islands: the importance of tradition. Environ. Conserv. 17: 29-38.

Carl, G. C. 1955. The green turtle in British Columbia. Report Provincial Museum Natural History and Anthropology, Victoria, British Columbia 1954: B77-78.

Carr, A. F. 1952. Handbook of turtles. The turtles of the United States, Canada, and Baja California. Cornell Univ. Press, Ithaca, New York, 542 pp.

Carr, A. 1965. The navigation of the green turtle. Scientific American 212(5): 79-86.

Carr, A. 1967a. So excellent a fishe: a natural history of sea turtles. Natural History Press, Garden City, N. Y., 249 pp.

Carr, A. 1967b. Imperiled gift of the sea. Nat. Geogr. 131(6): 876-890.

Carr, A. 1972a. The case for long-range chemoreceptive piloting in *Chelonia.* Pages 469-483 *in* S. R. Galler, K. Schmidt-Koenig, G. J. Jacobs and R. E. Belleville (eds.), Animal orientation and navigation. SP-262. National Aeronautics and Space Administration. Washington, DC, 606 pp.

Carr, A. 1972b. Great reptiles, great enigmas. Audubon 74(2): 24-35.

Carr, A. 1975. The Ascension Island green turtle colony. Copeia 1975(3): 547-555.

Carr, A. 1980. Some problems of sea turtle ecology. Amer. Zool. 20(3): 489-498.

Carr, A. 1982. Notes on the behavioral ecology of sea turtles. Pages 19-26 *in* K. A. Bjorndal (ed.), Biology and conservation of sea turtles. Smithsonian Institution Press, Washington, D. C., 583 pp.

Carr, A. 1983. *Chelonia mydas* (Tortugua, Tortuga Blanca, Green Turtle). Pages 390-392 *in* D. H. Janzen (ed.), Costa Rican Natural History. U. Chicago Press, 816 pp.

Carr, A. 1984. So excellent a fishe: a natural history of sea turtles. Revised edition. Charles Scribner's Sons, NY, 280 pp.

Carr, A. 1986. Rips, FADS, and little loggerheads. Bioscience 36(2): 92-100.

Carr, A. 1987a. New perspectives on the pelagic stage of sea turtle development. Conservation Biology 1(2): 103-121.

Carr, A. 1987b. Impact of nondegradable marine debris on the ecology and survival outlook of sea turtles. Marine Pollution Bull. 18(6B): 352-356.

Carr, A. and D. K. Caldwell. 1956. The ecology and migrations of sea turtles, 1. Results of fieldwork in Florida, 1955. Amer. Mus. Novitates No. 1793: 1-23.

Carr, A. and M. H. Carr. 1970a. Modulated reproductive periodicity in *Chelonia.* Ecology 51 (2): 335-337.

Carr, A. and M. H. Carr 1970b. Recruitment and remigration in a green turtle nesting colony. Biol. Conserv. 2: 282-284.

Carr, A. and M. H. Carr. 1972. Site fixity in the Caribbean green turtle. Ecology 53(3): 425-429.

Carr, A., M. H. Carr and A. B. Meylan. 1978. The ecology and migrations of sea turtles, 7. The West Caribbean green turtle colony. Bull. Amer. Mus. Nat. Hist. 162 (1): 1-46.

Carr, A. and P. J. Coleman. 1974. Seafloor spreading theory and the odyssey of the green turtle. Nature 249 (5453): 128-130.

Carr, A. and L. Giovannoli. 1957. The ecology and migrations of sea turtles, 2. Results of field work in Costa Rica, 1955. Amer. Mus. Novitates No. 1835, p. 1-32.

Carr, A. and D. Goodman. 1970. Ecologic implications of size and growth in *Chelonia.* Copeia 1970(4): 783-786.

Carr, A. and H. Hirth. 1961. Social facilitation in green turtle siblings. Animal Behaviour 9 (1-2): 68-70.

Carr, A. and H. Hirth. 1962. The ecology and migrations of sea turtles, 5. Comparative features of isolated green turtle colonies. Amer. Mus. Novitates 2091: 1-42.

Carr, A. and A. B. Meylan. 1980. Evidence of passive migration of green turtle hatchlings in Sargassum. Copeia 1980 (2):366-368.

Carr, A., A. Meylan, J. Mortimer, K. Bjorndal and T. Carr. 1982. Surveys of sea turtle populations and habitats in the Western Atlantic. NOAA Tech. Memo. NMFS-SEFC-91, 82 pp.

Carr, A. and L. Ogren. 1960. The ecology and migrations of sea turtles, 4. The green turtle in the Caribbean Sea. Bull. Amer. Mus. Nat. Hist. 121 (1): 1-48.

Carr, A. F. III and C. K. Dodd Jr. 1983. Sea turtles and the problem of hybridization. Pages 277-287 in C. M. Shonewald-Cox, S. M. Chambers, B. MacBryde and W. L. Thomas (eds.), Genetics and conservation: a reference for managing wild animal and plant populations. Benjamin/Cummings Publ. Co., Menlo Park, California, 722 pp.

Carr, T., and N. Carr. 1991. Surveys of the sea turtles of Angola. Biol. Conserv. 58(1): 19-29.

Center for Environmental Education. 1987. Plastics in the ocean: more than a litter problem. Center for Environmental Education, Washington D. C., 128 pp.

Chan, E. H. and H. C. Liew. 1988. A review on the effects of oil-based activities and oil pollution on sea turtles. Pages 159-167 in A. Sasekumar, R. D'Cruz and S. L. H. Lim (eds.), Thirty years of marine science research and development. Proceedings 11th annual seminar of the Malaysian Society of Marine Sciences, Kuala Lumpur, Malaysia.

Chan, E. H., H. C. Liew and A. G. Mazlan. 1988. The incidental capture of sea turtles in fishing gear in Terengganu, Malaysia. Biol. Conserv. 43(1): 1-7.

Chen, T. H. and I. J. Cheng. 1995. Breeding biology of the green turtle, Chelonia mydas, (Reptilia: Cheloniidae) on Wan-An Island, Peng-Hu Archipelago, Taiwan. I. Nesting ecology. Marine Biology 124(1): 9-15.

Cheong L. C. 1984. The national report for the country of Trinidad-Tobago. Pages 398-408 in P. Bacon, F. Berry, K. Bjorndal, H. Hirth, L. Ogren and M. Weber (eds.), Proc. Western Atlantic Turtle Symposium, Vol. 3, U. Miami Press, 514 pp.

Chester, A. J., J. Braun, F. A. Cross, S. P. Epperly, J. V. Merriner and P. A. Tester. 1994. AVHRR imagery and the near real-time conservation of endangered sea turtles in the western North Atlantic. Proceedings of the WMO/IOC Technical Conference on Space-Based Ocean Observations, September, 1993 (WMO/TD-No. 649), Bergen, Norway, pp. 184-189.

Chin, L. 1970. Notes on orang-utan and marine turtles. Sarawak Mus. J. 18 (36-37): 414-415.

Chin, L. 1971. Protected animals in Sarawak. Sarawak Mus. J. 19(38-39): 359-361.

CITES Secretariat. 1995. Convention on international trade in endangered species of wild fauna and flora (CITES). Ninth meeting of the conference of the parties, Fort Lauderdale (United States of America), 7 to 18 November 1994. Resolution of the conference of the parties. Guidelines for evaluating marine turtle ranching proposals submitted pursuant to resolution conf. 3.15. Marine Turtle Newsletter 69: 4-8.

Clark, D. R. Jr., and A. J. Krynitsky. 1980. Organochlorine residues in eggs of loggerhead and green sea turtles nesting at Merritt Island, Florida—July and August 1976. Pesticides Monitoring J. 14(1): 7-10.

Cliffton, K., D. O. Cornejo and R. S. Felger. 1982. Sea turtles of the Pacific coast of Mexico. Pages 199-209 in K. A. Bjorndal (ed.), Biology and conservation of sea turtles. Smithsonian Institution Press, Washington, D. C., 583 pp.

Cocteau, J. T. 1838. Reptiles de l'île de Cuba in R. de la Sagra, Historia fisica, politica y natural de la Isla de Cuba. IV. Reptiles y peces, Paris.

Code of Federal Regulations. 1992. Wildlife and Fisheries, Title 50, parts 1 to 199, revised as of October 1, 1992. Published by the Office of the Federal Register, U. S. Government Printing Office, Washington, D. C., 679 pp.

Cogger, H. G. 1992. Reptiles and Amphibians of Australia, Fifth edition. Cornell U. Press, Ithaca, NY, 775 pp.

Cogger, H. G., E. E. Cameron and H. M. Cogger. 1983. Amphibia and Reptilia, Vol. 1, Zoological Catalogue of Australia. Australian Government Publ. Service, Canberra, 313 pp.

Cogger, H. G. and D. A. Lindner. 1969. Marine turtles in Northern Australia. Australian Zoologist 15 (2): 150-159.

Coley, S. J. and A. C. Smart. 1992. The nesting success of green turtles on beaches at Kazanli, Turkey. Oryx 26 (3): 165-171.

Collard, S. B. 1992. Surface ocean fronts and the pelagic habitat of sea turtles: the question of food availability in non-frontal zones. Page 28 in M. Salmon and J. Wyneken (compilers), Proceedings of the eleventh annual workshop on sea turtle biology and conservation. NOAA Tech. Memo. NMFS-SEFSC-302, 195 pp.

Collazo, J. A., R. Boulon Jr., and T. L. Tallevast. 1992. Abundance and growth patterns of Chelonia mydas in Culebra, Puerto Rico. J. Herp. 26(3): 293-300.

Comuzzie, D. K. C. and D. W. Owens. 1990. A quantitative analysis of courtship behavior in captive green sea turtles (Chelonia mydas). Herpetologica 46(2): 195-202.

Congdon, J. D. 1989. Proximate and evolutionary constraints on energy relations of reptiles. Physiol. Zool. 62(2): 356-373.

Congdon, J. D., A. E. Dunham and R. C. Van Loben Sels. 1993. Delayed sexual maturity and demographics of Blanding's turtles (Emydoidea blandingii) : implications for conservation and management of long-lived organisms. Conservation Biology 7(4): 826-833.

Congdon, J. D., A. E. Dunham and R. C. Van Loben Sels. 1994. Demographics of common snapping turtles (Chelydra serpentina): implications for conservation and management of long-lived organisms. Amer. Zool. 34(3): 397-408.

Cooper, J. E. and O. F. Jackson (eds.). 1981a. Diseases of the reptilia. Vol. 1. Academic Press, N. Y., 383 pp.

Cooper, J. E. and O. F. Jackson (eds.). 1981b. Diseases of the reptilia. Vol. 2. Pages 387-584. Academic Press, N. Y.

Cornelius, S. E. 1976. Marine turtle nesting activity at Playa Naranjo, Costa Rica. Brenesia 8: 1-27.

Cornelius, S. E. 1982. Status of sea turtles along the Pacific coast of Middle America. Pages 211-219 in Biology and conservation of sea turtles, Smithsonian Institution Press, Washington D. C., 583 pp.

Cornelius, S. E. 1986. The sea turtles of Santa Rosa National Park. Fundacion de Parques Nacionales Costa Rica, 64 pp.

Coston-Clements, L. and D. E. Hoss. 1983. Synopsis of data on the impact of habitat alteration on sea turtles around the southeastern United States. NOAA Tech. Memo. NMFS-SEFC-117, 57 pp.

Coston-Clements, L., L. R. Settle, D. E. Hoss and F. A. Cross. 1991. Utilization of the *Sargassum* habitat by marine invertebrates and vertebrates—a review. NOAA Tech. Memo. NMFS-SEFSC-296, 32 pp.

Courtillot, V., and G. E. Vink. 1983. How continents break up. Scientific American 249(1): 43-49.

Cousteau, J. Y. 1971. Life and death in a coral sea. Doubleday Co., New York, 302 pp.

Coyne, M. S. and A. M. Landry Jr. 1994. Green sea turtle developmental habitat in south Texas. Page 51 *in* B. A. Schroeder and B. E. Witherington (compilers), Proceedings of the thirteenth annual symposium on sea turtle biology and conservation. NOAA Tech. Memo. NMFS-SEFSC-341, 281 pp.

Craig, P. 1994. Sea turtles migrate from American Samoa to Fiji. Marine Turtle Newsletter 66: 7-8.

Craig, P. and G. Balazs. 1995. Turtle travels from American Samoa to French Polynesia. Marine Turtle Newsletter 70: 5-6.

Crain, D. A., A. B. Bolten and K. A. Bjorndal. 1995. Effects of beach nourishment on sea turtles: review and research initiatives. Restoration Ecology 3(2): 95-104.

Crouse, D. 1993a. TEDs! At long last. Marine Conservation News 5(1): 1, 4.

Crouse, D. 1993b. TEDs in Mexico, too! Marine Conservation News 5(2): 4.

Crouse, D. T., L. B. Crowder and H. Caswell. 1987. A stage-based population model for loggerhead sea turtles and implications for conservation. Ecology 68 (5): 1412-1423.

Crouse, D. T., M. Donnelly, M. J. Bean, A. Clark, W. R. Irvin and C. E. Williams. 1992. The TED experience: claims and reality. Center for Marine Conservation, Environmental Defense Fund and National Wildlife Federation, Washington, DC, 17 pp.

Cuvier, G. L. C. F. D. 1829. Le Règne Animal. ed. 2, Paris, Détérville, 2, 406 pp.

Cuvier, G. L. C. F. D. 1832. Das Thierreich geordnet nach seiner Organization. Vol. 2. Die Reptilien und Fische enthaltend. F. U. Brodhous, Leipzig, 539 pp.

da Costa, R. S. 1969. Alguns dados biologicos da aruanã *Chelonia mydas* (Linnaeus), nas águas cearenses. Bol. Est. Pesca 9 (3): 21-34.

Dailey, M. D., M. L. Fast and G. H. Balazs. 1992. A survey of the trematoda (Platyhelminthes: Digenea) parasitic in green turtles, *Chelonia mydas* (L.) from Hawaii. Bull. Southern Calif. Acad. Sci. 91(2): 84-91.

Dailey, M. D., M. L. Fast and G. H. Balazs. 1993. *Hapalotrema dorsopora* sp. n. (Trematoda: Spirorchidae) from the heart of the green turtle (*Chelonia mydas*) with a redescription of *Hapalotrema postorchis*. J. Helminthol. Soc. Wash. 60(1): 5-9.

Dailey, M. D., and R. Morris. 1995. Relationship of parasites (Trematoda: Spirorchidae) and their eggs to the occurrence of fibropapillomas in the green turtle (*Chelonia mydas*). Canadian J. Fisheries and Aquatic Sci. 52(1): 84-89.

Daly, T. 1990. The development of a regional sea turtle program in the South Pacific. Pages 169-172 *in* T. H. Richardson, J. I. Richardson and M. Donnelly (compilers), Proceedings of the tenth annual workshop on sea turtle biology and conservation. NOAA Tech. Memo.

NMFS-SEFC-278, 286 pp.

D'Amato, A. F. and M. Marczwski. 1993. Aspectos da biologia de tartarugas marinhas (Cheloniidae) na região de Praia do Forte, Município de Mata de São João, Bahia, Brazil, durante o período reprodutivo 1990-1991. Arq. Biol. Tecnol. 36(3): 513-519.

Daniels, R. C., T. W. White and K. K. Chapman 1993. Sea-level rise: destruction of threatened and endangered species habitat in South Carolina. Environmental Management 17(3): 373-385.

Danielsson, B. 1956. Work and life on Raroia. George Allen and Unwin, London, 244 pp.

Daudin, F. M. 1801. Histoire naturelle, générale et particulière, des reptiles. Vol. 2. F. Dufart, Paris, 432 pp.

Davenport, J. 1989. Sea turtles and the greenhouse effect. British Herp. Soc. Bull. 29: 11-15.

Davenport, J., S. Antipas and E. Blake. 1989. Observations of gut function in young green turtles *Chelonia mydas* L. Herpetological J. 1(8): 336-342.

Davenport, J., G. Ingle and A. K. Hughes. 1982. Oxygen uptake and heart rate in young green turtles (*Chelonia mydas*). J. Zoology, London. 198(3): 399-412.

Davenport, J., S. A. Munks and P. J. Oxford. 1984. A comparison of the swimming of marine and freshwater turtles. Proc. Royal Soc. London B220(1220): 447-475.

Davenport J. and P. J. Oxford. 1984. Feeding, gut dynamics, digestion and oxygen consumption in hatchling green turtles (*Chelonia mydas* L.). British J. Herpetology 6(10): 351-358.

Davenport, J. and G. A. Pearson. 1994. Observations on the swimming of the Pacific ridley, *Lepidochelys olivacea* (Eschscholtz, 1829): comparisons with other sea turtles. Herpetological J. 4(2): 60-63.

Davenport, J. and C. R. Scott. 1993a. Individual growth and allometry of young green turtles (*Chelonia mydas* L.). Herpetological J. 3: 19-25.

Davenport, J. and C. R. Scott. 1993b. Individuality of growth, appetite, metabolic rate and assimilation of nutrients in young green turtles (*Chelonia mydas* L.) Herpetological J. 3: 26-31.

Dawes, C. J., E. D. McCoy and K. L. Heck Jr. 1991. The tropical western Atlantic including the Caribbean Sea. Pages 215-233 *in* A. C. Mathieson and P. H. Nienhuis (eds.), Ecosystems of the World 24, Intertidal and Littoral Ecosystems. Elsevier, Amsterdam, 564 pp.

de Celis, N. C. 1982. The status of research, exploitation, and conservation of marine turtles in the Philippines. Pages 323-326 *in* K. A. Bjorndal (ed.), Biology and conservation of sea turtles. Smithsonian Institution Press, Washington, D. C., 583 pp.

Delaugerre, M. 1987. Statut des tortues marines de la Corse (et de la Mediterrance). Vie Milieu 37(3/4): 243-264.

Demas, S., M. Duronslet, S. Wachtel, C. Caillouet and D. Nakamura. 1990. Sex-specific DNA in reptiles with temperature sex determination. J. Exp. Zoology 253: 319-324.

Demas, S. and S. Wachtel. 1991. DNA fingerprinting in reptiles: Bkm hybridization patterns in Crocodilia and Chelonia. Genome 34: 472-476.

Demetropoulos, A. and M. Hadjichristophorou. 1982. Turtle conservation in Cyprus. Bull. Biol. Soc. Cyprus (2): 23-28.

Demetropoulos, A. and M. Hadjichristophorou. 1995. Manual on marine turtle conservation in the Mediterranean.

UNEP (MAP) SPA/IUCN/CWS/Fisheries Dept., Manre (Cyprus), 77 pp.

Demetropoulos, A. and M. Lambert. 1986. Herpetology in Cyprus. British Herp. Soc. Bull. 17: 22-27.

den Hartog, C. 1970. The sea-grasses of the world. Verh. Konin. Nederl. Akad. Weten. Afd. Natuur. Tweede Reeks, 59(1): 1-275, North Holland Publ. Co., Amsterdam.

Derand, D. 1994. The "Coral Farm": farm for the fattening of marine turtles *Chelonia mydas* (the green turtle). Managing Company, The Societe Bourbonnaise d'Aquaculture (SBA), BP40-97436 Saint-Leu, Reunion Island (France, Indian Ocean), 31 pp.

Deraniyagala, P. E. P. 1939. The tetrapod reptiles of Ceylon. Vol. 1. Testudinates and crocodilians. Colombo Mus. Nat. Hist. Ser., Colombo, Ceylon, 412 pp.

Deraniyagala, P. E. P. 1956. Zoological collecting at the Maldives in 1932. Spolia Zeylanica 28: 7-16.

de Silva, G. S. 1969. Turtle conservation in Sabah. Sabah Soc. J. 5(1):6-26.

de Silva, G. S. 1970. Marine turtle conservation in Sabah. Ann. Rep. Res. Branch Forest Dept., 1969. Forest Dept., Sabah, Malaysia 1970: 125-136.

de Silva, G. S. 1982. The status of sea turtle populations in East Malaysia and the South China Sea. Pages 327-337 *in* K. A. Bjorndal (ed.), Biology and conservation of sea turtles. Smithsonian Institution Press, Washington, D. C, 583 pp.

de Silva, G. S. 1986. Turtle tagging and international tag returns for Sabah, East Malaysia. Sarawak Mus. J. 36(57): 263-271.

Despott, G. 1930. Herpetological Note: the green turtle (*Chelone mydas* Schw.). Bull. Museum Valletta 1: 80-82.

Dickerson, D. D., D. A. Nelson, M. Wolff and L. Manners. 1992. Summary of dredging impacts on sea turtles: King's Bay, Georgia and Cape Canaveral, Florida. Pages 148-151 *in* M. Salmon and J. Wyneken (compilers), Proceedings of the eleventh annual workshop on sea turtle biology and conservation. NOAA Tech. Memo. NMFS-SEFSC-302, 195 pp.

Didi, N. T. H. 1993. Sea turtles in the Maldives. Ministry of Fisheries and Agriculture of the Maldives, Male, 74 pp.

Dizon, A. E., and G. H. Balazs. 1982. Radio telemetry of Hawaiian green turtles at their breeding colony. Mar. Fish. Rev. 44(5): 13-20.

Dodd, C. K. Jr., 1982a. Nesting of the green turtle, *Chelonia mydas* (L.), in Florida: historic review and present trends. Brimleyana 7: 39-54.

Dodd, C. K. Jr., 1982b. Does sea turtle aquaculture benefit conservation? Pages 473-480 *in* K. A. Bjorndal (ed.), Biology and conservation of sea turtles. Smithsonian Institution Press, Washington D. C., 583 pp.

Dodd, C. K. Jr., 1995. Marine turtles in the Southeast. Pages 121-123 *in* E. T. LaRoe, G. S. Farris, C. E. Puckett, P. D. Doran and M. J. Mac (eds.), Our living resources: a report to the nation on the distribution, abundance, and health of the U. S. plants, animals, and ecosystems. National Biological Service, U. S. Dept. Interior, Washington D. C., 530 pp.

Dodd, C. K. Jr., and R. Byles. 1991. The status of loggerhead, *Caretta caretta*; Kemp's ridley, *Lepidochelys kempi*; and green, *Chelonia mydas*, sea turtles in U. S. waters: a reconsideration. Mar. Fish. Rev. 53(3): 30-31.

Domantay, J. S. 1952-1953. The turtle fisheries of the Turtle Islands. Bull. Fisheries Soc. Philippines 3-4: 3-27.

Donnelly, M. 1994. Sea turtle mariculture: a review of relevant information for conservation and commerce. Center for Marine Conservation, Washington D. C., 113 pp.

Doumenge, F. 1973. Development of the "turtle project" in French Polynesia. South Pacific Island Fisheries Newsletter 10: 37-39.

Drake, D. L. 1996. Marine turtle nesting, nest predation, hatch frequency, and nesting seasonality on the Osa Peninsula, Costa Rica. Chelonian Conservation and Biology 2(1): 89-92.

Dudley, S. F. J. and G. Cliff. 1993. Some effects of shark nets in the Natal nearshore environment. Environmental Biology of Fishes 36(3): 243-255.

Duméril, A. M. C. and G. Bibron. 1835. Erpétologie générale ou histoire naturelle complète des reptiles. Vol. 3. Librairie Encyclopedique de Roret, Paris, 680 pp.

Dunham, A. E., P. J. Morin and H. M. Wilbur. 1988. Methods for the study of reptile populations. Pages 332-386 *in* C. Gans and R. B. Huey (eds.), Biology of the Reptilia. Vol. 16, Ecology B: Defense and life history. A. R. Liss, Inc. N. Y. 659 pp.

Dunson, W. A. and F. J. Mazzotti. 1989. Salinity as a limiting factor in the distribution of reptiles in Florida Bay: a theory for the estuarine origin of marine snakes and turtles. Bull. Mar. Sci. 44 (1): 229-244.

Durako, M. J., W. J. Kenworthy, S. M. R. Fatemy, H. Valavi and G. W. Thayer. 1993. Assessment of the toxicity of Kuwait crude oil on the photosynthesis and respiration of seagrasses of the northern Gulf. Marine Pollution Bull. 27: 223-227.

Dupuy, A. R. 1986. The status of marine turtles in Senegal. Marine Turtle Newsletter 39: 4-7.

Dutton, P. and G. H. Balazs. 1995. Simple biopsy technique for sampling skin for DNA analysis of sea turtles. Marine Turtle Newsletter 69: 9-10.

Dutton, P. H., S. K. Davis, D. L. McDonald and T. Guerra. 1994. A genetic study to determine the origin of the sea turtles in San Diego Bay, California. Pages 55-56 *in* B. A. Schroeder and B. E. Witherington (compilers), Proceedings of the thirteenth annual symposium on sea turtle biology and conservation. NOAA Tech. Memo. NMFS-SEFSC-341, 28 pp.

Dutton, P. and D. McDonald. 1992. Tagging study of sea turtles in San Diego Bay, 1990-1991. Pages 35-38 *in* M. Salmon and J. Wyneken (compilers), Proceedings of the eleventh annual workshop on sea turtle biology and conservation. NOAA Tech. Memo. NMFS-SEFSC-302, 195 pp.

Dutton, P. and C. Whitmore. 1983. Saving doomed eggs in Suriname. Marine Turtle Newsletter 24: 8-10.

Dye, T. and D. W. Steadman. 1990. Polynesian ancestors and their animal world. Amer. Sci. 78(3): 207-215.

Dyer, W. G., E. H. Williams Jr. and L. Bunkley-Williams. 1991. Some digeneans (Trematoda) of the green turtle, *Chelonia mydas* (Testudines: Cheloniidae) from Puerto Rico. J. Helminthol. Soc. Wash. 58(2): 176-180.

Dyer, W. G., E. H. Williams Jr. and L. Bunkley-Williams. 1995. Digenea of the green turtle (*Chelonia mydas*) and the leatherback turtle (*Dermochelys coriacea*) from Puerto Rico. Caribbean J. Sci. 31(3-4): 269-273.

Eaton, P. 1985. Customary land tenure and conservation in Papua New Guinea. Pages 181-191 *in* J. A. McNeely and D. Pitt (eds.), Culture and conservation: the human dimension in environmental planning. Croom Helm, London, 308 pp.

Eaton, P. 1988. Reinforcing the land ethic: conservation and development through wildlife management areas. Pages 65-77 *in* P. J. Hughes and C. Thirlwall (eds.), The ethics of development: choices in development planning. Vol. 4, Univ. Papua New Guinea Press, Port Moresby, 300 pp.

Eckert, K. L. and T. D. Honebrink. 1992. WIDECAST sea turtle recovery action plan for St. Kitts and Nevis (K. L. Eckert, ed.). CEP Tech. Rep. No. 17. UNEP Caribbean Environment Programme, Kingston, Jamaica, 116 pp.

Eckert, K. L., J. A. Overing and B. B. Lettsome. 1992. WIDECAST sea turtle recovery action plan for the British Virgin Islands (K. L. Eckert, ed). CEP Technical Report No. 15. UNEP Caribbean Environment Programme, Kingston, Jamaica, 116 pp.

Edson, C. and F. Curren. 1987. Report from Oroluk. Marine Turtle Newsletter 41: 1-2.

Ehrenfeld, D. W. 1968. The role of vision in the sea-finding orientation of the green turtle (*Chelonia mydas*). 2. Orientation mechanism and range of spectral sensitivity. Animal Behaviour 16: 281-287.

Ehrenfeld, D. W. 1974. Conserving the edible sea turtle: can mariculture help? Amer. Sci. 62(1): 23-31.

Ehrenfeld, D. W. 1979. Behavior associated with nesting. Pages 417-434 *in* M. Harless and H. Morlock (eds.), Turtles: perspectives and research. John Wiley & Sons, New York, 695 pp.

Ehrenfeld, D. W. 1980. Commercial breeding of captive sea turtles: status and prospects. Pages 93-96 *in* J. B. Murphy and J. T. Collins (eds.), Reproductive biology and diseases of captive reptiles. Society for the study of amphibians and reptiles, Lawrence, Kansas, 277 pp.

Ehrenfeld, D. 1982. Options and limitations in the conservation of sea turtles. Pages 457-463 *in* K. A. Bjorndal (ed.), Biology and conservation of sea turtles. Smithsonian Institution Press, Washington D. C., 583 pp.

Ehrenfeld, D. W. 1990. The green turtle and hawksbill (Reptilia: Cheloniidae): world status, exploitation and trade. By B. Groombridge and R. Luxmoore. 1989. (Review). Copeia 1990(3): 898-900.

Ehrenfeld, D. W. and A. Carr. 1967. The role of vision in the sea-finding orientation of the green turtle (*Chelonia mydas*). Animal Behaviour 15: 25-36.

Ehrenfeld, J. G. and D. W. Ehrenfeld. 1973. Externally secreting glands of freshwater and sea turtles. Copeia 1973(2): 305-314.

Ehrenfeld, D. W. and A. L. Koch. 1967. Visual accomodation in the green turtle. Science 155 (3764): 827-828.

Ehrhardt, N. M. and R. Witham. 1992. Analysis of growth of the green sea turtle (*Chelonia mydas*) in the western central Atlantic. Bull. Mar. Sci. 50(2): 275-281.

Ehrhart, L. M. 1979a. Reproductive characteristics and management potential of the sea turtle rookery at Canaveral National Seashore, Florida. Pages 397-399 *in* R. M. Linn (ed.), Proceedings of the first conference on scientific research in the national parks, 9-12 November, 1976, New Orleans, LA. NPS Trans. Proc. Ser. No. 5.

Ehrhart, L. M. 1979b. Threatened and endangered species of the Kennedy Space Center. Vol. 5. Semi-annual report to the N. A. S. A., John F. Kennedy Space Center. Biomedical Office, Bioscience Operations, John F. Kennedy Space Center, Florida, 214 pp.

Ehrhart, L. M. 1982. A review of sea turtle reproduction. Pages 29-38 *in* K. A. Bjorndal (ed.), Biology and conservation of sea turtles. Smithsonian Institution Press, Washington, D. C., 583 pp.

Ehrhart, L. M. 1983. Marine turtles of the Indian River lagoon system. Florida Scientist 46 (3/4): 337-346.

Ehrhart, L. M. and W. E. Redfoot. 1995. Composition and status of the marine turtle assemblage of the Indian River lagoon system. Bull. Mar. Sci. 57(1): 279-280.

Ehrhart, L. M. and B. E. Witherington 1992. Green Turtle. Pages 90-94 *in* P. E. Moler (ed.), Rare and endangered biota of Florida. Vol. III. Amphibians and reptiles. Univ. Florida Press, Gainesville, 291 pp.

Eisentraut, M. 1964. Meeresschildkröten an der Küste von Fernando Poo. Natur und Museum 94: 471-475.

Encalada, S. E. 1994. Mitochondrial DNA structure of Atlantic green turtle nesting grounds. Pages 38-39 *in* K. A. Bjorndal, A. B. Bolten, D. A. Johnson and P. J. Eliazar (compilers), Proceedings of the fourteenth annual symposium on sea turtle biology and conservation. NOAA Tech. Memo. NMFS-SEFSC-351, 323 pp.

Engstrom, T. N. 1994. Observations on the testicular cycle of the green turtle, *Chelonia mydas*, in the Caribbean. Page 216 *in* K. A. Bjorndal, A. B. Bolten, D. A. Johnson and P. J. Eliazar (compilers), Proceedings of the fourteenth annual symposium on sea turtle biology and conservation. NOAA Tech. Memo. NMFS-SEFSC-351, 323 pp.

Epperly, S. P., J. Braun and A. J. Chester. 1995a. Aerial surveys for sea turtles in North Carolina inshore waters. Fish. Bull. 93(2): 254-261.

Epperly, S. P., J. Braun and A. Veishlow. 1995b. Sea turtles in North Carolina waters. Conservation Biology 9(2): 384-394.

Epperly, S. P., J. Braun and A. J. Chester, F. A. Cross, J. V. Merriner, and P. A. Tester. 1995c. Winter distribution of sea turtles in the vicinity of Cape Hatteras and their interactions with the summer flounder trawl fishery. Bull. Marine Sci. 56(2): 547-568.

Ernst, C. H. and R. W. Barbour. 1972. Turtles of the United States. University Press of Kentucky, Lexington, 347 pp.

Ernst, C. H. and R. W. Barbour. 1989. Turtles of the world. Smithsonian Institution Press, Washington, D. C., 313 pp.

Ernst, E. M. and C. H. Ernst. 1977. Synopsis of helminths endoparasitic in native turtles of the United States. Bull. Maryland Herp. Soc. 13(1): 1-75.

Ernst, C. H. and E. M. Ernst. 1979. Synopsis of protozoans parasitic in native turtles of the United States. Bull. Maryland Herp. Soc. 15(1): 1-15.

Ernst, C. H., J. E. Lovich and R. W. Barbour. 1994. Turtles of the United States and Canada. Smithsonian Institution Press, Washington, D. C., 578 pp.

Environmental Investigation Agency. 1995. Report on an investigation into threats to marine turtles in Sri Lanka and the Maldives. Environmental Investigation Agency, Washington, D.C., 28 pp.

Ewert, M. A., D. R. Jackson and C. E. Nelson. 1994. Patterns of temperature-dependent sex determination in turtles. J. Experimental Zoology 270(1):3-15.

Ewert, M. A. and C. E. Nelson. 1991. Sex determination in turtles: diverse patterns and some possible adaptive values. Copeia 1991(1): 50-69.

FAO. 1973. Report to the Government of the People's Democratic Republic of Yemen on marine turtle management, based on the work of H. F. Hirth and S. L. Hollingworth, marine turtle biologists. Rep. FAO/UNDP (TA), (3178), 51 pp.

Felger, R. S., K. Cliffton and P. J. Regal. 1976. Winter dormancy in sea turtles: independent discovery and exploitation in the Gulf of California by two local cultures. Science 191(4224): 283-285.

Felger, R. S. and M. B. Moser. 1985. People of the desert and sea: ethnobotany of the Seri Indians. U. Arizona Press, Tucson, 435 pp.

Fenchel, T. M. 1980. The protozoan fauna from the gut of the green turtle, *Chelonia mydas* L. with a description of *Balantidium bacteriophorus* sp. nov. Archiv. Protistenkunde 123(1): 22-26.

Fenchel, T. M., C. P. McRoy, J. C. Ogden, P. Parker and W. E. Rainey. 1979. Symbiotic cellulose degradation in green turtles, *Chelonia mydas* L. Applied and Environmental Microbiology 37(2): 348-350.

Ferreira, N. M. 1968. Sôbre a alimentação da aruanã, *Chelonia mydas* Linnaeus, ao longo da costa do estado do Ceará. Arq. Est. Biol. Mar. Univ. Fed. Ceará 8(1): 83-86.

Finley, J. 1984. The national report for the country of Grenada. Pages 184-196 *in* P. Bacon, F. Berry, K. Bjorndal, H. Hirth, L. Ogren and M. Weber (eds.) Proc. Western Atlantic Turtle Symposium, Vol. 3, U. Miami Press, 514 pp.

Fischer, K. 1964. Spontanes richtungsfinden nach dem sonnenstand bei *Chelonia mydas* L. (Suppenschildkröte). Naturwissenschaften 51(8): 203.

Fitzinger, L. J. 1843. Systema reptilium. Fasciculus primus. Amblyglossae. Braumüller and Seidel, Vienna, 106 pp.

Fitzsimmons, N. N., C. Moritz and S. S. Moore. 1993-94. Microsatellites in marine turtles: what they can tell us about species, populations and mating systems. Second World Congress of Herpetology, Abstract, page 88, University of Adelaide, Adelaide, Australia.

Fitzsimmons, N. N., C. Moritz, C. J. Limpus and S. S. Moore. 1994. Mating systems and male contribution to gene flow in marine turtles: preliminary evidence from microsatellite DNA analysis. Page 40 *in* K. A. Bjorndal, A. B. Bolten, D. A. Johnson and P. J. Eliazar (compilers), Proceedings of the fourteenth annual symposium on sea turtle biology and conservation. NOAA Tech. Memo. NMFS-SEFSC-351, 323 pp.

Fitzsimmons, N. N., C. Moritz and S. S. Moore. 1995a. Conservation and dynamics of microsatellite loci over 300 million years of marine turtle evolution. Molecular Biology and Evolution 12(3): 432-440.

Fitzsimmons, N. N., A. D. Tucker and C. J. Limpus. 1995b. Long-term breeding histories of male green turtles and fidelity to a breeding ground. Marine Turtle Newsletter 68: 2-4.

Fletemeyer, J. R. 1977. Rare albino turtle. Sea Frontiers 23: 233.

Fletemeyer, J. R. 1984a. The national report for the country of British Virgin Islands. Pages 70-117 *in* P. Bacon, F. Berry, K. Bjorndal, H. Hirth, L. Ogren and M. Weber (eds.), Proc. Western Atlantic Turtle Symposium, Vol. 3, Univ. Miami Press, 514 pp.

Fletemeyer, J. R. 1984b. The national report for the country of Turks-Caicos. Pages 409-422 *in* P. Bacon, F. Berry, K. Bjorndal, H. Hirth, L. Ogren and M. Weber (eds.), Proc. Western Atlantic Turtle Symposium, U. Miami Press,

514 pp.

Fontaine, C. T., T. D. Williams and J. D. Camper. 1987. Ridleys tagged with passive integrated transponder (PIT). Marine Turtle Newsletter 41: 6.

Forbes, G. A. 1994. The diet of the green turtle in an algalbased coral reef community—Heron Island, Australia. Pages 57-59 *in* B. A. Schroeder and B. E. Witherington (compilers), Proceedings of the thirteenth annual symposium on sea turtle biology and conservation. NOAA Tech. Memo. NMFS-SEFSC-341, 281 pp.

Forbes, G. A. and C. J. Limpus. 1993. A non-lethal method for retrieving stomach contents from sea turtles. Wildl. Res. 20: 339-343.

Fosberg, F. R. 1969. Observations on the green turtle in the Marshall Islands. Atoll Res. Bull. 135: 9-12.

Fosberg, F. R. 1990. A review of the natural history of the Marshall Islands. Atoll Res. Bull. 330: 1-100.

Fosberg, F. R., M-H Sachet and D. R. Stoddart. 1983. Henderson Island (Southeastern Polynesia): summary of current knowledge. Atoll Res. Bull. No. 272: 1-47.

Fosdick, P. D. and S. Fosdick. 1994. Last chance lost? Can and should farming save the green sea turtle? The story of Mariculture Ltd-Cayman Turtle Farm. Irvin S. Naylor, 100 Boxwood Lane, York, Pennsylvania 17402, USA, 338 pp.

Fowler, L. E. 1979. Hatching success and nest predation in the green sea turtle, *Chelonia mydas*, at Tortuguero, Costa Rica. Ecology 60 (5): 946-955.

Frair, W. 1977a. Turtle red blood cell packed volumes, sizes and numbers. Herpetologica 33: 167-190.

Frair, W. 1977b. Sea turtle red blood cell parameters correlated with carapace lengths. Comp. Biochem. Physiol. 56A: 467-472.

Frair, W. 1982. Serum electrophoresis and sea turtle classification. Comp. Biochem. Physiol. 72B: 1-4.

Frair, W. and B. K. Shah. 1982. Sea turtle blood serum protein concentrations correlated with carapace lengths. Comp. Biochem. Physiol. 73A: 337-339.

Frank. W., W. Sachsse and K. H. Winkelsträter. 1976. Aussergewöhnliche todesfälle durch amöbiasis bei einer brückenechse (*Sphenodon punctatus*), bei jungen suppenschildkröten (*Chelonia mydas*) und bei einer unechten karettschildkröte (*Caretta caretta*). Salamandra 12(3): 120-126.

Frazer, N. B. 1983. Survivorship of adult female loggerhead sea turtles, *Caretta caretta*, nesting on Little Cumberland Island, Georgia, USA. Herpetologica 39(4): 436-447.

Frazer, N. B. 1986. Survival from egg to adulthood in a declining population of loggerhead turtles, *Caretta caretta*. Herpetologica 42(1): 47-55.

Frazer, N. B. 1992. Sea turtle conservation and halfway technology. Conservation Biology 6(2): 179-184.

Frazer, N. B. 1994. Sea turtle headstarting and hatchery programs. Pages 374-380 *in* G. K. Meffe and C. R. Carroll (eds.), Principles of conservation biology. Sinauer Associates Inc., Sunderland, Massachusetts, USA, 600 pp.

Frazer, N. B. and L. M. Ehrhart. 1985. Preliminary growth models for green, *Chelonia mydas*, and loggerhead, *Caretta caretta*, turtles in the wild. Copeia 1985 (1): 73-79.

Frazer, N. B. and R. C. Ladner. 1986. A growth curve for green sea turtles, *Chelonia mydas*, in the U. S. Virgin Islands, 1913-14. Copeia 1986 (3): 798-802.

Frazier, J. 1971. Observations on sea turtles at Aldabra Atoll.

Phil. Trans. Royal Soc. London, B., 260: 373-410.

Frazier, J. 1980. Exploitation of marine turtles in the Indian Ocean. Human Ecology 8(4): 329-370.

Frazier, J. 1982a. Status of sea turtles in the Central Western Indian Ocean. Pages 385-389 in K. A. Bjorndal (ed.) Biology and conservation of sea turtles, Smithsonian Institution Press, Washington, D. C., 583 pp.

Frazier, J. 1982b. Subsistence hunting in the Indian Ocean. Pages 391-396 in K. A. Bjorndal (ed.), Biology and conservation of sea turtles. Smithsonian Institution Press, Washington, D. C., 583 pp.

Frazier J. 1984a. Las tortugas marinas en el oceano Atlantico sur occidental. Assoc. Herp. Argentina, Serie Divulgacion 2: 2-21.

Frazier, J. 1984b. Marine turtles in the Seychelles and adjacent territories. Pages 417-468 in D. R. Stoddart (ed.), Biogeography and ecology of the Seychelles Islands. Junk Publ., The Hague, Netherlands, 691 pp.

Frazier, J. 1985. Marine turtles in the Comoro Archipelago. Verh. Kon. Ned. Ak. Wet. Afd. Natuurk. Tweede Reeks 84: 1-177.

Frazier, J. 1989. Observations on stranded green turtles, Chelonia mydas, in the Gulf of Kutch. J. Bombay Nat. Hist. Soc. 86: 250-252.

Frazier, J. 1990. Biology and conservation of sea turtles in the Indian Ocean. Pages 364-386 in J. C. Daniel and J. S. Serrao (eds.), Conservation in developing countries: problems and prospects. Oxford Univ. Press, Oxford, 656 pp.

Frazier, J., G. C. Bertram and P. G. H. Evans. 1987. Turtles and marine mammals. Pages 288-314 in A. J. Edwards and S. M. Head (eds.), Key environments: Red Sea. Pergamon Press, New York, 441 pp.

Frazier, J. G., H. L. Fierstine, S. C. Beavers, F. Achaval, H. Suganuma, R. L. Pitman, Y. Yamaguchi and C. M. Prigioni. 1994. Impalement of marine turtles (Reptilia, Chelonia: Cheloniidae and Dermochelyidae) by billfishes (Osteichthyes, Perciformes: Istiophoridae and Xiphiidae). Envir. Biol. Fishes 39(1): 85-96.

Frazier, S. S., J. G. Frazier, H. Ding Z Huang, J. Zhong and L. Lu. 1988. Sea turtles in Fujian and Guangdong Provinces. Acta Herpetologica Sinica 3: 16-46.

Frazier, J., D. Margaritoulis, K. Muldoon, C. W. Potter, J. Rosewater, C. Ruckdeschel and S. Salas. 1985. Epizoan communities on marine turtles. I. Bivalve and gastropod mollusks. Marine Ecology 6(2): 127-140.

Frazier, J. G., J. E. Winston and C. A. Ruckdeschel. 1992. Epizoan communities on marine turtles. III. Bryozoa. Bull. Mar. Sci. 51(1): 1-8.

Freiberg, M. 1981. Turtles of South America. T. F. H. Publications Inc., New Jersey, 125 pp.

Fretey, J. 1984. The national report for the country of French Guiana. Pages 177-183 in P. Bacon, F. Berry, K. Bjorndal, H. Hirth, L. Ogren and M. Weber (eds.), Proc. Western Atlantic Turtle Symposium, Vol. 3, Univ. Miami Press, 514 pp.

Fretey, J. and N. Girardin. 1989. Donnees preliminaires sur les tortues marines au Gabon. Compte Rendu Seances Soc. Biogeographie 65(1): 39-57.

Frick, J. 1976. Orientation and behaviour of hatchling green turtles (Chelonia mydas) in the sea. Animal Behaviour 24(4): 849-857.

Friedman, J. M., S. R. Simon and T. W. Scott. 1985. Structure and function in sea turtle hemoglobins. Copeia 1985(3):

679-693.

Frith, C. B. 1975. Predation upon hatchlings and eggs of the green turtle, Chelonia mydas, on Aldabra Atoll, Indian Ocean. Atoll Res. Bull. 185: 11-12.

Fritts, T. H. 1981. Marine turtles of the Galápagos Islands and adjacent areas of the eastern Pacific on the basis of observations made by J. R. Slevin 1905-1906. J. Herpetology 15(3): 293-301.

Fuhn, I. E. and S. Vancea. 1961. Reptilia (Testoase, Sopirle, Serpi) in Fauna Republicii Populare Romine 14 (2): 1-352.

Fukada, H. 1965. Breeding habits of some Japanese reptiles (critical review). Bull. Kyoto Gakugei Univ. Ser. B. 27: 65-82.

Fuller, J. E., K. L. Eckert and J. I. Richardson. 1992. WIDECAST sea turtle recovery action plan for Antigua and Barbuda (K. L. Eckert, ed.). CEP Tech. Report No. 16. UNEP Caribbean Environment Programme, Kingston, Jamaica, 88 pp.

Gaffney, E. S. 1979. Comparative cranial morphology of recent and fossil turtles. Bull. Amer. Mus. Nat. Hist. 164(2): 65-376.

Gallagher, R. M., M. L. Hollinger, R. M. Ingle and C. R. Futch. 1972. Marine turtle nesting on Hutchinson Island, Florida in 1971. Special scientific report No. 37 Florida Dept. of Natural Resources, Marine Research Laboratory, St. Petersburg, Florida, 11 pp.

Gambarotta, J. C. and E. Gudynas. 1979. A new record of the green turtle Chelonia mydas mydas from Uruguay. C. E. D. Orione Contr. Biol. 1: 9-10.

Garnett, S. T., G. M. Crowley and N. Goudberg. 1985a. Observations of non-nesting emergence by green turtles in the Gulf of Carpentaria. Copeia 1985 (1): 262-264.

Garnett, S. T., I. R. Price and F. J. Scott. 1985b. The diet of the green turtle, Chelonia mydas (L.), in Torres Strait, Aust. Wildl. Res. 12: 103-112.

Gatz, R. N., M. L., Glass and S. C. Wood. 1987. Pulmonary function of the green sea turtle, Chelonia mydas. J. Applied Physiol. 62(2): 459-463.

Geldiay, R., T. Koray and S. Balik. 1982. Status of sea turtle populations (Caretta c. caretta and Chelonia m. mydas) in the northern Mediterranean Sea, Turkey. Pages 425-434 in K. A. Bjorndal (ed.), Biology and conservation of sea turtles. Smithsonian Institution Press, Washington, D. C, 583 pp.

Gervais, F. L. P. 1839-1849. Dictionnaire universel d' histoire naturelle. 16 vols., Paris.

Gibbons-Fly, W., C. Oravetz and W. Seidel, 1994. Public law 101-162 for the international conservation of sea turtles: a status report. Page 64 in B. A. Schroeder and B. E. Witherington (compilers), Proceedings of the thirteenth annual symposium on sea turtle biology and conservation. NOAA Tech. Memo. NMFS-SEFSC-341, 281 pp.

Gibson-Hill, C. A. 1950. A note on the reptiles occurring on the Cocos-Keeling Islands. Bull. Raffles Mus. Singapore, 22: 206-211.

Girard, C. F. 1858. Herpetology. Vol. 20. United States exploring expedition during the years 1838, 1839, 1840, 1841, 1842, under the command of Charles Wilkes, U.S.N., J. P. Lippincott Co., Philadelphia, 492 pp.

Girdler, R. W. 1984. The evolution of the Gulf of Aden and Red Sea in space and time. Deep Sea Research, Part A, Oceanographic Research Papers, Vol. 31 (No. 6-8A): 747-762.

Gistl, J. von N. F. X. 1848. Naturgeschichte des Thierreichs für höhere Schulen. Stuttgart, 216 pp.

Glazebrook, J. S. and R. S. F. Campbell. 1990a. A survey of the diseases of marine turtles in northern Australia. I. Farmed turtles. Diseases of Aquatic Organisms 9: 83-95.

Glazebrook, J. S. and R. S. F. Campbell. 1990b. A survey of the diseases of marine turtles in northern Australia. II. Oceanarium-reared and wild turtles. Diseases of Aquatic Organisms 9: 97-104.

Glazebrook, J. S., R. S. F. Campbell and D. Blair. 1981. Pathological changes associated with cardiovascular trematodes (Digenea: Spirorchidae) in a green turtle *Chelonia mydas* (L.). J. Comp. Path. 91(3): 361-368.

Glazebrook, J. S., R. S. F. Campbell and D. Blair. 1989. Studies on cardiovascular fluke (Digenea: Spirorchiidae) infections in sea turtles from the Great Barrier Reef, Queensland, Australia. J. Comp. Path. 101: 231-250.

Glazebrook, J. S., R. S. F. Campbell and A. T. Thomas. 1993. Studies on an ulcerative stomatitis-obstructive rhinitis-pneumonia disease complex in hatchling and juvenile sea turtles *Chelonia mydas* and *Caretta caretta*. Diseases Aquatic Organisms. 16: 133-147.

Godfrey, M. H. and R. Barreto. 1995. Beach vegetation and scafinding orientation of turtle hatchlings. Biol. Conserv. 74(1): 29-32.

Godfrey, M. H., R. Barreto and N. Mrosovsky. 1996. Estimating past and present sex ratios of sea turtles in Suriname. Canadian J. Zool. 74(2): 267-277.

Godfrey, M. H. and N. Mrosovsky. 1994. Simple method of estimating mean incubation temperatures on sea turtle beaches. Copeia 1994(3): 808-811.

Godley, B. and A. Broderick (eds.) 1993. Glasgow University turtle conservation expedition to northern Cyprus, 1992. Expedition Report, Dept. Veterinary Anatomy, Glasgow University Veterinary School, Glasgow, Scotland, 46 pp.

Godley, B. J. and A. C. Broderick (eds.). 1994. Glasgow University turtle conservation expedition to Northern Cyprus, 1994. Expedition Report. Dept. Veterinary Anatomy, Glasgow University Veterinary School, Glasgow, Scotland, 18 pp.

Godínez-Domínguez, E., R. E. Carretero-Montes, F. de A. Silva-Batíz, S. Ruiz and B. Aguilar. 1993. Crecimiento de neonatos de *Chelonia agassizi* (Testudines: Cheloniidae) en cautiverio. Revista de Biologia Tropical 41 (2): 253-260.

Gonzalez, J. G. 1984. The national report for the country of Puerto Rico. Pages 349-363 *in* P. Bacon, F. Berry, K. Bjorndal, H. Hirth, L. Ogren and M. Weber (eds.), Proc. Western Atlantic Turtle Symposium, Vol. 3, U. Miami Press, 514 pp.

González-de-la-Vega, A. M., J. A. Juarez and A. Pelaez. 1993-4. A panoramic view of sea turtle research and conservation in Mexico. Second World Congress of Herpetology, Abstract, pages 99-100, University of Adelaide, Adelaide, Australia.

Goodwin, M. M. 1971. Some aspects and problems of the use and exploitation of marine turtles. I. U. C. N. Publications New Series, Supplementary Paper No. 31: 98-101.

Gordon, A. N., W. R. Kelly and R. J. G. Lester. 1993. Epizootic mortality of free-living green turtles, *Chelonia mydas*, due to coccidiosis. J. Wildlife Diseases 29(3): 490-494.

Graff, D. 1995. Nesting and hunting survey of the marine turtles of the Island of São Tomé. ECOFAC, São Tomé, 35 pp.

Gramentz, D. 1989. Marine turtles in the Central Mediterranean Sea. Centro 1 (4): 41-56.

Granda, A. M. and P. J. O'Shea. 1972. Spectral sensitivity of the green turtle (*Chelonia mydas mydas*) determined by electrical responses to heterochromatic light. Brain, Behavior, Evolution 5: 143-154.

Grassman, M. 1993. Chemosensory orientation behavior in juvenile sea turtles. Brain, Behavior, Evolution 41: 224-228.

Grassman, M. and D. Owens. 1987. Chemosensory imprinting in juvenile green sea turtles, *Chelonia mydas*. Animal Behaviour 35(3): 929-931.

Green, D. 1979. Double tagging of green turtles in the Galápagos Islands. Marine Turtle Newsletter 13: 4-9.

Green, D., 1983. Galápagos sea turtles. Noticias Galápagos 38: 22-25.

Green, D., 1984. Long-distance movements of Galápagos green turtles. J. Herpetology 18(2): 121-130.

Green, D., 1993. Growth rates of wild immature green turtles in the Galápagos Islands, Ecuador. J. Herpetology 27(3): 338-341.

Green, D. 1994. Galapágos sea turtles: an overview. Pages 65-68 *in* B. A. Schroeder and B. E. Witherington (compilers), Proceedings of the thirteenth annual symposium on sea turtle biology and conservation. NOAA Tech. Memo. NMFS-SEFSC-341, 281 pp.

Green, D. and F. Ortiz-Crespo 1982. Status of sea turtle populations in the Central Eastern Pacific. Pages 221-233 *in* K. A. Bjorndal (ed.), Biology and conservation of sea turtles. Smithsonian Institution Press, Washington, D. C., 583 pp.

Green, R. H. 1971. The first record of the green turtle *Chelonia mydas* (Linne, 1758) and the hawksbill turtle *Eretmochelys imbricata bissa* (Ruppell, 1835) from Tasmanian waters. Records Queen Victoria Mus. 38: 1-4.

Gregory P. T. 1982. Reptilian hibernation. Pages 53-154 *in* C. Gans and F. H. Pough (eds.), Biology of the reptilia, Vol. 13 (Physiology D-physiological ecology). Academic Press, N. Y. 345 pp.

Greiner, E. C. 1995. Spirorchiid flukes in green turtles with fibropapillomas. Pages 44-46 *in* J. I. Richardson and T. H. Richardson (compilers), Proceedings of the twelfth annual workshop on sea turtle biology and conservation. NOAA Tech. Memo. NMFS-SEFSC-361, 274 pp.

Greiner, E. C., D. J. Forrester and E. R. Jacobson. 1980. Helminths of mariculture-reared green turtles (*Chelonia mydas mydas*) from Grand Cayman, British West Indies. Proc. Helminthol. Soc. Wash. 47(1): 142-144.

Groombridge B. 1990. Marine turtles in the Mediterranean: distribution, population status, and conservation. Council of Europe, Environment Conservation and Management Division, Strasbourg, 98 pp.

Groombridge, B., A. M. Kabraji and A. L. Rao. 1988. Marine turtles in Baluchistan (Pakistan). Marine Turtle Newsletter 42: 1-3.

Groombridge, B. and R. Luxmoore. 1989. The green turtle and hawksbill (Reptilia: Cheloniidae): world status, exploitation and trade. Secretariat of the Convention on International Trade in Endangered Species of Wild Fauna and Flora, Lausanne, Switzerland, 601 pp.

Grumbles, J., D. Rostal, J. Alvarado and D. Owens. 1990. Hematology study on the black turtle, *Chelonia agassizi*, at Playa Colola, Michoacan, Mexico. Pages 235-239 *in* T. H. Richardson, J. I. Richardson and M. Donnelly (compilers), Proceedings of the tenth annual workshop on sea turtle biology and conservation. NOAA Tech. Memo. NMFS-SEFC-278, 286 pp.

Guada, H. J. and P. Vernet. 1995. Sea turtle conservation in the national parks of Venezuela. Pages 192-194 *in* J. I. Richardson and T. H. Richardson (compilers), Proceedings of the twelfth annual workshop on sea turtle biology and conservation. NOAA Tech. Memo. NMFS-SEFSC-361, 274 pp.

Guada, H. J., P. J. Vernet, M. de Santana, A. Santana, and E. M. deAguilar. 1991. Fibropapillomas in a green turtle captured off Peninsula de Paraguana, Falcon State, Venezuela. Marine Turtle Newsletter 52: 24.

Gudynas, E. 1980. Notes on the sea turtles of Uruguay. A. S. R. A. Journal 1(3): 69-76.

Gupta, N. K. and V. Mehrotra. 1981. On two blood flukes (Trematoda) of the family Spirorchidae Stunkard, 1921, from Indian marine turtles. Acta Parasitologica (Polonica) 28: 11-20.

Gupta, S. P. 1961. On some trematodes from the intestine of the marine turtle, *Chelone mydas,* from the Caribbean Sea. Canadian J. Zool. 39(3): 293-298.

Guseman, J. L. and L. M. Ehrhart. 1992. Ecological geography of western Atlantic loggerheads and green turtles: evidence from remote tag recoveries. Page 50 *in* M. Salmon and J. Wyncken (compilers), Proceedings of the eleventh annual workshop on sea turtle biology and conservation. NOAA Tech. Memo. NMFS-SEFSC-302, 195 pp.

Gyuris, E. 1993. Factors that control the emergence of green turtle hatchlings from the nest. Wildl. Res. 20: 345-353.

Gyuris, E. 1994. The rate of predation by fishes on hatchlings of the green turtle (*Chelonia mydas*). Coral Reefs 13: 137-144.

Hadjichristophorou, M. and D. J. Grove. 1983. A study of appetitite, digestion and growth in juvenile green turtle (*Chelonia mydas* L.) fed on artificial diets. Aquaculture 30(1-4): 191-201.

Haines, H. 1988. Gray patch disease of green turtles. Pages 379-381 *in* C. J. Sindermann and D. V. Lightner (eds.), Disease diagnosis and control in North American marine aquaculture. Second, revised edition. Developments in Aquaculture and Fisheries Science, 17. Elsevier Science Publ. B. V., 431 pp.

Hallowell, R. 1979. Life's a shell game. Int. Wildlife 9(3): 12-13.

Halstead, B. W. 1988. Poisonous and venomous marine animals of the world (second revised edition). Darwin Press, Princeton, New Jersey, 1168 pp.

Halstead, B. W., P. S. Auerbach and D. R. Campbell. 1990. A color atlas of dangerous marine animals. CRC Press Inc., Boca Raton, Florida, 192 pp.

Harrisson, T. 1955. The edible turtle (*Chelonia mydas*) in Borneo 3. Young turtles (in captivity). Sarawak Mus. J. 6: 633-640.

Harrisson, T. 1960. Notes on the edible green turtle (*Chelonia mydas*): 8-First tag returns outside Sarawak, 1959. Sarawak Mus. J. 1960: 277-278.

Harrisson, T. 1963. Notes on marine turtles: 14-Albino green turtles and sacred ones. Sarawak Mus. J. (n. s.) 11: 304-306.

Hathaway, R. R. 1972. Sea turtles: unanswered questions about sea turtles in Turkey. Balik ve Balikcilik 20 (1): 1-8.

Hays, G. C., C. R. Adams and J. R. Speakman. 1993. Reproductive investment by green turtles nesting on Ascen-

sion Island. Canadian J. Zool. 71 (6): 1098-1103.

Hays, G. C., A. Mackay, C. R. Adams, J. A. Mortimer, J. R. Speakman and M. Boerema. 1995a. Nest site selection by sea turtles. J. Marine Biol. Assoc. U. K. 75(3): 667-674.

Hays, G. C., C. R. Adams, J. A. Mortimer and J. R. Speakman. 1995b. Inter-and intra-beach thermal variation for green turtle nests on Ascension Island, South Atlantic. J. Marine Biol. Assoc. U. K. 75(2): 405-411.

Heatwole, H. 1975. Biogeography of reptiles on some of the islands and cays of eastern Papua New Guinea. Atoll Res. Bull. 180: 1-39.

Heinsohn, G. E., J. Wake, H. Marsh and A. V. Spain. 1977. The dugong (*Dugong dugon* (Müller) in the seagrass system. Aquaculture 12(3): 235-248.

Hendrickson, J. R. 1958. The green sea turtle, *Chelonia mydas* (Linn.) in Malaya and Sarawak. Proc. Zool. Soc. London 130: 455-535.

Hendrickson, J. R. 1972. South Pacific Islands—Marine Turtle Resources. FI:SF/SOP/REG 102/6. A report prepared for the South Pacific Islands Fisheries Development Agency. FAO, Rome, 15 pp.

Hendrickson, J. R. 1980. The ecological strategies of sea turtles. Amer. Zool. 20(3): 597-608.

Hendrickson, J. R. 1982. Nesting behavior of sea turtles with emphasis on physical and behavioral determinants of nesting success or failure. Pages 53-57 *in* K. A. Bjorndal (ed.), Biology and conservation of sea turtles. Smithsonian Institution Press, Washington, D. C., 583 pp.

Hendrickson, L. P. and J. R. Hendrickson. 1981. A new method for marking sea turtles? Marine Turtle Newsletter 19: 6-7.

Hendrickson, J. R., J. R. Wood and R. S. Young. 1977. Lysine: histidine ratios in marine turtle shells. Comp. Biochem. Physiol. 57(4B): 285-286.

Henwood, T. A. and L. H. Ogren. 1987. Distribution and migrations of immature Kemp's ridley turtles (*Lepidochelys kempi*) and green turtles (*Chelonia mydas*) off Florida, Georgia and South Carolina. Northeast Gulf Sci. 9(2): 153-159.

Heppell, S. S., L. B. Crowder and D. T. Crouse. 1996. Models to evaluate headstarting as a management tool for long-lived turtles. Ecological Applications 6(2): 556-565.

Herbst, L. H., and E. R. Jacobson. 1995. Diseases of marine turtles. Pages 593-595 *in* K. A. Bjorndal (ed.), Biology and conservation of sea turtles, revised edition. Smithsonian Institution Press, Washington, D. C., 615 pp.

Herbst, L. H., E. R. Jacobson, R. Moretti, T. Brown, P. Klein and E. Greiner. 1994a. Progress in the experimental transmission of green turtle fibropapillomatosis. Page 238 *in* B. A. Schroeder and B. E. Witherington (compilers), Proceedings of the thirteenth annual symposium on sea turtle biology and conservation. NOAA Tech. Memo. NMFS-SEFSC-341, 28 pp.

Herbst, L. H., E. R. Jacobson, R. Moretti, T. Brown and P. A. Klein. 1994b. Green turtle fibropapillomatosis: transmission study update. Page 55 *in* K. A. Bjorndal, A. B. Bolten, D. A. Johnson and P. J. Eliazar (compilers), Proceedings of the fourteenth annual symposium on sea turtle biology and conservation. NOAA Tech. Memo. NMFS-SEFSC-351, 323 pp.

Herbst, L. H., E. R. Jacobson, R. Moretti, T. Brown, J. P.

101

Sundberg and P. A. Klein. 1995. Experimental transmission of green turtle fibropapillomatosis using cellfree tumor extracts. Diseases Aquatic Organisms 22(1): 1-12.

Herbst, L. H., and P. A. Klein. 1995a. Green turtle fibropapillomatosis: challenges to assessing the role of environmental cofactors. Environmental Health Prospectives 3(4): 27-30.

Herbst, L. H., and P. A. Klein. 1995b. Monoclonal antibodies for the measurement of class-specific antibody responses in the green turtle, *Chelonia mydas*. Veterinary Immunology and Immunopathology 46(3-4): 317-335.

Hewavisenthi, S. 1994a. The embryo and hatchling mortality of the green turtle (*Chelonia mydas*) and olive ridley (*Lepidochelys olivacea*) in relation to clutch size. Herpetological J. 4(3): 73-76.

Hewavisenthi, S. 1994b. Effect of retaining turtle hatchlings in tanks before their release. Pages 56-58 *in* K. A. Bjorndal, A. B. Bolten, D. A. Johnson and P. J. Eliazar (compilers), Proceedings of the fourteenth annual symposium on sea turtle biology and conservation. NOAA Tech. Memo. NMFS-SEFSC-351, 323 pp.

Hewavisenthi, S. 1994c. Bibliography of literature relating to marine turtles of Sri Lanka. Natural Resources, Energy and Science Authority of Sri Lanka, Colombo, Sri Lanka, 17 pp.

Hillestad, H. O., J. I. Richardson, C. McVea Jr., and J. M. Watson Jr. 1982. Worldwide incidental capture of sea turtles. Pages 489-495 *in* K. A. Bjorndal (ed.), Biology and conservation of sea turtles. Smithsonian Institution Press, Washington, D. C., 583 pp.

Hillman, J. C. and T. Gebremariam. 1995. The status of marine turtle conservation in Eritrea. Resources and Environment Division. Ministry of Marine Resources, Massawa, 11 pp.

Hirth, H. F. 1962. Cloacal temperatures of the green and hawksbill sea turtles. Copeia 1962 (3): 647-648.

Hirth, H. F. 1971a. South Pacific Islands—Marine Turtle Resources. A report prepared for the Fisheries Development Agency Project, Fl: SF/SOP/REG/102/2, FAO, Rome, 34 pp.

Hirth, H. F. 1971b. Synopsis of biological data on the green turtle, *Chelonia mydas* (Linnaeus) 1758. FAO Fisheries Synopsis No. 85: 1.1-8.19.

Hirth, H. F. 1978. A model of the evolution of green turtle (*Chelonia mydas*) remigrations. Herpetologica 34(2) 141-147.

Hirth, H. F. 1980a. *Chelonia*. Catalog. Amer. Amphibians and Reptiles. Society Study Amphibians and Reptiles. 248.1-248.2.

Hirth, H. F. 1980b. *Chelonia mydas*. Catalog. Amer. Amphibians and Reptiles. Society Study Amphibians and Reptiles 249.1-249.4.

Hirth, H. F. 1980c. Some aspects of the nesting behavior and reproductive biology of sea turtles. Amer. Zool. 20(3): 507-523.

Hirth, H. F. 1982. Weight and length relationships of some adult marine turtles. Bull. Mar. Sci. 32(1): 336-341.

Hirth, H. F. 1987. Pollution on the marine turtle nesting-beach in Tortuguero National Park, Costa Rica. Environ. Conserv. 14(1): 74-75.

Hirth, H. F. 1988. Intrapopulation reproductive traits of green turtles (*Chelonia mydas*) at Tortuguero, Costa Rica. Biotropica 20 (4): 322-325.

Hirth, H. F. 1993. Marine turtles. Pages 329-370 *in* A. Wright and L. Hill (eds.), Nearshore marine resources of the South Pacific: information for fisheries development and management. Institute of Pacific Studies, Suva; Forum Fisheries Agency, Honiara; and International Centre for Ocean Development, Canada. 710 pp.

Hirth, H. and A. Carr. 1970. The green turtle in the Gulf of Aden and the Seychelles Islands. Verh. Konin. Nederl. Akad. Weten., Afd. Natuur. Tweede Reeks 58: 1-44.

Hirth, H. F., M. Huber, T. Frohm and T. Mala. 1992. A natural assemblage of immature green (*Chelonia mydas*) and hawksbill (*Eretmochelys imbricata*) turtles on the fringing reef of Wuvulu Island, Papua New Guinea. Micronesica 25 (2): 145-153.

Hirth, H. F., L. G. Klikoff and K. T. Harper. 1973. Sea grasses at Khor Umaira, People's Democratic Republic of Yemen with reference to their role in the diet of the green turtle, *Chelonia mydas*. Fish. Bull. 71(4): 1093-1097.

Hirth, H. F. and L. H. Ogren. 1987. Some aspects of the ecology of the leatherback turtle *Demochelys coriacea* at Laguna Jalova, Costa Rica. NOAA Tech. Rep. NMFS, 56: 1-14.

Hirth, H. F. and D. L. H. Rohovit. 1992. Marketing patterns of green and hawksbill turtles in Port Moresby, Papua New Guinea. Oryx 26(1): 39-42.

Hirth, H. F. and D. A. Samson. 1987. Nesting behavior of green turtles (*Chelonia mydas*) at Tortuguero, Costa Rica. Caribbean J. Sci. 23 (3-4): 374-379.

Hirth, H. F. and W. M. Schaffer. 1974. Survival rate of the green turtle, *Chelonia mydas*, necessary to maintain stable populations. Copeia 1974 (2): 544-546.

Hodge, R. P. 1981. *Chelonia mydas agassizi* (Pacific green turtle). Herp. Rev. 12(3): 83-84.

Hoff, G. L., F. L. Frye and E. R. Jacobson (eds.). 1984. Diseases of amphibians and reptiles. Plenum Press, N. Y., 784 pp.

Hoffman, B. A. and W. J. Conley. 1987. Public aid to help assess nesting sea turtle populations in Florida. Pages 2230-2236 *in* O. T. Magoon, H. Converse, D. Miner, L. T. Tobin, D. Clark and G. Domurat (eds.), Coastal Zone '87. Vol. 2, Proceedings of the fifth symposium on coastal and ocean management. Amer. Soc. Civil Engineers, N. Y. 2452 pp.

Honegger, R. E. 1967. The green turtle (*Chelonia mydas japonica*) Thunberg in the Seychelle Islands. British J. Herpetology 4(1): 8-11.

Horikoshi, K. 1989. Egg survivorship and primary sex ratio of green turtles (*Chelonia mydas*) at Tortuguero, Costa Rica. Pages 328-329 *in* L. Ogren, F. Berry, K. Bjorndal, H. Kumpf, R. Mast, G. Medina, H. Reichart and R. Witham (eds.), Proceedings of the Second Western Atlantic Turtle Symposium. NOAA Tech. Memo. NMFS-SEFC-226, 401 pp.

Horikoshi, K. 1992. Sex ratio of green turtle hatchlings in Tortuguero, Costa Rica. Pages 59-60 *in* M. Salmon and J. Wyneken (compilers), Proceedings of the eleventh annual workshop on sea turtle biology and conservation. NOAA Tech. Memo. NMFS-SEFSC-302, 195 pp.

Horikoshi, K., H. Suganuma, H. Tachikawa, F. Sato and M. Yamaguchi. 1994. Decline of Ogasawara green turtle population in Japan. Pages 235-236 *in* K. A. Bjorndal, A. B. Bolten, D. A. Johnson and P. J. Eliazar (compilers), Proceedings of the fourteenth annual symposium on sea turtle biology and conservation. NOAA Tech.

Memo. NMFS-SEFSC-351, 323 pp.

Hornell, J. 1927. The turtle fisheries of the Seychelles Islands. H. M. S. O., London 55 pp.

Horrocks, J. A. 1992. WIDECAST sea turtle recovery action plan for Barbados (K. L. Eckert, ed.). CEP Technical Report No. 12. UNEP Caribbean Environment Programme, Kingston, Jamaica. 61 pp.

Houston, T. F. 1979. Sea turtles in South Australia. South Australian Naturalist 53 (3): 42-46.

Howlett, S. M. 1982. Saving turtles at Tarutao. CDC Newsletter 1 (1): 8-9.

Huang Chu-Chien, 1982. Distribution of sea turtles in China seas. Pages 321-322 in K. A. Bjorndal (ed.), Biology and conservation of sea turtles. Smithsonian Institution Press, Washington D. C., 583 pp.

Huff, J. A. 1989. Florida (USA) terminates "headstart" program. Marine Turtle Newsletter 46: 1-2.

Hughes G. 1971. Preliminary report on the sea turtles and dugongs of Mozambique. Veterinaria Mozambique, Lourenço Marques 4 (2): 45-62.

Hughes, G. R. 1974a. The sea turtles of south-east Africa. I. Status, morphology and distributions. South African Assoc. Marine Biol. Res., Ocean Res. Inst. 35: 1-144.

Hughes, G. R. 1974b. The sea turtles of south-east Africa. II. The biology of the Tongaland loggerhead turtle *Caretta caretta* L. with comments on the leatherback turtle *Dermochelys coriacea* L. and the green turtle *Chelonia mydas* L. in the study region. South African Assoc. Marine Biol. Res., Ocean Res. Inst. 36: 1-96.

Hughes, G. R. 1975. Fano! Defenders of Wildlife. 50(2): 159-163.

Hughes, G. R. 1976. The St. Brandon turtle fishery. Proc. Royal Soc. Arts Sciences Mauritius 3 (2): 165-189.

Hughes, G. R. 1982. Conservation of sea turtles in the southern African region. Pages 397-404 in K. A. Bjorndal (ed.), Biology and conservation of sea turtles. Smithsonian Institution Press, Washington, D. C, 583 pp.

Hughes, G. R. 1989. Sea turtles. Pages 230-243 in A. I. L. Payne and R. J. M. Crawford (eds.), Oceans of life off Southern Africa. Vlaeberg Publ., Capetown, South Africa, 380 pp.

Hykle, D. J. 1992. The migratory species (Bonn) Convention and marine turtle conservation. Pages 61-63 in M. Salmon and J. Wyneken (compilers), Proceedings of the eleventh annual workshop on sea turtle biology and conservation. NOAA Tech. Memo. NMFS-SEFSC- 302, 195 pp.

I.U.C.N. 1980. World Conservation Strategy: Living resource conservation for sustainable development. International Union for Conservation of Nature and Natural Resources. Gland, Switzerland.

I.U.C.N/U.N.E.P./W.W.F. 1991. Caring for the Earth: A strategy for sustainable living. International Union for Conservation of Nature and Natural Resources. Gland, Switzerland., 228 pp.

Ikai, A., T. Osada and M. Nishigai. 1988. Conformational changes of alpha-macroglobulin and ovomacroglobulin from the green turtle (*Chelonia mydas japonica*). J. Biochemistry 103(2): 218-224.

Ireland, L. C. 1979. Optokinetic behavior of the hatchling green turtle (*Chelonia mydas*) soon after leaving the nest. Herpetologica 35(4): 365-370.

Ireland, L. C. 1980. Homing behavior of juvenile green turtles, *Chelonia mydas*. Pages 761-764 in C. J. Amlaner and D. W. MacDonald (eds.), A handbook on biotelemetry and radio tracking. Pergamon Press, NY.

Irvine, F. R. 1947. The fishes and fisheries of the Gold Coast. Crown Agents for the Colonies, London, 352 pp.

Isaacks, R. E. and D. R. Harkness. 1980. Erythrocyte organic phosphates and hemoglobin function in birds, reptiles, and fishes. Amer. Zool. 20(1): 115-129.

Iverson, J. B. 1991. Patterns of survivorship in turtles (order Testudines). Canadian J. Zoology 69(2): 385-391.

Jackson, D. C. 1985. Respiration and respiratory control in the green turtle, *Chelonia mydas*. Copeia 1985(3): 664-671.

Jackson, D. C. and H. D. Prange. 1979. Ventilation and gas exchange during rest and exercise in adult green sea turtles. J. Comp. Physiol. 134(4): 315-319.

Jackson, M. E., L. U. Williamson and J. R. Spotila. 1987. Gross morphology vs. histology: sex determination of hatchling sea turtles. Marine Turtle Newsletter 40: 10-11.

Jacobson, E. R. 1990. An update on green turtle fibropapilloma. Marine Turtle Newsletter 49: 7-8.

Jacobson, E. R. 1996. Guest editorial: marine turtle farming and health issues. Marine Turtle Newsletter 72: 13-15.

Jacobson, E. R., C. Buergelt, B. Williams and R. K. Harris. 1991. Herpesvirus in cutaneous fibropapillomas of the green turtle *Chelonia mydas*. Diseases of Aquatic Organisms 12: 1-6.

Jacobson, E. R., J. M. Gaskin, R. P. Shields and F. H. White. 1979. Mycotic pneumonia in mariculture-reared green sea turtles. J. Amer. Vet. Med. Assoc. 175(9): 929-933.

Jacobson, E. R., J. M. Gaskin, M. Roelke, E. C. Greiner and J. Allen. 1986. Conjunctivitis, tracheitis, and pneumonia associated with herpesvirus infection in green sea turtles. J. Amer. Vet. Med. Assoc. 189 (9): 1020-1023.

Jacobson, E. R., J. L. Mansell, J. P. Sundberg, L. Hajjar, M. E. Reichmann, L. M. Ehrhart, M. Walsh and F. Murru. 1989. Cutaneous fibropapillomas of green turtles (*Chelonia mydas*). J. Comp. Path. 101: 39-52.

Jacobson, S. K. and A. F. Lopez. 1994. Biological impacts of ecotourism: tourists and nesting turtles in Tortuguero National Park, Costa Rica. Wildl. Soc. Bull. 22: 414-419.

Jacobson, S. K. and R. Robles. 1992. Ecotourism, sustainable development, and conservation education: development of a tour guide training program in Tortuguero, Costa Rica. Environmental Management 16(6): 701-713.

Jaffee, O. C. 1969. The development of the heart of the sea turtle (*Chelonia mydas*). Anat. Rec. 163(2): 203.

Janzen, F. J. 1994. Climate change and temperature-dependent sex determination in reptiles. Proc. National Academy Sciences (USA) 91(16): 7487-7490.

Janzen, F. J. and G. L. Paukstis. 1991. Environmental sex determination in reptiles: ecology, evolution, and experimental design. Quart. Rev. Biol. 66(2): 149-179.

Johannes, R. E. 1986. A review of information on the subsistence use of green and hawksbill sea turtles on islands under United States jurisdiction in the western Pacific Ocean. Adm. Rep. SWR-86-2, Pages 1-41, Nat. Mar. Fish. Ser. Southwest Region, California. USA.

Johnson, S. A., K. A. Bjorndal and A. B. Bolten. 1996a. A survey of organized turtle watch participants on sea turtle nesting beaches in Florida. Chelonian Conservation and Biology 2(1): 60-65.

Johnson, S. A., K. A. Bjorndal and A. B. Bolten. 1996b. Effects of organized turtle watches on loggerhead (*Caretta caretta*) nesting behavior and hatchling production in

Florida. Conservation Biology 10(2): 570-577.

Johnson, S. A. and L. M. Ehrhart. 1995. Reproductive ecology of the Florida green turtle (*Chelonia mydas*) at Melbourne Beach, Florida, 1991. Pages 54-56 in J. I. Richardson and T. H. Richardson (compilers), Proceedings of the twelfth annual workshop on sea turtle biology and conservation. NOAA Tech. Memo. NMFS-SEFSC-361, 274 pp.

Jones, B. and M. Shimlock. 1994. Turtle love. Wildlife Conservation 97(2): 52-57, 80.

Joseph, D., J. Fuller and R. Comacho. 1984. The national report for the country of Antigua and Barbuda. Pages 12-29 in P. Bacon, F. Berry, K. Bjorndal, H. Hirth, L. Ogren and M. Weber (eds.), Proc. Western Atlantic Turtle Symposium, Vol. 3, U. Miami Press, 514 pp.

Joseph, J. D., R. G. Ackman and G. T. Seaborn. 1985. Effect of diet on depot fatty acid composition in the green turtle *Chelonia mydas*. Comp. Biochem. Physiol. 80B(1): 15-22.

Joyner, C. C. and S. Frew. 1991. Plastic pollution in the marine environment. Ocean Development and International Law 22(1): 33-69.

Kam, A. K. H. 1984. An unusual example of basking by a green turtle in the northwestern Hawaiian Islands. Elepaio 45(1):3.

Kamezaki, N. and M. Matsui. 1995. Geographic variation in skull morphology of the green turtle, *Chelonia mydas*., with a taxonomic discussion. J. Herpetology 29(1): 51-60.

Kar, C. S. and S. Bhaskar. 1982. Status of sea turtles in the Eastern Indian Ocean. Pages 365-372 in K. A. Bjorndal (ed.), Biology and conservation of sea turtles. Smithsonian Institution Press, Washington D. C., 583 pp.

Karl, S. A. and J. C. Avise. 1993. PCR-based assays of Mendelian polymorphisms from anonymous single-copy nuclear DNA; techniques and applications for population genetics. Molecular Biology and Evolution 10(2): 342-361.

Karl, S. A., B. W. Bowen and J. C. Avise. 1992. Global population genetic structure and male-mediated gene flow in the green turtle (*Chelonia mydas*): RFLP analyses of anonymous nuclear loci. Genetics 131(1): 163-173.

Karl, S. A., B. W. Bowen and J. C. Avise. 1995. Hybridization among the ancient mariners: characterization of marine turtle hybrids with molecular genetic assays. J. Heredity 86(4): 262-268.

Kavanaght, R. 1984. The national report for the country of Haiti. Pages 216-219 in P. Bacon, F. Berry, K. Bjorndal, H. Hirth, L. Ogren and M. Weber (eds.), Proc. Western Atlantic Turtle Symposium, Vol. 3, U. Miami Press, 514 pp.

Kenworthy, W. J., M. J. Durako, S. M. R. Fatemy, H. Valavi and G. W. Thayer. 1993. Ecology of seagrasses in northeastern Saudi Arabia one year after the Gulf War oil spill. Marine Pollution Bull. 27: 213-222.

Kepler, C. B., A. K. Kepler and D. H. Ellis. 1994. The natural history of Caroline Atoll, Southern Line Islands, Part 2. Seabirds, other terrestrial animals, and conservation. Atoll Res. Bull. 398: 1-61.

Kikukawa, A., N. Kamezaki, K. Hirate and H. Ota. 1996. Distribution of nesting sites of sea turtles in Okinawajima and adjacent islands of the Central Ryukyus, Japan. Chelonian Conservation and Biology 2(1): 99-101.

King, F. W. 1982. Historical review of the decline of the green turtle and the hawksbill. Pages 183-188 in K. A. Bjorndal (ed.), Biology and conservation of sea turtles. Smithsonian Institution Press, Washington D. C., 583 pp.

Kinneary, J. J. 1996. The origin of marine turtles: a pluralistic view of evolution. Chelonian Conservation and Biology 2(1): 73-78.

Klima, E. F., G. R. Gitschlag and M. L. Renaud. 1988. Impacts of the explosive removal of offshore petroleum platforms on sea turtles and dolphins. Mar. Fish. Rev. 50(3): 33-42.

Knoepffler, L.-P. 1961. Contribution a l'etude des amphibiens et des reptiles de Provence. I.-Généralités. Vie Milieu 12: 67-76.

Koch, A. L., A. Carr and D. W. Ehrenfeld. 1969. The problem of open-sea navigation: the migration of the green turtle to Ascension Island. J. Theoret. Biol. 22: 163-179.

Kolinski, S. P. 1994a. Carapace lesions of *Chelonia mydas* breeding in Yap State are diagnosed to be fibropapilloma. Marine Turtle Newsletter 67: 26-27.

Kolinski, S. P. 1994b. *Chelonia mydas* (green turtle). Predation. Herp. Rev. 25(3): 120.

Kolinski, S. P. 1995. Migrations of the green turtle, *Chelonia mydas*, breeding in Yap State, Federated States of Micronesia. Micronesica 28(1): 1-8.

Koment, R. W. and H. Haines. 1982. Characterization of a reptilian epithelioid skin cell line derived from the green sea turtle, *Chelonia mydas*. In Vitro 18(3): 227-232.

Kooyman, G. L. 1989. Diverse divers: physiology and behavior. Springer-Verlag, New York, 200 pp.

Kowarsky, J. 1978. Observations on green turtles (*Chelonia mydas*) in north-eastern Australia during the 1975/76 nesting season. Biol. Conserv. 13 (1): 51-62.

Kowarsky, J. 1982. Subsistence hunting of sea turtles in Australia. Pages 305-313 in K. A. Bjorndal (ed.), Biology and conservation of sea turtles. Smithsonian Institution Press, Washington, D. C., 583 pp.

Krupp, F. and D. A. Jones. 1993. The creation of a marine sactuary after the 1991 Gulf War oil spill. Marine Pollution Bulletin 27: 315-323.

Kurata, Y., S. Yoneyama, K. Tsutsumi, J. Kimura and S. Hosokawa. 1978. Experiments to increase numbers of green turtles through the release of the young (VII. Aoumigame zōshoku horyu shiken). Ogasawara Fishery Center, Tokyo Metropolitan Government, Research Report No. 3: 58-80.

Kwan, D. 1994. Fat reserves and reproduction in the green turtle, *Chelonia mydas*. Wildl. Res. 21: 257-266.

Kwapena, N. 1982. Wildlife conservation, past and present, in the lowlands of Papua New Guinea. Pages 191-196 in L. Morauta, J. Pernetta and W. Heaney (eds.), Traditional conservation in Papua New Guinea: implications for today. Monograph 16, Inst. Appl. Social and Economic Res., Boroko, Papua New Guinea, 391 pp.

Lacépède, B. G. E. de. 1788. Histoire naturelle des quadrupèdes ovipares et des serpens. Vol. 1. Hotel de Thou, Paris, 651 pp.

Lahanas, P. N., M. M. Miyamoto, K. A. Bjorndal and A. B. Bolten. 1994. Molecular evolution and population genetics of Greater Caribbean green turtles (*Chelonia mydas*) as inferred from mitochondrial DNA control region sequences. Genetica 94(1): 57-67.

Lance, V. A. (ed.), 1994. Environmental sex determination in reptiles: patterns and processes. J. Experimental Zoology 270(1): 1-127.

Lance, V. A., T. Cort, J. Masuoka, R. Lawson and P. Saltman. 1995. Unusually high zinc concentrations in snake plasma, with observations on plasma zinc concentrations in lizards, turtles and alligators. J. Zoology 235(4): 577-585.

Lanyon, J. M., C. J. Limpus and H. Marsh. 1989. Dugongs and turtles: grazers in the seagrass system. Pages 610-634 in A. W. D. Larkum, A. J. McComb and S. A. Shepherd (eds.), Biology of seagrasses, Elsevier Publ., Amsterdam, 841 pp.

Laurent, L., and J. Lescure. 1992. The status of marine turtles in the Gulf of Gabès (South Tunisia). Pages 293-295 in Z. Korsós and I. Kiss (eds.). Proc. Sixth Ord. Meet. Soc. Europaea Herpetologica, Budapest, Hungary, 19-23 August 1991. Hungarian Natural History Museum, Budapest.

Laurent, L., S. Nouira, A. Jeudy de Grissac and M. N. Bradai. 1990. Les tortues marines de Tunisie: premieres donnees. Bull. Soc. Herp. Fr. 53: 1-17.

Lazell, Jr., J. D. 1980. New England waters: critical habitat for marine turtles. Copeia 1980 (2): 290-295.

Lebeau, A. 1985. Essai d' evaluation des pontes de la tortue verte Chelonia mydas (Linne) sur l' Atoll de Scilly (Iles-sous-le-vent, Polynésie française) au cours des saisons 1982-1983 et 1983-1984. Proc. Fifth Intern. Coral Reef Congress, Tahiti, Vol. 5, pp 487-493.

LeBourdiec, P. 1987. L' Acquaculture marine a la Reunion. Rev. Int. Oceanogr. Med. 85: 241-244.

LeGall, J-Y. 1985. Elevage de la tortue verte marine à l'île de la Réunion (1978-1985). La Peche Maritime (Juillet-Aout): 434-440.

LeGall, J.-Y., 1989. Tectonique des plaques, biogeographie et migrations: exemple de la tortue verte marine Chelonia mydas. Océanis 15(2): 143-160.

LeGall, J.-Y., P. Bosc, D. Chateau and M. Taquet 1986. Estimation du nombre de tortues vertes femelles adultes Chelonia mydas par saison de ponte á Tromelin et Europa (Océan Indien) (1973-1985). Oceanogr. Trop. 21 (1): 3-22.

LeGall, J-Y., D. Chateau and P. Bosc. 1985. Rythme de reproduction interannuel des tortues vertes Chelonia mydas sur les sites de ponte Tromelin et Europa (Océan Indien). C. R. Acad. Sci. Paris, t. 301, 3(5): 195-200.

LeGall, J.-Y. and G. R. Hughes. 1987. Migrations de la tortue verte Chelonia mydas dans l'Océan Indian Sud-Ouest observées à partir des marquages sur les sites de ponte Europa et Tromelin (1970-1985). Amphibia-Reptilia 8: 277-282.

Leh, C. M. U. 1994. Hatch rates of green turtle eggs in Sarawak. Hydrobiologia 285: 171-175.

Leh, C. M. U., S. K. Poon and Y. C. Siew. 1985. Temperature-related phenomena affecting the sex of green turtle (Chelonia mydas) hatchlings in the Sarawak Turtle Islands. Sarawak Mus. J. 34(55): 183-193.

Leibovitz, L., G. Rebell and G. C. Boucher. 1978. Caryospora cheloniae sp. n.: a coccidial pathogen of mariculture-reared green sea turtles (Chelonia mydas mydas). J. Wildlife Diseases 14: 269-275.

Lesson, R. P. 1834. Reptiles, Pages 289-336 in C. Bélanger, Voyage aux Indes-Orientales par le nord de l'Europe, les provinces de Caucase, la Géorgie, l'Arménie et la Perse, suivi de détails topographiques, statistiques et autres sur le cap-de-Bonne Esperance et Sainte-Helene, pendant les années 1825, 1826, 1827, 1828 et 1829. Zoologie. Arthus Bertrand, Paris, 535 pp.

Lewis, S. H., C. Ryder and K. Benirschke. 1992. Omphalopagus twins in Chelonia mydas. Herp. Rev. 23(3): 69-70.

Licht, P., R. J. Denver, S. Pavgi and B. Herrera. 1991. Seasonality in plasma thyroxine binding in turtles. J. Exp. Zoology 260(1): 59-65.

Licht, P. and H. Papkoff. 1985. Reevaluation of the relative activities of the pituitary glycoprotein hormones (follicle-stimulating hormone, luteinizing hormone, and thyrotrophin) from the green sea turtle, Chelonia mydas. Gen. Comp. Endocrin. 58: 443-451.

Licht, P., B. T. Pickering, H. Papkoff, A. Pearson and A. Bona-Gallo. 1984. Presence of a neurophysin-like precursor in the green turtle (Chelonia mydas). J. Endocrin. 103: 97-106.

Licht, P., J. F. Wood and F. E. Wood. 1985. Annual and diurnal cycles in plasma testosterone and thyroxine in the male green sea turtle Chelonia mydas. Gen. Comp. Endocrin. 57: 335-344.

Liebman, P. A. and A. M. Granda. 1971. Microspectrophotometric measurements of visual pigments in two species of turtle, Pseudemys scripta and Chelonia mydas. Vision Res. 11(2): 105-114.

Liebman, P. A. and A. M. Granda. 1975. Super dense carotenoid spectra resolved in single cone oil droplets. Nature 253(5490): 370-372.

Liew, H. C. and E. H. Chan. 1993. Biotelemetry of green turtles (Chelonia mydas) in Pulau Redang, Malaysia, during the internesting period. Pages 157-163 in M. Paolo, F. Sandro, C. Cristina and B. Remo (eds.), Biotelemetry XII: Proc. Twelfth Int. Symp. Biotelemetry, 31 August-5 September 1992, Ancona, Italy.

Light, P. R., M. Salmon, K. L. Lohmann and J. Wyneken. 1992. The magnetic compass of hatchling loggerhead sea turtles: evidence for detection of magnetic inclination. Page 72 in M. Salmon and J. Wyneken (compilers), Proceedings of the eleventh annual workshop on sea turtle biology and conservation. NOAA Tech. Memo. NMFS-SEFSC-302, 195 pp.

Light, P., M. Salmon and K. Lohmann. 1993. Geomagnetic orientation of loggerhead sea turtles: evidence for an inclination compass. J. Exp. Biol. 182: 1-10.

Limpus, C. J. 1980. The green turtle, Chelonia mydas (L) in eastern Australia. Pages 5-22 in Management of turtle resources, Research Monograph 1, James Cook Univ., Queensland, 72 pp.

Limpus, C. J. 1982a. The status of Australian sea turtle populations. Pages 297-303 in K. A. Bjorndal (ed.), Biology and conservation of sea turtles. Smithsonian Institution Press, Washington, D. C, 583 pp.

Limpus, C. J. 1982b. The reptiles of Lizard Island. Herpetofauna 13 (2): 1-6.

Limpus, C. J. 1987. A turtle fossil on Raine Island, Great Barrier Reef. Search 18 (5): 254-256.

Limpus, C. L. 1992. Estimation of tag loss in marine turtle research. Wildl. Res. 19: 457-469.

Limpus, C. 1993a. A marine resource case study: climate change and sea level rise probable impacts on marine turtles. Page 157 in J. E. Hay and C. Kaluwin (eds.), Climate change and sea level rise in the South Pacific region. Proceedings of the second SPREP meeting (Noumea, New Caledonia, 6-10 April 1992). Apia,

Western Samoa.

Limpus, C. J. 1993b. The green turtle, *Chelonia mydas*, in Queensland: breeding males in the southern Great Barrier Reef. Wildl. Res. 20(4): 513-523.

Limpus, C. J., P. J. Couper and M. A. Read. 1994b. The green turtle, *Chelonia mydas*, in Queensland: population structure in a warm temperate feeding area. Memoirs Queensland Museum 35(1): 139-154.

Limpus, C. J. and A. Fleay. 1983. Management and turtles. Pages 535-540 *in* J. T. Baker, R. M. Carter, P. W. Sammarco and K. P. Stark (eds.), Proceedings: Inaugural Great Barrier Reef Conference, Townsville, JCU Press, Australia.

Limpus, C. J. and J. D. Miller. 1993. Family Cheloniidae. Pages 133-138 *in* C. J. Glasby, G. J. B. Ross and P. L. Beesley (eds.) Fauna of Australia. Vol. 2A Amphibia and Reptilia. Australian Government Publishing Service, Canberra, Australia. 439 pp.

Limpus, C., J. D. Miller, and C. J. Parmenter. 1993. The northern Great Barrier Reef green turtle *Chelonia mydas* breeding population. Pages 47-50 *in* A. K. Smith (compiler), K. H. Zevering and C. E. Zevering (eds.), Raine Island and environs Great Barrier Reef: quest to preserve a fragile outpost of nature. Raine Island Corporation and Great Barrier Reef Marine Park Authority, Townsville, Queensland, Australia.

Limpus, C. J., J. D. Miller and N. Preece. 1994a. The basking greens of Bountiful Island: Kay's turtles revisited. Page 76 *in* K. A. Bjorndal, A. B. Bolten, D. A. Johnson and P. J. Eliazar (compilers), Proceedings of the fourteenth annual symposium on sea turtle biology and conservation. NOAA Tech. Memo. NMFS-SEFSC-351, 323 pp.

Limpus, C. J., J. D. Miller, P. C. Reed. 1993-94. Intra and inter specific variability in pivotal temperature during incubation of marine turtle eggs. Second World Congress of Herpetology, Abstract, pages 154-155, University of Adelaide, Adelaide, Australia.

Limpus, C. J., J. D. Miller, C. J. Parmenter, D. Reimer, N. McLachlan and R. Webb. 1992. Migration of green (*Chelonia mydas*) and loggerhead (*Caretta caretta*) turtles to and from eastern Australian rookeries. Wildl. Res. 19: 347-358.

Limpus, C. J. and N. Nicholls. 1988. The southern oscillation regulates the annual numbers of green turtles (*Chelonia mydas*) breeding around northern Australia. Aust. Wildl. Res. 15: 157-161.

Limpus, C. J. and C. J. Parmenter. 1986. The sea turtle resources of the Torres Strait region. Pages 95-107 *in* A. K. Haines, G. C. Williams and D. Coates (eds.), Torres Strait Fisheries Seminar, Port Moresby, 11-14 Feb. 1985. Australia Government Publishing Service, Canberra, Australia.

Limpus, C. J. and P. C. Reed. 1985a. The green turtle, *Chelonia mydas*, in Queensland: a preliminary description of the population structure in a coral reef feeding ground. Pages 47-52 *in* G. Grigg, R. Shine and H. Ehmann (eds.), Biology of Australasian frogs and reptiles. Royal Zool. Soc. New South Wales.

Limpus, C. J. and P. C. Reed. 1985b. Green sea turtles stranded by Cyclone Kathy on the south-western coast of the Gulf of Carpentaria. Austr. Wildl. Res. 12: 523-533.

Limpus, C. J., P. Reed and J. D. Miller. 1983. Islands and turtles: the influence of choice of nesting beach on sex ratio. Pages 397-402 *in* J. T. Baker, R. M. Carter, P. W.

Sammarco and K. P. Stark (eds.), Proceedings: inaugural Great Barrier Reef conference. JCU Press, Australia.

Limpus, C. J. and D. G. Walter. 1980. The growth of immature green turtles (*Chelonia mydas*) under natural conditions. Herpetologica 36(2): 162-165.

Lindsay, C. 1995. Turtle islands: Balinese ritual and the green turtle. Takarajima Books Inc., New York, 123 pp.

Lindsay, C. 1996. The green turtle's sacrifice. Natural History 105(1): 46-51.

Linnaeus, C. 1758. Systema naturae per regna tria naturae, secundum classes, ordines, genera, species, cum characteribus, differentiis, synonymis, locis, Ed. 10, Tomus 1. L. Salvii, Stockholm, 823 pp.

Linsley, N. B. and G. H. Balazs. 1994. Marine turtle postage stamps of the world. Page 246 *in* K. A. Bjorndal, A. B. Bolten, D. A. Johnson and P. J. Eliazar (compilers), Proceedings of the fourteenth annual symposium on sea turtle biology and conservation. NOAA Tech. Memo. NMFS-SEFSC-351, 323 pp.

Lockhart, R. 1989. Marine turtles of Papua New Guinea. Departmental Report 1-89, Dept. of Mathematics and Statistics, The Papua New Guinea University of Technology, Lae, Papua New Guinea, 88 pp.

Lohmann, K. J. 1991. Magnetic orientation by hatchling loggerhead sea turtles (*Caretta caretta*). J. Exp. Biol. 155: 37-49.

Lohmann, K. J. 1992. How sea turtles navigate. Scientific American 266 (1): 100-106.

Lohmann, K. J. and C. M. F. Lohmann. 1992. Orientation to oceanic waves by green turtle hatchlings. J. Exp. Biol. 171: 1-13.

Lohmann, K. J. and C. M. F. Lohmann. 1993. A light-independent magnetic compass in the leatherback sea turtle. Biol. Bull. 185(1): 149-151.

Lohmann, K. J. and C. M. F. Lohmann. 1994a. Acquisition of magnetic directional preference in hatchling loggerhead sea turtles. J. Exp. Biol. 190: 1-8.

Lohmann, K. J. and C. M. F. Lohmann. 1994b. Detection of magnetic inclination angle by sea turtles: a possible mechanism for determining latitude. J. Exp. Biol. 194: 23-32.

Lohmann, K. J. and C. M. F. Lohmann. 1996a. Detection of magnetic field intensity by sea turtles. Nature 380(6569): 59-61.

Lohmann, K. J. and C. M. F. Lohmann. 1996b. Orientation and open-sea navigation in sea turtles. J. Exp. Biol. 199(1): 73-81.

Lohmann, K. J., M. Salmon and J. Wyneken. 1990. Functional autonomy of land and sea orientation systems in sea turtle hatchlings. Biol. Bull. 179(2): 214-218.

Lohmann, K. J., A. W. Swartz and C. M. F. Lohmann. 1995. Perception of ocean wave direction by sea turtles. J. Exp. Biol. 198: 1079-1085.

Losey, G. S., G. H. Balazs and L. A. Privitera. 1994. Cleaning symbiosis between the wrasse, *Thalassoma duperry*, and the green turtle, *Chelonia mydas*. Copeia 1994 (3): 684-690.

Lovich, J. E. 1996. Possible demographic and ecological consequences of sex ratio manipulation in turtles. Chelonian Conservation and Biology 2(1): 114-117.

Low, T. 1985. Raine Island. Wildlife Australia 22 (2): 3-5.

Luschi, P., F. Papi, H. C. Liew, E. H. Chan and F. Bonadonna. 1996. Long-distance migration and homing after displacement in the green turtle (*Chelonia mydas*): a satellite tracking study. J. Comp. Physiol. A178(4): 447-452.

Lutz, P. L. 1990. Studies on the ingestion of plastic and latex by sea turtles. Pages 719-735 *in* R. S. Shomura and M. L. Godfrey (eds.), Proceedings of the second international conference on marine debris, 2-7 April 1989, Honolulu, Hawaii. NOAA Tech. Memo. NMFS-SWFSC-154, pp. 1274.

Lutz P. L. and T. B. Bentley. 1985. Respiratory physiology of diving in the sea turtle. Copeia 1985(3): 671-679.

Mack, D., N. Duplaix and S. Wells. 1982. Sea turtles, animals of divisible parts: international trade in sea turtle products. Pages 545-563 *in* K. A. Bjorndal (ed.), Biology and conservation of sea turtles. Smithsonian Institution Press, Washington, D. C., 583 pp.

Mackay, A. L. 1994. Sea turtle activity survey on St. Croix, U. S. Virgin Islands (1992-1993). Pages 247-248 *in* K. A. Bjorndal, A. B. Bolten, D. A. Johnson and P. J. Eliazar (compilers), Proceedings of the fourteenth annual symposium on sea turtle biology and conservation. NOAA Tech. Memo. NMFS-SEFSC-351, 323 pp.

Magnuson, J. J., K. A. Bjorndal, W. D. DuPaul, G. L. Graham, D. W. Owens, C. H. Peterson, P. C. H. Pritchard, J. I. Richardson, G. E. Saul and C. W. West. 1990. Decline of the sea turtles: causes and prevention. National Research Council, National Academy Press, Washington, D. C., 259 pp.

Maigret, J. 1977. Les tortues de mer au Senegal. Bull. Assoc. Avanc. Sci. (Senegal) 59: 7-14.

Maigret J. 1983. Répartition des tortues de mer sur les côtes ouest Africaines. Bull. Soc. Herp. Fr. 28: 22-34.

Manton, M. L., A. Karr and D. W. Ehrenfeld. 1972a. An operant method for the study of chemoreception in the green turtle, *Chelonia mydas.* Brain, Behavior and Evolution 5: 188-201.

Manton, M., A. Karr and D. W. Ehrenfeld. 1972b. Chemoreception in the migratory sea turtle, *Chelonia mydas.* Biol. Bull. 143(1): 184-195.

Manzella, S. A., J. A. Williams and C. W. Caillouet Jr. 1990. Radio and sonic tracking of juvenile sea turtles in inshore waters of Louisiana and Texas. Pages 115-120 *in* T. H. Richardson, J. I. Richardson and M. Donnelly (compilers), Proceedings of the tenth annual workshop on sea turtle biology and conservation. NOAA Tech. Memo. NMFS-SEFS-278, 286 pp.

Mao, S-H. and B-Y Chen. 1982. Serological relationships of turtles and evolutionary implications. Comp. Biochem. Physiol. 71B: 173-179.

Maragos, J. E. 1994. Description of reefs and corals for the 1988 protected area survey of the Northern Marshall Islands. Atoll Res. Bull. 419: 1-88.

Marcovaldi, M. A. and A. Laurent. 1996. A six season study of marine turtle nesting at Praia do Forte, Bahia, Brazil, with implications for conservation and management. Chelonian Conservation and Biology 2(1): 55-59.

Margaritoulis, D., T. Arapis, E. Kornaraki, and C. Mytilineou. 1986. Three specimens of the green sea turtle *Chelonia mydas* (L.) recorded in Greece. Biologia Gallo-hellenica 12: 237-243.

Margaritoulis D., N. Kousias, G. Nicolopoulou, and K. Teneketzis 1992. Incidental catch of sea turtles in Greece: the case of Lakonikos Bay. Pages 168-169 *in* M. Salmon and J. Wyneken (compilers), Proceedings of the eleventh annual workshop on sea turtle biology and

conservation. NOAA Tech. Memo. NMFS-SEFSC-302, 195 pp.

Márquez M., R. 1990. FAO species catalogue. Vol. 11: Sea turtles of the world. An annotated and illustrated catalogue of sea turtle species known to date. FAO Fisheries Synopsis. No. 125 Vol. 11, Rome, FAO, 81 pp.

Márquez, R., C. Peñaflores, A. Villanueva and J. Diaz. 1982. A model for diagnosis of populations of olive ridleys and green turtles of west Pacific tropical coasts. Pages 153-158 *in* K. A. Bjorndal (ed.), Biology and conservation of sea turtles. Smithsonian Institution Press, Washington, D. C. 583 pp.

Márquez, R., J. Vasconcelos and C. Peñaflores. 1990. XXV años de investigacion, conservacion y proteccion de la tortuga marina. Instituto Nacional de la Pesca, Secretaria de Pesca, Mexico, 49 pp.

Marshall, A. T. 1989. Intracellular and luminal ion concentrations in sea turtle salt glands determined by X-ray microanalysis. J. Comp. Physiol. 159B(5): 609-616.

Marshall, A. T. and P. D. Cooper. 1988. Secretory capacity of the lachrymal salt gland of hatchling sea turtles, *Chelonia mydas.* J. Comp. Physiol. 157B (6): 821-827.

Marshall, A. T. and S. R. Saddlier. 1989. The duct system of the lachrymal salt gland of the green sea turtle, *Chelonia mydas.* Cell and Tissue Research 257 (2): 399-404.

Maturbongs, J. A., H. Rumaikewi, J. Rumaropen and A. Sangganafa. 1993. Report of population and eggs laying place of turtles observation at Inggresau Beach, Yapen Waropen Regency, in Irian Jaya. WWF Project 1D0085-12 Yapen Tengah Mountains Strict Nature Reserve, in cooperation with subsection of Yapen Waropen Conservation Nature Resources and Group of Yapen Waropen Nature Lover. Jayapura, Irian Jaya, Indonesia, 32 pp.

McCoy, M. A. 1982. Subsistence hunting of turtles in the western Pacific: The Caroline Islands. Pages 275-280 *in* K. A. Bjorndal (ed.), Biology and conservation of sea turtles. Smithsonian Institution Press, Washington, D. C., 583 pp.

McDonald, D. and P. Dutton, 1990. Fibropapillomas on sea turtles in San Diego Bay, California. Marine Turtle Newsletter 51: 9-10.

McDonald, D. and P. Dutton, 1995. Ultrasonic tracking of sea turtles in San Diego Bay. Pages 218-221 *in* J. I. Richardson and T. H. Richardson (compilers), Proceedings of the twelfth annual workshop on sea turtle biology and conservation. NOAA Tech. Memo. NMFS-SEFSC-361, 274 pp.

McGehee, M. A. 1990. Effects of moisture on eggs and hatchlings of loggerhead sea turtles (*Caretta caretta*). Herpetologica 46(3): 251-258.

McKeown, A. 1977. Marine turtles of the Solomon Islands. Fisheries Div., Ministry Natural Resources, Honiara, Solomon Islands, 49 pp.

McKim, J. M. Jr., and K. L. Johnson. 1983. Polychlorinated biphenyls and p, p'-DDE in loggerhead and green postyearling Atlantic sea turtles. Bull. Environ. Contam. Toxicol. 31(1): 53-60.

McKinney E. C. and T. B. Bentley. 1985. Cell-mediated immune response of *Chelonia mydas.* Developmental Comparative Immunology 9: 445-452.

Mellgren, R. L., M. A. Mann, M. E. Bushong, S. R. Harkins and V. K. Krumke. 1994. Habitat selection in three species of captive sea turtle hatchlings. Pages 259-261 *in* K. A. Bjorndal, A. B. Bolten, D. A. Johnson and P. J. Eliazar (compilers), Proceedings of the fourteenth annual symposium on sea turtle biology and conservation. NOAA Tech. Memo. NMFS-SEFSC-351, 323 pp.

Mendonça, M. T. 1981. Comparative growth rates of wild immature *Chelonia mydas* and *Caretta caretta* in Florida. J. Herp. 15(4): 447-451.

Mendonça M. T. and L. M. Ehrhart. 1982. Activity, population size and structure of immature *Chelonia mydas* and *Caretta caretta* in Mosquito Lagoon, Florida. Copeia 1982 (1): 161-167.

Merrem, B. 1820. Versuch eines Systems der Amphibien. Tentamen systematis amphibiorum. Johann Christian Krieger, Marburg, 191 pp.

Meylan, A. 1982a. Behavioral ecology of the West Caribbean green turtle (*Chelonia mydas*) in the internesting habitat. Pages 67-80 *in* K. A. Bjorndal (ed.), Biology and conservation of sea turtles. Smithsonian Institution Press, Washington D. C. 583 pp.

Meylan, A. 1982b. Sea turtle migration-evidence from tag returns. Pages 91-100 *in* K. A. Bjorndal (ed.), Biology and conservation of sea turtles. Smithsonian Institution Press, Washington, D. C, 583 pp.

Meylan, A. B. 1983. Marine turtles of the Leeward Islands, Lesser Antilles. Atoll Res. Bull. 278: 1-24.

Meylan, A. B., B. W. Bowen and J. C. Avise. 1990. A genetic test of the natal homing versus social facilitation models for green turtle migration. Science 248: 724-727.

Meylan, A. B., P. A. Meylan, H. C. Frick and J. N. Burnett-Herkes. 1992a. Population structure of green turtles (*Chelonia mydas*) on foraging grounds in Bermuda. Page 73 *in* M. Salmon and J. Wyneken (compilers). Proceedings of the eleventh annual workshop on sea turtle biology and conservation. NOAA Tech. Memo. NMFS-SEFSC-302, 195 pp.

Meylan, P. A., A. B. Meylan and R. Yeomans. 1992b. Interception of Tortuguero-bound green turtles at Bocas Del Toro Province, Panama. Page 74 *in* M. Salmon and J. Wyneken (compilers), Proceedings of the eleventh annual workshop on sea turtle biology and conservation. NOAA Tech. Memo. NMFS-SEFSC-302, 195 pp.

Miller, J. D. 1985. Embryology of marine turtles. Pages 270-328 *in* C. Gans, F. Billett and P. F. A. Maderson (eds.), Biology of the Reptilia, Vol. 14, Development A. John Wiley & Sons, N. Y.

Miller, J. D. 1989. Marine turtles: Vol. 1: an assessment of the conservation status of marine turtles in the Kingdom of Saudi Arabia. MEPA Coastal and Marine Management Series, Report No. 9, pp. 1-209 Ministry of Defence and Aviation, Kingdom of Saudi Arabia.

Miller, J. D. and C. J. Limpus. 1981. Incubation period and sexual differentiation in the green turtle *Chelonia mydas* L. Pages 66-73 *in* C. Banks and A. Martin (eds.), Proceedings Melbourne Herpetological Symposium, The Royal Melbourne Zoological Gardens, Melbourne.

Miller, J. D. and C. J. Limpus. 1991. Torres Strait marine turtle resources. Pages 213-216 *in* D. Lawrence and T. Cansfield-Smith (eds.), Sustainable development for traditional inhabitants of the Torres Strait region. Workshop Series No. 16, Australian Government Publ. Service, Canberra, Australia.

Miller, J. D., C. J. Limpus and J. P. Ross 1989. Marine turtles: Vol. 2: Recommendations for the conservation of marine turtles in the Kingdom of Saudi Arabia. MEPA Coastal and Marine Management Series, Report No. 9,

pp 1-63, Ministry of Defence and Aviation, Kingdom of Saudi Arabia.

Miller, W. G., F. Berry and J. R. Fletemeyer. 1984. The national report for the country of Belize. Pages 41-48 *in* P. Bacon, F. Berry, K. Bjorndal, H. Hirth, L. Ogren and M. Weber (eds.), Proc. Western Atlantic Turtle Symposium Vol. 3, Univ. Miami Press, 514 pp.

Milton, S. L., S. Leone-Kabler, A. A. Schulman and P. L. Lutz. 1994. Effects of hurricane Andrew on the sea turtle nesting beaches of South Florida. Bull. Mar. Sci. 54(3): 974-981.

Minton Jr. S. A. 1966. A contribution to the herpetology of West Pakistan. Bull. Amer. Mus. Nat. Hist. 134(2): 27-184.

Mitchell, J. F., J. W. Watson, D. G. Foster and R. E. Caylor. 1995. The turtle excluder device (TED): a guide to better performance. NOAA Tech. Memo. NMFS-SEFSC-366, 35 pp.

Mittermeier, R. A., F. Medem and A. G. J. Rhodin. 1980. Vernacular names of South American turtles. Herpetological Circular No. 9. Society Study Amphibians and Reptiles, 44 pp.

Mohr, J. C. van der Meer. 1927. On anomalous eggs of the green turtle. Misc. Zool. Sumatrana 22: 1-2.

Moll, D. 1983. A proposed origin of nesting location divergence and a shared feeding range in Brazilian green turtle populations. Copeia 1983(1): 121-125.

Moll, D. 1985. The marine turtles of Belize. Oryx 19(3): 155-157.

Moorhouse, F. W. 1933. Notes on the green turtle (*Chelonia mydas*). Reports of the Great Barrier Reef Committee, 4(1): 1-22.

Moreira, L., C. Baptistotti, J. Scalfone, J. C. Thomé and A. P. L. S. de Almeida. 1995. Occurrence of *Chelonia mydas* on the Island of Trindade, Brazil. Marine Turtle Newsletter 70:2.

Moritz, C. 1994a. Defining "Evolutionary Significant Units" for conservation. Trends Ecology Evolution 9(10): 373-375.

Moritz, C. 1994b. Applications of mitochrondrial DNA analysis in conservation: a critical review. Molecular Ecology 3(4): 401-411.

Morreale, S. J., A. B. Meylan, S. S. Sadove and E. A. Standora. 1992. Annual occurrence and winter mortality of marine turtles in New York waters. J. Herpetology 26(3): 301-308.

Morreale, S. J., G. J. Ruiz, J. R. Spotila and E. A. Standora. 1982. Temperature-dependent sex determination: current practices threaten conservation of sea turtles. Science 216: 1245-1247.

Morris K. 1984. The national report for the country of St. Vincent. Pages 381-385 *in* P. Bacon, F. Berry, K. Bjorndal, H. Hirth, L. Ogren and M. Weber (eds.), Proc. Western Atlantic Turtle Symposium, Vol. 3, U. Miami Press 514 pp.

Morris, R. A. and G. H. Balazs. 1994. Experimental use of cryosurgery to treat fibropapillomas in the green turtle, *Chelonia mydas.* Pages 111-114 *in* B. A. Schroeder and B. E. Witherington (compilers), Proceedings of the thirteenth annual symposium on sea turtle biology and conservation. NOAA Tech. Memo. NMFS-SEFSC-341, 281 pp.

Mortimer, J. A. 1981. The feeding ecology of the west Caribbean green turtle (*Chelonia mydas*) in Nicaragua.

Biotropica 13(1): 49-58.

Mortimer, J. A. 1982a. Factors influencing beach selection by nesting sea turtles. Pages 45-51 *in* K. A. Bjorndal (ed.), Biology and conservation of sea turtles. Smithsonian Institution Press, Washington D. C., 583 pp.

Mortimer, J. A. 1982b. Feeding ecology of sea turtles. Pages 103-109 *in* K. A. Bjorndal (ed.), Biology and conservation of sea turtles, Smithsonian Institution Press, Washington, D. C., 583 pp.

Mortimer, J. A. 1984. Marine turtles in the Republic of the Seychelles: status and management. Report on Project 1809, I. U. C. N., Gland, Switzerland, 80 pp.

Mortimer, J. A. 1990. The influence of beach sand characteristics on the nesting behavior and clutch survival of green turtles (*Chelonia mydas*). Copeia 1990(3): 802-817.

Mortimer, J. A. 1992. Marine turtle conservation in Malaysia. Malayan Nature Journal 45 (1-4): 353-361.

Mortimer, J. A., Z. Ahmad and S. Kaslan. 1993. The status of the hawksbill *Eretmochelys imbricata* and green turtle *Chelonia mydas* of Melaka and Negeri Sembilan. Malayan Nature J. 46: 243-253.

Mortimer, J. A. and A. Carr. 1987. Reproduction and migrations of the Ascension Island green turtle (*Chelonia mydas*). Copeia 1987 (1): 103-113.

Mortimer, J. A. and K. M. Portier 1989. Reproductive homing and internesting behavior of the green turtle (*Chelonia mydas*) at Ascension Island, South Atlantic Ocean. Copeia 1989 (4): 962-977.

Morton, B. 1992. China's turtles. Marine Pollution Bull. 24(12): 576-577.

Mosier, A. E. 1994. What is GIS and how can it benefit sea turtle research and conservation? Pages 97-98 *in* K. A. Bjorndal, A. B. Bolten, D. A. Johnson and P. J. Eliazar (compilers), Proceedings of the fourteenth annual symposium on sea turtle biology and conservation. NOAA Tech. Memo. NMFS-SEFSC-351, 323 pp.

Mrosovsky, N. 1967. How turtles find the sea. Sci. J. 3(11): 53-57.

Mrosovsky, N. 1968. Nocturnal emergence of hatchling sea turtles: control by thermal inhibition of activity. Nature 220(5174): 1338-39.

Mrosovsky, N. 1970. The influence of the sun's position and elevated cues on the orientation of hatchling sea turtles. Animal Behaviour 18(4): 648-651.

Mrosovsky, N. 1972. The water-finding ability of sea turtles. Brain, Behavior and Evolution 5(2-3): 202-225.

Mrosovsky, N. 1978a. Effects of flashing lights on sea-finding behavior of green turtles. Behavioral Biology 22: 85-91.

Mrosovsky, N. 1978b. Orientation mechanisms of marine turtles. Pages 413-419 *in* K. Schmidt-Koenig and W. T. Keeton (eds.), Animal migration, navigation and homing. Springer-Verlag, NY 462 pp.

Mrosovsky, N. 1980. Thermal biology of sea turtles. Amer. Zool. 20(3): 531-547.

Mrsovsky, N. 1982. Sex ratio bias in hatchling sea turtles from artificially incubated eggs. Biol. Conserv. 23(4): 309-314.

Mrosovsky, N. 1983. Conserving Sea Turtles. The British Herpetological Society, London, U. K., 176 pp.

Mrosovsky, N. 1994. Sex ratios of sea turtles. J. Experimental Zoology 270 (1): 16-27.

Mrosovsky, N. and A. Carr. 1967. Preference for light of short wavelengths in hatchling green sea turtles, *Chelonia*

mydas, tested on their natural nesting beaches. Behaviour 28(3-4): 217-231.

Mrosovsky, N., P. H. Dutton and C. P. Whitmore. 1984. Sex ratios of two species of sea turtle nesting in Suriname. Canadian J. Zool. 62(11): 2227-2239.

Mrosovsky, N., and M. H. Godfrey. 1995. Manipulating sex ratios: turtle speed ahead! Chelonian Conservation and Biology 1(3): 238-240.

Mrosovsky, N., A. M. Granda and T. Hay. 1979. Seaward orientation of hatchling turtles: turning systems in the optic tectum. Brain, Behavior and Evolution 16(3): 203-221.

Mrosovsky, N. and S. F. Kingsmill. 1985. How turtles find the sea. Zeit. Tierpsychol. 67(1-4): 237-256.

Mrosovsky, N., C. Lavin and M. H. Godfrey. 1994. Thermal effects of condominiums on a Florida beach: potential impact on sex ratios. Page 99 *in* K. A. Bjorndal, A. B. Bolten, D. A. Johnson and P. J. Eliazar (compilers), Proceedings of the fourteenth annual symposium on sea turtle biology and conservation. NOAA Tech. Memo. NMFS-SEFSC-351, 323 pp.

Mrosovsky, N. and C. Pieau. 1991. Transitional range of temperature, pivotal temperatures and thermosensitive stages for sex determination in reptiles. Amphibia-Reptilia 12: 169-179.

Mrosovsky, N. and P. C. H. Pritchard. 1971. Body temperatures of *Dermochelys coriacea* and other sea turtles. Copeia 1971 (4): 624-631.

Mrosovsky, N., and J. Provancha. 1992. Sex ratio of hatchling loggerhead sea turtles: data and estimates from a 5-year study. Canadian J. Zoology 70: 530-538.

Mrosovsky, N. and S. J. Shettleworth. 1968. Wavelength preferences and brightness cues in the water finding behaviour of sea turtles. Behaviour 32(4): 211-257.

Mukai, H. 1993. Biogeography of the tropical seagrasses in the western Pacific. Australian J. Marine and Freshwater Research 44(1): 1-17.

Murphy, T. M. and S. R. Hopkins-Murphy. 1989. Sea turtle and shrimp fishing interactions: a summary and critique of relevant information. Center for Marine Conservation, Washington, D. C., 52 pp.

Murray, P. A. 1984. The national report for the country of Saint Lucia. Pages 370-380 *in* P. Bacon, F. Berry, K. Bjorndal, H. Hirth, L. Ogren and M. Weber (eds.), Proc. Western Atlantic Turtle Symposium, Vol. 3, U. Miami Press, 514 pp.

Nájera, J. J. D. 1991. Anidación de la tortuga blanca, *Chelonia mydas* (Linnaeus, 1758) (Testudines: Cheloniidae), en Isla Contoy, Mexico. Rev. Biol. Trop. 39(1): 149-152.

Nakamura, K. 1980. Carotenoids in serum of Pacific green turtle, *Chelonia mydas*. Bull. Japanese Soc. Scientific Fisheries 46(7): 909.

Nardo, G. D. 1864. Nuova rarissima specie di Cheloniano pescato nelle nostre spiaggie: *Chelonia mydas*. Atti Int. Veneto Sci. Lett. Art. (3)9: 1418-1427.

National Marine Fisheries Service. 1993. Satellites used to study the oceanic migrations of Hawaii's green sea turtles. Marine Turtle Newsletter 61: 7-9.

National Marine Fisheries Service and U. S. Fish and Wildlife Service. 1991. Recovery Plan for U. S. Population of Atlantic Green Turtle. National Marine Fisheries Service, Washington, D. C. 52 pp.

Navid, D. 1982. Conservation and management of sea turtles: a legal overview. Pages 523-535 *in* K. A. Bjorndal (ed.),

Biology and conservation of sea turtles. Smithsonian Institution Press, Washington D. C., 583 pp.

Nelson, D. A. 1994. Preliminary assessment of juvenile green sea turtle behavior in the Trident Submarine Basin Patrick AFB, Florida. Pages 104-108 *in* K. A. Bjorndal, A. B. Bolten, D. A. Johnson and P. J. Eliazar (compilers), Proceedings of the fourteenth annual symposium on sea turtle biology and conservation. NOAA Tech. Memo. NMFS-SEFSC-351, 323 pp.

Nicolson, S. W. and P. L. Lutz. 1989. Salt gland function in the green sea turtle *Chelonia mydas*. J. Exp. Biol. 144: 171-184.

Nietschmann, B. 1973. Between land and water: the subsistence ecology of the Miskito Indians, Eastern Nicaragua. Seminar Press, New York, 277 pp.

Nietschmann, B. 1982. The cultural context of sea turtle subsistence hunting in the Caribbean and problems caused by commercial exploitation. Pages 439-445 *in* K. A. Bjorndal (ed.), Biology and conservation of sea turtles. Smithsonian Institution Press, Washington D. C., 583 pp.

Nietschmann, B. 1989. Traditional sea territories, resources and rights in Torres Strait. Pages 60-93 *in* J. Cordell (ed.), A sea of small boats. Cultural Survival Report 26, Cultural Survival, Inc., Cambridge, Mass., 418 pp.

Nigrelli, R. F. and G. M. Smith. 1943. The occurrence of leeches, *Ozobranchus branchiatus* (Menzies), on fibro-epithelial tumors of marine turtles, *Chelonia mydas* (Linnaeus). Zoologica 28(2): 107-108.

Norman, J., C. Limpus, J. Miller and C. Moritz. 1993-94. Inferences about feeding ground distributions from genetic markers. Second World Congress of Herpetology, Abstract, page 182, University of Adelaide, Adelaide, Australia.

Norman, J. A., C. Moritz and C. J. Limpus. 1994. Mitochondrial DNA control region polymorphisms: genetic markers for ecological studies of marine turtles. Molecular Ecology 3(4): 363-373.

Northmore, D. P. M. and A. M. Granda. 1991. Ocular dimensions and schematic eyes of freshwater and sea turtles. Visual Neuroscience 7: 627-635.

Nuitja, I. N. S. 1993-94. The ecology of the green turtle *Chelonia mydas* L. on Sukumade Beach, East Java. Second World Congress of Herpetology, Abstract, Appendix (no pagination), University of Adelaide, Adelaide, Australia.

Nuitja, N. S. and J. D. Lazell. 1982. Marine turtle nesting in Indonesia. Copeia 3: 708-710.

Nutaphand, W. 1979. The turtles of Thailand. Siamfarm Zoological Garden, Bangkok, Thailand, 222 pp.

Ogren, L. H. 1989. Status report of the green turtle. Pages 89-94 *in* L. Ogren, F. Berry, K. Bjorndal, H. Kumpf, R. Mast, G. Medina, H. Reichart and R. Witham (eds.), Proc. Second Western Atlantic Turtle Symposium, NOAA Tech. Memo. NMFS-SEFC-226, 401 pp.

Ogren, L., F. Berry, K. Bjorndal, H. Kumpf, R. Mast, G. Medina, H. Reichart and R. Witham (eds.), 1989. Proceedings of the Second Western Atlantic Turtle Symposium, NOAA Tech. Memo. NMFS-SEFC-226, 401 pp.

Ogren, L. and C. McVea Jr. 1982. Apparent hibernation by sea turtles in North American waters. Pages 127-132 *in* K. A. Bjorndal (ed.), Biology and conservation of sea turtles. Smithsonian Institution Press, Washington, D. C., 583 pp.

Olson, S. L. 1981. Natural history of vertebrates on the Brazilian Islands of the mid-south Atlantic. Nat. Geogr. Soc. Res. Rep. 13: 481-492.

Osada, T., T. Sasaki and A. Ikai. 1988. Purification and characterization of alpha-macroglobulin and ovomacroglobulin of the green turtle (*Chelonia mydas japonica*). J. Biochemistry 103(2): 212-217.

Osorio de Castro, J. 1954. Glossario de nomes dos peixes. Publ. No. 20. Gabinete de estudos das pescas, Lisbon. 249 pp.

Ottenwalder, J. A. and J. P. Ross 1992. The Cuban sea turtle fishery: description and needs for management. Pages 90-92 *in* M. Salmon and J. Wyneken (compilers) Proc. eleventh annual workshop on sea turtle biology and conservation. NOAA Tech. Memo. NMFS-SEFSC-302, 195 pp.

Owen, R. D., S. A. Johnson, W. E. Redfoot and L. M. Ehrhart. 1994. Marine turtle nest production and reproductive success at Archie Carr NWR: 1982-1993. Pages 109-111 *in* K. A. Bjorndal, A. B. Bolten, D. A. Johnson and P. J. Eliazar (compilers), Proceedings of the fourteenth annual symposium on sea turtle biology and conservation. NOAA Tech. Memo. NMFS-SEFSC-351, 323 pp.

Owens, D. W. 1980. The comparative reproductive physiology of sea turtles. Amer. Zool. 20(3): 549-563.

Owens, D. W. 1982. The role of reproductive physiology in the conservation of sea turtles. Pages 39-44 *in* K. A. Bjorndal (ed.), Biology and conservation of sea turtles. Smithsonian Institution Press, Washington D. C., 583 pp.

Owens, D. W. 1993-94. Endocrine effects on sea turtle behavior. Second World Congress of Herpetology, Abstract, pages 189-190, University of Adelaide, Adelaide, Australia.

Owens, D., D. C. Comuzzie and M. Grassman. 1986. Chemoreception in the homing and orientation behavior of amphibians and reptiles, with special reference to sea turtles. Pages 341-355 *in* D. Duvall, D. Müller-Schwarze and R. M. Silverstein (eds.), Chemical signals in vertebrates, 4. Ecology, evolution and comparative biology. Plenum Press, NY, 742 pp.

Owens, D. W. and W. A. Gern. 1985. The pineal gland and melatonin in sea turtles. Pages 645-648 *in* B. Lofts and W. N. Holms (eds.), Current trends in comparative endocrinology. Hong Kong Univ. Press, Hong Kong, 1266 pp.

Owens, D. W., W. A. Gern and C. L. Ralph. 1980. Melatonin in the blood and cerebrospinal fluid of the green sea turtle (*Chelonia mydas*). Gen. Comp. Endocrin. 40(2): 180-187.

Owens, D. W., M. A. Grassman and J. R. Hendrickson. 1982. The imprinting hypothesis and sea turtle reproduction. Herpetologica 38(1): 124-135.

Owens, D. W. and Y. A. Morris. 1985. The comparative endocrinology of sea turtles. Copeia 1985 (3): 723-735.

Owens, D. W. and C. L. Ralph. 1978. The pineal-paraphyseal complex of sea turtles. 1. Light microscopic description. J. Morphology 158(2): 169-180.

Owens, D. W. and G. J. Ruiz. 1980. New methods of obtaining blood and cerebrospinal fluid from marine turtles. Herpetologica 36(1): 17-20.

Packard, G. C., K. Miller and M. J. Packard. 1992. A protocol for measuring water potential in subterranean nests of reptiles. Herpetologica 48(2): 202-209.

Packard, G. C. and M. J. Packard 1988. The physiological ecology of reptilian eggs and embryos. Pages 523-605 *in* C. Gans and R. B. Huey (eds.), Biology of the reptilia. Vol. 16, Ecology B: Defense and life history. A. R. Liss, Inc. N. Y., 659 pp.

Papadi, G. P., G. H. Balazs and E. R. Jacobson. 1995. Flow cytometric DNA content analysis of fibropapillomas in green turtles *Chelonia mydas*. Diseases Aquatic Organisms 22(1): 13-18.

Papi, F., H. C. Liew, P. Luschi and E. H. Chan. 1995. Long-range migratory travel of a green turtle tracked by satellite: evidence for navigational ability in the open sea. Marine Biology 122(2): 171-175.

Papi, F. and P. Luschi. 1996. Pinpointing "Isla Meta": the case of sea turtles and albatrosses. J. Exp. Biol. 199(1): 65-71.

Parham, J. F. and G. R. Zug. 1996. *Chelonia agassizi*-valid or not? Marine Turtle Newsletter 72: 2-6.

Parmenter, C. J. 1993a. A preliminary evaluation of the performance of passive integrated transponders and metal tags in a population study of the flatback sea turtle (*Natator depressus*). Wildl. Res. 20: 375-381.

Parmenter, C. J. 1993b. Australian sea turtle research, conservation and management: a 1993 status review. Pages 321-325 *in* D. Lunney and D. Ayers (eds.), Herpetology in Australia: a diverse discipline. Royal Zoological Society of New South Wales: Mosman, New South Wales, Australia, 414 pp.

Parsons, J. J. 1962. The green turtle and man. Univ. Florida Press, Gainesville, Florida, 126 pp.

Parsons, T. S. 1968. Variation in the choanal structure of recent turtles. Canadian J. Zool. 46(6): 1235-1263.

Parsons, T. S. 1970. The nose and Jacobson's organ. Pages 99-191 *in* C. Gans and T. S. Parsons (eds.), Biology of the Reptilia. Vol. 2, Morphology B. Academic Press, New York, 374 pp.

Pascual, X. 1985. Contribución al estudio de las tortugas marinas en las costas españolas. I. Distribución. Misc. Zool. 9: 287-294.

Patel, T. 1995. France falls into line over turtle ranch. New Scientist 145 (1960): 10.

Patterson , R. 1973. Why tortoises float. J. Herpetology 7(4): 373-375.

Pawikan Conservation Project Staff. 1993. Marine turtles in the Philippines. Pawikan Conservation Project, Protected Areas and Wildlife Bureau, NAPWNC, Quezon City, Philippines, 10 pp.

Peare, T., P. G. Parker and T. A. Waite. 1994. Multiple paternity in green turtles (*Chelonia mydas*): conservation implications. Pages 115-118 *in* K. A. Bjorndal, A. B. Bolten, D. A. Johnson and P. J. Eliazar (compilers), Proceedings of the fourteenth annual symposium on sea turtle biology and conservation. NOAA Tech. Memo. NMFS-SEFSC-351, 323 pp.

Penhallurick, R. D. 1990. Turtles off Cornwall, The Isles of Scilly and Devonshire. Dyllansow Pengwella, Cornwall, U. K., 95 pp.

Penick, D. N., F. V. Paladino, A. C. Steyermark and J. R. Spotila. 1996. Thermal dependence of tissue metabolism in the green turtle, *Chelonia mydas*. Comp. Biochem. Physiol. 113A(3): 293-296.

Penny, D. G. 1987. Frogs and turtles: different ectotherm overwintering strategies. Comp. Biochem. Physiol. 86A(4): 609-615.

Penyapol, A. 1958. A preliminary study of the sea turtles in the Gulf of Thailand. Nat. Hist. Bull. Siam Soc. 17: 23-36.

Perry, A., G. B. Bauer and A. E. Dizon. 1985. Magnetoreception and biomineralization of magnetite in amphibians and reptiles. Pages 439-453 *in* J. L. Kirschvink, D. S. Jones and B. J. MacFadden (eds.), Magnetite biomineralization and magnetoreception in organisms: a new biomagnetism. Plenum Press, NY. 682 pp.

Peters, A. J. and J. F. G. Lionnet. 1973. Central Western Indian Ocean bibliography. Atoll Res. Bull. 165: 1-322.

Peterson, C., G. Monahan and F. Schwartz 1985. Tagged green turtle returns and nests again in North Carolina. Marine Turtle Newsletter 35: 5-6.

Philander, S. G. 1990. El Niño, La Niña and the Southern Oscillation. Academic Press, N. Y., 293 pp.

Philippi, R. A. 1887. Vorlaufige Nachricht über die chilenischen Seeschildkröten und einige Fische der chilenischen Küste. Zool. Garten 28: 84-88.

Pinckney, J. 1990. Correlation analysis of adult female, egg and hatchling sizes in the loggerhead turtle, *Caretta caretta* (L.), nesting at Kiawah Island, South Carolina, USA. Bull. Mar. Sci. 47(3): 670-679.

Pinto-Rodríquez, B., A. A. Mignucci-Giannoni and K. V. Hall. 1995. Sea turtle mortality assessment and the newly established Caribbean stranding network. Pages 92-93 *in* J. I. Richardson and T. H. Richardson (compilers), Proceedings of the twelfth annual workshop on sea turtle biology and conservation. NOAA Tech. Memo. NMFS-SEFSC-361, 274 pp.

Pitman R. L. 1992. Sea turtle associations with flotsam in the eastern tropical Pacific Ocean. Page 94 *in* M. Salmon and J. Wyneken (compilers), Proceedings of the eleventh annual workshop on sea turtle biology and conservation. NOAA Tech. Memo. NMFS-SEFSC-302, 195 pp.

Plotkin, P. and A. F. Amos. 1990. Effects of anthropogenic debris on sea turtles in the northwestern Gulf of Mexico. Pages 736-743 *in* R. S. Shomura and M. L. Godfrey (eds.), Proceedings of the second international conference on marine debris, 2-7 April 1989, Honolulu, Hawaii. NOAA Tech. Memo. NMFS-SWFSC-154, 1274 pp.

Poiner, I. R., R. C. Buckworth and A. N. M. Harris. 1990. Incidental capture and mortality of sea turtles in Australia's northern prawn fishery. Aust. J. Mar. Freshwater Res. 41: 97-110.

Polunin, N.V.C. 1975. Sea turtles: reports on Thailand, West Malaysia and Indonesia, with a synopsis of data on the "conservation status" of sea turtles in the Indo-West Pacific Region. Mimeo report, I. U. C. N. Gland, Switzerland, 113 pp.

Polunin, N. V. C. 1983. The marine resources of Indonesia. Pages 455-531 *in* M. Barnes (ed.), Oceanography and Marine Biology: An Annual Review. Vol. 21, Aberdeen Univ. Press, U. K., 590 pp.

Polunin, N. V. C. 1985. Traditional marine practices in Indonesia and their bearing on conservation. Pages 155-179 *in* J. A. McNeely and D. Pitt (eds.), Culture and conservation: the human dimension in environmental planning. Croom Helm, London, 308 pp.

Polunin, N. V. C. and N. S. Nuitja. 1982. Sea turtle populations of Indonesia and Thailand. Pages 353-362 *in* K. A. Bjorndal (ed.), Biology and conservation of sea turtles. Smithsonian Institution Press, Washington, D. C., 583 pp.

Powell, R. 1957. Breeding turtles for profit. South Pacific Commission Quarterly Bull. 7(3): 41-42.

Prange, H. D. 1976. Energetics of swimming of a sea turtle. J. Exp. Biol. 64(1): 1-12.

Prange, H. D. 1985. Renal and extra-renal mechanisms of salt and water regulation of sea turtles: a speculative review. Copeia 1985 (3): 771-776.

Price, E. W. 1939. A new genus and two new species of digenetic trematodes from a marine turtle. Proc. Helminthol. Soc. Wash. 6(1): 24-25.

Prince, R. I. T. 1993. Western Australian marine turtle conservation project: an outline of scope and an invitation to participate. Marine Turtle Newsletter 60: 8-14.

Pritchard, P. C. H. 1969. Sea turtles of the Guianas. Bull. Florida State Mus. 13(2): 85-140.

Pritchard, P. C. H. 1971. Galápagos sea turtles—preliminary findings. J. Herpetology 5(1-2): 1-9.

Pritchard, P. C. H. 1976. Post-nesting movements of marine turtles (Cheloniidae and Dermochelyidae) tagged in the Guianas. Copeia 1976(4): 749-754.

Pritchard, P. C. H. 1977. Marine turtles of Micronesia. Chelonia Press, San Francisco, California, 83 pp.

Pritchard, P. C. H. 1979a. Marine turtles of Papua New Guinea. Report on a consultancy. Wildlife Division, Dept. of Lands and Environment, Konedobu, Papua New Guinea, 122 pp.

Pritchard, P. C. H. 1979b. Encyclopedia of turtles. T. F. H. Publications, Neptune, New Jersey, 895 pp.

Pritchard, P. C. H. 1982a. Marine turtles of the South Pacific. Pages 253-262 in K. A. Bjorndal (ed.), Biology and conservation of sea turtles. Smithsonian Institution Press, Washington, D. C., 583 pp.

Pritchard, P. C. H. 1982b. Marine turtles of Micronesia. Pages 263-274 in K. A. Bjorndal (ed.), Biology and conservation of sea turtles. Smithsonian Institution Press, Washington, D. C., 583 pp.

Pritchard, P. C. H. 1982c. Recovered sea turtle populations and U. S. recovery team efforts. Pages 503-511 in K. A. Bjorndal (ed.), Biology and conservation of sea turtles. Smithsonian Institution Press, Washington, D. C., 583 pp.

Pritchard, P. C. H. 1987. Sea turtles in New Caledonia. Unpublished report of a literature survey and field investigation, 25 pp.

Pritchard, P. C. H. 1994. Les D'Entrecasteaux enfin! Report of an expedition to study the sea turtles of the D'Entrecasteaux Reefs, north of New Calendonia. Pages 143-145 in B. A. Schroeder and B. E. Witherington (compilers), Proceedings of the thirteenth annual symposium on sea turtle biology and conservation. NOAA Tech. Memo. NMFS-SEFSC-341, 281 pp.

Pritchard, P., P. Bacon, F. Berry, A. Carr, J. Fletemeyer, R. Gallagher, S. Hopkins, R. Lankford, R. Marquez, L. Ogren, W. Pringle Jr., H. Reichart and R. Witham. 1983. Manual of sea turtle research and conservation techniques, second edition. K. A. Bjorndal and G. H. Balazs, editors. Center for Environmental Education, Washington, D. C., 126 pp.

Pritchard, P. C. H. and P. Trebbau. 1984. The turtles of Venezuela. Society for Study of Amphibians and Reptiles, Oxford, Ohio, 403 pp.

Quesada, R. and L. F. Madriz. 1986. Vascularización coronaria de la tortuga marina Chelonia mydas. Rev. Biol. Trop. 34(2): 253-258.

Radovich, J. 1961. Relationships of some marine organisms of the northeast Pacific to water temperatures particularly during 1957 through 1959. State of California, Dept. Fish and Game, Marine Resources Operations, Fish. Bull. 112: 1-62.

Rafinesque, C. S. 1814. Specchio della scienze o giornale enciclopedico di Sicilia. 2 vols. Palermo.

Rainey W. E. 1971. Reconnaissance of the green turtle, Chelonia mydas, nesting aggregation at Aves Island, Lesser Antilles. Caribbean Res. Inst., College of the Virgin Islands, St. Thomas, Virgin Islands, 20 pp.

Rainey, W. E. 1981. Guide to sea turtle visceral anatomy. NOAA Tech. Memo. NMFS-SEFC-82, 82 pp.

Rakotonirina, B. and A. Cooke. 1994. Sea turtles of Madagascar—their status, exploitation and conservation. Oryx 28(1): 51-61.

Ramirez de Veyra, R. T. D. 1994a. Foreign tag recoveries from the Philippines. Marine Turtle Newsletter 64: 6-9.

Ramirez de Veyra, R. T. D. 1994b. Status of marine turtles in the Philippines. Pages 123-125 in K. A. Bjorndal, A. B. Bolten, D. A. Johnson and P. J. Eliazar (compilers), Proceedings of the fourteenth annual symposium on sea turtle biology and conservation. NOAA Tech. Memo. NMFS-SEFSC-351, 323 pp.

Rand, T. G. and M. Wiles. 1985. Histopathology of infections by Learedius learedi Price, 1934 and Neospirorchis schistosomatoides Price, 1934 (Digenea: Spirorchiidae) in wild green turtles, Chelonia mydas L., from Bermuda. J. Wildlife Diseases 21(4): 461-463.

Raven, H. C. 1946. Predators eating turtle eggs in the East Indies. Copeia 1946(1): 48.

Raymond, P. W. 1984. Sea turtle hatchling disorientation and artificial beachfront lighting: a review of the problem and potential solutions. Center for Environmental Education, Washington, D. C., 72 pp.

Read, M. A., G. C. Grigg and C. J. Limpus. 1996. Body temperatures and winter feeding in immature green turtles, Chelonia mydas, in Moreton Bay, Southeastern Australia. J. Herpetology 30(2): 262-265.

Rebel, T. 1974. Sea turtles and the turtle industry of the West Indies, Florida, and the Gulf of Mexico. U. Miami Press, Florida, 250 pp.

Reichart, H. A. 1982. Farming and ranching as a strategy for sea turtle conservation. Pages 465-471 in K. A. Bjorndal (ed.), Biology and conservation of sea turtles. Smithsonian Institution Press, Washington D. C., 583 pp.

Reichart, H. A. and J. Fretey. 1993. WIDECAST sea turtle recovery action plan for Suriname (K. L. Eckert, ed.). CEP Tech. Report No. 24. UNEP Caribbean Environment Programme, Kingston, Jamaica, 65 pp.

Reina, R. D. 1994. Comparison of blood ionic composition between Australian populations of Chelonia mydas. Pages 270-273 in K. A. Bjorndal, A. B. Bolten, D. A. Johnson and P. J. Eliazar (compilers), Proceedings of the fourteenth annual symposium on sea turtle biology and conservation. NOAA Tech. Memo. NMFS-SEFSC-351, 323 pp.

Renaud, M. L., J. A. Carpenter, S. A. Manzella and J. A. Williams. 1994. Radio and sonic telemetric monitoring of immature green sea turtles in the Brazos-Santiago Pass area, South Padre Island, Texas. Page 148 in B. A. Schroeder and B. E. Witherington (compilers), Proceedings of the thirteenth annual symposium on sea turtle biology and conservation. NOAA Tech. Memo. NMFS-SEFSC-341, 281 pp.

Renaud, M. L., J. A. Carpenter, J. A. Williams and S. A. Manzella-Tirpak. 1995. Activities of juvenile green turtles, *Chelonia mydas*, at a jettied pass in South Texas. Fish. Bull. 93(3): 586-593.

Renaud, M. L., G. R. Gitschlag and J. K. Hale. 1993a. Retention of imitation satellite transmitters fiberglassed to the carapace of sea turtles. Herpet. Rev. 24(3): 94-95, 98-99.

Renaud, M., G. Gitschlag, E. Klima, A. Shah, D. Koi and J. Nance. 1993b. Loss of shrimp by turtle excluder devices (TEDs) in coastal waters of the United States, North Carolina to Texas: March 1988-August 1990. Fish. Bull. 91(1): 129-137.

Rhodin, A. G. J. 1985. Comparative chondro-osseous development and growth of marine turtles. Copeia 1985(3): 752-771.

Rhodin, A. G. J., P. C. H. Pritchard and R. A. Mittermeier. 1984. The incidence of spinal deformities in marine turtles, with notes on the prevalence of kyphosis in Indonesian *Chelonia mydas*. British J. Herp. 6(10): 369-373.

Rhodin, A. G. J., S. Spring and P. C. H. Pritchard 1980. Glossary of turtle vernacular names used in the New Guinea region. J. Polynesian Soc. 89(1): 105-117.

Richard, E., and H. R. Moulin. 1990. Captura y primeros datos de *Chelonia mydas* (Cheloniidae) para la localidad de mar de ajo (Buenos Aires, Argentina). Spheniscus (8): 9-10.

Ridgway, S. H., E. G. Wever, J. G. McCormick, J. Palin and J. H. Anderson. 1969. Hearing in the giant sea turtle, *Chelonia mydas*. Proc. Nat. Acad. Sci. 64: 884-890.

Rimkus, T. A. and R. A. Ackerman. 1995. The impact of beach renourishment on the hydric climate of sea turtle nesting beaches along the Atlantic coast of Florida. Pages 97-102 *in* J. I. Richardson and T. H. Richardson (compilers), Proceedings of the twelfth annual workshop on sea turtle biology and conservation. NOAA Tech. Memo. NMFS-SEFSC-361, 274 pp.

Robins, J. B. 1995. Estimated catch and mortality of sea turtles from the east coast otter trawl fishery of Queensland, Australia. Biol. Conserv. 74(3): 157-167.

Rodda, G. H., T. H. Fritts and J. D. Reichel. 1991. The distributional patterns of reptiles and amphibians in the Mariana Islands. Micronesica 24(2): 195-210.

Rodriquez, E. and R. Zambrano. 1991. Caracterizacion de la temporada de anidacion de tortuga carey (*Eretmochelys imbricata*) y tortuga blanca (*Chelonia mydas*) en El Cuyo, Yucatan. Internal report, 28 pp. ProNatura Peninsula de Yucatan, Merida, Yucatan, Mexico.

Rogers, R. W. 1989. The influence of sea turtles on the terrestrial vegetation of Heron Island, Great Barrier Reef. Proc. Royal Soc. Queensland 100: 67-70.

Rosa, H. Jr. 1965. Preparation of synopses on the biology of species of living aquatic organisms. FAO Fish. Synopsis No. 1, Revision 1, 75 pp.

Ross, J. P. 1984. Adult sex ratio in the green sea turtle. Copeia 1984 (3): 774-776.

Ross, J. P. 1985. Biology of the green turtle, *Chelonia mydas*, on an Arabian feeding ground. J. Herp. 19(4): 459-468.

Ross, J. P. 1987. Sea turtle management plan for the Sultanate of Oman. Marine Science and Fisheries Center, Ministry of Agriculture and Fisheries, Sultanate of Oman and the Omani-American Joint Commission, 27 pp.

Ross J. P. and M. A. Barwani. 1982. Review of sea turtles in the Arabian area. Pages 373-383 *in* K. A. Bjorndal (ed.) Biology and conservation of sea turtles, Smithsonian Institution Press, Washington D. C., 583 pp.

Rostal, D., J. Alvarado, J. Grumbles and D. Owens. 1990. Observations on the reproductive biology of the black turtle, *Chelonia agassizi*, at Playa Colola, Michoacan, Mexico. Pages 255-258 *in* T. H. Richardson, J. I. Richardson and M. Donnelly (compilers), Proceedings of the tenth annual workshop on sea turtle biology and conservation. NOAA Tech. Memo. NMFS-SEFC-278, 286 pp.

Rudloe, A. and J. Rudloe. 1994. Sea turtles: in a race for survival. Nat. Geographic 185(2): 94-121.

Rueda-Almonacid, J. V., J. E. Mayorga and G. Ulloa. 1992. Observaciones sobre la captura comercial de tortugas marinas en La Peninsula de la Guajira, Colombia. Pages 133-153 *in* Contribucion al conocimiento de las tortugas marinas de Colombia, No. 4. Inst. Nacional Recursos Naturales, Bogota, Colombia, 190 pp.

Russell, D. J. and G. H. Balazs. 1994. Colonization by the alien marine alga *Hypnea musciformis* (Wulfen) J. Ag. (Rhodophyta: Gigartinales) in the Hawaiian Islands and its utilization by the green turtle, *Chelonia mydas* L. Aquatic Botany 47 (1994): 53-60.

Ryder, C. 1995. The effect of beach renourishment on sea turtle nesting and hatching success at Sebastian Inlet State Recreation Area, east-central Florida. Pages 230-233 *in* J. I. Richardson and T. H. Richardson (compilers), Proceedings of the twelfth annual workshop on sea turtle biology and conservation. NOAA Tech. Memo. NMFS-SEFSC-361, 274 pp.

Sachet, M-H. 1954. A summary of information on Rose Atoll. Atoll Res. Bull. 29: 1-25.

Sachet, M.-H. 1983. Natural history of Mopelia Atoll, Society Islands. Atoll Res. Bull. 274: 1-37.

Sage, H. and W. R. Gray. 1979. Studies on the evolution of elastin-I. Phylogenetic distribution. Comp. Biochem. Physiol. 64B: 313-327.

Saint-Girons, H. 1991. Histologie comparée des fosses nasales de quelques tortues marines (*Dermochelys coriacea* et *Chelonia mydas*) et d'eaux douces (*Emys orbicularis* et *Pseudemys scripta*) (Reptilia, Dermochelyidae, Cheloniidae, Emydidae). Bijdragen tot de Dierkunde 61(1): 51-61.

Salm, R. and S. Salm. 1991. Sea turtles in the Sultanate of Oman. The Historical Association of Oman, Ruwi, Sultanate of Oman, 40 pp.

Salmon, M. and K. J. Lohmann. 1989. Orientation cues used by hatchling loggerhead sea turtles (*Caretta caretta* L.) during their offshore migration. Ethology 83(3): 215-228.

Salmon, M., J. Wyneken, E. Fritz and M. Lucas. 1992. Seafinding by hatchling sea turtles: role of brightness, silhouette and beach slope as orientation cues. Behaviour 122(1-2): 56-77.

Salvat, F. and B. Salvat. 1992. Nukutipipi Atoll, Tuamotu Archipelago; geomorphology, land and marine flora and fauna and interrelationships. Atoll Res. Bull. 357: 1-43.

Sandys-Winsch, C. and P. J. C. Harris. 1994. "Green" development on the Cape Verde Islands. Env. Conserv. 21(3): 225-230.

Sapsford, C. W. 1978. Anatomical evidence for intracardiac blood shunting in marine turtles. Zoologica Africana 13(1): 57-62.

Sawyer, R. T., A. R. Lawler and R. M. Overstreet. 1975. Marine leeches of the eastern United States and the Gulf of Mexico with a key to the species. J. Nat. Hist. 9(5): 633-667.

Sazima, I. and M. Sazima. 1983. Aspectos de comportamento alimentar e dieta da tartaruga marinha, *Chelonia mydas*, no litoral norte paulista. Bolm. Inst. Oceanogr. S. Paulo 32(2): 199-203.

Schmid, J. R. 1995. Marine turtle populations on the east-central coast of Florida: results of tagging studies at Cape Canaveral, Florida, 1986-1991. Fish. Bull. 93(1): 139-151.

Schmidt, J. 1916. Marking experiments with turtles in the Danish West Indies. Meddelelser Kommissionen Havundersogelser, Serie Fiskeri 5: 1-26.

Schneider, J. G. 1783. Allgemeine Naturgeschichte der Schildkröten, nebst einem systematischen Verzeichnisse der einzelnen Arten. J. C. Müller, Leipzig, 364 pp.

Schroeder, B. A., L. M. Ehrhart, J. L. Guseman, R. D. Owen and W. E. Redfoot. 1990. Cold stunning of marine turtles in the Indian River Lagoon system, Florida, December 1989. Pages 67-69 *in* T. H. Richardson, J. I. Richardson and M. Donnelly (compilers), Proceedings of the tenth annual workshop on sea turtle biology and conservation. NOAA Tech. Memo. NMFS-SEFC-278, 286 pp.

Schroeder, B. A. and A. M. Foley. 1995. Population studies of marine turtles in Florida Bay. Page 117 *in* J. I. Richardson and T. H. Richardson (compilers), Proceedings of the twelfth annual workshop on sea turtle biology and conservation. NOAA Tech. Memo. NMFS-SEFSC-361, 274 pp.

Schroeder, B. A. and D. W. Owens. 1994. Sex ratio of immature green turtles in an east central Florida developmental habitat. Pages 157-161 *in* B. A. Schroeder and B. E. Witherington (compilers), Proceedings of the thirteenth annual symposium on sea turtle biology and conservation. NOAA Tech. Memo. NMFS-SEFSC-341, 281 pp.

Schroeder, R. E. 1995. Observations and data from Mariculture Ltd., Grand Cayman Island. Pages 118-121 *in* J. I. Richardson and T. H. Richardson (compilers), Proceedings of the twelfth annual workshop on sea turtle biology and conservation. NOAA Tech. Memo. NMFS-SEFSC-361, 274 pp.

Schulman, A. A. and P. Lutz. 1995. The effect of plastic ingestion on lipid metabolism in the green sea turtle (*Chelonia mydas*). Pages 122-124 *in* J. I. Richardson and T. H. Richardson (compilers), Proceedings of the twelfth annual workshop on sea turtle biology and conservation. NOAA Tech. Memo. NMFS-SEFSC-361, 274 pp.

Schulz, J. P. 1975. Sea turtles nesting in Suriname. Neder. Com. Int. Natuur. Med. No. 23, STINASU, Verh. No. 3, 143 pp.

Schulz, J. P. 1982. Status of sea turtle populations nesting in Suriname with notes on sea turtles nesting in Guyana and French Guiana. Pages 435-437 *in* K. A. Bjorndal (ed.) Biology and conservation of sea turtles, Smithsonian Institution Press, Washington, D. C., 583 pp.

Schwartz, F. J. 1960. The barnacle, *Platylepas hexastylos,* encrusting a green turtle, *Chelonia mydas mydas,* from Chincoteague Bay, Maryland. Chesapeake Sci. 1: 116-117.

Schwartz, F. J. 1974. The marine leech *Ozobranchus margoi* (Hirudinea: Pisciocolidae), epizootic on *Chelonia* and *Caretta* sea turtles from North Carolina. J. Parasitology 60(5): 889-890.

Schwartz, F. J. 1978. Behavioral and tolerance responses to cold water temperatures by three species of sea turtles (Reptilia, Cheloniidae) in North Carolina. Florida Marine Research Publ., 33: 16-18.

Schwartz, F. J. 1981. A long term internal tag for sea turtles. Northeast Gulf Science 5(1): 87-93.

Schwartz, F. J. 1989. Biology and ecology of sea turtles frequenting North Carolina. NOAA-NURP Rept. 89-2: 307-331.

Schwartz, F. J. 1992. Algal-diatom growths associated with the marine fish sheepshead, *Archosargus probatocephalus,* and loggerhead, *Caretta caretta,* and green, *Chelonia mydas,* sea turtles held in captivity in North Carolina. Bull. Mar. Sci. 51(3): 466-474.

Schwartz, F. J. and C. Peterson. 1984. Color and teratological abnormalities of green turtle, *Chelonia mydas,* hatchlings from North Carolina. Florida Scientist 47(1): 65-68.

Schweigger, A. F. 1812. Prodromus monographiae cheloniorum. Königsberger Arch. Naturw. Math. 1: 271-368, 406-458.

Scolaro, J. A. 1990. *Chelonia mydas* (green sea turtle). Herp. Rev. 21 (1): 24.

Scott, N. and J. A. Horrocks 1993. WIDECAST sea turtle recovery action plan for St. Vincent and the Grenadines. (K. A. Eckert, ed.). CEP Technical Report No. 27, UNEP Caribbean Environment Programme, Kingston, Jamaica, 80 pp.

Sea Turtle Research Unit. 1995. Research activities of the Sea Turtle Research Unit (SEATRU) of Universiti Pertanian Malaysia. Chelonian Conservation and Biology 1(3): 248-249.

Seaborn, G. T. and M. K. Moore. 1994. Unscrambled eggs: a biochemical method of species identification to aid in the prosecution of marine turtle egg poachers. Page 162 *in* B. A. Schroeder and B. E. Witherington (compilers), Proceedings of the thirteenth annual symposium on sea turtle biology and conservation. NOAA Tech. Memo. NMFS-SEFSC-341, 281 pp.

Seabrook, W. 1989a. The seasonal pattern and distribution of green turtle (*Chelonia mydas*) nesting activity on Aldabra Atoll, Indian Ocean. J. Zoology (London), 219(1): 71-81.

Seabrook, W. 1989b. Feral cats (*Felis catus*) as predators of hatchling green turtles (*Chelonia mydas*). J. Zoology 219(1): 83-88.

Seabrook, W. 1991. How many green turtles nest on Aldabra? Oryx 25(2): 96-98.

Segura, A. and R. M. Arauz. 1995. By-catch capture of sea turtles by two kinds of experimental longline gears in Pacific Costa Rica waters. Pages 125-127 *in* J. I. Richardson and T. H. Richardson (compilers), Proceedings of the twelfth annual workshop on sea turtle biology and conservation. NOAA Tech. Memo. NMFS-SEFSC-361, 274 pp.

Sella, I. 1982. Sea turtles in the eastern Mediterranean and northern Red Sea. Pages 417-423 *in* K. A. Bjorndal (ed.), Biology and conservation of sea turtles, Smithsonian Institution Press, Washington, D. C., 583 pp.

Servan, J. 1976. Ecologie de la tortue verte a l'Ile Europa (Canal de Mozambique). Terre Vie 30(3): 421-464.

Sey, O. 1977. Examination of helminth parasites of marine turtles caught along the Egyptian coast. Acta Zool. Acad. Sci. Hungaricae 23(3-4): 387-394.

Shabika, S. V. 1982. Planning for protection of sea turtle habitat. Pages 513-518 in K. A. Bjorndal (ed.), Biology and conservation of sea turtles. Smithsonian Institution Press, Washington, D. C., 583 pp.

Shannon, F. A. 1956. The reptiles and amphibians of Korea. Herpetologica 12: 22-49.

Shannon, S. and J. R. Morgan. 1993. Management of insular Pacific marine ecosystems. Pages 196-213 in E. M. Borgese, N. Ginsburg and J. R. Morgan (eds.), Ocean Yearbook 10. University of Chicago Press, Chicago, 545 pp.

Shaver, D. J. 1994. Relative abundance, temporal patterns, and growth of sea turtles at the Mansfield Channel, Texas. J. Herpetology 28(4): 491-497.

Shaw, S. L., S. Leone-Kabler, A. Alfaro and P. L. Lutz. 1995a. Isoflurane: a safe and effective anesthetic for sea turtles. Pages 240-241 in J. I. Richardson and T. H. Richardson (compilers), Proceedings of the twelfth annual workshop on sea turtle biology and conservation. NOAA Tech. Memo. NMFS-SEFSC-361, 274 pp.

Shaw, S. L., A. Schulman and P. L. Lutz. 1995b. A comparison of Florida silicate and Bahamian aragonite sand as substrates for sea turtle nesting. Pages 128-131 in J. I. Richardson and T. H. Richardson (compilers), Proceedings of the twelfth annual workshop on sea turtle biology and conservation. NOAA Tech. Memo. NMFS-SEFSC-361, 274 pp.

Sheppard, C. 1983. A surfeit of turtles. Sea Frontiers. 29(6): 329-334.

Sheppard, C., A. Price and C. Roberts. 1992. Marine ecology of the Arabian region: patterns and processes in extreme tropical environments. Academic Press, N. Y., 359 pp.

Siddeek, S. M. and R. M. Baldwin. 1996. Assessment of the Oman green turtle (Chelonia mydas) stock using a stage-class matrix model. Herpetological J. 6(1): 1-8.

Silas, E. G. and A. B. Fernando. 1984. Turtle poisoning. Bull. Central Marine Fisheries Research Institute 35: 62-75.

Simha, S. S. and D. R. Chattopadhyaya. 1970. A new genus and species of a blood fluke, Squaroacetabulum solus, from the ventricle of the heart of a marine turtle, Chelone mydas. Zoologischer Anzeiger 184: 290-294.

Simon, M. H. and A. S. Parkes. 1976. The green sea turtle (Chelonia mydas): nesting on Ascension Island, 1973-1974. J. Zool. London 179: 153-163.

Sindermann, C. J. 1988. Coccidian disease of green turtles. Pages 384-385 in C. J. Sindermann and D. V. Lightner (eds.), Disease diagnosis and control in North American marine aquaculture. Second, revised edition. Developments in Aquaculture and Fisheries Science, 17. Elsevier Science Publ. B. V., 431 pp.

Slater, J. R. 1963. Distribution of Washington reptiles. Occ. Pap. Dept. Biol. College Puget Sound 24: 212-233.

Smith, E. N., N. C. Long and J. Wood. 1986. Thermoregulation and evaporative water loss of green sea turtles, Chelonia mydas. J. Herpetology 20(3): 325-332.

Smith, H. M. and R. B. Smith. 1979. Synopsis of the herpetofauna of Mexico. Vol. VI. Guide to Mexican turtles. Bibliographic Addendum III. John Johnson, North Bennington, Vermont, 1044 pp.

Smith, H. M. and R. B. Smith. 1993. Synopsis of the herpetofauna of Mexico. Vol. VII. Bibliographic Addendum IV and Index, Bibliographic Addenda II-IV 1979-1991. Univ. Press of Colorado, Niwot, Colorado, 1082 pp.

Smith, H. M. and E. H. Taylor. 1950. An annotated checklist and key to the reptiles of Mexico exclusive of the snakes. U. S. Nat. Mus. Bull. (199): 1-253.

Smith, J. W. 1972. The flood flukes (Digenea: Sanguinicolidae and Spirorchidae) of cold-blooded vertebrates and some comparisons with the schistosomes. Helminthological Abstracts, Series A, 41(2): 161-204.

Smith, M. H., H. O. Hillestad, M. N. Manlove, D. O. Straney and J. M. Dean. 1978. Management implications of genetic variability in loggerhead and green turtles. XIIIth Congress of Game Biologists, pp. 302-312.

Snell, H. L. and T. H. Fritts. 1983. The significance of diurnal terrestrial emergence of green turtles (Chelonia mydas) in the Galápagos Archipelogo. Biotropica 15(4): 285-291.

Society for the Protection of Nature. 1992. Kazanli sea turtle hatchling rescue project. Coastal management section and Alice Carswell, Istanbul, Turkey, 20 pp.

Solé, G. 1994. Migration of the Chelonia mydas population from Aves Island. Pages 283-286 in K. A. Bjorndal, A. B. Bolten, D. A. Johnson and P. J. Eliazar (compilers), Proceedings of the fourteenth annual symposium on sea turtle biology and conservation. NOAA Tech. Memo. NMFS-SEFSC-351, 323 pp.

Solomon, S. E. 1984. The characterization and distribution of cells lining the axillary gland of the adult green turtle (Chelonia mydas L.). J. Anat. 138(2): 267-279.

Solomon, S. E. 1985. The morphology of the kidney of the green turtle (Chelonia mydas L.). J. Anat. 140(3): 355-369.

Solomon, S. E. and T. Baird. 1979. Aspects of the biology of Chelonia mydas. Oceanog. Mar. Biol. Ann. Rev. 17: 347-361.

Solomon, S. E. and T. Baird. 1980. The effect of fungal penetration on the egg shell of the green turtle. Electron Microscopy 2: 434-435.

Solomon, S. E., J. R. Hendrickson and L. P. Hendrickson. 1986. The structure of the carapace and plastron of juvenile turtles, Chelonia mydas (the green turtle) and Caretta caretta (the loggerhead turtle). J. Anat. 145: 123-131.

Solomon, S. E. and M. Purton. 1984. The respiratory epithelium of the lung in the green turtle (Chelonia mydas L.) J. Anat. 139(2): 353-370.

Solomon, S. E. and R. Tippett. 1991. Lipid inclusion in the livers of captive reared marine turtles. Animal Technology 42(2): 77-81.

Sonnini, C. S. and P. A. Latreille. 1802. Histoire naturelle des reptiles avec figures dessinées d'apres nature. I. Deterville, Paris, 280 pp.

Soulé, M. E. (ed.). 1987. Viable populations for conservation. Cambridge University Press, Cambridge, 189 pp.

Spotila, J. R., L. D. Spotila and N. F. Kaufer. 1994. Molecular mechanisms of TSD in reptiles: a search for the magic bullet. J. Experimental Zoology 270(1): 117-127.

Spotila, J. R., E. A. Standora, S. J. Morreale and G. J. Ruiz. 1987. Temperature dependent sex determination in the green turtle (Chelonia mydas): effects on the sex ratio on a natural nesting beach. Herpetologica 43(1): 74-81.

Spotila, J. R., E. J. Standora, S. J. Morreale, G. J. Ruiz, and C. Puccia. 1983. Methodology for the study of temperature related phenomena affecting sea turtle eggs. Endangered species report 11, U. S. Fish Wildlife Service, Albuquerque, New Mexico, 51 pp.

Sprent, J. F. A. 1977. Ascaridoid nematodes of amphibians and reptiles: *Sulcascaris.* J. Helminthology 51: 379-387.

Spring, C. S. 1980. Turtles, men & magic. Wildlife Division, Konedobu, Papua New Guinea, 26 pp.

Spring, S. 1981. Marine turtles in the Manus Province. Wildlife in Papua New Guinea 81/13. Wildlife Div., Dept. Lands and Environment, Konedobu, Papua New Guinea, 15 pp.

Spring, S. 1982a. Status of marine turtle populations in Papua New Guinea. Pages 281-289 *in* K. A. Bjorndal (ed.), Biology and conservation of sea turtles. Smithsonian Institution Press, Washington, D. C. 583 pp.

Spring, S. 1982b. Subsistence hunting of marine turtles in Papua New Guinea. Pages 291-295 *in* K. A. Bjorndal (ed.), Biology and conservation of sea turtles. Smithsonian Institution Press, Washington, D. C., 583 pp.

Spring, S. C. 1982c. Marine turtle conservation in Papua New Guinea. Pages 303-306 *in* L. Morauta, J. Pernetta and W. Heaney (eds.), Traditional conservation in Papua New Guinea: implications for today. Monograph 16, Inst. Appl. Social and Economic Res., Boroko, Papua New Guinea, 391 pp.

Spring, C. S. 1983. Marine turtles of Long Island. Unpublished report on an IUCN/WWF sponsored tagging project. Project No. 1683, IUCN, Gland, Switzerland, 39 pp.

Stabenau, E. K., P. F. Moon and T. A. Heming. 1993. Resuscitation of sea turtles. Marine Turtle Newsletter 62: 3-5.

Stancyk, S. S. 1982. Non-human predators of sea turtles and their control. Pages 139-152 *in* K. A. Bjorndal (ed.), Biology and conservation of sea turtles, Smithsonian Institution Press, Washington D. C., 583 pp.

Standora, E. A., S. J. Morreale, G. J. Ruiz and J. R. Spotila. 1982a. Sex determination in green turtle (*Chelonia mydas*) hatchlings can be influenced by egg position within the nest. Bull. Ecol. Soc. Amer. 63(2): 83-84.

Standora, E. A. and J. R. Spotila. 1985. Temperature dependent sex determination in sea turtles. Copeia 1985(3): 711-722.

Standora, E. A., J. R. Spotila and R. E. Foley. 1982b. Regional endothermy in the sea turtle, *Chelonia mydas.* J. Therm. Biol. 7: 159-165.

Stearns, S. C. 1992. The evolution of life histories. Oxford Univ. Press, Oxford, 249 pp.

Stebbins, R. C. 1985. A field guide to western reptiles and amphibians. Houghton Mifflin Co., Boston, 336 pp.

Steiner, T. 1994. International implementation of TEDS Law PL 101-162 by the U. S. Government: fact or science fiction. Pages 178-181 *in* B. A. Schroeder and B. E. Witherington (compilers), Proceedings of the thirteenth annual symposium on sea turtle biology and conservation. NOAA Tech. Memo. NMFS-SEFSC-341, 281 pp.

Steiner, T., D. Dobson, K. Nielsen and J. J. Siegel. 1995. TEDS: international implementation? Pages 246-248 *in* J. I. Richardson and T. H. Richardson (compilers), Proceedings of the twelfth annual workshop on sea turtle biology and conservation. NOAA Tech. Memo. NMFS-SEFSC-361, 274 pp.

Sternberg, J. 1981. The worldwide distribution of sea turtle nesting beaches. Center for Environmental Education, Washington, D. C.

Sternberg, J. 1982. Sea turtle hunts throughout the world. Center for Environmental Education, Washington, D. C., 16 pp.

Stoddart, D. R. (ed.). 1967. Ecology of Aldabra Atoll, Indian Ocean. Atoll Res. Bull. 118: 1-141.

Stoddart, D. R. 1971. Scientific studies at Aldabra and neighbouring islands. Phil. Trans. Royal Soc. London; B, 260: 5-29.

Stoddart, D. R., P. E. Gibbs and D. Hopley. 1981. Natural History of Raine Island, Great Barrier Reef. Atoll Res. Bull. 254: 1-44.

Storr, G. M. 1960. The physiography, vegetation and vertebrate fauna of North Island, Houtman Abrolhos. J. Royal Soc. West. Australia 43: 59-62.

Suganuma, H. 1985. Green turtle research program in Ogasawara. Marine Turtle Newsletter 33: 2-3.

Suganuma, H. 1989. The green turtle (*Chelonia mydas*) in Ogasawara Islands, Japan. Page 344 *in* L. Ogren, F. Berry, K. Bjorndal, H. Kumpf, R. Mast, G. Medina, H. Reichart and R. Witham (eds.), Proceedings of the Second Western Atlantic Turtle Symposium. NOAA Tech. Memo. NMFS-SEFC-226, 401 pp.

Suganuma, H., K. Horikoshi and H. Tachikawa. 1994. Scute deviation of green turtle hatchlings from a hatchery in the Ogasawara Islands, Japan. Page 148 *in* K. A. Bjorndal, A. B. Bolten, D. A. Johnson and P. J. Eliazar (compilers), Proceedings of the fourteenth annual symposium on sea turtle biology and conservation. NOAA Tech. Memo. NMFS-SEFSC-351, 323 pp.

Suwelo, I. S. 1975. Peternakan penyu di Sukamade, Banyuwangi. Oseanologi di Indonesia 4: 13-20.

Suwelo, I. S. and Kuntjoro. 1969. Penju laut, produktivitas dan pembinaannya di Indonesia. Rimba Indonesia 14: 18-49.

Suwelo, I. S., N. S. Nuitja and I. Soetrisno. 1982. Marine turtles in Indonesia. Pages 349-351 *in* K. A. Bjorndal (ed.), Biology and conservation of sea turtles. Smithsonian Institution Press, Washington, D. C., 583 pp.

Sybesma, J. 1992. WIDECAST sea turtle recovery action plan for the Netherlands Antilles (K. L. Eckert, ed.). CEP Technical Report No. 11. UNEP Caribbean Environment Programme, Kingston, Jamaica, 63 pp.

Tachikawa, H., H. Suganuma, F. Sato, M. Yamaguchi, K. Horikoshi, Y. Kurata and J. Kimura. 1994. Long distance dispersal and remigration of adult green turtles in the Ogasawara Islands, Japan. Page 265 *in* B. A. Schroeder and B. E. Witherington (compilers), Proceedings of the thirteenth annual symposium on sea turtle biology and conservation. NOAA Tech. Memo. NMFS-SEFSC-341, 281 pp.

Taft, C. 1996. Growing solid waste crisis in Tortuguero. Pages 4-6 *in* Velador: Newsletter of the Caribbean Conservation Corporation. Winter 1996. Caribbean Conservation Corporation, Gainesville, Florida, 8 pp.

Tambiah, C. R. 1995. Integrated management of sea turtles among the indigenous people of Guyana: planning beyond recovery and towards sustainability. Pages 138-141 *in* J. I. Richardson and T. H. Richardson (compilers), Proceedings of the twelfth annual workshop on sea turtle biology and conservation. NOAA Tech. Memo. NMFS-SEFSC-361, 274 pp.

Tarr, P. W. 1987. Non-nesting emergence by green turtles *Chelonia mydas* at the Cunene River mouth, South West Africa/Namibia. Madoqua 15(3): 267-268.

Teas, W. G. 1992a. 1990 Annual report of the sea turtle stranding and salvage network: Atlantic and Gulf coasts of the United States. NOAA-NMFS-SEFSC, Miami Laboratory, Contribution No. MIA-91/92-60, 48 pp.

Teas, W. G. 1992b. 1991 Annual report of the sea turtle stranding and salvage network: Atlantic and Gulf coasts of the United States. NOAA-NMFS-SEFSC, Miami Laboratory, Contribution No. MIA-91/92-62, 48 pp.

Teas, W. G. 1993. 1992 Annual report of the sea turtle stranding and salvage network: Atlantic and Gulf coasts of the United States. NOAA-NMFS-SEFSC, Miami Laboratory, Contribution No. MIA-92/93-73, 43 pp.

Teas, W. G. 1994. 1993 Annual report of the sea turtle stranding and salvage network: Atlantic and Gulf coasts of the United States. NOAA-NMFS-SEFSC, Miami Laboratory, Contribution No. MIA-94/95-12, 46 pp.

Thayer, G. W., K. A. Bjorndal, J. C. Ogden, S. L. Williams and J. C. Zieman. 1984. Role of larger herbivores in seagrass communities. Estuaries 7(4A): 351-376.

Thompson, N. B. 1988. The status of loggerhead, *Caretta caretta;* Kemp's ridley, *Lepidochelys kempi;* and green, *Chelonia mydas,* sea turtles in U. S. waters. Mar. Fish. Rev. 50(3): 16-23.

Thompson, N. B. 1991. A response to Dodd and Byles. Mar. Fish. Rev. 53(3): 31-33.

Thompson, N. P., P. W. Rankin and D. W. Johnston. 1974. Polychlorinated biphenyls and p, p' DDE in green turtle eggs from Ascension Island, South Atlantic Ocean. Bull. Environ. Contam. Toxicol. 11(5): 399-406.

Thunberg, C. P. 1787. Befkrifring pa Trenne Skold-paddor. Kongl. Vetenskaps Acad. NYA Handl. 8: 178-180.

Tiwari, M. 1994. A survey of sea turtles in the Andaman and Nicobar Islands. Pages 152-153 *in* K. A. Bjorndal, A. B. Bolten, D. A. Johnson and P. J. Eliazar (compilers), Proceedings of the fourteenth annual symposium on sea turtle biology and conservation. NOAA Tech. Memo. NMFS-SEFSC-351, 323 pp.

Toda, T., Y. Toda and F. A. Kummerow. 1984. Spontaneous aortic lesions in marine turtles. Tohoku J. Exp. Med. 144(2): 139-142.

Tow, S. K. and E. O. Moll. 1982. Status and conservation of estuarine and sea turtles in West Malaysian waters. Pages 339-347 *in* K. A. Bjorndal (ed.), Biology and conservation of sea turtles. Smithsonian Institution Press, Washington, D. C., 583 pp.

Trono, R. B. 1991. Philippine marine turtle conservation program. Marine Turtle Newsletter 53: 5-7.

Tschudi, J. J. von. 1846. Untersuchungen über die Fauna Peruana. Herpetologie & Ichthyologie. Berlin, 113 pp.

Tuato'o-Bartley, N., T. E. Morrell and P. Craig. 1993. Status of sea turtles in American Samoa in 1991. Pacific Science 47(3): 215-221.

Uchida, I. 1990. On the synthetic materials found in the digestive systems of, and discharged by, sea turtles collected in waters adjacent to Japan. Page 744 *in* R. S. Shomura and M. L. Godfrey (eds.), Proceedings of the second international conference on marine debris, 2-7 April 1989, Honolulu, Hawaii. NOAA Tech. Memo. NMFS-SWFSC-154, 1274 pp.

Umezu, T., M. Murai, M. Miki and Y. Kurata. 1991. Long-term marking of green turtles with Ir. Nippon Suisan Gakkaishi 57(6): 1115-1120.

UNEP/IUCN 1988a. Coral Reefs of the World. Vol. 1: Atlantic and Eastern Pacific. UNEP Regional Seas Directories and Bibliographies. IUCN, Gland, Switzerland and Cambridge, UK/UNEP, Nairobi, Kenya, 373 pp.

UNEP/IUCN 1988b. Coral Reefs of the World. Vol. 2: Indian Ocean, Red Sea and Gulf. UNEP Regional Seas Direc-

tories and Bibliographies. IUCN, Gland, Switzerland and Cambridge, UK/UNEP, Nairobi, Kenya, 389 pp.

UNEP/IUCN 1988c. Coral Reefs of the World. Vol. 3: Central and Western Pacific. UNEP Regional Seas Directories and Bibliographies. IUCN, Gland, Switzerland and Cambridge, UK/UNEP, Nairobi, Kenya, 329 pp.

Urban, E. K. 1970. Nesting of the green turtle (*Chelonia mydas*) in the Dahlak Archipelago, Ethiopia. Copeia 1970(2): 393-394.

Valkanov, A. 1949. Die Seeschildkröten des Schwarzen Meeres. Arb. Biol. Meeresst. Varna, 14: 99-102.

Van Buskirk, J. and L. B. Crowder. 1994. Life-history variation in marine turtles. Copeia 1994(1): 66-81.

Van der Heiden, A. M., R. Briseño-Dueñas and D. Rios-Olmeda. 1985. A simplified method for determining sex in hatchling sea turtles. Copeia 1985(3): 779-782.

Van Dyke, J. M. 1993. International governance and stewardship of the high seas and its resources. Pages 13-22 *in* J. M. Van Dyke, D. Zaelke and G. Hewison (eds.), Freedom for the seas in the 21st century: ocean governance and environmental harmony. Island Press, Washington D. C., 504 pp.

Van Piggelen, D. C. G. and H. Strijbosch. 1993. The nesting of sea turtles (*Caretta caretta* and *Chelonia mydas*) in the Göksu Delta, Turkey (June-August, 1991). Doga-Tr. J. Zoology 17: 137-149.

Van Rhijn, F. A. 1979. Optic orientation in hatchlings of the sea turtle, *Chelonia mydas.* I. Brightness: not the only optic cue in sea-finding orientation. Mar. Behav. Physiol. 6: 105-121.

Van Rhijn, F. A. and J. C. Van Gorkom. 1983. Optic orientation in hatchlings of the sea turtle, *Chelonia mydas.* III. Sea-finding behaviour: the role of photic and visual orientation in animals walking on the spot under laboratory conditions. Mar. Behav. Physiol. 9: 211-228.

Van Vleet, E. S. and G. G. Pauly. 1987. Characterization of oil residues scrapped from stranded sea turtles from the Gulf of Mexico. Caribbean J. Sci. 23(1): 77-83.

Vargas, P., P. Tello and C. Aranda. 1994. Sea turtle conservation in Peru: the present situation and a strategy for immediate action. Pages 159-162 *in* K. A. Bjorndal, A. B. Bolten, D. A. Johnson and P. J. Eliazar (compilers), Proceedings of the fourteenth annual symposium on sea turtle biology and conservation. NOAA Tech. Memo. NMFS-SEFSC-351, 323 pp.

Vaughan, P. W. 1981. Marine turtles: a review of their status and management in the Solomon Islands. Fisheries Div. Ministry Natural Resources, Honiara, Solomon Islands, 70 pp.

Venizelos, L. E. 1991. Pressure on the endangered Mediterranean marine turtles is increasing. The role of MEDASSET. Marine Pollution Bull. 23: 613-616.

Verheijen, F. J. 1985. Photopollution: artificial light optic spatial control systems fail to cope with. Incidents, causations, remedies. Exp. Biol. 44: 1-18.

Vicente, V. P. and T. Tallevast. 1995. Characteristics of green turtle (*Chelonia mydas*) grazing grounds in some Caribbean Islands. Pages 145-149 *in* J. I. Richardson and T. H. Richardson (compilers), Proceedings of the twelfth annual workshop on sea turtle biology and conservation. NOAA Tech. Memo. NMFS-SEFSC-361, 274 pp.

Villiers, A. 1958. Tortues et crocodiles de l'Afrique Noire Française. Initiations Africaines, Institut Français D'Afrique Noire 15: 1-354.

Vogt, R. C. 1994. Temperature controlled sex determination as a tool for turtle conservation. Chelonian Conservation and Biology 1(2): 159-162.

Walbaum, J. J. 1782. Chelonographia oder beschreibung einiger Schildkröten nach natürlichen Urbildern. Johann Friedrich Gleditsch, Lubeck und Leipzig, 132 pp.

Walker, T. A., and C. J. Parmenter. 1990. Absence of a pelagic phase in the life cycle of the flatback turtle, *Natator depressa* (Garman). J. Biogeography 17(3): 275-278.

Wallin, L. 1985. A survey of Linnaeus's material of *Chelone mydas, Caretta caretta* and *Eretmochelys imbricata* (Reptilia, Cheloniidae). Zool. J. Linnean Soc. 85(2): 121-130.

Walsh, M. T., T. W. Campbell and B. Phillips. 1994. Treatment of traumatic carapace injuries of sea turtles. Pages 297-298 *in* K. A. Bjorndal, A. B. Bolten, D. A. Johnson and P. J. Eliazar (compilers), Proceedings of the fourteenth annual symposium on sea turtle biology and conservation. NOAA Tech. Memo. NMFS-SEFSC-351, 323 pp.

Watts, D. A., T. Angelides and W. D. Brown. 1983. The primary structure of myoglobin from Pacific green sea turtle (*Chelonia mydas caranigra*). Biochimica et Biophysica Acta 742(1983): 310-317.

Weisler, M. I. 1995. Henderson Island prehistory: colonization and extinction on a remote Polynesian island. Biological J. Linnean Soc. 56(1-2): 377-404.

Wellins, D. J. 1987. Use of an H-Y antigen assay for sex determination in sea turtles. Copeia 1987(1): 46-52.

Wells, R. M. G. and J. Baldwin. 1994. Oxygen transport in marine green turtle (*Chelonia mydas*) hatchlings: blood viscosity and control of hemoglobin oxygen-affinity. J. Exp. Biol. 188: 103-114.

Wells, S. 1987. New marine park proposed for Brazil. Oryx 21(3): 140-141.

Wells, S. M. and J. G. Barzdo. 1991. International trade in marine species: Is CITES a useful control mechanism? Coastal Management 19(1): 135-154.

Wermuth, H. and R. Mertens. 1977. Liste der rezenten Amphibien und Reptilien. Testudines, Crocodylia, Rhynchocephalia. Das Tierreich 100: 1-174.

Wershoven, J. L., and R. W. Wershoven. 1992. Juvenile green turtles in their nearshore habitat of Broward County, Florida: a five year review. Pages 121-123 *in* M. Salmon and J. Wyneken (compilers), Proceedings of the eleventh annual workshop on sea turtle biology and conservation. NOAA Tech. Memo. NMFS-SEFSC-302, 195 pp.

West, N. P. H., P. J. Butler and R. M. Bevan. 1992. Pulmonary blood flow at rest and during swimming in the green turtle, *Chelonia mydas*. Physiol. Zool. 65(2): 287-310.

Wetherall, J. A., G. H. Balazs, R. A. Tokunaga and M. Y. Y. Yong. 1993. Bycatch of marine turtles in North Pacific high-seas driftnet fisheries and impacts on the stocks. International North Pacific Fisheries Commission Bull. 53 (III): 519-538.

Wever, E. G. 1978. The Reptile Ear. Princeton U. Press, Princeton, New Jersey, 1024 pp.

Whitmore, C. P. and P. H. Dutton. 1985. Infertility, embryonic mortality and nest-site selection in leatherback and green sea turtles in Suriname. Biol. Conserv. 34(3): 251-272.

Whittow, G. C. and G. H. Balazs. 1982. Basking behavior of the Hawaiian green turtle (*Chelonia mydas*). Pacific Science 36(2): 129-139.

Wibbels, T., G. H. Balazs, D. W. Owens and M. S. Amoss, Jr.

1993. Sex ratio of immature green turtles inhabiting the Hawaiian Archipelago. J. Herpetology 27(3): 327-329.

Wibbels, T., D. W. Owens, P. Licht, C. Limpus, P. C. Reed and M. S. Amoss Jr. 1992. Serum gonadotropins and gonadal steroids associated with ovulation and egg production in sea turtles. Gen. Comp. Endocrin. 87: 71-78.

Wibbels, T., D. W. Owens and D. Rostal. 1991. Soft plastra of adult male sea turtles: an apparent secondary sexual characteristic. Herp. Rev. 22(2): 47-49.

Wibbels, T., J. J. Bull and D. Crews. 1994. Temperature-dependent sex determination: a mechanistic approach. J. Experimental Zoology 270(1): 71-78.

Wiens, H. J. 1962. Atoll environment and ecology, Yale Univ. Press, New Haven, Conn., 532 pp.

Wilbur, H. M., and P. J. Morin. 1988. Life history evolution in turtles. Pages 387-439 *in* C. Gans and R. B. Huey (eds.), Biology of the reptilia. Vol. 16, Ecology B: Defense and life history. A. R. Liss, Inc. N. Y. 659 pp.

Wilkins, R. and A. Meylan. 1984. The national report for the country of Saint Kitts-Nevis. Pages 364-369 *in* P. Bacon, F. Berry, K. Bjorndal, H. Hirth, L. Ogren and M. Weber (eds.). Proc. Western Atlantic Turtle Symposium. Vol. 3, U. Miami Press, 514 pp.

Williams D. G. 1990. An annotated bibliography of the natural history of the Cocos (Keeling) Islands, Indian Ocean. Atoll Res. Bull. 331: 1-17.

Williams, D. G. 1994. Marine habitats of the Cocos (Keeling) Islands. Atoll Res. Bull. No. 406: 1-10.

Williams, E. H. Jr., L. Bunkley-Williams, E. C. Peters, B. Pinto-Rodríguez, R. Matos-Morales, A. A. Mignucci-Giannoni, K. V. Hall, J. V. Rueda-Almonacid, J. Sybesma, I. Bonnelly de Calventi and R. H. Boulon. 1994. An epizootic of cutaneous fibropapillomas in green turtles *Chelonia mydas* of the Caribbean: Part of a panzootic? J. Aquatic Animal Health 6: 70-78.

Williams, J. D. Jr., and W. D. Brown. 1976. Characterization of myoglobins from Atlantic and Pacific green sea turtles. Comp. Biochem. Physiol. 54B(2): 253-259.

Williams S. L. 1988. *Thalassia testudinum* productivity and grazing by green turtles in a highly disturbed seagrass bed. Marine Biology 98(3): 447-455.

Wilmers, T. J. 1994. Characteristics and management potential of sea turtle nesting areas in the Florida Keys National Wildlife Refuges. Pages 164-165 *in* K. A. Bjorndal, A. B. Bolten, D. A. Johnson and P. J. Eliazar (compilers), Proceedings of the fourteenth annual symposium on sea turtle biology and conservation. NOAA Tech. Memo. NMFS-SEFSC-351, 323 pp.

Wilson, P. T. 1976. Conservation problems in Micronesia. Oceans 9(3): 34-41.

Winokur, R. M. 1988. The buccopharyngeal mucosa of the turtles (Testudines). J. Morphology 196(1): 33-52.

Winokur, R. M. and J. M. Legler. 1974. Rostral pores in turtles. J. Morphology 143(1): 107-119.

Witham, R. 1974. Neonate sea turtles from the stomach of a pelagic fish. Copeia 1974(2): 548.

Witham R. 1980. The "lost year" question in young sea turtles. Amer. Zool. 20(3): 525-530.

Witham, R. 1982. Disruption of sea turtle habitat with emphasis on human influence. Pages 519-522 *in* K. A. Bjorndal (ed.), Biology and conservation of sea turtles. Smithsonian Institution Press, Washington, D. C. 583 pp.

Witham, R. 1990. A case report on beach erosion, beach nourishment and sea turtle nesting. Pages 157-160 *in* T. H. Richardson, J. I. Richardson, and M. Donnelly (compilers), Proceedings of the tenth annual workshop on sea turtle biology and conservation. NOAA Tech. Memo. NMFS-SEFC-278, 286 pp.

Witham R. 1991. On the ecology of young sea turtles. Florida Scientist 54(3/4): 179-190.

Witherington, B. E. 1992. Behavioral responses of nesting sea turtles to artificial lighting. Herpetologica 48(1): 31-39.

Witherington, B. E. and K. A. Bjorndal. 1991. Influences of wavelength and intensity on hatchling sea turtle phototaxis: implications for sea-finding behavior. Copeia 1991(4): 1060-1069.

Witherington, B. E. and L. M. Ehrhart 1989a. Status and reproductive characteristics of green turtles (*Chelonia mydas*) nesting in Florida. Pages 351-352 *in* L. Ogren, F. Berry, K. Bjorndal, H. Kumpf, R. Mast, G. Medina, H. Reichart and R. Witham (eds.), Proceedings of the second Western Atlantic turtle symposium. NOAA Tech. Memo. NMFS-SEFC-226, 401 pp.

Witherington, B. E. and L. M. Ehrhart. 1989b. Hypothermic stunning and mortality of marine turtles in the Indian River lagoon system, Florida. Copeia 1989(3): 696-703.

Witzell, W. N. 1981. Predation on juvenile green sea turtles, *Chelonia mydas*, by a grouper, *Promicrops lanceolatus* (Pisces: Serranidae) in the Kingdom of Tonga, South Pacific. Bull. Mar. Sci. 31(4): 935-936.

Witzell, W. N. 1982. Observations on the green sea turtle (*Chelonia mydas*) in Western Samoa. Copeia 1982 (1): 183-185.

Witzell, W. N. 1987. Selective predation on large cheloniid sea turtles by tiger sharks (*Galeocerdo cuvier*). Japanese J. Herpetology 12(1): 22-29.

Wolke, R. E. and A. George. 1981. Sea turtle necropsy manual. NOAA Tech.. Memo. NMFS-SEFC-24, 20 pp.

Wood F. 1991. Turtle culture. Pages 225-234 *in* C. E. Nash (ed.), Production of aquatic animals: crustaceans, molluscs, amphibians and reptiles. Elsevier Publ., Amsterdam, 244 pp.

Wood, F. E. and G. K. Ebanks. 1984. Blood cytology and hematology of the green sea turtle, *Chelonia mydas*. Herpetologica 40(3): 331-336.

Wood, F. E. and J. R. Wood. 1977. Quantitative requirements of the hatchling green sea turtle, *Chelonia mydas*, for valine, leucine, isoleucine and phenylalanine. J. Nutrition 107(8): 1502-1506.

Wood, F. and J. Wood. 1990. Successful production of captive F_2 generation of the green sea turtle. Marine Turtle Newsletter 50: 3-4.

Wood, F. and J. Wood. 1993a. Growth curve for captive-reared green sea turtles, *Chelonia mydas*. Herpetological J. 3(2): 49-54.

Wood, F. and J. Wood. 1993b. Release and recapture of captive-reared green sea turtles, *Chelonia mydas*, in the waters surrounding the Cayman Islands. Herpetological J. 3: 84-89.

Wood, J. R. and F. E. Wood. 1977. Quantitative requirements of the hatchling green sea turtle for lysine, tryptophan, and methionine. J. Nutrition 107(2): 171-175.

Wood, J. R. and F. E. Wood. 1980. Reproductive biology of captive green sea turtles *Chelonia mydas*. Amer. Zool. 20(3): 499-505.

Wood, J. R. and F. E. Wood. 1981. Growth and digestibility for the green turtle (*Chelonia mydas*) fed diets containing varying protein levels. Aquaculture 25: 269-274.

Wood, J. R., F. E. Wood and K. Critchley. 1983a. Hybridization of *Chelonia mydas* and *Eretmochelys imbricata*. Copeia 1983(3): 839-842.

Wood, J. R., F. E. Wood, K. H. Critchley, D. E. Wildt and M. Bush. 1983b. Laparoscopy of the green sea turtle, *Chelonia mydas*. British J. Herp. 6(9): 323-327.

World Resources Institute. 1994. World resources 1994-95. Oxford University Press, Oxford, 403 pp.

Wuethrich, B. 1993. Tracking turtles' ocean highways. New Scientist 138(1868): 8.

Wuethrich, B. 1996. Into dangerous waters. International Wildlife 26(2): 2, 44-51.

Wyneken, J. 1994. Ontogenetic changes in sea turtle body shape: morphological analyses and adaptive implications. J. Morphology 220 (3): 413.

Wyneken, J., M. Goff and L. Glenn. 1994. The trials and tribulations of swimming in the near-shore environment. Pages 169-171 *in* K. A. Bjorndal, A. B. Bolten, D. A. Johnson and P. J. Eliazar (compilers), Proceedings of the fourteenth annual symposium on sea turtle biology and conservation. NOAA Tech. Memo. NMFS-SEFSC-351, 323 pp.

Wyneken, J., and M. Salmon. 1992. Frenzy and postfrenzy swimming activity in loggerhead, green, and leatherback hatchling sea turtles. Copeia 1992(2): 478-484.

Wyneken, J., M. Salmon and K. J. Lohmann. 1990. Orientation by hatchling loggerhead sea turtles *Caretta caretta* L. in a wave tank. J. Exp. Mar. Biol. Ecol. 139(1-2): 43-50.

Yasuda, A., H. Kawauchi and H. Papkoff. 1990. The complete amino acid sequence of prolactin from the sea turtle (*Chelonia mydas*). Gen. Comp. Endocrin. 80: 363-371.

Yasuda, A., K. Yamaguchi, H. Papkoff, Y. Yokoo and H. Kawauchi. 1989. The complete amino acid sequence of growth hormone from the sea turtle (*Chelonia mydas*). Gen. Comp. Endocrin. 73: 242-251.

Zangerl, R. 1969. The turtle shell. Pages 311-339 *in* C. Gans (ed.), Biology of the reptilia, Vol. 1, Morphology A, Academic Press, New York, 373 pp.

Zangerl, R. 1980. Patterns of phylogenetic differentiation in the toxochelyid and cheloniid sea turtles. Amer. Zool. 20(3): 585-596.

Zann, L. P. 1994. The status of coral reefs in South Western Pacific Islands. Marine Pollution Bull. 29(1-3): 52-61.

Zhao, E-M. and K. Adler 1993. Herpetology of China. Society for the Study of Amphibians and Reptiles. Oxford, Ohio, 522 pp.

Zieman, J. C., R. L. Iverson and J. C. Ogden. 1984. Herbivory effects on *Thalassia testudinum* leaf growth and nitrogen content. Marine Ecology-Progress Series 15: 151-158.

Zug, G. R. 1966. The penial morphology and the relationships of cryptodiran turtles. Occ. Pap. Mus. Zool. Univ. Mich. No. 647, 24 pp.

Zug, G. R. and G. H. Balazs. 1985. Skeletochronological age estimates for Hawaiian green turtles. Marine Turtle Newsletter 33: 9-10.

Zurita G., J. C., A. César-Dachary and E. Suárez. 1992. Aspectos historicos de la pesqueria de las tortugas marinas en las costas del Mar Caribe Mexicano. Pages 75-81 *in* M. Benabib and L. Sarti (eds.), Memorias del VI encuentro interuniversitario sobre tortugas marinas. Publ. Soc. Herpetologica Mexicana No. 1, 96 pp.

Zurita G., J. C., R. Herrera and B. Prezas. 1993. Tortugas marinas del Caribe. Pages 735-751 *in* S. I. Salazar-Vallejo
and N. E. González (eds.), Biodiversidad Marina y
Costera de México. Com. Nal. Biodiversidad y CIQRO,
Mexico, 865 pp.

Zurita G., J. C., B. Prezas, R. Herrera and J. L. Miranda. 1994.
Sea turtle tagging program in Quintana Roo, Mexico.
Pages 300-303 *in* K. A. Bjorndal, A. B. Bolten, D. A.
Johnson and P. J. Eliazar (compilers), Proceedings of
the fourteenth annual symposium on sea turtle biology
and conservation. NOAA Tech. Memo. NMFS-SEFSC-
351, 323 pp.